1st 33046
    502

Voluntary Agencies
in the Welfare State

RALPH M. KRAMER

Voluntary Agencies in the Welfare State

With a Foreword
by Harold L. Wilensky

UNIVERSITY OF CALIFORNIA PRESS
Berkeley · Los Angeles · London

University of California Press
Berkeley and Los Angeles, California
University of California Press, Ltd.
London, England
© 1981 by
The Regents of the University of California

Printed in the United States of America

1   2   3   4   5   6   7   8   9

Library of Congress Cataloging in Publication Data

Kramer, Ralph M
    Voluntary agencies in the welfare state.

    Bibliography: p.
    Includes index.
    1. Social service.   2. Social policy.
3. Voluntarism.   4. Welfare state.   I. Title.
HV40.K68   361.3'7   80-5918
ISBN 0-520-04290-5

For the Kramer, Shalev, and Shein families

CONTENTS

Part II: Internal Factors:
How Voluntary Agencies are Constituted and Maintained

TABLES AND FIGURES

Tables

Figures

FOREWORD

In the stormy political climate and tight economic circumstances of the early 1980s, a recurrent problem in social theory acquires new urgency: the relative effectiveness of markets, governments, and voluntary associations in coping with social issues — the question of what each sector can do well or badly or not at all. As they tackle this question, American social scientists and policy analysts have given us an abundance of ideological passion, a minimum of serious analysis, and few cross-national comparisons. Their work has inspired a vast confusion in political language and action. In the 1970s, Governor Jerry Brown of California initially urged austerity in an era of limits. When confronted with dramatic erosion of the tax base for social services (Proposition 13), he invoked the spirit of good neighborliness as the solution: a collective volunteer effort would restore services lost by major cuts. At the same time, other enthusiasts for small government were saying that we must save the "non-profit sector," revive voluntarism, and "do more with less" by "getting public service into private hands." More recently a group of executives of foundations and national voluntary associations, including John Gardner of Common Cause, established a new association to promote the "Independent Sector."

In this book, Ralph Kramer cuts through the conceptual confusion and presents a detailed account of the actual operation of voluntary agencies serving the handicapped in four countries. He thereby puts American experience in wider perspective, bringing into view the gains and costs of the major policy options for relating government to the voluntary agency and the market. Anyone who wants to think clearly about the desirable and feasible functions, financing, and organization of voluntary agencies and volunteers should examine his results. I offer a few reflections on the larger implications of his research for public policy and the social sciences.

Upon close inspection, the "voluntary," "private" sector turns out to be neither voluntary nor private. This is yet another sign of a major tendency of modern democratic political economies: the blurring of old distinctions between the public and the private. The growth of paid volunteers, such as child minders and Peace Corps members, and of the public funding of private agencies — long apparent in countries with substantial Catholic party power (Belgium, Italy, the Netherlands) but now spreading everywhere — underscores the obsolescence of older concepts.

The need to disentangle various meanings of *voluntarism* is evident when we try to answer such questions as, "Is voluntarism an obstacle to welfare-state development?" Or, conversely, "Does the expansion of the welfare state threaten the autonomy and functions of the voluntary agency?" A sensible answer depends on distinctions among at least three concepts of "voluntarism."

1. *Voluntarism as an ideology* justifying reliance on free markets. It is hostile to state intervention generally and to social policy in particular. It emphasizes the role of philanthropy and self-help in the solution of social problems. In this view government should deliver cash and services only when normal structures of supply, the family and the market, break down. The likely effect: to slow down welfare-state development, especially income maintenance programs.

2. *Voluntarism as voluntary associations* that extend, improve, complement, supplement, or sometimes substitute entirely for the delivery of social services by government. These services are typically labor intensive; they require both local intelligence (knowledge of particular needs of specialized clientele) and local consensus (community support of the program). The main targets: the aged, the young, and the handicapped of any age. Typical services for the handicapped are sheltered workshops, job training, transportation, day care centers, homemaker chore services, nutritional programs, and social, recreational, and camping activities. The likely impact: to make the welfare state more effective. The expansion of the welfare state has, in fact, everywhere meant the growth of voluntary agencies with increased reliance on government funding. (Only in the United States and only until the 1930s did voluntarism as voluntary organizations retard the development of the welfare state.)

3. *Voluntarism as volunteerism* — the mobilization and deployment of volunteers, paid or unpaid, in money-raising campaigns or direct service, in private or public agencies. Advocates of greater vol-

unteer participation say that it humanizes the welfare state, re-
vives the sense of community, combats big government, and
even reduces inflation. But, as Kramer suggests, the realization
of one or another of these benign effects depends upon what kind
of volunteers we are talking about: unpaid staff, unpaid fund-
raisers, paid service volunteers, peer self-helpers, mutual aid
associations, neighborhood service organizations, religious institutions, etc. The label volunteers obscures these differences.

In addition to clarifying such conceptual confusion, Kramer's work
again demonstrates the power of comparative analysis. He spells out
five major strategies for relating government to the voluntary agency
in the delivery of personal social services: (1) nationalization (Montreal
recently incorporated fifteen voluntary agencies into three new government Social Service Centers); (2) government dominance (the
British government has assumed financial responsibility for a fifth social service system, the "personal social services," added to education,
income maintenance, health, and housing); (3) "pragmatic partnership," the alternative the author seems to favor; (4) "empowerment" (a
variant on the Dutch system, with advocates in the United States);
and (5) "reprivatization" (very popular in the rhetoric of American
politics). The following is a highly selective account of the Dutch,
British, and American experience with these strategies, drawing the
lessons for American policy analysts as I see them.

Are you attracted to the idea of total reliance on voluntary associations, religious institutions, neighborhoods, and the family as a way to
cut the costs of government and make social services accountable to
the consumer? (It is called "empowerment" and involves the delega-
tion of policing power, education, and social service to such local
community groups.) Then you ought to examine the case of the
Netherlands, where voluntary agencies constitute the primary system
of service delivery. The cost, of course, is huge government subsidies
out of current operating budgets and compulsory insurance premiums
funneled through voluntary agencies — money to finance all their
staff, administration, and services. In fact, the Netherlands has one of
the costliest public sectors among modern democracies. Whatever the
gains in local autonomy, professionalism, and stable, high-quality services, which are considerable, the Dutch way is definitely not a way
out of the fiscal crisis. Nor does it increase citizen control or participation. The Dutch agencies, dominated by professionals, have experienced a decline in citizen participation. Indeed, from Kramer's
account, I infer that the almost complete reliance on voluntary agen-

cies in the Netherlands has led to greater than usual fragmentation, duplication, and inflexibility. Some of Kramer's informants also claim that there is a lack of "quality control," but there is wide consensus that the Dutch are among the leaders in actual delivery of high-quality services.

Or maybe you prefer the "statist" option of the British, a statutory system of comprehensive, universal, personal social service. Exemplifying the scope of entitlement for the disabled is a long list of services under Section 2 of the Chronic Sick and Disabled Persons Act of 1970, including meals; practical assistance in the home and modifications of the home for greater safety, comfort, and convenience; holidays, outings, transportation to social events, and other recreational and educational activities and facilities in and outside the home; radio and tv; phone; and necessary equipment. In theory, the central government funds and local governments deliver these services, with the voluntary agency acting as a supplement, making up for resource deficiencies. In contrast to the Dutch system, the British government gives a small number of voluntary agencies only very limited grants-in-aid for administration. The burden of financing services is shifted to local authorities, whose budget constraints force them to set priorities and ration social services. Thus, in practice, lack of funds and lack of coordination between the statutory programs in health, housing, education, and employment, on the one hand, and the social services, on the other, make universal coverage an impossible dream. The services one gets in Britain as elsewhere vary enormously by location and type of disability. And neither the Dutch dependence on voluntary agencies nor the British reliance on local government reduces the problem of cost and coherence.

From even a glance at these other cases, we can put the American experience in perspective. Kramer describes the turbulent, competitive era of "private federalism" — an American policy of "guided innovation" fueled by a grants economy. This system has forced voluntary agencies to become more opportunistic, entrepreneurial, and political than their counterparts in other countries.

American tendencies in the funding and delivery of personal social services resemble both "empowerment" and "reprivatization." In our increasing reliance on voluntary agencies and government subsidies, we move toward the Dutch model. In our emphasis on the profit-making sector and market competition to assure the best quality at the lowest price, we are embracing theories of reprivatization. The first tendency is evident in increased government funding of voluntary agencies, many with mandated citizen participation. The second tendency is evident in the spread of service contracts and payments to private vendors (e.g., the Job Corps, Medicare, day care, nursing homes, dialysis centers). Unfortunately, there is no evidence that either trend has reduced the cost of delivering service, enhanced consumer choice, or even improved "accountability."

Because Kramer makes an heroic effort to maintain balance in his treatment of gains and costs of these tendencies, his work is an eloquent indictment of the pathologies of a politicized grants economy. The new alliance between voluntarism and vendorism, he reports, does not threaten agency autonomy or even advocacy as much as it deflects resources to the scramble for subsidies and then to rituals of reporting and accountability—the often meaningless counts of "outputs," such as number of interviews, hospital days, or meals served.

In no country has the government been able to monitor the activities of a maze of voluntary associations and private vendors. But the greater effort to do so in the United States has perhaps resulted in less service delivered at a greater unit cost. Apparently we are shooting for the Netherlands' level of dependence on voluntary agencies without the advantage of adequate, stable funding. The results: service functions are overwhelmed by grantsmanship, budget-justification research, and accountability rituals. The agencies become "fund raising instruments in search of a program"; agency volunteers are chiefly assigned to fund raising; public relations and marketing techniques are prominent. Kramer concludes that in the United States and, to a lesser extent, England, this arrangement diverts resources away from improved services, innovative programs, and leadership development, although it may increase citizen participation.

Although Kramer is persuasive on the costs of bureaucratic pathologies that afflict the "private" as much as the "public" sector, when he offers his recommendations for administrative reform of voluntary agencies, he is attracted to more of what the American government typically demands—more systematic record keeping, more program evaluation, more rational planning and priorities. To me, this part of his agenda applies best to countries whose service system is more stably funded than that of the United States. Perhaps the Netherlands, Britain, and Israel need a bit more of our preoccupation with demonstration projects and evaluation research while we need a bit less.

Students of organizational theory and practice will appreciate
Kramer's penchant for myth shattering. Consider the notion that
small- to medium-sized private voluntary associations are pioneers in
program and service delivery, that they are dynamic innovators, light-
ing the way. At least for the United States, and for the established
agencies he studies, Kramer casts doubt on this common image. It is
true that the "alternative agencies" not included in the author's sample
have sometimes introduced an original mode of intervention or service
delivery (e.g., "hot lines" for suicide prevention) or a program change
that extends existing programs to a new clientele (e.g., rape victims,
battered wives). But many significant program innovations — e.g.,
community care of the mentally ill, community action programs —
were inspired by government. More important, in all four countries
(1) the voluntary agencies do not report many major innovations; and
(2) very few voluntary agency innovations of any kind are adopted by
government. Finally, the most innovative vanguard agencies are
among the largest, most bureaucratized, and most professionalized,
although newer groups in their early stages of growth, whether professionalized or not, have often been service innovators. In my view,
Kramer could make more of this important finding.

If by "innovation" we merely mean expansion of or changes in existing programs, then the most vigorously innovative country is the
United States. Because income from community campaigns is static,
many voluntary agencies in the United States are engaged in a constant search for new funds; when approaching funding sources, public
and private alike, the symbols "innovation" and "demonstration project" are expedient; the assumption is that new is better. In practice,
the proposals are typically a means of carrying out the agencies' existing function. Here, as in the rest of American culture, the "cult of the
new" runs rampant. In contrast, other countries place a higher value
on government funding for implementation of existing programs.
Perhaps this illustrates Wilensky's law: the more demonstration, the
less follow-through; the more entrepreneurial spirit, the less service
delivery. As Kramer concludes, "The exaggerated emphasis on innovation by funding bodies may detract attention from other, more
critical aspects of the social services system, such as access, continuity,
choice, coherence, effectiveness, equity, and efficiency."

If it is a myth that the small, established private voluntary agency in
the United States is typically a pioneer and program innovator, it is an
even more misleading myth that government funding constrains

agency operations in general and active advocacy in particular. Kramer shows that with some exceptions he who pays the piper does *not* call the tune. In fact, many of the American agencies that receive the largest funding from government are among the most assertive advocates. An example is the Center for Independent Living in the San Francisco Bay Area. Both militant advocate and effective innovator, this consumer-managed organization of disabled persons has a budget of over $3,000,000, almost all from government sources. The point is general: the government of the Netherlands, where voluntary agencies are most dependent on government funding, places fewer constraints on agency operations than the governments of Britain or the United States, where agencies have more diversified sources of funds.

In an especially subtle explanation of this problem of financing and constraint, Kramer makes two points I find revealing. First, the degree of government control depends on the method of payment: strong constraint with categorical grants and subsidies, moderate constraint with fees for service or service contracts, and least constraint (and most potential for abuse) with third-party payment and vouchers. Whatever the form of payment, however — and this is a caution to all proponents of a businesslike management and accountability for voluntary agencies — government bureaucrats in all four countries lack the incentive and the capacity for stricter forms of accountability. He who pays the piper does not call the tune because he does not know the score. And where government tries for tight control, the bureaucratic pathologies discussed above metastasize. For instance, Kramer describes the interaction between agencies with different accounting practices and their government regulators, who in good faith issue guidelines under Title XX of the Social Security Act. Among the resulting administrative complexities are eight different payment mechanisms and eleven different variables the rational regulator can weigh in rate determination — enough to blow the mind of a computer.

For students interested in convergence theory — the question of whether as rich countries develop they become more alike in social structure and culture or less alike — Kramer shows how the larger context (civic culture, government structure, and professional ideology) explains national differences in the behavior of voluntary agencies as well as similarities in their structure and function.

Civic culture in the United States and England encourages various forms of citizen participation; these countries much more than the

Netherlands and Israel use volunteers. Regarding government structure, the decentralized and fragmented federalism of the United States
makes the targets of agency advocates more numerous; their aim, the
passage of detailed legislation; the means, political coalitions of voluntary agencies and citizens' committees using lobbying and the media.
All this is in sharp contrast to the other three countries, where parliaments produce fewer, more general laws, investing more power in
central government bureaucrats, who then become a simpler, more
stable target of pressure, more amenable to negotiation.

Regarding convergence, we emerge with a picture of what the
seventy-five voluntary agencies under study are and are not. Few are
pioneering, few offer choices alternative to government provision, and
none have a monopoly on volunteerism. Except for the Netherlands,
they are all subordinate to government, and they tend to be smaller,
somewhat less bureaucratic, and — their great advantage — much
more specialized in function than their government counterparts.

Kramer brings to his task two decades of firsthand experience as a
social worker, agency executive, and social planner before his
academic career. Combining this experience with the constraining dis-
cipline of comparative analysis and his impressions from hundreds of
interviews he conducted in four countries, he concludes with a message to the voluntary agency. As the social services of the welfare state
become more universal and adequate, the voluntary agency, he argues, should concentrate more on the "improver" role — prodding,
pressuring, monitoring, articulating the interests of neglected groups,
to achieve delivery of higher quality, better distributed services.
Kramer suggests that types and goals of pressure should depend on
how much government has assumed responsibility for comprehensive
coverage of the population of concern to the agency. The more nearly
universal the coverage, the more the watchdog function is appropriate
(and he spells out the specific aims and types of action, including more
effective regulatory control, consumer participation, and grievance
management). The more meager or narrow the coverage, the more
need to prod government for legal entitlement and adequacy of service. It is apparent that we have much to learn from abroad about
adequate funding and equitable distribution, while the Netherlands,
Israel, and England could learn from us some of the strategies for
citizen participation and advocacy.

To keep his study manageable, Kramer concentrates on agencies
dealing with the handicapped. Can his findings be applied to other
specialized clientele — the nonhandicapped elderly, single parents,

children, teenage youth? In discussing the weakness of advocacy in England, the Netherlands, and Israel relative to advocacy in the United States, especially efforts to improve government programs, Kramer notes a big exception: in all four countries there were persistent and successful campaigns to upgrade programs for the mentally handicapped. One reason: because the incidence of severe mental retardation is more evenly spread throughout the population than other handicaps, there is more potential for activism — a cadre of educated people "directly affected as parents who have both the incentive and the necessary organizational skills to influence public policy." Does this mean that the more evenly spread across classes or the more "middle class" *any* disease, *any* social or personal difficulty, the more voluntary agencies and activists will pressure government and the more government will deliver? If true, other things being equal, we would expect blindness, breast cancer, and ulcers to elicit effective government support, but not such afflictions of the poor as tuberculosis, youth unemployment, or diabetes and the infant mortality due to inadequate prenatal care and nutrition. Kramer's book cannot settle these questions, but it is packed with stimulating hypotheses and leads. He provides a solid base from which other students of the burgeoning service sector can take off.

What Kramer concludes about his agencies — they are not necessarily authentic pioneers — cannot be said about his study, a long-needed analysis of the distinctive competence, vulnerability, and potential of the voluntary agency. It will surely fill, as they say, a glaring gap in the literature. It is perhaps too much to hope that it will also modify the simplistic slogans that now guide the tortured development of the American welfare state.

HAROLD L. WILENSKY

PREFACE

This book seeks to contribute to the continuing debate about the role of voluntary nonprofit organizations in democratic welfare states. Most discussions of voluntary organizations tend to be long on sentiment and short on evidence. I have tried to correct this imbalance and to dispel the mystique surrounding voluntary agencies by using as the core of the book empirical data from a comparative analysis of 75 voluntary agencies serving the physically and mentally handicapped in the United States, England, the Netherlands, and Israel. The findings and the generalizations I have drawn from them will, I hope, suggest some new ways of thinking about the issues of governmental-voluntary relationships that face all welfare states.

Throughout history the determination of what rightfully belongs to Caesar has been one of the fundamental challenges facing all social institutions. In the field of social welfare there has been a recurrent quest for principles that would maintain a balance between the state and the interests of the individuals and groups comprising it. Despite the importance of voluntary agencies, however, there have been few analyses of the policy issues concerning them and little data that might suggest what can be realistically expected of them. If the welfare state is to continue — and there are no signs of its disappearance, although its growth rate has slowed — then pressures to make greater use of nongovernmental organizations to carry out public purposes will probably continue. Under these circumstances, it would be desirable to make a more persuasive case for voluntary organizations than the usual mix of expediency — more elegantly, pragmatism — and the values of pluralism.

This study, the first of its kind, is inevitably exploratory. I am aware of the inadequacies of some of the cross-national data and of the hazards of generalizing from limited and occasionally imprecise findings. I offer this report and its conclusions with the understanding that the results stand as hypotheses to be discussed, evaluated, and tested in other settings or fields of service.

In the process of demystifying the voluntary agency, I take a fresh look at such concepts as voluntarism, innovation and pioneering, autonomy, the "partnership" with government, accountability, and advocacy. Because the focus of the study is on the voluntary agency as an organization and the similarities and differences in agencies' respective sociopolitical contexts, the design does not include an assessment of community needs and resources or an analysis of the problems and perceptions of clientele.

I have attempted to write for readers with a variety of interests in governmental-voluntary relationships. These include social scientists who have a special concern with organization theory and with the convergence of modern societies and welfare states. As a research monograph, this book offers some comparative empirical data on the effects of selected environmental and organizational variables on the performance of voluntary agencies as innovators, advocates, promoters of citizen participation, and providers of social services. Voluntary agencies, like all other organizations, fall short of achieving their multiple goals, and I examine some of the possible explanations.

In the spirit of Richard M. Titmuss, who urged us to combine the pessimism of social science with the optimism of social policy, I have also addressed myself to those directly involved with the use of the voluntary agency as a nongovernmental provider of public services. This includes board and executive staff members of voluntary agencies and their professional counterparts in government — legislators and public officials who decide who should provide what social services to whom. Perhaps the findings and the conceptual clarification I present may be useful in evaluating the costs and benefits of utilizing government, voluntary, or profit-making organizations, or informal social networks, for service delivery.

In such a value-laden area, it is important to make one's preferences clear. Although I have tried to be objective, I regard myself as a supporter of voluntarism, strongly committed to the importance of maintaining an effective and influential nonprofit sector. At the same time, I do not believe in elevating voluntarism by denigrating government or in exaggerating the virtues and minimizing the inherent deficiencies of voluntary action. Injustice, inequity, and inefficiency are found in both the voluntary and governmental sectors. I see a place for both, as well as a role for profit-making organizations and informal social networks, as major channels for helping people to cope with the problems of living in an industrial society. What should be the proper role and interrelationships of each sector remains to be discovered, and perhaps this book can contribute to that quest by providing a rough map of the area. Naturally, there is no single correct map, but the ideas developed here may be a guide to more systematic efforts in developing a theory of voluntary organizations in the welfare state.

I began this research to follow up a study of government-sponsored programs of citizen participation in community development in Israel and the Netherlands. In the course of my research, I became interested in the influence that Israeli voluntary organizations outside the political structure have on social policy. I then decided to broaden the scope of the inquiry to include other functions of voluntary organizations: pioneering, the promotion of citizen participation, and service delivery. Because of my long-standing concern about the future of voluntary organizations in welfare states, a broader international comparative dimension was added by including England and the United States, countries with which I had some familiarity. Because of its small size, Israel was selected for the pilot study in 1972–73, and from this start I developed the theoretical framework and methodology that was subsequently used for the other three countries.

In the years between the inception of this study and its completion, I acquired many debts to persons whose help was indispensable to me. In England, my work would have not been possible without the sponsorship and encouragement of David Jones, Principal of the National Institute of Social Work. Stephen Hatch, Senior Research Officer of the Wolfenden Committee, also was always willing to exchange ideas and information with me. I am grateful to the following persons who were so generous with their time and from whom I learned much about the British social services: Jonathan Bradshaw, Raymond Clarke, Duncan Guthrie, Professor Roger Hadley, A. R. Isserlis, Robin Huws Jones, George Lee, Elizabeth Littlejohn, James Loring, Foster Murphy, Professor Robert Pinker, Professor Jack Tizard, and John Ward. That so much data was collected in England in such a short time was due in great measure to Pamela Llewelyn and David Thomas.

In the Netherlands, my work was facilitated by a grant from the Ministry of Culture, Recreation and Social Welfare to the National Council on Social Welfare for the research assistance of the Netherlands' Institute for Social Work Research (NIMAWO). Gerrit Kronjee of the NIMAWO staff supervised the interviewing and wrote the

Dutch report published by NIMAWO on some of the findings. Many useful suggestions and a great deal of information were provided by: Dr. Annie Huisman-van Bergen, P. J. Blommestijn, Professor Elie Lopes Cardozo, W. Fransen, Kees van Gelder, Dr. G. Hendriks, C. J. Moulijn, J. B. Meirsonne, and Professor Bram Peper. The assistance of Esther van Bemmelen, Bronka Horenblas, and Esther Wolfe is also much appreciated.

In Israel Dr. Uri Aviram, Mrs. Judy Rand, Mrs. Barbara Beram, and Dr. Benjamin Gidron helped complete the interviewing under rather difficult conditions. Others who reviewed drafts of the material dealing with Israel were: Dr. Joseph Ben Or, Emanuel Chigier, M.D., Professor Abraham Doron, Professor Ben Lappin, Professor David Macarov, Dr. Joseph Neipris, Dr. Chagit Shlonsky, Dr. Benjamin Yanoov, and Mrs. Laura Yarblom.

Having been deeply involved in voluntary agencies for most of my professional life, I am singularly appreciative of the support of the Institute of International Studies at the University of California, Berkeley for enabling me to study these organizations on a cross-national basis. I want particularly to thank Nadine Zelinski, who cheerfully retyped innumerable drafts of the manuscript, and Mrs. Cleo Stoker, who was invariably helpful with the administrative and fiscal details.

I am grateful to Professor Harold L. Wilensky and Dr. Paul Terrell for unsparing critical reviews of the entire manuscript and to some of my other colleagues in the School of Social Welfare at Berkeley who reviewed earlier versions of several chapters: Dean Harry Specht, Professor Neal Gilbert, Professor Martin Wolins, and Mrs. Riva Specht. My editor, Karen Reeds, provided a well-balanced diet of encouragement and constructive suggestions.

I could not have completed this work without the help and advice of all of these people and many others. I owe a special thanks to the hundreds of respondents in the voluntary and governmental sectors in the four countries who contributed so much of their time. Of course, I take full responsibility for the use of the data and for any errors of fact or interpretation.

Some of the material and portions of several chapters have previously appeared in different form in the following journals: *The Journal of Social Policy, The Netherlands' Journal of Sociology, Journal of Voluntary Action Research, Social Work, Social Service Review*, and *Administration in Social Work*. Papers based on some of the findings were presented at

the American Sociological Association in 1978, at the Ninth World
Congress of Sociology in Sweden in 1978, and at the Annual Confer-
ence of the Association of Voluntary Action Scholars in 1977. A
Dutch version of portions of chapter 1 appears in *Organisatie van de
Gehandicaptenzorg*, edited by G. J. Kronjee (Assen, The Netherlands:
Van Gorcum, 1980). Portions of chapter 4 and some of the material on
Israel previously appeared in a 1976 monograph published by the In-
stitute for International Studies.

Finally, I want to express my gratitude to my wife Hadassah,
whose life has been intertwined with this book for many years. She
has served as an interviewer, critic, and editor, and has assisted me in
one or another of those seemingly endless research tasks. Always patient, encouraging, and loving, she is indeed a woman of valor.

ACRONYMS AND FOREIGN WORDS

ABW	Algemene Bijstandswet, Public Assistance Act, 1965, the Netherlands
ACTION	Federal agency, United States, established under the Domestic Volunteer Service Act (PL 93-113) to oversee federally sponsored volunteer programs of state and local governments
AFL-CIO	American Federation of Labor-Congress of Industrial Organizations
AKIM	Israel Association for the Rehabilitation of the Mentally Handicapped
ANAT	Israel Association for Rehabilitation of Traffic Accident Victims
AWBZ	Algemene Wet Bijzondere Ziekenkosten, the Netherlands
CCD	Central Council for the Disabled, England
CIL	Center for Independent Living, United States
COS	Charity Organization Society, United States
CRM	Ministry of Culture, Recreation, and Social Welfare, the Netherlands
CSDPA	Chronic Sick and Disabled Persons Act of 1970, England
DHSS	Department of Health and Social Security, England
DIG	Disablement Income Group, England
Histadrut	General Federation of Labor, Israel
ILAN	Israel Foundation for Handicapped Children
JDC-Malben	Joint Distribution Committee-Malben, Israel
Knesset	Parliament of Israel
Knelpuntennota	Literally "policy bottlenecks," title of 1974 social policy report in the Netherlands
LASSA	Local Authority Social Service Act of 1970, England
MATAV	Homemaker Services Association, Israel
MICHA	Association for the Rehabilitation of Deaf Children, Israel
Migdal Or	American-Israel Lighthouse for the Blind
NCSS	National Council of Social Service, England
Nechei Zahal	Disabled Veterans Association, Israel
NIMAWO	Netherlands' Institute for Social Work Research
NISW	National Institute of Social Work, England
NITZAN	Organization for Children with Developmental and Learning Difficulties, Israel
NOZ	Nationaal Orgaan Zwakzinnigenzorg, National Association for the Care of the Mentally Retarded, the Netherlands

NSMHC	National Society for Mentally Handicapped Children, England
NVR	De Nederlandse Vereniging voor Revalidatie, Netherlands Society for Rehabilitation
ORT	Organization for Rehabilitation and Training, Israel
Particulier initiatief (PI)	Dutch term corresponding to voluntary agency
PSSC	Personal Social Service Council, England
QUANGO	Quasi-nongovernmental organization
RNIB	Royal National Institute for the Blind, England
RSVP	Retired Senior Volunteer Program, United States
SHEMA	Organization of Parents of Deaf and Hard-of-Hearing Children, Israel
SSD	Local Authority Social Service Department, England
TVMD	Tijdelijke Verstrekkingenwet Maatschappelijke Dienstverlening, Temporary Act for Social Service Provision, the Netherlands
Vaad Leumi	National Council of the Jewish Community in Palestine under the British Mandate
Verzuiling	Literally, "pillarization," the compartmentalization of the social structure of the Netherlands according to religious affiliation; also referred to as "segmented integration"
VISTA	Volunteers in Service to America
VSU	Voluntary Services Unit, England
Yishuv	Jewish community in Palestine prior to the establishment of the state of Israel
WAO	Wet op de arbeidsongeschiktheidsverzekering (incapacity insurance law), the Netherlands
WIZO	Women's International Zionist Organization, Israel
Zuilen	"Pillars," the various religious blocs and their institutional structure in the Netherlands

Introduction

> Since Henry VIII dissolved the
> monasteries people have been talking
> gloomily about the declining role of
> voluntary organizations in the
> provision of social welfare services.
> W. B. HARBERT

Among the more distinctive and frequently celebrated features of American life is a pluralism that takes the form of a vast array of voluntary nongovernmental, noncommercial organizations. Known variously as the private, independent, philanthropic, nonprofit, or third sector — after government and business — voluntary organizations serve an astonishing diversity of interests that in other countries are the responsibility of the government. The economic, as well as the social and political, importance of the voluntary sector is not always appreciated. The legendary American propensity to organize for collective purposes has resulted in an estimated 37,000 human service agencies, 3,500 private hospitals, 1,514 private institutions of higher education, 4,600 privately supported secondary schools, 1,100 symphonies, 6,000 museums, and 5,500 libraries, in addition to 350,000 religious organizations. The total income of the nonprofit sector was estimated at over $80 billion in 1974; it is equally noteworthy that government funds accounted for $23 billion, while contributions provided $25 billion,[1] and $32 billion was obtained from user charges and endowment income.

Since the 1960s each voluntary organization, whether a hospital, a college, an arts program, or a social service agency, in its own way has been significantly affected by an increased reliance on government funds and functions. Threatened by budgetary strains, by a growing demand for services, and by persistent inflation, nonprofit health,

---

1. Commission on Private Philanthropy and Public Needs, *Giving in America: Toward a Stronger Voluntary Sector*, pp. 34–36. This report of the Filer Commission, together with the research studies it sponsored, constitutes the most comprehensive study of the nongovernmental, philanthropic sector in the United States. (It will be subsequently cited as Filer.) See also Waldemar A. Nielsen, *The Endangered Sector*. On the particular problems of voluntary social agencies, see Gordon Manser and Rosemary Cass, *Voluntarism at the Crossroads*.

welfare, and educational organizations are, as providers of public services, confronted by the same dilemmas stemming from the rise of the state, which has become the major philanthropist. Essentially, they must cope with an ever-increasing financial dependency on government funds and with a need to preserve the degree of independence essential to their status as a nongovernment organization. In a political context of mounting resistance to taxation and public spending, it is not surprising that leaders in the third sector see governmental-voluntary relations as their foremost concern.

In the field of social welfare, there is a long tradition in the United States of viewing with alarm the future of the voluntary sector. Periodically during the last fifty years, the situation of voluntary social service agencies has been described by its leadership as a crisis, a catastrophe, and a threat to survival. The calamity is usually defined in fiscal terms, and much evidence of increasing difficulty in raising funds is cited, as is the consequent necessity of budget cuts resulting in staff reductions, fewer services to the community, and much suffering for the needy, the ill, the handicapped, and the troubled. The crisis is also described in organizational terms, with frequent accusations of government encroachment on the domain of voluntary organizations and unfair tax policies that discourage voluntary giving. Finally, the crisis is perceived in ideological terms as a threat to the values of voluntarism and pluralism essential to a democratic society.

At the same time, when laments about the "unrelenting deterioration" of voluntarism were heard during the 1970s, there was a contrasting picture of voluntary organizations as an expanding and vigorous sector of American life. According to the findings of the Filer Commission in 1975, the number of voluntary organizations has increased every year, more money is being raised, and more and different types of persons are involved as volunteers and as board members. Which of these views is correct? Part of the confusion may be due to the global character of the concept of "the voluntary sector," which includes all types of nongovernmental, nonprofit organizations. It is important, however, to distinguish between *volunteerism*, i.e., the freely given service of individuals to help others; *voluntary associations*, which include unions, churches, civic and professional organizations, philanthropic foundations, and private universities; and *voluntary social agencies*, which are the subject of this book. The future of these nongovernmental, nonprofit voluntary organizations and the ways in which they relate to government may be quite different. So, are things getting better or worse for voluntary social agencies?

In appearance, at least, both views are correct. Underlying the dual condition of scarcity and growth in the field of social welfare is a parallel process in Western democracies of the simultaneous expansion of the public and the private sectors in the economy and in society and a blurring of the boundaries between them. A progressive and pervasive mingling of public and private funds and functions has resulted in a mixed economy in the social services that renders obsolete conventional conceptions of governmental and voluntary roles. Increasingly, there is a call for the design of new and more appropriate models of interorganizational relationships that will help maintain the independence and integrity of voluntary agencies and, at the same time, will lead to better methods of public accountability. For voluntary agencies, this would mean the redefinition of their mission on the basis of a more realistic reassessment of their capabilities. In this way, they would be in a stronger position to assert the vitality and leadership expected from them.

Despite concern for the preservation of voluntarism and pluralism in welfare states and the need for new concepts to reflect the fading dichotomy between public and private, there is little research that can contribute to a theory of voluntary provision in a democratic, postindustrial society that has a substantial system of public social services. The research upon which much of this book is based — a comparative study of voluntary agencies serving the physically and mentally handicapped in the United States, England, the Netherlands, and Israel — may lead to a better understanding of the factors that influence the character and role of voluntary agencies in welfare states. My findings and the generalizations they suggest provide a map of a partially explored territory to guide future policymaking and theory development.

The Context of the Welfare State

The welfare state is generally recognized as one of the dominant features of our time.[2] While among Western democracies the welfare

2. Among the many definitions of the welfare state, the following one is generally accepted: government-protected, minimum standards of income, health, nutrition, housing, and education for all citizens as a legal right, not as a charity. Harold L. Wilensky, *The Welfare State and Equality: Structural and Ideological Roots of Public Expenditures*, p. 1. In other definitions, employment and the personal social services are included in the social services provided by the welfare state. The personal social services are those required by individuals with physical or psychosocial deficits. They include: homemaker services, day and foster care, hospital and institutional facilities, hostels, counseling, protective services, sheltered workshops, and other employment training programs, social and recreational programs, etc. They are usually administered by agencies employing social workers. See Eric Sainsbury, *The Personal Social Services*, pp. 3–4, 23–24.

states have converged in the development of social services, there is still a wide range of roles in social welfare for the nongovernmental sector. The Netherlands, where voluntary agencies constitute the primary social service delivery system, stands at one end of a continuum; Sweden, where practically no voluntary agencies are used although some are subsidized for purposes of advocacy, stands at the other. Not only is it possible to do without a voluntary sector for social service delivery, as Sweden has demonstrated, but much of the voluntary sector can be nationalized and incorporated as part of the government, as Quebec did in 1974. Closer to the Netherlands is West Germany, where about half of the social services are subsidized by government but are provided by voluntary agencies. The United States is in the middle, preferring the voluntary agency as an agent and sometime partner to complement a dominant governmental system that uses a variety of service providers. England stands close to Sweden because of the dominance of its statutory agencies, while France, Israel, and Canada stand somewhere between it and the United States.[3]

In each country, the particular division of responsibility between governmental and voluntary agencies is not formalized, but it reflects a distinctive history and sociopolitical context. While the welfare states differ in the extent of their reliance on nongovernmental organizations for the provision of social services, they all share a basic perception of voluntary agencies: these agencies are expected to be innovative and flexible, to protect particularistic interests, to promote volunteer citizen participation, and to meet needs not met by government. Through provision of opportunities for citizen participation, sponsorship of social services, dispersal of social power, and an increased sense of civic efficacy, voluntary social agencies are believed to strengthen the pluralist and democratic forces of a society. Together with government and profit-making organizations, voluntary agencies may relieve, replace, or reinforce the primary social systems of family, neighbors, and friends.

Though their importance is acknowledged, voluntary agencies, particularly in the United States and in England, are increasingly ap-

3. With the exception of Sweden, these countries are the focus of Alfred J. Kahn and Sheila B. Kamerman, *Social Services in International Perspective: The Emergence of the Sixth System.* The convergence of welfare states in their social services is analyzed in Ramesh Mishra, "Welfare and Industrial Man: A Study of Welfare in Western Industrial Societies in Relation to a Hypothesis of Convergence." See also Gaston V. Rimlinger, *Welfare Policy and Industrialization in Europe, America and Russia.*

prehensive about survival in the face of substantial changes in their organizational environment. Since 1950 the inexorable and accelerating growth of the public sector has been accompanied by an increasing reliance by voluntary agencies on government funds. The change in sources of funding, which compensates somewhat for a declining income from contributions, has resulted in a major shift in the balance of power, resources, and functions. With the decline of the historical preeminence of voluntary agencies has come a blurring of the boundaries between the public and private sectors that raises questions about the preservation of the autonomy of voluntary agencies and the accountability of public agencies. Furthermore, new types of nonprofit organizations — alternative agencies, quasi-nongovernmental organizations (QUANGOS), and peer self-help groups — have proliferated, particularly in the United States and England, while profit-making organizations have entered the social service market.

The result is a more complex and competitive system of social welfare, which poses a challenge to the distinctive competence of the voluntary agency. While voluntary agencies have traditionally stressed innovation, flexibility, and a capacity to promote volunteerism, there is little evidence of their monopoly over these organizational virtues today. It is estimated that in the United States there are now over thirty federal programs involving three million volunteers. Similarly, in England, the Netherlands, and Israel government-sponsored volunteer programs established in recent years complement, if not compete with, those of nongovernmental agencies.

As the domain of government expands in financing the social services, if not in directly providing them, and in moving toward greater coverage and equity and toward services as a right, there has been growing pressure on voluntary agencies receiving public funds for more accountability, coordination, and cost-efficiency. This trend is reflected in a series of national commissions established during the 1970s in England, the Netherlands, Canada, Quebec, and the United States that sought to chart the future of voluntary organizations in relation to the government. Until recently, issues regarding the future of the voluntary agency were considered in the light of an expanding welfare state. However, most of the national commissions assumed that we have come to the end of an era of welfare state expansion and that at least the growth rate of the social services will be reduced. While there are various explanations for this trend, it is widely believed that the welfare state inevitably generates more demand for social services than it can realistically (fiscally or politically) provide. Among the built-in, almost uncontrollable factors conducive to expansion of the welfare state have been: (1) the increasing division of labor in society within roles, status, and organizations, leading to new demands and categories for concern and new areas of the "service society"; (2) the growth of professional cadres and the differentiation of new programs at an exponential rate; (3) an accelerating demand resulting from public relations, which raises standards and expectations; (4) an increased sophistication in clientele claims for new services and programs, leading to still further differentiation and professionalization. Contributing to the contraction of the welfare state are: (1) ever-mounting costs (which have fueled taxpayer revolts in several countries) attributable to the labor-intensive character of the social services; (2) antibureaucratic sentiments and widespread disillusionment over the persistence of social problems despite substantial investments of resources; (3) past successes in universalizing certain services so that fewer groups remain to be included.[4]

Not surprisingly, in this struggle there has been a revival of "reprivatization" in the United States and growing support for the advantages of nongovernmental organizations in carrying out public purposes. Some see the voluntary agency as a bulwark against further governmental intervention, or at least as an alternative to, if not a substitute for, it.[5] On the other hand, a few perceive the voluntary agency as an obstacle to the development of a more equitable, comprehensive, and universal system of personal social services similar to that of England.

Although the historical source of the democratic welfare state has been described as "voluntary action crystallized and made universal,"[6] the subsequent role of voluntary social agencies in welfare states is still uncertain. It has become increasingly difficult to use Lord Beveridge's guideline, that voluntary agencies should be "doing those things which the State should not do"[7] because the limit of governmental

4. Meyer N. Zald, "Demographics, Politics and the Future of the Welfare State."
5. The concept of "reprivatization," or the greater use of the profit-making sector, has been advocated, notably by Peter Drucker, *The Age of Discontinuity: Guidelines to Our Changing Society,* and Richard Cornuelle, *Reclaiming the American Dream.* Greater use of the nonprofit sector, which includes voluntary agencies and church and neighborhood groups, as well as the family, is urged in Peter L. Berger and Richard John Neuhaus, *To Empower People: The Role of Mediating Structures in Public Policy.* I discuss the strategies of reprivatization and empowerment in chapter 14.
6. The phrase is used in the 1960 Nathan Report on the Charity Law in England, as cited in David Owen, *English Philanthropy, 1660–1960,* p. 534.
7. Lord Beveridge, *Voluntary Action: A Report on Methods of Social Advance,* pp. 301–2.

actions is no longer clear. These ambiguities are reinforced because there is no accepted philosophy regarding the use of voluntary organizations. In none of the welfare states is there a theory that would specify the role of voluntary organizations in a complex industrial society.

There has been, however, a growing consensus during the last twenty years that the presumed differences between voluntary and governmental services have diminished and in many cases are indistinguishable.

> Certain attributes may belong indifferently to both voluntary and statutory services . . . it is oversimplistic to assume that voluntary social services are either better or worse than statutory ones.[8]

T. H. Marshall has also questioned the importance and feasibility of any division of function:

> The bulk of the work done by voluntary agencies falls within areas in which the state recognizes its overall responsibility . . . if the voluntary body did not do it, the state would have to take over as much of it as it could . . . there is no clear case for assigning some areas wholly to one and some wholly to the other.[9]

Others argue, however, that the governmental services may be stretched to their limits within existing resources and therefore that it is necessary to reexamine and redefine the respective roles of voluntary and government agencies. At least there is a need to clarify the changing social service economy and to search for new models of governmental-voluntary relationships. How is this to be done?

Definitions and Concepts

Despite concern over the future of the voluntary sector and its relationship to government, there is a scarcity of comparative empirical research or theory that might contribute to a more realistic assessment of the distinctive organizational competence, vulnerability, and potential of the voluntary agency and might assist in policymaking and planning. Academics and researchers have neglected the voluntary sector, and it has not been treated seriously or included in the social policymaking process in most countries. This may be due to the ambiguity of the voluntary sector, its complexity, and its diversity, as

---

8. Joyce Warham, *Social Policy in Context*, p. 19.
9. T. H. Marshall, *Social Policy in the Twentieth Century*, p. 184.

well as to the ambivalence with which it is regarded.[10] As a result, there is no coherent theory of voluntary organization, development, or organizational change. The methodology of many studies of voluntary organizations — and social agencies are rarely included in the sample — is often badly flawed, making comparisons invalid. Different definitions of variables and their indicators, different units, different levels of analysis, the absence of replication, and highly equivocal findings characterize this field of social science research.[11]

On the other hand, most comparative studies of the welfare state focus on social policies and programs or on the public bureaucracies responsible for the delivery of social services.[12] Generally neglected and still awaiting an adequate typology is an array of nonprofit organizations, including voluntary social agencies, alternative agencies, and QUANGOS. While the field of voluntary associations, including self-help groups, is well cultivated, relatively little attention has been given to the voluntary social agencies that, at least in the United States, provide a growing proportion of the government-financed, personal social services through purchase arrangements typical of the "contract State." Characterized by a heavy ideological overlay, vested interests, and lack of data, most discussions of voluntary agencies tend to be hortatory, often confusing what the voluntary agency should or could be with what it is or was.

Because there is no generally accepted taxonomy of voluntary organizations, there is a frequent failure to distinguish between voluntarism, volunteerism, voluntary associations, and voluntary agencies. Voluntarism consists of both a set of values (volunteerism) and a set of structures (voluntary organizations). The values can be expressed in such behavior as citizen participation in policymaking, planning, advocacy, administration, and fund-raising, and in freely giving oneself

10. There is a growing interest by public choice economists in the role of the third sector in the economy as a provider of public goods. See Burton A. Weisbrod, *The Voluntary Non-Profit Sector: An Economic Analysis.* Although there are theories concerning the private sector and public collective goods, for nongovernmental organizations whose programs are not financed by fees from users or taxes there is no theory besides pluralism apart from the beginning efforts of a few economists such as Weisbrod. The absence of a suitable conceptual framework for the role of nonprofit organizations as providers of public goods has contributed to the ambiguity surrounding the function of voluntarism in welfare states.

11. James Q. Wilson, *Political Organizations*, pp. 12–13; John R. Kimberly, "Hospital Adoption of Innovation: The Role of Integration into External Informational Environments," p. 361.

12. Typical of these studies are: P. R. Kaim-Caudle, *Comparative Social Policy and Social Security: A Ten-Country Study;* Barbara N. Rodgers, John Greve, and John S. Morgan, *Comparative Social Administration;* Dorothy Lally, *National Social Service Systems: A Comparative Study and Analysis of Selected Countries;* Kahn and Kamerman; and Wilensky.

to directly help another person or group. Voluntary organizations fall into two classes according to the primacy of their social welfare functions. First, *voluntary associations* are membership organizations which usually have a social purpose — a "cause" — and usually seek to benefit their constituency. They include service and fraternal organizations, religious and charitable societies, political parties, and unions. Second, *voluntary agencies* are also of many different types, depending, for example, on the degree of participation of consumers in their governance. We are concerned with those that are essentially bureaucratic in structure, governed by an elected volunteer board of directors, employing professional or volunteer staff to provide a continuing social service to a clientele in the community. At various times volunteer agencies have also been known as "private agencies," "nonprofit organizations," and even as "public agencies." Closely related to voluntary agencies are various forms of self-help or mutual aid groups, some of which may provide services for their members. At the risk of some confusion but in the interest of avoiding repetition, *voluntary agency* and *voluntary organization* will be used interchangeably in this book, even though the voluntary agency is the primary focus of my research.

Most discussions of the character, goals, and functions of voluntary agencies imply the performance of four organizational *roles*.[13] (1) As *vanguard*, the purpose of the voluntary agency is to innovate, pioneer, experiment, and demonstrate programs, some of which may eventually be taken over by the government. (2) As *improver* or *advocate*, the agency is expected to serve as a critic, watchdog, or gadfly as it pressures a governmental body to extend, improve, or establish needed services. (3) As *value guardian* of voluntaristic, particularistic, and sectarian values, a voluntary agency is expected to promote citizen participation, to develop leadership, and to protect the special interests of social, religious, cultural, or other minority groups. (4) As *service provider*, the voluntary agency delivers certain services it has selected, some of which may be a public responsibility that government is unable, is unwilling, or prefers not to assume directly or fully.

I shall try to answer the question, To what extent do voluntary agencies in the United States, England, the Netherlands, and Israel

13. In the interests of avoiding the terminological confusion associated with the concept of *function* — a term that has been preempted by several disciplines — I prefer to use *role* to refer to the pattern of expected organizational behavior relating to the position of the voluntary agency in the social welfare system. Role is also the traditional term used in most discussions of governmental-voluntary relationships, even though social scientists tend to restrict its use to the behavior of individuals.

perform these four roles? I shall also ask, by extension, Under what conditions might agencies be expected to perform these roles in the future? By analyzing the structure and functioning of voluntary agencies in four welfare democracies and the factors influencing their organizational behavior, I will suggest some implications for social policy. For example, the experience of the Netherlands illuminates some of the likely consequences of reprivatization, a policy that has strong adherents in the United States who urge the transfer of many functions to the nongovernmental sector. On the other hand, the voluntary agencies in England operate in the shadow of a comprehensive statutory system of personal social services, a statist solution that many in the United States regard as an equally controversial model. The benefits and costs of an extremely close partnership or bureaucratic symbiosis between governmental and voluntary organizations can be analyzed in Israel. In the United States, one can observe the contract state fueled by a grants economy.

The four countries were chosen because they illustrate some of the leading patterns of governmental and voluntary agency relationships, evolving out of different sociopolitical contexts and reflecting varying stages of development. Thus, in Israel the voluntary sector predated and provided the basis for the present governmental structure and virtually all other social institutions. Since statehood, however, Israeli voluntary organizations have been overshadowed by a highly centralized and politicized group of service bureaucracies, although there is a resurgence of interest in reviving volunteerism and a search for ways of strengthening the nongovernmental sector.

In the Netherlands, the situation is reversed. There the primary social service structure is composed of voluntary organizations that are almost completely subsidized by the government with, until now, little loss of autonomy. In recent years, changes in government policies, together with a trend toward secularization, have created many uncertainties for the future of voluntary organizations because of the possibilities of greater control by municipal government. Comparison of the Netherlands and Israel is useful because of such similarities as small size, high degree of urbanization and industrialization, and historical social cleavages based on religion (in Israel, on sociocultural grounds as well). They are among the few countries in the world with separate but integrated religious and secular political party systems. In both countries, the civic culture is increasingly influenced by American and English conceptions of citizen participation. The Netherlands and Israel represent examples of "vertical pluralism," in which state and society are divided into a number of separate spheres, relatively independent of each other but together constituting a democratic polity. Other states characterized by this pattern include Austria, Belgium, Switzerland, and parts of Canada.[14]

In England, the voluntary organizations, which were expected to diminish in importance as the welfare state emerged in the years following World War II, believe that they have forged a new partnership with government. As their own sources of support have declined, they have been relying more on grants and payments for services, supplementing many functions government has been unable to provide. Since 1970 major structural changes have taken place in the reorganization of the Local Authority Social Service Departments; these government agencies have become a freestanding source of personal social services for all citizens. At the same time, in certain quarters there is a tendency to place more emphasis on utilizing the voluntary sector than on expanding the statutory agencies.

In the United States the distinctions between public and private have faded as government has taken on numerous social welfare and health responsibilities previously assumed by voluntary groups. There are greatly increased use of public funds by voluntary agencies, new forms of client participation in policymaking and staff roles as part of government-mandated citizen participation, and the emergence of new quasi-public organizations as conduits for federal funds. There is growing disillusionment with the welfare state, as well as strong support for "private federalism," with its reliance on nongovernmental organizations to perform public functions.[15]

The rationale for this inquiry is both ideological and technical. On one level it is based on a mounting concern over the future of voluntary agencies in welfare states, whose ever-widening scope of responsibility and power appears to overshadow and challenge the viability of the nongovernmental sector. As an editorial in the British weekly *New Society* expressed it:

> A central theme in any discussion of the role of voluntary organizations today is whether or not they are a healthy antidote to the rigidity of statu-

14. These four countries are the subject of Kenneth D. McRae, editor, *Consociational Democracy: Political Accommodation in Segmented Societies.*

15. "Private federalism" refers to direct, national grants to voluntary nonprofit institutions; it is used by Charles Gilbert in "Welfare Policy," p. 167. Implications of the blurring of the boundaries between the governmental and voluntary sectors are cogently analyzed in: Eleanor L. Brilliant, "Private or Public: A Model of Ambiguities," and Bertram M. Beck, "The Voluntary Social Welfare Agency: A Reassessment." A broader perspective is given in Ira Sharkansky, *Wither the State? Politics and Public Enterprise in Three Countries.*

tory services, and a central pillar of the pluralist society, or a silly append-
age which serves merely to relieve the State of a few responsibilities.[16]

The concern with the voluntary agency is part of a continuing debate over the proper place of government in the affairs of society and
in the lives of individuals. At odds are two opposing models of the
state originally conceived in the seventeenth century by Hobbes and
Locke. For Hobbes, individuals have assigned to the state the powers
of total administration and, on this assumption, progress is measured
in the degree to which services become statutory (i.e., universal, im-
partial, and subject to democratic control). In the Lockean version, the
state is only a means, one of several covenants that people have constituted for their governance, along with a variety of other institutions.
Later, in the 1840s, de Tocqueville's seminal observations on voluntary associations laid the foundations for the theory of pluralism. In
this conception, nongovernmental organizations serve as mediating
and empowering instruments between the individual and the state and
as a countervailing force to the mass society.[17] A more extreme expression of this idea is found in the concept of *subsidiarity* formulated by
Pope Pius XI in the encyclical *Quadragesimo Anno*, which states no
function is to be performed by a higher, more complex and distant
system that can be carried out by more primary groups such as family,
neighbors, friends, and church. This principle underlies the social
service s.ucture in the Netherlands, and it is also invoked frequently
by Catholic spokesmen in the United States and by leaders of the
voluntary sector in England. These conflicting political philosophies
are also involved in the debate on the redistributional functions of the
welfare state and the justification for the priority of its tax claims on
discretionary income for public goods.

On another level the study is related in a more technical way to the
significance of auspice in the social services. What difference does it
make if a service is financed and provided by a governmental or voluntary agency — or, it might be added, by the family or a profit-making

16. "Friendly Satellites," p. 11.

17. The literature on voluntary associations and the political theory of pluralism is volumin-
ous. A useful collection of essays is J. Rowland Pennock and John W. Chapman, eds., *Voluntary
Associations, Nomos*, XI, Yearbook of the American Society for Political and Legal Philosophy.
See also Constance Smith and Ann Freedman, *Voluntary Associations: Perspectives on the Literature*,
pp. 33–85. Robert A. Nisbet has written eloquently on the conflict between the state, voluntary
associations, and the individual in *The Quest for Community: A Study in the Ethics of Order and
Freedom* and *The Sociological Tradition*.

organization? Unfortunately, virtually no research bears on this critical question. Most consumers believe that whether sponsorship is governmental or voluntary is not nearly as important as the manner in which the service is delivered — i.e., *how* is more important than *who*. It has been asserted that there are as many differences among voluntary agencies as between them and governmental organizations; hence, auspices are unimportant per se, and such organizational factors as size, complexity, level of professionalization, bureaucratization, leadership, and ideology may be more significant. Yet many claim that nongovernmental organizations are intrinsically preferable to those under public sponsorship because of their greater discretion, responsiveness, and innovative capacity. Others are concerned that in substituting for, instead of supplementing, the governmental services or in providing an alternative, the voluntary agency may perpetuate second-rate services and mask basic weaknesses in governmental services. Another point of view is that competition should be encouraged between governmental, nonprofit, and profit-making organizations operating as parallel systems to assure the rapid development of needed services, while recognizing that only government can provide universal services as a matter of right.

Underlying these beliefs is another difference of opinion on what should belong to Caesar and on the desirability and feasibility of a more formal division of labor between governmental and voluntary organizations.

Regardless of the merit of each position, social policy decisions must be made regarding who shall be served, on what basis, and by whom — governmental or nongovernmental organizations. It is desirable, therefore, to have a more rational basis for making these decisions and to be able to know more realistically what can be expected from voluntary services.

Design of the Research

Accordingly, I undertook the first international comparative analysis of the structure and functioning of voluntary agencies, focusing on agencies serving the physically, sensorially, and mentally handicapped in England, the Netherlands, Israel, and the United States. The goal of the study was to identify distinctive organizational competence, vulnerability, and potential. The study was designed to analyze the principal internal and external factors affecting performance of the four major roles attributed to voluntary agencies: pioneering (vanguard), promoting social change and advocacy (improver), encouraging volunteer citizen participation (value guardian), and providing services.

Although the term *handicapped* may be considered pejorative by the disabled, I use it because it reflects common usage in legislation and by organizations in this field.

A total of seventy-five case studies was conducted between 1972 and 1975 in the four democratic welfare states, which differ in sociopolitical context and public policy environment, as well as in the extent of reliance on nongovernmental organizations for service delivery.

To avoid the usual global generalizations about voluntarism, I confined the study to one particular field of service, that for the physically and mentally handicapped. A purposive sample of fifteen to twenty agencies in each country, representing from 50 to 90 percent of the agencies serving the physically and mentally handicapped, was selected with the aid of experts for a series of case studies. The agencies are national in scope, with the exception of those in the United States, which provide services in one or more counties in the San Francisco Bay Area. In England, the agencies selected are based in the Greater London area; in the Netherlands, in the Randstad (Amsterdam, Rotterdam, The Hague, and Utrecht); and in Israel, in Tel Aviv or Jerusalem. (The list of agencies studied in each county can be found in the Appendix, together with information regarding the sample selection and the types of respondents.)

The agencies displayed considerable diversity. They included organizations both *of* and *for* the blind, deaf, and other handicapped groups; "health" agencies, such as those for cancer, heart disease, and tuberculosis; and counterparts in each country of organizations serving the mentally handicapped and victims of such neuromuscular conditions as poliomyelitis, cerebral palsy, muscular dystrophy, and multiple sclerosis. While the same types of voluntary agency were studied in each country, the agencies varied in the extent to which they operated institutions, provided care or rehabilitation, and supported research. Data were collected from documents and from extensive, structured interviews with agency executive directors, government officials, and "significant others" in the organizational environment regarding the process of program development, episodes of social action, and utilization of volunteers during the last twenty years. Information was also obtained about internal organizational structure, fiscal resources, policymaking, and operating systems, in addition to the public policy environment and political context.

I employed an organizational perspective. The voluntary agency was studied as an organization having the characteristics of both a mutual-benefit and a service organization, to use P. M. Blau and W. R. Scott's designation, with a distinctive character of its own that has yet to be determined.[18] Because of the relative absence of theory and empirical research, the case studies were exploratory in character though descriptive-analytical in form — i.e., hypotheses were used to guide the process of data collection, not as propositions to be tested. As D. J. Palumbo has stated, "Comparative analysis should be used as a heuristic device, not a testing method. The end product of comparative research should be the creation of new hypotheses and concepts."[19] Similarly, Arend Lijphart has stressed the value of hypothesis-generating studies in areas where no theory yet exists.[20]

Although I make some generalizations, my findings, strictly speaking, pertain only to agencies serving the physically and mentally handicapped, but one cell within a larger matrix of voluntary organizations. The style of this kind of an inquiry has been described by Eveline Burns as

> The "it looks as if" kind of research where one cannot hope to prove the validity of one's hypotheses rigorously, but where, by the marshalling of a variety of pieces of evidence, one can establish a probability which has some relevance to the major problems of social welfare and which may exert some influence on social policy or professional practice.[21]

Plan of the Book

The book is divided into four parts. Part I (chapters 1–4) consists of four case studies that describe for each country the historical and sociopolitical context, as well as the public policy and organizational environment, that affects the roles of voluntary agencies. Part II

18. Peter M. Blau and W. Richard Scott, *Formal Organizations: A Comparative Approach*, pp. 42–58.

19. Dennis J. Palumbo, "Comparative Analysis: Quasimethodology or New Science?," p. 49.

20. Arend Lijphart, "Comparative Politics and the Comparative Method." The use of the comparative method as a sensitizing device is also recommended by John Carrier and Ian Kendall, "The Development of Welfare States: The Production of Plausible Accounts." The advantages and limitations of comparative methods are discussed in Donald T. Warwick and Samuel Osherson, editors, *Comparative Research Methods*.

21. Eveline M. Burns, "Letter to the Editor," *Social Service Review*.

(chapters 5–8) includes comparisons of the internal organizational structures of the voluntary agencies; their size, formalization, and professionalization; and their governance and fiscal resource systems. These four chapters deal with the maintenance or survival functions of voluntary organizations. In Part III I examine organizational functions by comparing performance patterns in the four roles attributed to voluntary agencies: vanguard (chapter 9); value guardian (chapter 10); improver (chapter 11); and service provider (chapter 12). Part IV contains two concluding chapters on implications for theory and social policy. On the basis of the study findings, in chapter 13 the four organizational roles are reformulated, and some generalizations are made on the distinctive competence and vulnerability of the voluntary agency. The last chapter considers various policy choices involving voluntary agencies in relation to the future of the welfare state.

PART I

Four National Studies:
The Sociopolitical Context

Chapters 1 through 4 present some background information essential for the subsequent analysis of the structure and functioning of voluntary agencies serving the physically and mentally handicapped in the Netherlands, England, the United States, and Israel. The historical development of each welfare state is viewed from the perspective of the changing pattern of governmental and voluntary effort, in general and with specific reference to the handicapped. In each country a distinctive ideology underlies the relationship between the governmental and voluntary sectors. This ideology reflects political structure, civic culture, and system of public policymaking, the key external factors that help account for similarities and differences in the governance and fiscal resource systems of voluntary agencies, discussed in part II, and for the pattern of performance of their organizational roles, treated in part III.

1. The Netherlands: The Primacy of Private Initiative

In the Netherlands the division of function between governmental and voluntary agencies is the reverse of the pattern in the United States and England. Although the size, scope, and rate of growth of governmental programs in the United States and England dwarf those of programs in the voluntary sector, nongovernmental organizations are still expected to supplement, to fill gaps, and to serve as advocates, monitors, sources of innovation, and standard setters. In contrast, a highly complex network of private agencies[1] in the Netherlands, still mostly organized along denominational lines, has undisputed responsibility for the provision of virtually all social services. The clear priority of private over state initiative is evident in the restriction of the authority of government to finance this system and to supervise, set standards, and plan. Only about 10 percent of all health, education, and social welfare services are provided directly by local or provincial governments. That the social services are organized predominantly under religious auspices has not, however, prevented the Netherlands from evolving a comprehensive state system of social insurance based on legal rights, as well as numerous high-quality, personal social services for the physically and mentally handicapped.

The organizing principle underlying the social services in the Netherlands reflects the unique phenomenon of *verzuiling*, which is the central motif of Dutch social structure. Variously translated as "pillarization," "compartmentalization," "segmented integration," or "vertical pluralism," *verzuiling* refers to the idea that "the various blocs of the population represent pillars *(zuilen)*, each valuable in its own

---

1. The nongovernmental, nonprofit social service organizations in the Netherlands are not generally known as private or as voluntary agencies. The term that comes closest is *particulier initiatief*, which will be shortened to PI for the remainder of this chapter. This is, as far as I know, the first analysis in English of these social service organizations in the Netherlands.

right and together indispensable in supporting the national structure."[2] The Netherlands has been a religiously divided country ever since the Reformation. Each of the three largest denominational blocs — Roman Catholic, Neo-Calvinist, and Liberal Protestant, as well as the Humanists and other secular groups — has established for its adherents an array of organizations encompassing every sphere of social and political life, including schools and universities, political parties, trade unions, employer associations, sick funds, health and welfare agencies, sports and leisure time associations, newspapers, and radio and television stations.

Governmental responsibility for social welfare is largely a post-World War II development because, historically, voluntary organizations under religious auspices provided most forms of social welfare. Although the roots of the Dutch system of vertical pluralism go back to the Reformation, its immediate antecedents are in the nineteenth century, when the concept of *particulier initiatief* (PI) was coined and acquired ideological overtones that prevailed until recently.[3]

Precedents in Education and Public Health

Despite the sharp cleavages in social class and religious belief between the Roman Catholics and the two major Protestant sects, a system of public education prevailed during the first half of the nineteenth century. The desire to receive governmental subsidies for educational and welfare institutions led to political collaboration between these previously hostile groups. As a result, the Roman Catholics and the Neo-Calvinist Protestants founded political parties that cooperated in a Christian coalition from 1888 to 1938 and governed the Netherlands for most of the fifty-year period.

Both religious groups invoked an ideology that asserted the primacy of the individual and group over the state. The Neo-Calvinist theological doctrine of "sphere sovereignty" proclaimed the sovereignty of God over the family, the state, the church, and society, each of which had its own sphere of influence. This doctrine is equivalent to the Roman Catholic principle of subsidiarity, contained in the statement

2. Johan Goudsblom, *Dutch Society*, p. 30; see also pp. 50–127. The description of the social structure in the Netherlands that follows is drawn largely from Goudsblom and the following: J. P. Kruijt, "The Netherlands: The Influence of Denominationalism on Social Life and Organizational Patterns"; Arend Lijphart, *The Politics of Accommodation: Pluralism and Accommodation in the Netherlands;* and Christopher Bagley, *The Dutch Plural Society: A Comparative Study in Race Relations.*

3. David O. Moberg, "Social Differentiation in the Netherlands."

by Pope Pius XI in the encyclical "Quadragesimo Anno" in 1931 that "it is an injustice, a grave evil, and a disturbance of right order for a larger and higher organization to arrogate to itself functions which can be performed by smaller and lower bodies."[4]

Although both doctrines supported the belief that education should be under the control of parents, not of government, the battle over the schools did not end until 1917, when total financial equality was approved for both public education and religious schools. State support brought about a dramatic shift in the proportion of students attending religious schools. At present, about two-thirds of all parents — divided roughly equally between Roman Catholics and Protestants — send their children to religious primary schools. In the field of special education for the physically and the mentally handicapped, there are 714 schools, of which 304 are under Roman Catholic auspices, 156 are Protestant, 188 are operated by the state, and 66 are independent. The role of government is to finance and to set minimum standards regarding admissions, curriculum, degrees, and numbers of teachers and their qualifications.[5]

In the 1920s the historic breakdown of the separation of church and state and the new recognition of the principle of state aid for education sponsored by the denominations set a precedent that was gradually extended to all other health, welfare, cultural, and recreational activities sponsored by each denomination.

A second prototype of the present system of governmental subsidies to denominational organizations that perform a public function is the public health movement in the Netherlands.[6] The public health system has its roots in the fight led against epidemics of infectious diseases by voluntary associations in the late nineteenth century. In 1875 the White Cross was founded in North Holland by an inspector of the government public health service who was convinced that typhoid could only be combated by improving the nursing of patients in their own homes. Around the turn of the century, other provinces of the Netherlands followed with similar denominational organizations that not only provided home nursing but also took on other public health and hygiene functions. In addition to the Green Cross in the twentieth century, the Roman Catholic White-Yellow Cross and the Protestant

4. Quoted in Michael P. Fogarty, *Christian Democracy in Western Europe, 1820–1953*, p. 41.
5. *Educational Care of the Handicapped Child*, pp. 44–45.
6. A. Querido, *The Development of Socio-Medical Care in the Netherlands*, pp. 23–42. See also *Public Health in the Netherlands*, pp. 3–24.

Orange-Green Cross Associations were established. In the beginning these Cross organizations encouraged visiting the sick and rendering assistance during epidemics; gradually they began raising funds for sanitariums, clinics, medical aid, and welfare work. Later, district nurses were attached to the local Cross organizations. Beginning in 1920, preventive medical care, first provided for tuberculosis and for maternal and child health, was also extended to cover mental health, rheumatism, venereal disease, cancer, and the care of the physically handicapped.

Today, 73 percent of the Dutch population are members of a Cross organization, and together these organizations employ over four thousand district nurses. Except in the four large cities (Amsterdam, Rotterdam, The Hague, and Utrecht), where there are municipal public health departments, preventive health care in the Netherlands is completely in the hands of the nongovernmental Cross organizations.

In addition to public health, which in most Western countries is a governmental function, in the criminal justice system of the Netherlands probation has also been the responsibility of many small voluntary organizations since the early part of the nineteenth century. It is now the domain of four large denominational organizations subsidized by the Ministry of Justice.

Historical Development of Particulier Initiatief

The very late evolution of governmental responsibility for health and welfare services in the Netherlands is evident in the fact that not until 1854 was a poor law adopted. The first legislation applying to the handicapped was not adopted until the first decade of the twentieth century, when a series of parliamentary acts were passed dealing with industrial accidents, invalidism, and sickness benefits. It should be remembered, however, that during the nineteenth century Holland was a rather stagnant, small, agrarian country with a population of about three million. Since then its population has increased fourfold as a result of industrialization and modernization.

As in pre-Elizabethan England, in the Netherlands aid to the sick and disabled was considered a religious duty to be performed by individuals motivated by Christian piety. For the physically and mentally handicapped, beginning with the deaf and the blind in the early part of the nineteenth century and extending to the mentally handicapped around 1890, each denomination established local societies known as *particulier initiatief* (PI), which provided limited aid for their own members. By 1908, there were more than two-hundred PIs, which together formed the Netherlands Association for Poor Relief and Charity, the predecessor of the present National Council for Social Welfare.

Until World War II, there were very few schools or sheltered workshops for mentally handicapped, hard-of-hearing, partially sighted, or physically handicapped children and adults. Nursing homes for the elderly also took care of the physically handicapped. Not until after World War II were rehabilitation services sponsored by any of the denominational organizations, and before the war the social welfare organizations associated with the churches were generally regarded as inefficient and relatively unimportant, in sharp contrast to today's government-subsidized, professionalized, bureaucratic agencies of the *zuilen*.

Not all forms of social service were originally the monopoly of the confessional blocs. Before World War II, the denominational PIs did not employ social workers; and various forms of public assistance, psychiatric social work, and child welfare were sponsored by local government or by private organizations not affiliated with religious groups. During the war, however, when the Nazis deported most of the men as slave laborers, many churches organized home-help services, and later family welfare agencies, to provide material assistance and practical help to families. After the war, the churches began to enlarge these programs, partly for political reasons and partly as a response to what was seen as the declining role of religion in a modern, urbanized society. It was widely believed that sponsorship of social work services would be a means of strengthening the various denominations.

Underlying and supporting the great expansion of church-operated social service programs in the postwar period was a welfare ideology based on the Thomistic principle of subsidiarity and the Protestant equivalent, sphere sovereignty. In practice, this has been taken to mean that if an individual citizen or a lower social unit is unable to carry out a desirable objective, then the obligation of higher authority is restricted to providing the necessary financial support. In this conception, government is viewed as a residual, last-resort institution when other, more primary ones are unable to function.[7] Government

7. On "sphere sovereignty," see David O. Moberg, "Religion and Society in the Netherlands and in America." A British view of the concept of subsidiarity is R. E. B. Leaper, "Subsidiarity and the Welfare State."

becomes the financier, relying on the individual, the family, and the church as primary providers of a service, on the assumption that the service should stay as close as possible to the person in need. A corollary belief is that government should interfere as little as possible in the work of the more primary social units; "give us the money, but hands-off" is a crude statement of the operating principle, which is reinforced by a theological rationale and by the organized religious interests involved.[8]

This ideology grew out of a nineteenth-century context in which government represented power, law, and order, while the religious denominations stood for mercy, goodwill, love of one's neighbor, and compassion. The traditional division of responsibility between government and the denominational sponsors of the social services was in accord with the divine order of human society. This meant that the state could finance and encourage, now and again cautiously taking the initiative, but that it could never implement or interfere with what the voluntary organizations were doing. Evolved over a period of 300 years, the political framework in the Netherlands contributes to a stable and integrated society, despite a high degree of religious stratification.

Political System and Civic Culture

The Netherlands has been described as a "consociational democracy." The term refers to a pattern in which the political elites of distinct religious, sociocultural, or ethnic social groups succeed in establishing a viable pluralism by a process of mutual toleration and accommodation.[9] Formally a constitutional monarchy since 1848, the Netherlands, like Israel, is a unitary state with the central government possessing more authority than most federal structures. Regardless of the particular composition of party coalitions, the scope of government has grown over the years. While some allowance is made for decentralized authority in the provincial and local governments, all major taxes are collected by the national government, and in every important field of activity, policy is determined nationally. There are still over 800 municipalities, many of which have fewer than 1,000

8. A typical expression of the principle of subsidiarity as invoked in the United States by Catholic spokesmen is Bernard J. Coughlin, *Church and State in Social Welfare.* The principle of subsidiarity is a more extreme statement of the philosophies of reprivatization and empowerment. See footnote 5, Introduction and chapter 14.

9. In addition to Lijphart, other useful sources in English on the political system in the Netherlands are: Hans Daalder, "On Building Consociational Nations: The Cases of the Netherlands and Switzerland," and "The Netherlands: Opposition in a Segmented Society."

inhabitants, and while there is recognition in The Hague of the need for regional government and consolidation of marginal local units, this proceeds very slowly. Along with the centralization of governmental powers, there is an old tradition of planned cooperation in the creation of the largely man-made environment in the Netherlands; however, there are still strong feelings of local autonomy and resentment of outside authorities and their attempts to influence the community.

The sociopolitical structure is characterized by a limited popular participation and a general lack of interest in politics. For example, attendance by private citizens at local city council meetings is a rarity, even when controversial topics are discussed. Numerous studies have confirmed the existence of considerable apathy and lack of knowledge among the citizens. Moreover, in the political system of the Netherlands, there is little direct popular control.[10] Only the local and provincial legislatures and one house of the national legislature are elected directly by the people.

There is a high degree of congruence between the political and social structures: both are elitist and support deferential patterns of authority that until recently have not encouraged much citizen activity outside of or across the boundaries of the various religiopolitical blocs. Despite a reluctance to take overt individual action, there is a deeply rooted tradition of voluntary association within the historical framework of the *zuilen*. With the gradual decline of the *verzuiling*, however, there are more signs of departures from this tradition.

Beginning in the late 1960s, the structure of vertical pluralism in the Netherlands has increasingly been called into question. Secularization has proceeded apace in Dutch society, along with a tendency for the central government to take a stronger initiative in reviewing and making policy. The rise of modern secular ideologies in the Netherlands has accelerated the pace of "depillarization" *(ontzuiling)* or "deconfessionalization," and throughout the society there has been a resurgence of interest in democratization.[11] There are many signs that *verzuiling* is changing rapidly as it comes under increasing criticism as a result of pleas for ecumenism and of the pressures of a modern society. It has been estimated that at least one-third of the population in urban areas is now "unchurched," and that this proportion has increased to at least two-thirds among the younger generation, intellectuals, professionals,

10. Daalder, "The Netherlands," pp. 189–90.

11. G. P. A. Braam, "Social Work as a Means to Social Change." On the process of secularization, see Ralph M. Kramer, *Community Development in Israel and the Netherlands*, pp. 71–72, and Wolfenden Committee, "Report on Visit to the Netherlands," in *The Future of Voluntary Organisations*, pp. 275–78. This report will subsequently be cited as Wolfenden.

and industrial workers. Trends toward depillarization persist, despite the government's continuing policy of allocating most subsidies on a proportional basis to the organizations of the religious subculture.

Although the confessional blocs and their social welfare agencies, which may represent the last vestige of their influence, are still the foremost power structures outside the largest cities, most Dutch social scientists believe the *verzuiling* has reached its peak. Secularization and interbloc cooperation are proceeding more rapidly in some fields of social service than in others, but that they are well under way is indisputable. The course of secularization is now a matter of varying rates of change.

Public Fiscal Policy and the Statutory Framework

The distinctive relationship between the government and PIs in the Netherlands can be better understood through the evolution of the subsidy policy. The precedent established for education in 1917 was adopted in the field of social welfare services in 1953. As the scope of denominationally sponsored welfare services increased rapidly in the post-World War II years, it became more and more difficult to acquire the necessary funds through the usual methods of public appeals and special events. In particular, the increased cost of a professionalized staff exceeded the funding capacities of the church groups. In 1953 the Ministry of Social Work was established by a coalition government that included representatives of the Catholic parties, and, although no statute was passed, subsidies began to be made available as an administrative policy. Over the next decade there was a rapid growth in the number and scope of subsidies to denominationally sponsored agencies.

The next major change occurred in 1965, when the Public Assistance Act (ABW) replaced the 1912 poor law. The ABW established government responsibility for a minimum income for all citizens, including payments to the disabled under the incapacity insurance law (WAO).[12] Financial assistance, which had been a heavy item in the

12. The comprehensive social security system of the Netherlands is discussed in P.R. Kaim-Caudle, *Comparative Social Policy and Social Security: A Ten-Country Study*, pp. 153–56, 223–25, 271–72. This legislation is summarized in two 1977 fact sheets: The Netherlands, Ministry of Culture, Recreation, and Social Welfare, *The Public Assistance Act in the Netherlands* and *Social Policy on the Handicapped in the Netherlands*. The information provided by Dr. G. Hendriks, Director-General for Social Development, P. J. Blommestijn, Head, Department for Aged Care and Social Rehabilitation, and Professor Bram Peper of Erasmus Universitiet, Rotterdam, is gratefully acknowledged.

budgets of the PIs that had supplemented the old poor law provisions, became a governmental function through the establishment of an income maintenance system of social insurance and public assistance similar to that established in the United States thirty years earlier. Also in 1964, the Ministry of Social Work was expanded to include cultural affairs and recreation, becoming the Ministry of Culture, Recreation, and Social Welfare (CRM). The 1965 ABW separated social work from financial assistance, and most of the social services came under the jurisdiction of the new CRM, although several other services for the physically and mentally handicapped were also provided by the Ministries of Education, Health, and Social Affairs.

In addition to ending PIs' involvement with financial aid, the subsidy system also to a great extent relieved the nongovernmental organizations of the necessity of obtaining public contributions. The percentage of the budget paid by governmental subsidies for staff services has increased five times since 1965, so that subsidies now average between 80 to 90 percent of the costs of the twenty-thousand staff members employed by over 2,500 PIs.

As a consequence of the subsidy policy, only a few social service programs, usually those no PI is interested in sponsoring, are operated directly by government. These include institutions for emotionally disturbed youth, employment exchanges, and vocational training programs. Almost all of the two-hundred sheltered workshops for the physically and mentally handicapped are under municipal sponsorship. They represent one of the very few instances of a service program originally developed by a PI being adopted by government.[13] On the whole, however, there is no strong pressure or even sanction for direct governmental provision of services, although an increasing number of municipalities undertake social service functions where nongovernmental initiative is not forthcoming. In this process, the municipalities have sought to obtain the same rate of subsidy as PIs, but they claim that the PIs receive more favorable treatment, particularly in sponsoring generic social work, which also includes nonspecialized services for the physically handicapped.[14]

13. The sheltered workshops in the Netherlands are the subject of two empirical studies by Robert H. Haveman: *A Benefit-Cost and Policy Analysis of the Netherlands Social Employment Program* and *Public Employment of Less Productive Workers — Lessons for the U.S. from the Dutch Experience.*
14. Despite the existence of 340 organizations providing generic social work, with a combined staff of 1,625 persons and a budget representing 6 percent of all funds expended for the social services in the Netherlands, only 2 percent of the population made use of this service during 1972–1974. (Social and Cultural Planning Office, *Social and Cultural Report.*)

Beginning in the 1960s, many new forms of PI have appeared. "Alternative" service organizations, self-help, and action groups that are nonprofessional, secular, or nonsectarian have been started. Some of these also receive subsidies from municipal or national government. Falling somewhere between the relatively small organizations and the large denominationally sponsored agencies is a new, hybrid form, the "fusion" organization, which consists of the merger or federation of several organizations under religious auspices that have been providing the same service in a community to members of different denominations. Special subsidies are a strong incentive to create such organizations. In addition to some proprietary organizations, still another group of nonsubsidized social services is provided through the industrial welfare system by large corporations that employ their own social workers.

The PIs in the Netherlands function as primary service providers within a statutory context of a comprehensive system of social and health insurance, providing almost complete protection from the risks of old age, unemployment, sickness, and work incapacity. In addition, there is provision for children's allowances, vocational rehabilitation, and exceptional medical expenses. Although the subsidies that are the chief source of fiscal support for the PIs have been given annually by the government since 1952, when they were introduced as an "experiment," there is still no statutory basis for this primary method of financing social services. Also, there is no separate, general act to prescribe the organization, planning, coordination, research, or financing of social services for the handicapped.

Despite the seemingly precarious statutory basis of the subsidy policy and the uncertainties inherent in the annual negotiations between CRM and the Treasury, there has been considerable resistance over the years to adopting a law that would clearly establish the legal right of the PIs to these subsidies. In the last 20 years, six attempts have been made by CRM to draft legislation, but it was never possible to develop sufficient agreement on the bill between the ministry and the PIs to assure successful passage. Because of the importance of the confessional parties to which most of the PIs are indirectly attached, legislation that does not have their support will not ordinarily be adopted by the Parliament. It seems that the government and the PIs prefer to live with the absence of statutory provision rather than to make more explicit the distribution of power between them, which would also formalize and make less flexible the informal processes of negotiation and bargaining.

Apart from the laws pertaining to social insurance, there are a large number of administrative regulations regarding program subsidies that describe the conditions under which staff and operating costs will be paid for such programs as day care centers, boarding homes, hostels, residential centers, and social work services, as well as the administrative expenses of the organizations of parents and the national federations of PIs.

While many of the regulations provide for fifty-fifty support by the national and municipal governments or require that at least 10 percent of the funds of a PI be obtained from nongovernmental sources, these requirements have not always been implemented. Because sociopedagogical work for the mentally handicapped, which enjoyed a high priority in CRM, varied greatly in the financial support it received from municipalities, the conditional requirement that a PI obtain a matching grant was frequently overlooked when a grant was not forthcoming. Eventually 100 percent salary support of the sociopedagogues was adopted by CRM in 1976.

Even though subsidies are budgeted on a year-to-year basis, they represent in fact a long-term commitment because they are rarely revoked. Hence, officials in CRM tend to move slowly and cautiously before providing new subsidies, and it is not unusual for five years to pass before this occurs. The relatively small investment of staff in governmental supervision and inspection in the provincial bureaus also contributes to the enduring quality of subsidy decisions. While annual financial reports are required, organizations that do not submit such statements continue to receive subsidies. With a few exceptions, there is no system of mandatory, uniform service statistics or other forms of program accountability. CRM generally assumes that the boards of directors, the municipalities, the organizations of parents, and the national federations of PIs, as well as the norms of professional responsibility, will serve as effective monitors for service programs, even though there is no structural provision for feedback to government.

Among other outcomes, the subsidy policy has three related consequences. First, a tremendous expansion of most social services took place. The expansion is particularly noticeable in programs in which the government has a special interest. For example, during 1969–1972, the number of day care centers for the mentally handicapped almost doubled and served three times as many persons.[15] There is also a

15. The best account in English on the mentally handicapped is Jan B. Meiresonne, *Care for the Mentally Retarded in the Netherlands*.

progressive inclusion of subsidies for new types of professionals, as well as for additional psychologists, social workers, and game leaders, many of whom were proposed for inclusion by PIs that first demonstrated their value and absorbed the costs from their own funds. The range of subsidies was also extended in response to a cumulative push for higher personnel standards by agencies as they become more professionalized.

Second, beginning in the 1970s there has been a steep rise in the cost of subsidizing social services. In 1977 the government noted with dismay that there had been a thousandfold increase in the amount of subsidies over a twenty-five-year period.[16] Efforts are being made to transfer some of the costs of the personal social services from the current operating budgets of the ministries to the social insurance system, using third-party per capita payments for services. This first occurred in 1968, when day care centers for the mentally handicapped became eligible as an exceptional medical expense. The policy is since spreading to other forms of care and treatment, including hostels, social work, and hospital care.[17]

Third, the increased number of subsidized organizations and the accelerating cost of their programs is resulting in more pressure from government for a greater measure of efficiency, coherence, and consistency, and for more planning and coordination to reduce fragmentation and duplication.[18] To understand the significance of these trends, we must first examine certain features of the interorganizational environment of the PIs and the government.

Central Government and the National PIs

Responsibility for financing and supervising services to the physically and mentally handicapped is divided among four ministries: Social Affairs (social insurance, sheltered workshops, and employment services); Education and Science (special education); Public Health and Environmental Hygiene (hospitals, rehabilitation centers, and institutions); and Culture, Recreation, and Social Welfare (personal social

16. Pieter J. Blommestijn, "Implementation and Administration of Legislation concerning the Handicapped," p. 4.

17. "Outline of the Policy of CRM with Regard to the Handicapped." This legislation, Algemene Wet Bijzondere Zicktenkosten (AWBZ), provides for insurance against extraordinary medical expenses. See also A. Linde in *Talking about Integration* (Ministry of Culture, Recreation, and Social Welfare, Social Rehabilitation Department, 1973), p. 81.

18. A typical expression of this concern is found in G. Hendriks, "Scale Enlargement and Democratization."

services, including home help, day care, hostels, holidays, short-stay homes, leisure and sports programs, and professional social work).[19]

Differences between the Ministry of Health and CRM affect their relationships with the PIs. They differ in their primary mode of financing the PIs (health insurance versus CRM subsidies), in their budgeting, planning, and policymaking processes, in their relationships with local government, and in their ability to secure compliance with their standards. While the Ministry of Health is dominated by the medical profession, CRM is oriented more toward social services and social work. CRM also has a stronger policy commitment to community care, citizen participation, and decentralization. Each ministry has introduced separate, comprehensive draft legislation for its future programs, which may be difficult to reconcile because of opposing attitudes toward central-local governmental relationships.

As a relatively new and less powerful multidisciplinary ministry, CRM is generally perceived as being among the more progressive government departments. It characteristically proclaims itself to be the "mother Ministry" for national organizations in the field of rehabilitation. However, the growing movement from subsidies to health-related social insurance is circumscribing the domain of CRM because PIs now have more extensive contact with the Ministry of Health, under whose auspices reimbursement rates are set.

The central government usually consults with the national organizations of the PIs in the formulation of administrative regulations concerning the allocation of funds. This is consistent with the Dutch political system, which provides for extensive consultation with many policy advisory bodies and spokesmen for the various officially recognized sectors of community life that constitute "the fifth power" in the state. The national organizations with which CRM consults on policy present a staggering and highly complex "iron ring" of 256 "roof" or "umbrella" federations in the field of social welfare. Referring to the number of federations with which a PI may be affiliated, a Dutchman with a sense of humor put it this way: "We are all under at least three umbrellas; but nevertheless we get wetter and wetter."[20]

Among the most prominent of the CRM-subsidized interest groups are a federation of 8 national organizations for the mentally handi-

19. Unless otherwise indicated, what follows is based on my interviews with government officials in CRM.

20. A. Linde, "Services for the Mentally Handicapped in the Netherlands: A General Review."

capped and 150 associations in the field of rehabilitation. Efforts have been under way for several years to create a council of 25 national organizations for the physically and sensorially handicapped. Organized according to denomination, functional specialization based on specific disability, group or service modality, and geographic area, these national corporate interest groups — the umbrella organizations — do not find it easy to impose standards or ensure quality control in the local community because the PIs are quite autonomous and may not even choose to be affiliated with them.

There is a conscious government attempt to guide program development, to set priorities, and to raise standards. Government fiscal policy determines the budget for professional staffing of the PIs and thus affects standards of service delivery. Because fiscal policies are usually developed in consultation with the PIs or their national federations, almost all differences are regarded as negotiable by both parties, who stress the consensual character of their relationship. Most respondents agree that individuals and organizations have easy access to CRM and that there is more communication at the higher levels between the CRM officials and the national federations than there is on the lower echelons.

Despite the belief that he who pays the piper usually calls the tune, CRM evidently exerts relatively little central control over the PIs. Four factors may account for this. First, politically it is not feasible for the ministries to exert much power because the interests of the PIs are strongly defended in Parliament by the denominational political parties, which are almost invariably included in coalition governments.[21] Second, administratively it is not practical for the small staff in the provincial office of CRM to monitor the activities of a large number of small, autonomous agencies. Often presented with faits accomplis by PIs who claim to be entitled to a subsidy, CRM usually responds by financing the PIs and later trying to influence their policies and practices. Third, there is no comprehensive social plan, explicit set of governmental priorities, or standardized service statistics to serve as a basis for program evaluation. Fourth, the government is dependent on the PIs for service delivery, and it has few viable alternatives to the status quo and the traditional principle of live and let live.

A question of particular interest in a system relying almost exclusively on subsidized, nongovernmental organizations to provide ser-

21. In addition, 5 of the 150 members of Parliament in recent years have themselves been physically handicapped, and 2 others were presidents of associations of the handicapped. A CRM minister was also president of the League of Parents of the Mentally Handicapped.

vices pertains to the sources of, and incentives for, innovation and change. In contrast to the ideology of the United States or England, in which a voluntary agency is expected to lead with the government agency following and adopting the demonstrated service, in the Netherlands there is only one system of service delivery with no likelihood of governmental adoption or the diffusion of an innovation into another system. At the same time, there is no expectation that the PIs will be the only source of innovation, although they are recognized as the major instigators of change. Administratively, there is strong professional support for innovation by the CRM staff, and until recently there were special funds for research and program development and for statistics and planning.

One strategy of those officials in CRM who are interested in promoting both administrative and service improvements is the familiar one of cooptation — i.e., of seeking allies among the PI professionals, "planting" ideas and then later acknowledging them as coming from the PIs. In this way, government does not appear to be too assertive; rather, it works quietly and indirectly behind the scenes. This approach makes good sense on many grounds, not the least of which is the reality of the balance of power, which tends to favor the PIs. If there is any major difference between the government and the PIs regarding innovation and change, it may be the greater concern of the government with more progressive and efficient management, technical improvements, professionalization, and interdisciplinary cooperation, in contrast to the more programmatic and substantive interests of the PIs themselves.

Future Policy Changes

Two major policy issues affect the PIs in the mid-seventies. One consists of national problems in the financing, administration, planning, and delivery of services; the other pertains to structure and governance. In 1974 both were the subject of a comprehensive governmental critique of the social services entitled *Knelpuntennota* (literally, "policy bottlenecks").[22] The discussions of this document in Parliament between CRM and representatives of the national PIs and the

22. The account that follows is based on an English translation of the original report, which has been reviewed by various CRM staff members who are, of course, not responsible for my interpretation of the document known officially as the *Rapport van de Beraadsgroep knelpunten harmonisatie welzijnsbeleid en welzijnswetgeving* of 1974. Both the report and a summary in Dutch prepared by Paul Beugels and Bram Peper are issued by CRM. Some of the implications of these developments are discussed in Ralph M. Kramer, "Governmental-Voluntary Relationships in the Netherlands."

steps taken to implement it suggest that it will have considerable influence on the pattern of development of the social services over the next decade.

The *Nota* strongly criticizes the subsidy system for encouraging the uncontrolled growth of nongovernmental organizations, many of which are regarded as too small and specialized to be effective. In addition to diseconomies of scale, the multiplicity of the PIs results in a highly fragmented system with extensive duplication, inefficient services, inequities among groups and regions, and considerable over- and underuse. Constantly rising costs of subsidies reduce policy options and the possibility of change, making it difficult to fund any new or revitalized programs. In addition, inspection and supervision are spotty and restricted, limited to financial accountability with few means of assuring program quality control. Finally, because subsidies lack a basis in legislation, administrative regulations and the budgeting process produce insecurity and inequality among the PIs, their staffs, and their clientele.

Within the government structure itself, wide differences in funding and personnel practices between the various ministries and provincial and municipal governments result in uneven provision of services throughout the country. Because of excessive centralization of authority, the ministries have to deal with hundreds of national organizations on an individual basis, which creates formidable obstacles to communication, efficient administration, and citizen participation in policy-making and planning.

The *Nota* particularly faults the present service pattern for its failure to encourage democratic citizen participation in administration and planning. The document further cites an increasing number of conflicts between professionals and board members, with relatively little citizen involvement in the processes of PI governance and policymaking.

The *Nota* proposed three reforms. First, it recommended a new welfare policy that would provide for decentralized policymaking and for financing based upon an explicit division of function between various governmental levels and all types of PIs, and that would require citizen participation in municipal social planning. Second, the *Nota* proposed that the small size, multiplicity, and fragmentation of most of the PIs be countered by a policy of mergers. Third, it recommended decentralization of the entire structure through the formation of new budgeting and planning bodies on the municipal level. This recommendation was implemented in the Temporary Act for Social Service Provision (TVMD) of February 26, 1975, which established a precedent for municipal responsibility for certain social services. If a voluntary agency is unable or unwilling to implement a previously adopted plan, then the municipality may establish its own organization for this purpose or may undertake to do the work itself with national government loan guarantees. This act represents the first legislative recognition of the principle of subsidiarity and sets an important precedent by requiring a planning process that includes client representation and the formulation of service goals as a means of determining necessary community facilities. Thus this legislation and the recommendations of the *Knelpuntennota* seek to put together what the subsidy system has kept asunder over the years.

The process has proceeded slowly because of opposition to the devolution of authority by other ministries, the national associations of the PIs, professionals, and even local government officials. In view of past lack of interest and experience, the capacity of local government to take on its new function is questionable. It is also unclear how the allocation of several hundred million guilden in block grants to over 400 separate municipalities would result in a more coherent and efficient pattern of social services, particularly since many agencies will continue to receive all or most of their funds from central government through the social insurance system.

What is more likely is that many of the PIs will be worse off because of increased competition and politicization of a decentralized, local subsidy process guided by CRM-formulated spending ratios. The PIs will be confronted with a new locus and different distribution of power if the traditional influence of their national organizations in the central government and in Parliament wanes. It also seems likely that local government will impose a greater measure of control and will increase demands for accountability. Local government may also be reluctant to support the newer, more controversial programs of certain PIs, and some municipalities may decide to operate their own programs instead of financing a PI.

Conclusions

Although the PIs will continue to be almost exclusive providers of the social services in the Netherlands, a new pattern of relationships between them and the government seems to be emerging. It reflects the slowed growth rate of the welfare state and a shift from subsidies to social insurance in the mode of financing the social services. In the course of achieving financial security and a high degree of professionalization, the PIs may have lost something of their original voluntaristic character. If, as seems likely, their connection to central government will weaken in the future, with more demands for accountability and greater citizen participation, they will no longer enjoy the degree of autonomy that they have in the past.

2. England:
Statutory Supplementer

The pattern of development of the British welfare state can be viewed as two streams of governmental and voluntary initiative that occasionally intersect and that, even when parallel, affect each others' courses. In the beginning charity was sponsored by the church; later, because of the inability of private philanthropy to confront the ever-increasing scale and complexity of social problems, the government was forced to take increasing responsibility for the poor and the disabled.[1] After a century of Tudor experience with the problems of poverty, both the Elizabethan Poor Law Act and the Statute of Charitable Uses, the starting point of the modern British law of charities, were adopted in 1601. Although parishes were empowered by the Poor Law to provide for the education and care of the disabled (the blind, the lame, and the impotent poor) if their families were unable to provide for them, very little was actually done: state help was available more in principle than in practice. For the next three hundred years, apart from parish poor relief and some types of public institutional care, religious and philanthropic organizations were almost alone in the social services. They established numerous homes, hospitals, schools, training institutions, workshops, and clubs and organized visiting and other forms of what are now called the personal social services.

The Changing Pattern of Statutory and Voluntary Effort
In the context of laissez-faire individualism and underdevelopment of statutory services, voluntary agencies pioneered in the care of the handicapped until the end of the nineteenth century, when the state slowly began to take responsibility for some essential public health

1. The following are the primary sources for the historical account of the changing pattern of statutory and voluntary effort: Maurice Bruce, *The Coming of the Welfare State;* Derek Fraser, *The Evolution of the British Welfare State: A History of Social Policy since the Industrial Revolution;* M. Penelope Hall, *The Social Services of Modern England;* David Owen, *English Philanthropy 1660–1960;* Kathleen Woodroofe, *From Charity to Social Work in England and the United States.*

and welfare services. During this period the sensorially handicapped first were singled out for special attention.[2] Initial statutory recognition of disability as a distinct category of need occurred when educational responsibility for blind and deaf children was assumed by local government in 1893. Although the Poor Law guardians had been authorized since 1834 to pay the fees for handicapped children of poor families at charity schools, such as those founded by the Shaftesbury Society, in 1889 a royal commission discovered that these powers had been very sparingly used. The commission recommended mandatory education for the blind and deaf and permissive powers to provide funds to the existing voluntary schools for the mentally handicapped, some of which had been founded as early as the 1840s. Education for the mentally handicapped was not made mandatory until another inquiry in 1899, and not until 1918 was it brought into line with educational provisions for blind and deaf children. Despite a 600-year history of voluntary care for the blind in England, statutory recognition and provision for the blind also was long delayed. The Royal National Institute of the Blind (RNIB) was founded in 1868, but not until 1920 did the Blind Persons Law establish a registry, define blindness, and authorize some welfare and employment services.

Significant variations occurred in the pattern of service development for different disabilities. The first institutions for the mentally handicapped were established by voluntary associations beginning in 1848, and, by the 1930s, most had been transferred to the central government. In contrast, schools, homes, and workshops established for the blind beginning in 1834 continue to be maintained by voluntary bodies at present, when they number over 250.

The first modern statutory social services evolved at about the same time as a similar period of social reform in the United States, 1905–14, when considerable social legislation was passed by the Liberal Party under the leadership of Lloyd George. Although statutory responsibility was assumed for pensions, school meals, school medical services, unemployment, and health insurance for certain sections of the population, voluntary organizations continued to provide the major personal social services, particularly for the handicapped and for children.

2. On the development of specialized services to the mentally handicapped and the blind, see Madeline Rooff, *Voluntary Societies and Social Policy*, pp. 79–158 and 176–250; June Rose, *Changing Focus: The Development of Blind Welfare in Britain*, pp. 11–44; and Eda Topliss, *Provision for the Disabled*, pp. 1–11 and 29–33. The mentally handicapped are included in Kathleen Jones, *A History of the Mental Health Services*.

By 1911 both sectors had developed sufficiently for Sidney and Beatrice Webb to formulate a set of principles for a functional division of responsibility that is still regarded as valid. They rejected the 1869 "parallel bars" theory of two mutually exclusive sectors in which private charity was more highly valued, aiding the deserving and the helpable while the hopeless and undeserving were assigned to the Poor Law. Instead they proposed the "extension ladder" theory, in which voluntary organizations supplement the basic statutory services that provide a minimum standard of life for all.[3] This became one of the major assumptions of the widely accepted "partnership" concept of statutory-voluntary relationships.

In the period between the two world wars, the state began to take increasing responsibility for some welfare services. Because voluntary organizations already existed, the state paid them for services rendered and began to use them as delegate agencies in serving the blind and the deaf, and to utilize voluntary residential institutions for the physically and mentally handicapped. During the 1920s and 1930s the number of voluntary facilities and programs for the mentally handicapped greatly exceeded those of the statutory sector.[4]

Whereas the nineteenth century was marked by the expansion of voluntary services and the first quarter of the twentieth century was characterized by the emergence of the statutory services, the postwar period, beginning in 1946, can be viewed as the consolidation of the welfare state. Beginning with the passage in 1946 of the National Health Service and the National Insurance acts, and in 1948 of the National Assistance and the Children's acts, the foundations of the postwar welfare state were laid, apparently ending the supremacy of the voluntary agency. The social philosophy behind the implementation of the Beveridge Report was Fabian in its commitment to the superiority of statutory responsibility over private charity. At the same time, welfare was not regarded as altogether a state monopoly.[5]

Although some feared that private philanthropy and voluntary organizations would be displaced as unnecessary by cradle-to-grave legislation, voluntary agencies did not diminish in importance. Instead, the number and scope of voluntary organizations increased tremendously, and they took on even more varied functions. New

3. The Webbs developed these ideas in their Minority Report of The Poor Law Commission, 1905–1909 and in their book *The Prevention of Destitution*, pp. 226–38.

4. Rooff, pp. 112–218.

5. The deep commitment of Lord Beveridge to voluntary organizations and his belief in their future is evident in his *Voluntary Action: A Report on Methods of Social Advance* and in Lord Beveridge and A. F. Wells, eds., *The Evidence for Voluntary Action.*

types of voluntary organizations were established in the postwar years, in particular, organizations concerned with a single handicap, whose major constituency consisted of the victims themselves and members of their families. The peer self-help groups, rooted in the tradition of mutual aid, also became pressure groups on behalf of persons suffering from a specific disability. Before this time, most voluntary organizations were much less specialized and had an undifferentiated concern for "cripples," all types of disabled or handicapped persons.

These organizational developments were part of a movement taking place simultaneously in other European countries and in the United States during the 1950s. The rapid growth in the number of such organizations can be seen in our sample of the twenty national agencies. The first nine organizations emerged over a period of 120 years, but it took only 16 years for the next ten to emerge. Six agencies were established during 1948–57, and another four were founded in 1958–65. Contributing to the growth of such agencies was the increasing awareness of such diseases as polio and multiple sclerosis, the higher birth rate, and reduced infant mortality, which resulted in the survival of more children with handicaps.

In the postwar period voluntary organizations continued to play an important role due to the perennial insufficiency of statutory resources. A series of legislative precedents in both statutes and Circular Letters acknowledged the value of voluntary organizations and encouraged local authorities to provide services directly or to rely on voluntary agencies. For example, a Circular Letter of August 1962 from the Department of Health lists over fifty different voluntary agencies' services as eligible for support from local authorities. In the mid-1950s, 92 percent of the local authorities relied on voluntary organizations to serve the deaf; almost three-quarters of the local authorities used voluntary agencies for some services to the physically handicapped, and until 1970 over 70 percent of the local authorities used voluntary societies as their agents for the blind.[6] This was the era of the development of residential facilities by national voluntary organizations. By 1975, only twenty local authority homes were desig-

6. Margot Jefferys, *An Anatomy of Social Services*, p. 155. For a picture of statutory-voluntary relationships during the 1950s, see Barbara N. Rodgers and Julia Dixon, *A Portrait of Social Work: A Study of Social Services in a Northern Town*. Some of the changes that took place during the 1960s are reflected in Barbara N. Rodgers and June Stevenson, *A New Portrait of Social Work: A Study of the Social Services in a Northern Town from Younghusband to Seebohm*.

nated specifically for the physically handicapped, and less than half of all the physically handicapped were in residential care in statutory homes.

When local authorities took on services to the physically handicapped in the 1960s, they used methods originated and developed by voluntary agencies. These included providing advice and guidance, social centers and clubs, transportation, home helps, recreation, aids, holidays, and employment in a workshop or center or at home, as well as assisting in the marketing of products and providing handicraft teachers. In addition, most physically and mentally handicapped children benefit from special education provided by local authorities. Since 1960, local authorities have had the power to spend public money from the taxes on local property to provide these services, but not until 1967 were they authorized to provide directly domiciliary meals and recreational facilities for the disabled and aged, activities that have traditionally been a voluntary prerogative. The expanding scope of statutory programs is reflected in a 1958 report, which acknowledges that if all local authorities exercised their welfare powers fully, the need for voluntary agencies would be drastically reduced.[7] This has not occurred, not only because of inadequate statutory funds and staff shortages, but also because of the more economical charges of the voluntary agencies, which are supposed to be 75 percent of costs, but usually are much lower. The wide use of voluntary agencies also contributes to unevenness and lack of coherence in the pattern of statutory services, which is aggravated by minimal coordination between statutory and voluntary agencies.[8]

Summary of Service Patterns

Over the last two-hundred years, the pace was first set by the voluntary sector; in the last thirty or forty years, it has been set by the state. Five features of service patterns from 1960 to 1975 are especially noteworthy.

First, there has been a substantial expansion of both statutory and voluntary services of all kinds, with perhaps more being done for the physically than for the mentally handicapped. While there is con-

7. J. H. Nicholson, *Help for the Handicapped: An Inquiry into the Opportunities of the Voluntary Services*, p. 102.

8. Rooff, pp. 234–92; and Samuel Mencher, "Factors Affecting the Relationship of the Voluntary and Statutory Child Care Services in England" and "Financial Relationships between Voluntary and Statutory Bodies in the British Social Services."

siderable variation in the provision of services from one handicap to another, the statutory system has the broadest obligations and, with a few exceptions, is the major service provider, as well as the primary source of funds. Although a few voluntary agencies continue to hold a significant place because of their highly specialized character, the comprehensive scope and volume of the statutory personal social services exceeds that of the voluntary sector. Statutory bodies do pay for services and make grants to voluntary organizations, but this is marginal in comparison with the more widespread public programs.

In part, the lesser scale of voluntary effort is due to a concern with small populations at risk. With a low, and in several cases declining, incidence of handicaps resulting from such diseases as polio, spina bifida, autism, and muscular dystrophy, from a statutory purview the handicapped represent a numerically marginal group. A Local Authority Social Service Department (SSD) is likely to have only a few cases among thousands of clientele.[9]

The second noteworthy feature is that there is no clear separation of function between voluntary and statutory services. Both continue to operate very similar institutional and community-based programs, although their scope and volume differ considerably. Few social services are the unique property of one or the other sector, but leisure time and recreational programs for the mentally handicapped are almost invariably operated by voluntary, not statutory, agencies.

Statutory programs for the physically and mentally handicapped tend to be more universalistic and generic than the specialized and particularistic programs of a voluntary agency. The SSD is charged by law to serve all classes of the handicapped, regardless of the cause of their condition or the particular medical label attached to it. Apart from the blind, the deaf, and the mentally handicapped, the statutory services have been concerned more with degree of disability and possibility of rehabilitation than with a particular medical rubric. In practice, the same types of personal social service — for example,

9. The low incidence of some of these handicaps can be seen from the projection that for every 250,000 persons (90,000 households), one can expect to find 500 very severely handicapped children, including 200 mentally handicapped ones, but only 25 deaf, 20 blind, and 5 autistic children, and 20 cases of muscular dystrophy. The incidence of many of these conditions is expected to decline in the future due to the lowered birth rate, greater use of amniocentesis and other prenatal diagnostic techniques, and genetic counseling. A 20 percent reduction in the number of disabled children needing care in the 1980s has been predicted, with an increase in the number of handicapped over sixty-five. It is expected that 70 percent of the disabled will be seventy-five and over by 1984. (Family Fund Research Project, *The Prevalence of Children with Very Severe Disabilities in the United Kingdom*, p. 18.)

nurseries, day care, home helps, sheltered workshops, hostels, and residential care — are required by most handicapped persons.[10]

Despite the fact that most handicapped persons have multiple disabilities, virtually all the national voluntary agencies are organized on behalf of a single handicap. This is less true in local communities, where there are indigenous, less specialized associations. While voluntary agencies are concerned with a specific disability, their focus is still on the person as a whole and on the totality of his social, educational, health, employment, and housing requirements. Unlike statutory agencies, which are organized on a functional basis, voluntary agencies tend to be organized on the basis of clientele.

The third feature is that, apart from size, there is a basic disparity between the voluntary and statutory service systems in degree of bureaucratization, complexity, and professionalization. Statutory organizations present a contrast to the looser structure of voluntary organizations, particularly on the local level. Judged by number of staff, by operating budget, and by assets, some of the national agencies are also complex, large service bureaucracies, but even these exceptions cannot be compared to the typical formal, hierarchical, and decentralized statutory organization, with four to five thousand staff members and a £20,000,000 budget. For example, a study of social service manpower resources found that voluntary organizations employ a paid work force equal to one-sixth of the comparable local authority staff. Nationally, only 13 to 14 percent of all professional social workers are employed by voluntary organizations, according to recent estimates.[11]

A fourth feature of the personal social services for the physically and mentally handicapped is the great variability in both sectors, both geographically and by disability. The quantity and quality of the personal social services differ between urban and rural areas and within

10. The characteristics of these programs are analyzed in Eric Sainsbury, *The Personal Social Services*, pp. 23–83; Michael Bayley, *Mental Handicap and Community Care*; and Robert Pinker, *Research Priorities in the Personal Social Services: A Report to the Research Initiatives Board*, pp. 2–35. An excellent compendium of articles dealing with the conditions, services and needs of handicapped persons is David M. Boswell and Janet M. Wingrove, eds., *The Handicapped Person in the Community*.

11. While the Social Service Departments employ almost 85 percent of all professionally educated social workers, only 40 percent of their total social work staff is trained. (Adrian Webb, Lesley Day, and Douglas Weller, *Voluntary Social Service Manpower Resources*, p. 20.) On the organizational character and structure of the Local Authority Social Service Department, see R. G. S. Brown, *The Management of Welfare: A Study of British Social Service Administration*, pp. 108–37. For an American perspective, see Robert Morris, *Toward a Caring Society*.

regions. The persistent differences, often referred to as "territorial in-justice," detract from the universality of public provision. The major factor affecting service delivery is still where one lives.[12] Many localities have a paucity of voluntary agencies, and the scope and con-tent of their services varies in quality and quantity on an almost idiosyncratic basis.

The last characteristic feature is the low "take-up" of services in both the statutory and voluntary sectors. Despite the existence of over forty handicap-specific national voluntary associations and a long list of mandated and practically unlimited permissive statutory services, it is estimated that 72 percent of all seriously handicapped persons re-ceive no welfare services from *any* source.[13] While not all impaired persons require or want such services, there is evidence of a high degree of underutilization. Apart from the low incidence of some disabilities, resource and communication deficiencies, as well as dis-crepant individual and organizational perceptions of a handicap, contribute to low utilization.[14]

Current Trends and Issues

Service patterns must be viewed against a rapid succession of struc-tural, social policy, and economic changes since 1970 that have made the organizational environment in both voluntary and statutory sec-tors turbulent and uncertain. Reorganization of local government, first in London in 1965 and in the rest of England in 1974, reduced the number of social service departments by almost one-fourth. Legisla-tion in 1968 and 1970 gave more explicit power to the local authorities to aid and use voluntary agencies and permitted the use of local statu-tory funds to provide vehicles, home helps, laundry services, and at-tendant allowances to the physically and mentally handicapped.[15] The 1970 Education Act also shifted the responsibility from the Health Department to the Local Education Authority for the training

12. Family Fund Research Project, *Variations in Provision by Local Authority Social Service Departments for Families with Handicapped Children.*

13. A. I. Harris, *Handicapped and Impaired in Great Britain*, Part I, Table 38, p. 50. Topliss, pp. 129–43, also reports on a 1973 survey of over one thousand disabled persons, consisting of all disabled people in Southhampton under the age of sixty-five. Two-thirds of them received no service, but only 25 percent receiving no help wanted any.

14. Mildred Blaxter, *The Meaning of Disability: A Sociological Study of Impairment.*

15. Health Service & Public Health Act of 1968, Sections 13, 33, and 45. On implementation of some of these supporting services by the local authorities, see Topliss, pp. 102–15. A list of the acts of Parliament giving statutory powers for government to provide funds to voluntary organi-zations is found in Wolfenden, pp. 232–41.

of all mentally handicapped children, and this was followed in 1971 by an influential White Paper, *Better Services for the Mentally Handicapped* (Cmnd 4683).

The foremost step in restructuring the personal social services occurred in 1970 with passage of the Local Authority Social Service Act (LASSA), implementing most of the recommendations of the Seebohm Committee, which completed its work in 1968.[16] Although it did not create any new programs, the LASSA brought together under one new administration in each local government previously independent services offered by the local children's committee, the welfare, and the health departments. In 1974 hospital social work was also brought within the province of the personal social services of the SSD. The new SSDs became the welfare instruments of reorganized local governments and were authorized to provide a wide array of personal social services administered by social workers. As a generic, one-stop agency, the SSD is expected to improve the coordination of services, as well as to become a center for prevention and voluntary activity.

A long-standing governmental policy of making maximum use of voluntary agencies was reaffirmed by the LASSA,[17] and voluntary agencies continue to fill some of the financial and service gaps that persist despite a 71 percent increase in funds allocated for the personal social services between 1970 and 1976. Part of the difficulty resulted from the fact that funds from central government were not earmarked and that the 12 percent increase each year to local authority for expanding welfare services could be used for a variety of other purposes.

Because existing staff and facilities have been inherited from previously separate agencies, the development of services is highly uneven for the disabled, the chronically ill, handicapped children, and the aged. This is reinforced by the lack of central government guidance

16. A definitive analysis of the work of the Seebohm Committee is Phoebe Hall, *Reforming the Welfare: The Politics of Change in the Personal Social Services.* The independent Committee on Local Authority and Allied Personal Social Services, better known after its chairman as the Seebohm Committee, was appointed by Parliament in 1966 to review the existing statutory programs and to recommend the changes necessary "to secure an effective family service." In retrospect, LASSA has been viewed by many as essentially an administrative change, which does not embody the philosophy of the Seebohm Report concerning the family and the informal helping processes in the community. Many of these ideas were stressed in the Wolfenden Report a decade later.

17. Sainsbury, pp. 101–2, believes that the Seebohm Report represents a turning point in defining the respective roles of statutory and voluntary services. The latter offer a quality of help that is not just an extension of statutory services, but is different in kind—e.g., developing citizen participation, revealing new needs, and exposing shortcomings in the services.

on priorities, so that differences in services reflect variations in local priorities and the self-selection inevitable when services are available only by request and do not reach out.

In addition, an initial emphasis on a generic approach by the new SSDs means that if a voluntary agency has expertise or another specialized resource, it is likely to be used. This tendency is particularly pronounced with respect to the blind, the deaf, and the mentally handicapped. Many of the most professionally qualified social workers who formerly provided specialized care of children, for mental illness, and for mental handicaps have moved into administrative, middle-management, and supervisory posts or have become consultants and advisors, leaving generic tasks to those who have less experience and training, among whom there is also a rapid turnover. The use of voluntary agencies is limited by emphasis on services for which they have fewer resources, such as community care, home helps, and day care centers, instead of institutional placement. Another factor that affects the relationship of voluntary agencies to the new SSDs is the post-1970 administrative reorganization, which has resulted in large, complex, hierarchical structures, making communication and access more difficult.

Another landmark law of 1970 was the Chronic Sick and Disabled Persons Act (CSDPA), which represented the first clear recognition of comprehensive statutory responsibility for the disabled since 1948. Although authorized since 1948 to provide supporting welfare services for the elderly and the handicapped, most local authorities had made little progress in offering the range of services needed by the disabled. Consequently, in a departure from the usual process of social policy development, the leadership of a group of voluntary organizations generated pressure to secure passage of a private members' bill that capitalized on public sympathy for the disabled. Over the strong objections of central government officials who feared that the legislation could not be properly implemented, the CSDPA was passed by a resounding majority in Parliament.[18]

The act has not been well received by local authorities who were initially charged with conducting surveys to determine the number of disabled persons and to provide for their special needs, but who were not given guidelines and additional or earmarked funds by the Department of Health and Social Security (DHSS) for these purposes.

18. A personal account of this process is Alfred Morris and Arthur Butler, pp. 7–23. A somewhat different perspective is found in Topliss, pp. 12, 111–14, and 146–47.

There has been considerable controversy over the intent of the act, which in the judgment of its supporters obligated the local authority to meet the special needs of all disabled persons identified. Even under the best of circumstances, this cannot be done without giving a higher priority to services for the chronic sick and disabled than to such other local needs as roads, schools, libraries, and housing, over and above the interests of such other clientele as children, families, and the aged.

In general, implementation of the CSDPA is spotty and inadequate. A five-year review by the Central Council for the Disabled condemned the local authorities and central government for failure to carry out the intent of the CSDPA.[19] Because of the limited powers of central government and traditional local autonomy, neither DHSS nor the Minister for the Disabled, who was appointed in 1974, has made a concerted effort to secure greater compliance by local authorities. Also, few voluntary agencies press hard, either nationally or locally, for implementation.

The timing of the CSDPA was most unfortunate because it coincided with an accelerating inflation rate and the subsequent retrenchment of government social service expenditures.[20] The economic difficulties of the mid-1970s increased the demand for, and the cost of, social services, while inflation reduced the value of contributed funds to voluntary agencies. To compensate for their loss of income, some national voluntary agencies sought increased grants from central government and additional tax relief. Their financial plight was, in part, a stimulus to the appointment of two citizen committees by leading national bodies to help chart the future of voluntary organizations.

The National Council of Social Service appointed an independent committee of inquiry of seventeen members, headed by Lord Goodman, that from 1974 to 1976 examined the effect of charity law and practice on voluntary organizations. After reviewing current fund raising, tax exemptions, political activity, and accounting practices in the light of the Law of Charities of 1960, the Goodman Committee decided not to recommend any substantial changes in policy. It offered instead some guidelines for the definition of *charitable purposes*

19. "Five Years of Enabling Legislation: The 1970 Act and Its Consequences," *Contact* No. 10 (June–July 1975):3–9. The Central Council for the Disabled has merged with the British Council for Rehabilitation of the Disabled and is now known as the Royal Association for Disability and Rehabilitation. See also Walter Jaehnig, "Seeking Out the Disabled."

20. Sainsbury, pp. 128–34. A more detailed analysis of this process is Ken Judge, *Rationing Social Services: A Study of the Allocation of the Personal Social Services.*

and suggested a more liberal interpretation of the existing restrictions on the lobbying activity of charitable organizations.[21]

A nine-member committee headed by Lord Wolfenden was jointly appointed by the Rowntree Memorial Trust and the Carnegie United Kingdom Trust to review the role of voluntary organizations over the next twenty-five years. The committee collected information from 320 organizations dealing with the personal social services and the environment as the basis for its principal recommendations for greater statutory funding of the voluntary sector, directly and through aiding local coordinating bodies.[22]

The Public Policymaking Process

Three major groups make public policy in England: the House of Commons, pressure groups, and the career civil servants of central government.[23] Although the House of Commons is the supreme authority in the United Kingdom, it is not a law-initiating body like the United States Congress, but is more an extension of the executive branch of government. Ninety percent of the bills enacted — and they are relatively few in number — are government bills proposed by a cabinet minister, but actually emanating from the departments of central government. The most important function of the House of Commons is to examine proposals, to criticize them, and to probe, using such devices as the parliamentary question, which requires the government to justify its actions. Members tend to vote in predetermined ways strictly according to party lines. No private member of Parliament can propose legislation that would increase taxation, and the members exercise little control over the spending of public money. Parliamentary committees do not have the power or the quasi-judicial status of their American counterparts; for example, bills are referred to committees only after the second reading.

21. Goodman Committee, *Charity Law and Voluntary Organisations.* The subject is also discussed by the former chief charity commissioner, Christopher P. Hill, "The English System of Charity." See also Benedict Nightingale, *Charities*, pp. 34–67.

22. Representative of some of the criticism of the Wolfenden Report are: Nicholas Hinton, "Building for the Future"; F. J. Amos, "An Opportunity Missed"; and Adrian Webb, "Voluntary Action: In Search of a Policy?" Some of the major recommendations of the report are summarized in the *London Times* of November 23, 1977, "Why Our Social Service Volunteers Deserve More Backing."

23. The following are the sources for the description of the governmental structure and public policymaking system in this section. S. E. Finer, *Comparative Government*, pp. 138–86; Phoebe Hall et. al., *Change, Choice and Conflict in Social Policy*, pp. 1–153; R. G. S. Brown, pp. 175–210; and Jay Darlove, *The Politics of Policy in Local Government.*

A second influence on social policy consists of a stable subsystem of pressure groups that are in close contact with the executive branch (civil servants and ministers) and to a lesser extent are in contact with members of Parliament. Groups traditionally are invited to testify before royal commissions and departmental committees of inquiry, and more than five-hundred advisory committees are attached to the departments, in addition to interest groups that have attained consultative status. The government clearly accepts the role of voluntary organizations as advocates for particular constituencies, and two all-party parliamentary groups are devoted to the physically and the mentally handicapped.

The primary policymakers, however, are the civil service staffs of the departments of central government. They tend to operate independently of public control and beyond the range of public scrutiny. Although ministers have final responsibility, the permanent, politically neutral civil service has the greatest influence, particularly those civil servants in the higher ranks who are protected by a tradition of secrecy regarding intradepartmental activity and who cannot be criticized by name. This code of secrecy not only protects any civil servant from revealing or commenting on the affairs of a department, but it also legally protects the department from scrutiny by the courts of law.[24] Although in theory it is the minister who acts and the civil servant who informs and advises, the enormous size of the civil service (for example, the DHSS has seven thousand employees) and its possession of information, expertise, and other sources of power protected by the code of secrecy make it the dominant element in policymaking.

At the same time, neither the civil servants nor the departments of central government are monolithic, and they do not form a single hierarchy. "Government exhibits an administrative pluralism which strengthens the polycentric nature of the policy processes . . . there are divergences of interest, priorities, and values between the authorities and even within the government itself."[25]

The other side of this pluralism is a perennial lack of coherence and coordination among the departments that has been the subject of many parliamentary inquiries and debates. For example, seven out of the more than twenty departments are involved in rehabilitation, and service to the mentally handicapped is within the province of four

24. G. W. Keeton, *Government in Action in the United Kingdom*, p. 146.
25. Hall et al., p. 128.

departments. Two recent efforts at coordination are the establishment of the Minister for the Disabled in the DHSS and the Voluntary Services Unit (VSU). The Minister for the Disabled, a member of Parliament with a long career of service to the handicapped, was appointed in 1974 and became a major point of contact for voluntary organizations in their relationships with government. In addition, he serves an advocate function within DHSS and between it and other departments.

Whereas the Minister for the Disabled is concerned with advancing the interests of one particular group served by voluntary organizations, the VSU has a general concern with the relationship of voluntary organizations to all departments. Originally set up under the Conservative government in 1972, it was continued under the Labour government following a prolonged struggle over its appropriate administrative form and locus.[26] The VSU has four functions. First, within central government it coordinates the diverse interests of the voluntary sector that cut across different government boundaries. Second, it helps voluntary agencies to find their way around central government and keeps them informed. Third, it promotes volunteerism through its financial support of the Volunteer Centre, Volunteer Bureaux, the National Council of Social Service, and the Women's Royal Voluntary Service. Finally, as the "financier of last resort in Whitehall," it makes allocations to a limited number of voluntary organizations. Essentially, the VSU has a liaison rather than a coordinative function, providing some interdepartmental linkages in addition to allocating £4,600,000 to voluntary organizations in 1976–77.

Despite the existence of the VSU, each department of central government makes annual allocations to national voluntary agencies quite independently of the others.[27] In recent years the grants have increased substantially — to over £38,000,000 in 1976 — and are made primarily to meet administrative and other expenses of the headquarters offices of several hundred national organizations, not for provision of services. Since 1973, the issue of central government's financing of voluntary agencies has become increasingly controversial as agencies press to make their budgets proof against inflation. While there is strong ideological support in Parliament for voluntary agencies, as

---

26. Andrew Rowe, "The Voluntary Service Unit."
27. The process whereby these allocations are made to the national voluntary agencies is described in Wolfenden Committee, *The Future of Voluntary Organisations*, pp. 219–30. (Hereafter cited as Wolfenden.)

well as considerable concern about their finances, no substantial change has occurred in the pattern of governmental support.[28]

DHSS stands between Parliament and statutory and voluntary agencies, professional organizations, and consumer groups. It has four major tasks: representing the health and social services to Parliament and obtaining resources; allocating funds to local authorities, the National Health Service, individuals, and voluntary organizations; policymaking, supervision, monitoring, and some provision of services.

Within DHSS is a large and complex administrative structure involving multidisciplinary teams of administrators and professionals devoted to specific populations at risk, including separate divisions for physical and mental health.[29] They are divided into a series of health and social service development groups, which advise the secretary of state on objectives, priorities, and standards for the health and social services. Typical of these numerous advisory and consultative bodies in DHSS was the appointment in 1975 of the National Development Group for the Mentally Handicapped, consisting of scientists and representatives of voluntary agencies and statutory organizations. The Personal Social Service Council (PSSC) was set up by DHSS in 1974 to provide an independent structure for advice and research. Jointly financed by central and local authorities, the PSSC appointed its own staff and was one of the few forums for representatives from government and from professional and voluntary organizations until it was terminated by the Conservative government in 1980. On a day-to-day basis within DHSS, representatives of voluntary agencies interact with members of the Social Work Service and its regional offices, which are also divided into specialized staff for the mentally, physically, and sensorially handicapped.

The English pattern of relationship between central and local government differs from that in the United States in the absence of an intermediate third layer, such as state governments. The central government offices are restricted to controlling some resource allocations and, to a lesser extent, to planning. The direct administrative authority of DHSS over a local SSD is confined to veto power over the appointment of the director (who must be a social worker) and to control over the size and content of the capital building program. Indirect power is exerted by DHSS in its ability to delay decision making and

28. The high regard for voluntary organizations and the way in which they are regarded as almost *sancta* is evident in *House of Lords Debates*, Hansard, 1975, vol. 361, no. 110, cols. 1389 and 1397; and *House of Commons Debates*, Hansard, 1975, vol. 895, no. 154. cols. 345–405.
    29. R. G. S. Brown, pp. 52–78.

the allocation of funds, along with the influence of its suggested guidelines. Apart from this authority, central government does not control directly the day-to-day operations of local authority, and there is relative little supervision, inspection, or responsibility for securing conformity to a national plan, to priorities, or to guidelines. However, although the hand of central government is gentle, it is firm. Eventually most local authorities do what the central government asks, particularly when they are requested to reduce their budgets.

Most legislation pertaining to the handicapped is permissive, and the guidelines and circulars of DHSS are considered to be suggestive only. Failure to use the power of central government to inspect local health and welfare facilities has been criticized, and, periodically, there have been scandals. These administrative conditions result in a high degree of local discretion in the social services that explains much of the variation among local authorities in their provision of the personal social services that are supposed to be available as a matter of right in each community.

The central government's major resource for influence is the block grant to local authorities to supplement the local property tax, the primary income source for local government. These block grants average nationally about 60 percent, varying from 20 to 80 percent, and average 40 percent in the London area. Central government has not been able to keep to the plan for raising expenditures for the personal social services to meet the level of demand, even though their funding has increased to a greater extent than any other function of local authority.[30] Since 1973, cutbacks of 25 percent are not unknown, and voluntary agencies, which also suffer severely from the economic pinch, are called upon to step in and help to fill the breach.

In general, few local or national structures bring together statutory and voluntary agencies for joint planning. Instead, voluntary organizations have such federations as the National Council of Social Service (NCSS) and the Central Council for the Disabled (CCD), while local authorities have their own associations. There may be a greater need for intra- than for inter-sectoral planning and coordination, particularly in light of disparity in resources and responsibilities.

Ideology of Governmental-Voluntary Relationships

In these developments, the prevailing ideology of governmental-voluntary relationships in England can be identified. Strictly speak-

30. Wolfenden, 255–58.

ing, it is true that "there is no positive accepted philosophy regarding the use of voluntary organizations."[31] Yet a set of guiding principles, not necessarily formalized or made explicit, does seem to exist. On the one hand, the government clearly accepts the obligation of administering a system of universal social services. On the other, a history of pragmatic collaboration with the voluntary sector is recognized. The frequently invoked concept of a partnership between the two sectors, however, seems to imply parity and a degree of interdependence that does not always conform to reality, in which the voluntary agency is at best a junior and usually silent partner. Although the popular view of the social service system can be expressed in holistic terms, in practice, because the two sectors interact less than is believed, there is considerable evidence for its being dualistic. Historically, the socialist ideology of the Labour Party has led to a stronger emphasis on direct governmental administration and to regarding voluntary organizations as a residual irrelevancy. The Conservatives, on the other hand, have often stressed voluntary organizations, at the expense of allocating insufficient resources to the statutory agencies.[32]

Some, however, believe that the growth of the statutory system has peaked and that the next twenty-five years will see greater utilization of the voluntary and informal sectors. This point of view, which seeks to change the current balance of power, is incorporated in the recommendations of the Wolfenden Committee. It has a natural appeal to many diverse groups, particularly those who believe that policies based on such a view might result in reducing taxes, as well as the power of central government. However, its adoption might rekindle the historical working-class antagonism to the modern version of "private charities."

Certain unique and indispensable features of the voluntary agency are recognized. The Wolfenden Committee, for example, identified five "special contributions" by the voluntary sector: (1) providing services that are complementary, additional, or alternative to statutory services, such as day centers, children's homes, advice centers, housing associations, and residential care; (2) responding to new needs and pioneering services that may later be incorporated in the welfare state, such as family planning and, more recently, refuges for battered wives; (3) acting as a pressure group to bring about changes in social policies; (4) reinforcing the extensive informal caring arrangements of

31. George J. Murray, *Voluntary Organizations and Social Welfare*, p. 15.
32. Sainsbury, p. 219.

families and neighbors; (5) in some places, acting as the sole agent providing services.[33]

In a more limited context, Barbara Rodgers has proposed five "strategic tasks" as particularly suitable for voluntary agencies: (1) social and recreational services that do not call for large financial resources but in which volunteer and community involvement is at a premium; (2) controversial services; (3) mutual aid and interest and pressure group activities; (4) experiments in helping or treating the most difficult and hard-to-reach groups, particularly those that have a strong antiauthority feeling; (5) extralegal additional benefits and services that a particular group needs or wants to provide as mutual aid over and above what can be obtained from the state.[34]

Civic Culture

The evolution of the British welfare state from its religious and philanthropic origins to the present statutory structure occurred within the context of a set of values and norms regarding citizen participation that has become a prototype for other Western democracies. This civic culture not only sanctions, but strongly encourages, two related forms of altruistic and voluntary action. One is interpersonal, rooted in religious-humanitarian values and expressed in the tradition of charity and self-help within the social services. The other is sociopolitical, originating in the classical pluralist philosophies of Locke and Mill asserting the rights of individuals to freely associate and to seek to influence public policy on behalf of their members and constituents. In the development of the social services in England, as well as in the United States, these two components of the civic culture are closely linked in the historical relationship between private philanthropy and social reform.

The British civic culture is associated with a highly stable, liberal democratic form of government based on a relatively homogeneous and moderately consensual society and on the common-law rights of free expression, free assembly, and free association. Political scientists have noted that in Britain "the culture of democratic citizenship with its emphasis on initiative and participation was amalgamated with an

33. Wolfenden, pp. 26–29. These five functions are also featured in the official press release of November 22, 1977 issued by the Committee on Voluntary Organisations. The first paragraph begins with a call for greater statutory funding of the voluntary sector.

34. Barbara Rodgers, *Cross-National Studies of Social Service Systems*, pp. 41–42.

older political culture that stressed the rights of the subject."[35] Hence, one finds a more deferential attitude toward authority than in the United States, combined with a tendency to play the part of respectful subject rather than that of active participant. For example, studies show that about half as many Britons as Americans report that they have attempted to influence a local political or governmental decision.

Nevertheless, there is no shortage of organizations in Britain; studies suggest that the incidence of voluntary associations of all types is from one to three per thousand persons in towns and cities, and that the number increases by at least 5 percent each year.[36] It is estimated that there are over 100,000 nonstatutory, nonprofit organizations, with an aggregate annual income of over £1,500,000,000.

The more personal type of volunteerism is evident in the participation in some form of volunteer work reported by an average of 15–20 percent of the adult population, amounting to almost 5,000,000 individuals. The percentage of volunteer participation varies among social classes, ranging from about 30 percent among managerial, administrative, and professional persons to 8.6 percent among low-skilled workers. Most of the voluntary citizen participation is in work with the elderly, the handicapped, children, youth, and families.[37]

Conclusions

Moving from a dominant and initiatory role that lasted well into the twentieth century, voluntary agencies in England have been overshadowed by the rapid rise of the welfare state. Despite the growth and comprehensive scope of the statutory services, voluntary agencies have not become redundant. In contrast to changes in the health, education, and income maintenance sectors, voluntary agencies continue to provide such basic services as residential care and to fill gaps due to lags in the development of the statutory services. Because the demand for individualized and specialized forms of personal care is always present, voluntary agencies that can provide such resources are utilized and valued by statutory agencies. With the end of the era of rapid growth in government welfare expenditures, the promise of a

35. Gabriel A. Almond and Sidney Verba, *The Civic Culture: Political Attitudes and Democracy in Five Nations*, p. 315. See also Arnold J. Heidenheimer, Hugh Heclo, and Carolyn Adams, *Comparative Public Policy: The Politics of Social Choice in Europe and America*, pp. 109–10 and 114.

36. Stephen Hatch and Ian Mocroft, "Factors Affecting the Location of Voluntary Organization Branches."

37. Stephen Hatch, *Voluntary Work: A Report of A Survey*, p. 2.

universalized statutory system of personal social services is unlikely to be fulfilled. In a context of statutory rationing and more explicit setting of priorities, the function of voluntary agencies as supplementary services, will continue to be an essential part of the social service system.

Relations between statutory and voluntary organizations remain ambiguous, partly because of great disparities in their power. Whether the statutory system can change its direction and make substantially greater use of voluntary organizations and the informal sector, as recommended in the Wolfenden Report, is questionable.

3. The United States: A Mixed Economy

The origins of the social services in the United States, as in England, are rooted in a combination of governmental and voluntary action. Private charity and the poor law coexisted side by side for hundreds of years in these countries, each developing at its own pace and with gradually increasing influence over the other. For example, the era of voluntary agency predominance in the United States lasted until the 1930s, when there was a massive expansion of governmental social welfare programs. Despite the centrality of the public sector since then, a parallel, though not commensurate, growth of voluntary organizations and profit-making organizations has occurred, producing a mixed economy in the field of social welfare.

In the past one-hundred years, there has been a special concern with appropriate roles and the differentiation of functions between governmental and voluntary organizations during three particular eras. Out of the controversy over public subsidies to private children's institutions and the efforts of the Charity Organization Societies (COS) to eliminate public relief in the last quarter of the nineteenth century arose conceptions of the respective character and functions of the governmental and voluntary organizations that persisted for over fifty years. On the basis of a faith in the superiority and primacy of private charity, many believed that government should play a limited role, restricting itself to protective and large-scale custodial programs.

Another reevaluation of functions took place during the 1930s, when unemployment relief and basic income maintenance were acknowledged as a public obligation and no longer as within the capabilities of voluntary agencies. A proposed division of labor resulted, stressing a vanguard and standard-setting role for the voluntary agency, while government had primary responsibility for income maintenance.

The third era — the "take-off" period for the welfare state — began after World War II. It can be divided into two phases, 1946–66 and

1967–80. During these years, the feasibility of, and interest in, a more formal separation of functions has declined as voluntary agencies increasingly are used to carry out public purposes, and there appear to be fewer significant organizational differences between them.

These three periods can serve as convenient anchoring points for a brief sketch of historical trends. Because the history of the changing relations between governmental and voluntary efforts to cope with the "dependent, defective and delinquent classes" (as the objects of public and private charity were known in the nineteenth century) is not as well known as recent developments, more attention will be given to the period preceding 1930.[1]

Early Beginnings

From the beginning of the colonization of what was to become the United States, there have been both governmental and voluntary modes of coping with the problems of economic dependency. The harsh conditions of colonial life meant that families and neighbors were rarely in a position to assume responsibility for anyone else; hence, some governmental provision for the relief of destitution was assumed from the start. The legal framework for such assistance was the English poor laws with which the colonists were familiar. The poor laws provided a meager, last-resort help when family and individual resources were exhausted, but only under restrictive conditions of residence. That government was not expected or able to monopolize the means of dealing with the problems of living is evident in the almost parallel, simultaneous development of voluntary forms of assistance in the church, in mutual-benefit societies, and in private philanthropy. As the historian Daniel Boorstin notes, "Communities existed before governments were there to care for public needs," with the result that voluntary collaborative activities were first set up to provide basic social services and that government followed later.[2]

The slump after the Revolutionary War and the depressions following the Embargo, the War of 1812, and the panic of 1819, together with epidemics and substantial immigration, resulted in widespread destitution that taxed the capacity of the poor law and the all-purpose

---

1. The historical summary of the development of governmental and voluntary social welfare draws on many sources including: James Leiby, *A History of Social Welfare and Social Work in the United States;* Nathan E. Cohen, *Social Work in the American Tradition;* Ralph E. Pumphrey and Muriel W. Pumphrey, *The Heritage of American Social Work;* Frank J. Bruno, *Trends in Social Work;* Samuel Mencher, *Poor Law to Poverty Program;* and Kathleen Woodroofe, *From Charity to Social Work in England and the United States,* pp. 77–101.

2. Daniel J. Boorstin, *The Americans: the National Experience,* p. 121.

almshouse to deal with the extraordinary number of persons forced to ask for aid. Because the established public means of dealing with destitution were unable to cope with the unprecedented demand, voluntary associations were organized to promote more humane measures for dealing with the indigent and neglected, as well as with handicapped children and adults.

In many instances the voluntary organization, even when originally conceived as a supplement, was a sectarian or humanitarian expression of dissatisfaction with inadequate public resources and sought to supplant government. At other times, in the first half of the nineteenth century, the voluntary agency filled a vacuum due to the absence of governmental responsibility.[3] The prevailing sentiment was that private philanthropy provided services and facilities that relieved government of a burden and that it should be encouraged to do so. This belief was reinforced by the absence of an established church in America, which facilitated the organization of a host of charitable, educational, and religious institutions under voluntary auspices. These included institutions for the handicapped; shelters for children; houses of refuge for homeless and transient persons; orphanages; hospitals; reform schools; settlement houses; homes for unmarried mothers; agencies to aid prisoners, the destitute, or runaway children; summer camps; seamen's missions; and youth organizations.

The establishment of facilities for special classes of handicapped persons was due in large part to the commitment of local government to an undifferentiated institutional solution for a wide variety of social problems, all of which ended up in the all-purpose almshouse. While more or less functional for a static, homogeneous, rural community, the almshouse was ill-adapted to the consequences of nineteenth-century urbanization, immigration, and the rapid shift from an agricultural to an industrial economy.

Two principal factors shaped the relationship between public and private effort in the last quarter of the nineteenth century: (1) the subsidy system and (2) the efforts of the COS to eliminate public "outdoor relief," i.e., financial aid to persons living outside of institutions for whom the public was responsible. Both of these factors had considerable influence on the proliferation and rapid professionalization of the voluntary agency and on the persistent underdevelopment of government social service organizations until the 1930s.

3. The status of government during much of the nineteenth century is revealed in the statement of Justice Marshall that "These eleemosynary institutions do not fill the place which would otherwise be occupied by government, but that which would otherwise remain vacant." (*Trustees of Dartmouth College* vs. *Woodward*)

The Subsidy System

Historically, the subsidy system has its roots in the eighteenth-century practice of boarding out and contracting for the care of the poor and the handicapped, for whom the poor law made little provision. Auctioning off the care of the dependent and of defective children and adults, as well as contracting out, usually occurred when the number of persons was insufficient to warrant constructing a public institution. Because voluntary sectarian institutions antedated the assumption of governmental responsibility, it was natural for a municipality or state either to utilize preexisting facilities rather than construct its own or to provide land and subsidies, particularly when the governmental unit was too impoverished to make substantial capital expenditures.[4]

By the 1820s, several states had entered into agreements with private residential institutions to serve indigent, deaf, and handicapped children, many of whom were victims of epidemics that ravaged the population at the beginning of the nineteenth century. The first institution of this kind was the American Asylum for the Education and Instruction of the Deaf and Dumb in Hartford, which was started in 1817 with philanthropic contributions and later received a land grant from Congress. New England was also the site of the first private institution for the blind, which was established in 1829 and set a precedent for other schools initiated by volunteers that later were assisted or taken over by the state.[5] In California lump-sum subsidies were given to many private orphanages established for abandoned children and orphans who were casualties of the gold rush. The first state institution in California for deaf, dumb, and blind children (established in 1860), as well as the first one for the mentally handicapped (established in 1885) were founded by voluntary associations and were initially subsidized, and then taken over and administered by, the state.[6]

As a result of immigration, population growth, and urbanization in

4. The granting of a charter to private groups that would carry out some public purpose was a widespread practice in the nineteenth century. This included groups of businessmen that built bridges, ferries, and turnpikes or organized banks and land companies that bought and redistributed public land. The American business corporation began as a type of body politic that had a public charter to do a public job. (Boorstin, pp 250–54.)

5. Harry Best, *Deafness and the Deaf in the United States*, pp. 389–414. On the development of schools for the blind, see Gabriel Farrell, *The Story of Blindness*, pp. 41–52. On mental retardation see M. Rosen et. al., *The History of Mental Retardation: Collected Papers*.

6. Frances Cahn and Valeska Bary, *Welfare Activities of Federal, State and Local Governments in California 1850–1934*, pp. 103–36, 183–97. A definitive study of subsidies in the United States before 1930 is Arlien Johnson, *Public Policy and Public Charities*.

the latter half of the nineteenth century, there were an increasing number of public wards whose care was beyond the capacity of local government. There were two chief means of coping with the growing number of the blind, the deaf, the insane, and other "defectives," who had all been mixed together in the almshouse. Dependent children and, to a lesser extent, some of the blind and the deaf were progressively taken out of the almshouse and cared for by voluntary organizations. Such other groups as the insane, the deaf, the mentally retarded, and the tubercular were transferred from the care of local government to the custodial care of the state. State government, which was in slightly better repute than local government, was seen as the protector of society, best qualified to provide congregate care in one centralized facility for the unfortunate and the handicapped. Thus, the number of state institutions for the deaf, the blind, and the mentally handicapped slowly grew, although federal responsibility for their support was delayed until the 1930s.

Leaders in the voluntary sector were critical of state institutions, many of which acquired an unsavory reputation because of their corrupt character and the stigma attached to their residents. Voluntary leaders pressed for the creation of state boards of charities and corrections to improve administration and to develop standards for the care of inmates. These boards represented an early transfer to government of a model taken from the voluntary sector, i.e., the advisory or policymaking board, to which an executive reported.[7]

Despite the growth of state institutions and the transfer of care of handicapped persons from the local to the state level, the use of subsidies accelerated from the mid-nineteenth century on. In the last quarter of the century, subsidies became the prevailing method of financing most voluntary institutions. Apart from the prior existence of private sectarian institutions and their lesser costs — reasons that are still given today for the use of voluntary agencies to carry out a public purpose — there were three other reasons for a readiness to use public tax funds to subsidize existing voluntary institutions rather than to build new public ones: (1) political pressures exerted by voluntary leaders, who had a vested interest in utilizing their own facilities to the fullest; (2) an individualistic and moralistic approach to the care of the poor and the handicapped that implied an active concern for the religious life of the persons being aided, a concern for which government was considered intrinsically unsuited; (3) a pervasive distrust of gov-

7. Leiby, pp. 97–101.

ernmental machinery (much of which was justified, given the prevalence of the spoils system and the low level of public administration).
In short, "private philanthropy flourished in America partly because
of the benevolence of the pious and well-to-do and partly because public charity was afflicted with political abuse and corruption."[8]

The arguments advanced for and against subsidies in the nineteenth
century are not unlike those advanced in the 1980s regarding the use
of public funds by voluntary agencies. In the voluntary institutions'
favor were the facts that they were more economical, that they were
reputed to have a better effect on inmates, and that politics played a
lesser role in the selection of staff. Subsidies were opposed on the
grounds that there was no real economy because of the necessity of
duplicate sectarian institutions and because of the lack of government
control over policies. In addition, it was claimed that subsidies tended
to dry up the sources of private funds, to encourage undesirable political pressures on the legislature, and to destroy the freedom of voluntary organizations.[9]

The subsidy policy prevailed until the 1930s. It assumed the superiority and primacy of voluntary agencies and the residual role of
government. Government was believed to be either incapable or inappropriate as a provider of services other than institutional care for the
most handicapped and the most hopeless cases, while voluntary agencies worked with more hopeful and deserving persons. In this way,
voluntary organizations could act in their self-assigned roles as guardians of religious and moral values and as vanguards. Voluntary agencies saw themselves as individualizing, sensitive, intrinsically more
humane, and uplifting — stereotypes that still persist in the United
States and many other countries.

The Charity Organization Society

Stereotypes about voluntary agencies were reinforced by a second set
of influences, exerted in large urban centers in the last quarter of the
nineteenth century by the COS.[10] The severe depression in 1873 pro-

8. Leiby, p. 274.
9. An authoritative analysis of the subsidy policy and the state of municipal charity at the
time is Amos G. Warner, *American Charities: A Study in Philanthropy and Economics*, pp. 334–56.
10. In addition to the sources cited in footnote 1, see Frank Watson, *The Charity Organization
Movement in the U.S.: A Study in American Philanthropy*; Warner, pp. 372–94; Helen Witmer,
Social Work: An Analysis of a Social Institution, p. 127–82; Roy Lubove, *The Professional Altruist: The
Emergence of Social Work as a Career*, pp. 1–21; and Robert Bremner, "Scientific Philanthropy
1873–93."

duced a national unemployment problem for which the numerous private relief societies with their meager resources were clearly inadequate. As part of a reform of private charity, COSs based on the London model were established in many cities. Underlying the COS belief in "scientific philanthropy" was a conviction that pauperism was a result of individual character defects and that the dependent poor needed "not alms but a friend." Although handicapped persons were generally classified as "defective," their condition was viewed as an act of God not, like pauperism, as a sign of moral weakness. Consequently, the development of specialized institutions and services for the handicapped did not need to overcome the ideological barriers faced in assisting other types of dependent persons.

Despairing of any success in eliminating corruption from local government, the COS concentrated on eliminating public relief as a municipal function and on allocating assistance to persons in their own homes through private charitable organizations. As the COS movement spread throughout the country between 1878 and 1890, this objective was accomplished in over twelve large cities, including New York and San Francisco, and, in some cases, the COS even received subsidies for saving the municipal treasury the expenses of public relief.

The controversy over the elimination of public outdoor relief raged for almost a quarter of a century. Governmental and voluntary agencies came to be identified with the following polarities.[11]

Governmental Agency	*Voluntary Agency*
Indoor relief — the almshouse	Outdoor relief — assistance for deserving unfortunates in their own homes
chronic and hopeless cases	temporary need
relief	treatment and prevention
inferior, mass approach, generally corrupt and corrupting	morally superior and individualizing approach
residual function	primary and preferred resource

In ascribing to the COS the discrediting of public assistance and the chronic tensions between public and private welfare, Lubove adds that "this legacy of suspicion provided one explanation for the philan-

11. These characterizations are reflected in the successive proceedings of the National Conference of Charities and Corrections for over fifty years beginning in 1881. Bruno summarizes the leading trends.

thropic division of labor which prevailed until the Great Depression."[12] On the other hand, many significant developments in the voluntary sector owed their origin to the COS. They included family and child welfare services, the professionalization of social work, and the methods of case work. The first schools of social work were started by the COS, and until the 1950s professional education for social work was dominated by the special interests of the voluntary sector. Other organizations that evolved out of COS experience were family service agencies, the federated fund-raising movement, including community chests, and the first councils of social agencies for coordination and planning.

A strong link between private philanthropy and social reform was forged toward the end of the nineteenth century and strengthened the advocacy role of the voluntary agency. The aggressive, uncompromising opposition of the COS to public relief diminished around the turn of the century, and there was less concern with abolition, more with the improvement of the administration of poor relief. Citizen leaders and voluntary agency executives also worked for social legislation that would eliminate child labor and promote public health.[13]

The movement for social change initiated by leaders of voluntary organizations resulted in the founding of several national health agencies. Tuberculosis, mental illness, infant mortality, venereal disease, and blindness were increasingly regarded as products of poverty and neglect. From the beginning, the approach of health agencies was distinguished from the moralistic approach of the private charities. Disease was regarded as a social phenomenon to be attacked by legislation and research, as well as by social services.[14]

In the 1920s, case work and other professional methods pioneered by voluntary agencies were gradually introduced into public settings

12. Lubove, p. 52.

13. Somewhat more active than the COS in both pioneering and advocacy were the leaders of the settlement house movement who, together with other social reformers in the two decades before World War I, were influential in securing legislation to bring about improvements in working conditions, housing, and in some of the early forms of social insurance. Pumphrey, pp. 258–77 documents the rivalry of the COS and the settlements for the support of the philanthropic public. See also Jane Addams, *Twenty Years at Hull House*, pp. 126, 198–230. The growth in the number of settlements to one hundred by 1900 is cited as another example of the attack on laissez-faire and Spencerian individualism and, conversely, as evidence of support for the general welfare concept of government by Sidney Fine, *Laissez-faire and the General Welfare State*, pp. 347–49.

14. Richard Carter, *The Gentle Legions*, p. 37.

and broke down the long-held belief that government could deal only with mass programs. Voluntary agencies, including many new organizations for the handicapped, grew rapidly on both national and local levels. New government agencies were established on state and municipal levels, and state powers to regulate, supervise, and license voluntary agencies were granted. In the 1920s, increase in public expenditure for social services surpassed for the first time the amount expended by voluntary agencies. The relative importance of public subsidies to voluntary agencies began to decline because of the gradual expansion of programs administered directly by government, such as those authorized by the Vocational Rehabilitation Act of 1920.

The Great Depression and Its Aftermath

Until the 1930s voluntarism was the American substitute for a genuine social policy. It delayed the establishment of public programs for income maintenance, housing, medical care, and other benefits instituted decades earlier in Europe. The Great Depression finally made clear that voluntary institutions had been assigned a task they could not meet — "to serve as a substitute for and to the exclusion of, a broad program in dealing with poverty, misery, distress, and economic maladjustment."[15] Because of the inability of voluntary agencies and local and state governments to cope with the Great Depression, the federal government was given greater authority over relief, culminating in the passage of the Social Security Act in 1935. Accompanying the supervision of relief funds by the federal government was a policy of restricting public funds to public agencies, which was adopted because of past abuses in the subsidy system.

When a new era of government responsibility was inaugurated during the 1930s, the functions of governmental and voluntary agencies were reevaluated. Some saw only an emergency role for public services and refused to grant them permanent status. At the other extreme, with the advent of new public programs, others no longer saw any place for private voluntary services. They pointed to the decrease in private expenditures during the 1930s as a sign of the beginning of the demise of the voluntary sector. Contributions grew only minimally as the nation came out of the Great Depression, and, at the same

15. I. M. Rubinow, cited in Roy Lubove, "The Welfare Industry: Social Work and the Life of the Poor," p. 610. One of the best descriptions of the development of the public relief program is Josephine C. Brown, *Public Relief 1929–39.*

time, voluntary expenditures for relief — formerly about a quarter of the national total — dropped to less than 1 percent. A prevalent opinion was that it was necessary to integrate public and private services. A division of labor was advocated by Linton B. Swift, one of the leaders in the family service movement, whereby voluntary agencies would supplement, experiment, innovate, and specialize, whereas government would provide funds and services relating to basic economic needs.[16] This principle was based on an analysis of organizational characteristics in which the voluntary agency was conceived of as a vanguard and a minority agency in the community, concerned with needs not yet recognized or accepted by the majority as meriting public support. While redefinition of function varied among fields of service, most social work spokesmen assigned to the governmental agency the mass, routine, and remedial tasks, while the voluntary agency was free to experiment, set the pace and standards, and assert its superiority in quality if not in quantity.

With respect to the handicapped, perhaps the most significant event during the 1930s was the creation of the National Foundation for Infantile Paralysis in 1938. Preceded by four annual birthday balls sponsored by President Franklin D. Roosevelt, himself a polio victim, a March of Dimes was inaugurated on a national basis by the five founders of the National Foundation. Within a few years a local chapter and a Mothers' March on Polio could be found in almost every county in the United States. Enlisting the largest number of volunteers and contributors in the country, the National Foundation set a precedent for other health agencies in its style of fund raising, publicity, research, and service donations.

Earlier health organizations, such as the American Cancer Society (1913), the National Society for Crippled Children (1921), the American Heart Association (1924), the National Committee for the Prevention of Blindness (1915), and the American Society for the Hard of Hearing (1919), struggled for many years with relatively little effect. During the post-World War II years, however, they were revitalized as they adopted many of the methods that had worked successfully in the polio campaign. In addition, there was an organizational explosion in the health field as new national associations were formed to combat

16. Cohen, 182–206. The classic statement of the proposed division of responsibility is: Linton B. Swift, *New Alignments between Public and Private Agencies in a Community Family Welfare and Relief Program*.

multiple sclerosis (1946), cerebral palsy (1958), muscular dystrophy (1950), mental retardation (1953), and a host of other diseases.[17]

Recent Trends

The postwar years have marked the expansion of the United States welfare state, with an enormous increase in governmental expenditures for social welfare. Five major trends affect the pattern of development of the U.S. welfare state and its relationship to voluntary organizations. First, a "disproportionate" expansion of the public sector has reduced the domain of voluntary agencies so that most of them serve a much smaller share of the market. During the last twenty-five years the growth rate of government has been at least four times that of the voluntary sector, with a ten-to-one spending ratio of government to nongovernmental organizations.[18] Beginning with the passage of the National Institute of Mental Health Act in 1946, there has been a steady stream of social legislation, and, by the end of the 1970s, there are almost 500 different categorical social service programs under federal auspices. The expansion of federal programs for the direct provision of social services has been accompanied by a widened scope of governmental functions, which include monitoring, evaluation, research, demonstration, standard setting, citizen participation, planning, and coordination.

A second trend is the relative decline in voluntary fund raising. Although the amount of money raised has increased in actual dollars, purchasing power has been eroded by a steadily increasing rate of inflation and by a tripling of costs over the twenty-year period from

17. Carter, pp. 189–216. A lively account of the organization of these health agencies is Selskar M. Gunn and Philip S. Platt, *Voluntary Health Agencies, an Interpretive Study*, which also includes a critical evaluation of the health agencies up to the end of World War II. The fundraising problems of the national health agencies in the years following World War II are reviewed in Robert Hamlin, *Voluntary Health and Welfare Agencies in the U.S.: An Exploratory Study by an Ad Hoc Committee*. This was one of a series of such investigations sponsored by the Rockefeller Foundation. A more recent popular account of the fund raising patterns of the national health (or disease) agencies is Carl Bakal, *Charity U.S.A.: An Investigation into the Hidden World of the Multi-Billion Dollar Charity Industry*, pp. 119–209.

18. Alfred M. Skolnick and Sophie R. Dales, "Social Welfare Expenditures, 1950–1975," p. 19. A fivefold increase in governmental child welfare and institutional expenditures for 1950–1967 is reported in Alvin L. Schorr, "The Tasks for Volunteerism in the Next Decade." In the field of health, the federal government spent only 15 percent more than private philanthropy in 1930; in 1973, it spent nearly seven times as much. (Commission on Private Philanthropy and Public Needs, *Giving in America: Toward a Stronger Voluntary Sector*, p. 90. Hereafter cited as Filer.)

1955 to 1975. At the same time, the level of giving by individuals has declined markedly in proportion to personal income and to the GNP.[19] Corporate contributions — which have always been very low, amounting to less than 3 percent of all giving — have tended to remain static and have averaged about 1 percent of net profits. Individual giving as a proportion of personal income dropped 13 percent between 1960 and 1976, and similarly the proportion of philanthropic giving devoted to social welfare dropped from 15 percent to 6 percent. The combined effects of these trends have spurred voluntary agencies to search for additional sources of income.

Third, a landmark shift in the relationship between the two sectors occurred in the 1960s, when many voluntary agencies virtually backed into the more extensive use of public funds with little consideration of the consequences.[20] Beginning with a limited amount of purchase of service indirectly authorized by the 1962 Public Welfare Amendments, the practice of purchasing services rapidly accelerated with the passage of the Economic Opportunity Act of 1964 and because of the 1967 amendments to the Social Security Act (P.L. 90-248) and its regulations. The original restrictions on matching funds in Title IV A and B of the amendments were interpreted to mean that United Way allocations and other local contributions to voluntary agencies could be used as part of a 25 percent required matching share, thus producing three federal dollars for every one voluntary dollar.

The open-ended nature of appropriations for these purposes resulted in several years of uncontrolled growth in expenditures, as well as in the diversion in some states of social service funds to other purposes. In 1972 Congress finally enacted a ceiling on such expenditures, and two years later Title XX of the 1974 Social Security Amendments provided a new framework for purchase of service from nongovernmental organizations. Essentially, it encouraged the policy by legitimating local share practices and by specifying types of services and conditions under which they might be purchased. As a result, govern-

19. The causes of the relative decline in individual giving are not known. Some have ascribed it to inflation, the increased privatism of society, the expansion of governmental social programs, and federal income tax policies, all of which are believed to have a damping effect. See Filer, pp. 53–75 and 79–87; and Burton A. Abrams and Mark D. Schitz, "The 'Crowding-out' Effect of Governmental Transfers on Private Charitable Contributions."

20. A lucid account of this process is Elizabeth Wickenden, "A Perspective on Social Services: An Essay Review." A broader view is given by Martha Derthick in *Uncontrollable Spending for Social Service Grants.* See also Paul Terrell, "Private Alternatives to Public Human Services Administration," and Bill Benton et. al., *Social Service Federal Legislation versus State Implementation.*

ment purchase of service has become the principal mode of financing service delivery in the United States. The scope of government support of the voluntary sector can be seen in the estimate of the Filer Commission that tax funds of all types accounted for $23,000,000,000 of the revenues of all nonprofit organizations in 1974, compared with about $25,000,000,000 that they receive from all other sources of giving combined.[21]

A fourth set of changes is the appearance of new types of voluntary organization, such as alternative agencies, quasi-nongovernmental organizations, and a proliferation of self-help, mutual aid, and consumer-oriented associations. This has made the voluntary sector exceedingly lively and competitive. The continual establishment of new organizations, viewed with dismay by some, reflects the strength of voluntarism in the United States, as well as the impetus given to citizen participation by the Great Society legislation. The expanding volume of publicly financed social services also accounts for the increased number of profit-making organizations in this field.

At the same time, growing out of the War on Poverty and the civil rights movement of the 1960s was an attack by both social activists and academic critics on established social agencies in the voluntary sector.[22] Voluntary agencies were accused of marginality, overspecialization, selectivity, low accountability, and ineffectiveness. In the 1970s, some of the same groups, joined by representatives of minority and ethnic organizations, have attacked the United Way because of its alleged monopoly of corporate giving and contributions by federal employees through payroll-deduction plans. Drawn together by criticism of the Filer Commission report, social activist groups have formed the National Committee for Responsive Philanthropy to oppose the established organizations.

Finally, there have been basic changes in service policies. In addition to the greater use of public funds by nongovernmental organizations to carry out public responsibilities, eligibility for the social services has progressively broadened, and the use of selective means tests has decreased. Federal social service programs emphasize such tangible, care-oriented services as homemaker services, meals-on-

21. Filer, p. 89. These estimates are for all types of nonprofit organizatons and all forms of government funds.
22. Representative of this criticism of voluntary agencies is Richard A. Cloward and Irwin Epstein, "Private Social Welfare's Disengagement from the Poor: The Case of Family Adjustment Agencies," and Esther Stanton, *Clients Come Last: Volunteers and Welfare Organizations*.

wheels, and transportation, rather than counseling and other "soft" services. Beginning in the 1960s, public policy has been committed to deinstitutionalization and "mainstreaming" of the handicapped, which encourages the use of community care facilities. In addition, the rights of the handicapped to education, rehabilitation, and independent living have been embodied in a series of major pieces of social legislation, including the Rehabilitation Act of 1973, the Education of All Handicapped Children Act of 1975, and the Developmental Disabilities Assistance Bill of Rights Act of 1975. All of this legislation, together with the major financing provisions of Title XX and the General Revenue Sharing Act of 1972, requires more evidence of planning, evaluation, and accountability from the states, and stresses involving local government in the coordination and integration of services.[23]

A comparative analysis concludes that the social service pattern in the United States consists of many layers of programs added incrementally over the years through special legislation promoted by different constituencies, each competing for funds. The large number of categorical programs for favored groups developed under governmental auspices, together with the specialized interests of voluntary agencies, has resulted in some of the most complex and multiproblem cases falling to the overextended and poorly staffed public welfare departments in each county.[24] Despite the inequities and lack of coherence in the system, there does not appear to be any resolution of ambiguous role relationships between governmental and voluntary agencies.

Public Policy System

The distinguishing feature of the American political system is its structure as a three-level federal system with strong constitutional provision for a separation of powers between the federal and state governments and between the executive, legislative, and judicial branches on each level.[25] Characterized by a unique division of function with built-in checks and balances, authority, power, and responsibility are widely dispersed throughout the United States. *Fragmented*

23. The leading trends are analyzed by Neil Gilbert, "The Transformation of the Social Services."

24. Alfred J. Kahn and Sheila B. Kamerman, *Social Services in International Perspective: The Emergence of the Sixth System*, p. 349.

25. Standard accounts of the governmental structure and political system in the United States are found in Robert Sherrill et. al., *Governing America*, and William Ebenstein et al., *American Democracy in World Perspective*. See also Eric Redman, *The Dance of Legislation*, and Michael J. Bevier, *Politics Backstage: Inside the California Legislature*.

is the term most frequently used to describe the distinctive pluralism that is both the despair and pride of the United States.

The American penchant for legislation and prolific regulations is well known. For example, 25,000 bills are introduced annually in the United States Congress, and upwards of 7,000 are introduced in the California State Legislature. Many of these bills are reviewed through an elaborate network of legislative committees and public hearings or in the Congress itself. The initiative for legislation can come from within the government bureaucracy, as well as from interested groups and individuals who can offer testimony.

Most significant social service legislation originates on the federal level, and it typically provides for both state and local participation in financing and administration. Therefore, voluntary organizations must be represented in Washington and in the state capital, as well as in their local communities. This helps explain why national voluntary agencies in the United States stress advocacy, standard setting, and research and do not operate service programs, as is the case in England where pressure groups and public opinion are less important in the policymaking process. In this respect, the national voluntary agencies in the United States most resemble their counterparts in the Netherlands.

In contrast to other democracies, the United States has only two major political parties, and these appeal to a broad group of constituents. Although ideological differences between them continue to be asserted, the influence of political parties has declined. Single-issue politics based on ad hoc coalitions of pressure groups seeking to influence public policy on one specialized issue, such as abortion, pollution, welfare reform, or state aid to parochial schools, is growing in importance. Lobbying by pressure groups is expected, and it is out of the interaction between them, the bureaucracy, and the legislature that laws are fashioned.[26]

United States legislative bodies are not only more prolific than their counterparts in other countries, but the bills they introduce also tend to be lengthy because of their specificity. Laws are supplemented by detailed administrative regulations developed by federal and state departments, which usually invite comments from affected organizations and governmental agencies, thus providing another channel for

26. A critical view of this interest-group pluralism is presented by Theodore J. Lowi, *The End of Liberalism: Ideology, Policy and the Crisis of Public Authority*, pp. 238–73. See also Morris P. Fiorina, "The Decline of Collective Responsibility in American Politics."

involvement in the policymaking process. It was estimated, for example, that there are 12,000 pages of regulations and guidelines for the more than 300 programs within the Department of Health, Education and Welfare.[27]

Despite the vast powers and resources of the federal government, there is a greater reliance on financial inducement than on direct control and less capacity to monitor implementation than is suggested by complaints about overregulation.

Welfare Ideology

The United States has been characterized as a "reluctant welfare state" because of a persistent conflict between two opposing sets of values.[28] At one pole is a cluster of ideas associated with Social Darwinism, laissez-faire, individualism, free enterprise, and a distrust of government. At the other is the American creed of humanistic liberalism and a belief in progress and in governmental intervention to achieve security and equality. Related ideological dualisms in the United States are those between self-reliance and dependency, charity and justice, philanthropy and taxation, and volunteerism and bureaucracy and professionalism. The separation of church and state, once an important factor militating against the use of public funds by sectarian agencies, seems less important in the personal social services.

As Wilensky and Lebeaux stated: "American culture (especially those values shaping economic action: our individualism, our ideas about private property, the free market, and the role of government) affects not only the amount of cash we spend for welfare services but also the kind of services we assign to private vs. public agencies, local and state vs. federal agencies."[29] Historically, although community preceded government in the United States, the resources of state and federal governments have been used to help Americans cope with every type of economic and social problem. Since early in the nineteenth century, Americans, typically, have wanted to have their cake and to eat it, too — proclaiming that government best which governs least, and at the same time seeking to use its powers for their own particular benefit. Eveline M. Burns has observed that "in contrast to [those countries, such as] Great Britain, which appear to regard gov-

27. Eliot L. Richardson, *Responsibility and Responsiveness, II*, p. 19, as cited in Sheila B. Kamerman and Alfred J. Kahn, *Social Services in the U.S.*, p. 441.
28. Harold L. Wilensky and Charles N. Lebeaux, *Industrial Society and Social Welfare*, p. xvii
29. Wilensky and Lebeaux, p. 15.

ernment merely as the most effective of several possible institutions for the administration of income security programs or the provision of services . . . a society like the U.S. that distrusts its government is likely to organize its social security services in such a way as to keep government to a minimum."[30] Consequently, in the United States voluntary effort remains a larger part of total welfare effort than in other advanced societies.

Conflicting ideologies underlie the two conceptions of social welfare dominant today. The "residual" view that prevailed before the 1930s holds that social welfare institutions should only come into play when the normal structure of the family and the market breaks down. It stresses self-reliance, charity, philanthropy, and voluntarism. The "institutional" view of social welfare sees the social services as essential requirements to meet the needs of all persons — not just the unfortunate and the handicapped — and it is the philosophical basis for the welfare state. In practice, these conflicting philosophies coexist uneasily, with the residual view periodically revived in protest against increased taxation and spending. Basically, they reflect opposing views of the extent to which government has a claim on discretionary personal income for public purposes.[31]

While some public-sector programs — such as education, public health, social insurance, and mortgage guarantees for federally financed housing — are accepted as essential to normal living by normal people, other social service programs are regarded with distaste or, at best, ambivalence.[32] To resolve the dilemma created by a continuing desire for social services provided by the welfare state and opposition to taxation and spending by government bureaucracies, distinctions have been made between public financing and public provision. The public more readily accepts government funding and standard setting if nongovernmental organizations deliver the public goods and services. A separation between financing and administration is evident in the decentralization policies of the New Federalism in the 1970s, which assigned more decision-making authority to the states and local communities, with the federal government responsible for major funding. Additional support for the use of nongovernmental organizations has come from those who favor "reprivatization" and the "empower-

30. Eveline M. Burns, *Social Security and Public Policy*, p. 274.

31. Wilensky and Lebeaux, pp. 138–40. See also Mencher, pp. 241–66, on the historical background of the ideologies affecting welfare policy.

32. Kamerman and Kahn, pp. 20–22.

ment of mediating structures" and invoke the values of volunteerism, self-help, and independence, which have historically been pitted
against reliance on government. While voluntary organizations have
been viewed as bulwarks against, and alternatives to, government,
they have at the same time benefited greatly from the "private federalism" that has been public policy since the 1960s.[33]

Because of the ever-expanding domain of government and the extensive tangible benefits to nongovernmental organizations, there is
little support for a serious attempt to delineate more rational lines of
demarcation between government and the voluntary sector. This may
change, however, as the availability of public funds decreases and
more emphasis is placed on the setting of priorities, greater accountability, and the more efficient allocation of funds.

Civic Culture

While the civic culture in the United States has the same philosophical
roots as that in England, it has been shaped by distinctive American
constitutional and historical factors. As de Tocqueville said: "A single
Englishman will often carry through some great undertaking, whereas
Americans form associations for no matter how small a matter."[34] The
American penchant for turning to voluntary action as a solution to
social, political, and personal problems has intensified since de Tocqueville made his observations in the first part of the nineteenth
century. Americans place a high value on volunteerism and they
participate extensively in giving direct services to others, through
an estimated 500,000 self-help and mutual aid groups and over
6,000,000 voluntary associations for a bewildering variety of purposes.
There are at least 100,000 national organizations in the United States,
37,000 of which are human service agencies. A Census Bureau study
estimated that 37,000,000 volunteers contributed their time in 1974.
Approximately seven in ten adults living in urban America say they
would be willing to serve on committees, to participate in neighborhood betterment activities, or to assist in rendering social services.[35]

So strong is the commitment to citizen participation that beginning
in the mid-1960s the federal government has mandated various forms
of resident or consumer representation on the advisory committees

33. See footnote 14, Introduction; and Daryl Vorwaller, "The Voluntary Agency as a Vendor of Social Services."

34. Alexis de Tocqueville, *Democracy in America*, pp. 513–14.

35. U.S. Census Bureau, *Americans Volunteer 1974*. See also James N. Morgan, Richard F.
Dye, and Judith H. Hybels, "Results from Two National Surveys of Philanthropic Activity,"
pp. 169–72.

and boards of directors of one-fourth of all the categorical grant programs funded by the Department of Health, Education and Welfare. This policy has brought about more active involvement by ethnic, consumer, neighborhood, and other groups excluded from community decision making in the past.[36] It has also encouraged the physically handicapped to organize themselves, and in the 1970s they, too, began to take the initiative and to create self-help organizations and agencies.

The American civic culture, which encourages the belief that every citizen has the right and duty to be involved, helps explain the finding that twice as many Americans as Britons report trying to influence local governmental decisions. The greater proclivity to citizen action in the United States is also related to a traditional lack of deference to government officials and politicians, as well as to a strong bias against government bureaucracy.[37] As an essential part of the political culture of representative democracy, voluntary organizations are regarded not only as desirable, but as necessary prerequisites for the satisfactory functioning of the polity and the society.

Conclusions

Two sources of social welfare provision have always existed in the United States — governmental and voluntary initiative — and their relationships have reflected changing ideas about organizational character, human nature, and the purpose of the state. The growth rate of the two systems was disparate until the Great Depression of the 1930s, with private charities proliferating in all fields of service while the public welfare agency remained very limited in scope and was guided by poor law principles. Then the preeminence of the voluntary agency was shattered by an unprecedented expansion of governmental social service functions in what later was designated the "welfare state." However, voluntary nonprofit organizations continue to play an important role in a social service economy that remains essentially pluralistic, despite the dominant influence of government funds and policies.

Just as conceptions of governmental and voluntary roles and relationships were influenced by the nineteenth-century system of public subsidies to private institutions, future interorganizational patterns

36. On mandated citizen participation, see John J. Strange, "Citizen Participation in Community Action and Model City Programs," and Robert K. Yin et. al., *Citizen Organizations: Increasing Client Control over Services* and *Citizen Participation*.

37. Almond and Verba, pp. 35–36, 179–80, 351.

will be shaped by contemporary public fiscal policies, which raise many of the same issues as their predecessors. Once again, voluntary agencies have become increasingly dependent on government funds for support and are vulnerable to reductions in public spending. Coupled with inflation, a growing reliance on government funds endangers the future of many voluntary agencies. Also, although their relationship is essentially symbiotic because of the preference in the United States for nongovernmental service providers, the need of voluntary agencies for autonomy can conflict with governmental requirements for accountability. The role of the voluntary agency in the U.S. welfare state will therefore depend on the ways it copes with major challenges to its organizational and fiscal integrity.

4. Israel:
The Close Partnership

Prestate Background

The welfare state in Israel has its roots in the millennial history of the Jewish people and, more recently, in the development of political Zionism in the latter part of the nineteenth century, which led to the reestablishment of the Jewish state in 1948. Most social institutions in present-day Israel originated in the Yishuv, the Jewish community that emerged under Turkish and, after World War I, British rule. Known as the "State-on-the-way," the Yishuv was distinguished by the voluntary character of its self-governing institutions, most of which were eventually transferred to the state.[1]

The early settlers who came from Eastern Europe at the turn of the century to rebuild the Jewish homeland were strongly influenced by the ideology of Labor Zionism, which stressed pioneering, collective responsibility, productivity, and egalitarianism — ideals that were eminently suited to the tasks of nation building and the creation of a "new society." Israel has been characterized by Eisenstadt as an "ideological society," and by others as one of a handful of "new societies," such as the United States, Canada, the Republic of South Africa, Australia, and New Zealand. Each of these nations was founded by pioneering settlers who migrated to a new territory and underwent a frontier experience in which they created a modern social order, unfettered by traditional or feudal ways.[2] This experience particularly encourages self-discipline and mutual aid, and in Israel it led to the formation of an extraordinarily large number of highly politicized voluntary associ-

---

1. Useful accounts in English of the prestate Jewish community in Palestine and the continuities in the new State of Israel can be found in S. N. Eisenstadt, *Israeli Society*, pp. 2–68; Amitai Etzioni, "The Decline of Neo-Feudalism: The Case of Israel"; Aharon K. Kleinberger, *Society, Schools and Progress in Israel*, pp. 1–37; and Amos Elon, *The Israelis: Founders and Sons*, pp. 3–147.
2. The concept of "new societies" is based partly on Louis Hartz, *The Founding of New Societies*, as cited in Daniel J. Elazar, *Israel: From Ideological to Territorial Democracy*, pp. 1–3.

ations, such as trade unions, sick funds, social insurance schemes, and a variety of social service organizations.

By 1927, the self-governing organ of the Jewish community, Vaad Leumi (National Council), to which 95 percent of the Jewish settlers belonged voluntarily, was officially recognized by the British Mandatory Government and was given limited powers of taxation. Dozens of political parties represented a wide array of labor, middle-class, Zionist, and religious interests, each of which undertook its own projects in agricultural settlement, urban and economic development, social services, education, culture, health, recreation, and defense. The Jewish political parties emerged under a foreign rule that was unsympathetic, if not hostile, to the Zionist enterprise and within the framework of a communal self-government that lacked power. Because these parties could not achieve their ideological objectives by influencing governmental policies in the usual ways, they strove to attain their goals by direct social action. Thus, voluntarism and political partisanship were pervasive influences in the prestate period, and they have persisted, giving a distinctive character to Israeli society.

In the prestate period, three different and competing social service systems emerged.[3] The oldest voluntary organizations were those sponsored by orthodox religious groups, some of whose adherents had lived in the Holy Land for generations and who depended almost completely on charitable contributions from abroad. During the 1920s, a second group of programs was created by secular, socialist-labor pioneers who totally rejected philanthropy and supported instead the mutual aid societies of the union movement. A third group of services came into being in 1931, when the Vaad Leumi overcame ideological resistance and established a Social Welfare Department that sought to aid families and children without regard to their membership in either the religious or the labor community. This principle, which had been espoused by some of the women's voluntary organizations, together with other policies established by the Vaad Leumi, such as local administration, set a precedent that was incorporated into the Ministry of Social Welfare when it was organized in 1950.

From its inception, however, the General Federation of Labor (Histadrut) denigrated government welfare because it represented a threat to the values and vested interests of the unions in their struggle for

3. Joseph Neipris, "Social Services in Israel." This is the best account in English of the development of the social services in Israel, and a 1978 update is available from the Paul Baerwald School of Social Work, Hebrew University, Jerusalem. See also Eliezer D. Jaffe, "Substitutes for Family: On the Development of Institutional Care for Dependent Children in Israel."

power. Because of a stress on agricultural labor, the early Zionist ideology had no place for those who were unable to contribute productively to the building of a Jewish state. Although rooted in Eastern European socialism, this "religion of work" had much in common with the Protestant ethic in denigrating the "nonproductive" elements of the population. The stigma attached to the public social services continues despite the fact that most of the million or more immigrants to Israel since the establishment of the state have been aided by the government in their resettlement.[4]

Under these circumstances, very few services for the handicapped emerged during the prestate period, apart from a few religious institutions for the blind and the deaf. Among the most significant developments during the 1920s was the pioneering work of the Hadassah Medical Organization in establishing the first maternal and child care clinics, a hospital, and nursing, public health, and research programs. This precedent was followed in the 1950s by the Joint Distribution Committee-Malben (JDC-Malben), which took primary responsibility for the institutional care of the aged and of handicapped immigrants. Both of these American voluntary organizations initiated services that in other states are provided by government. In Israel, voluntary associations filled the gap between settlers who came without resources and Jewish philanthropic funds from abroad that were available only to organizations, not to individuals. For this reason, Prime Minister David Ben-Gurion said when the state came into existence — and he has been echoed in succeeding years — "if we had not had voluntary institutions, we would have had to create them."

Statehood and New Voluntary Organizations

One of the reasons for the remarkable stability and development of the state of Israel is the continuity of the social, political, and economic infrastructure, which included a wide range of social services developed under voluntary auspices and then rapidly, though often reluctantly, transferred to governmental sponsorship after 1948. While most of the social services administered by voluntary organizations in the prestate period were taken over by the government, certain fields of service — preschool education, day care, medical programs, many services to the aged, and noncustodial care for the retarded and the

4. Reuben Schindler, "The Pioneering Ideology and the Roots of Social Welfare in the Pre-State Period of Israel," and Abraham Doron and Ralph M. Kramer, "Ideology, Programme and Organizational Factors in Public Assistance: The Case of Israel." In both Israel and the United States, the pioneering ideology has served to delay and constrain the passage of welfare legislation, in addition to adding to the stigma attached to certain governmental assistance programs.

physically handicapped — remained in the hands of nongovernmental bodies. Immediately after the establishment of the state in 1948, there was a strong feeling, similar to that in England at the same time, that voluntary organizations might no longer be needed. However, because of the immensity of the tasks facing the new government — such as the resettlement of over a million immigrants from eighty countries that quadrupled the population, defense requirements, economic development, and housing — the government was unable to fulfill many of the new and unprecedented expectations. As a result, in the early 1950s, despite the tremendously expanded scope of governmental authority, many new voluntary agencies concerned with mental retardation, cerebral palsy, brain damage, polio, cancer, the sensorially handicapped, and the victims of traffic accidents were organized.

Being autonomous and problem-centered, the new voluntary agencies represented a substantial departure from those that flourished during the Yishuv. The new organizations were nonpolitical, were highly specialized in function, employed professionals, and were dependent on the public at large for their funds. Concerned mainly with handicapped groups whose special needs were not receiving sufficient attention from the public and the government, most of the voluntary agencies were consciously modeled after counterparts in the United States and England, particularly those organized by the parents of handicapped children. JDC-Malben was among the most important influences in this field. It helped mobilize public interest and pressure by stimulating the establishment of three parent groups; it initiated surveys to record the existing needs for services; and it established new types of services, such as assessment and rehabilitation centers, which were later taken over by the government. JDC-Malben also provided seed money for demonstration and pilot projects, consultation, and subsidies to help voluntary agencies upgrade the quality of their professional services. JDC-Malben served a function similar to that of a private foundation, and it had considerable influence in promoting the ideology of volunteerism.[5]

Over the years, a division of labor between voluntary agencies and government has evolved. One distinction is based on the age of the group served, with voluntary agencies, particularly women's organizations, expected to serve preschool children, whereas the government takes over as children enter school. In addition to diagnostic, medical,

5. J. Marcus and A. Russell, "The Vulnerable and the Handicapped." This is the best survey in English of the pattern of services to the physically and mentally handicapped in Israel. See also Th. Grushka, ed., *Health Services in Israel*, pp. 253–78.

and treatment services, as well as custodial and institutional programs (particularly if these have a social control function), the government provides children and youth with services necessary for assuming adult roles, such as financial aid, schooling, and training. Handicaps defined in medical terms tend to become the responsibility of voluntary agencies, while services for conditions with a social character were developed under government auspices. Still another division of responsibility has resulted in the existence of two distinct child welfare systems, with the voluntary one predominantly supported from abroad, eschewing asocial and difficult children, and concentrating on such philanthropically appealing groups as babies, orphans, and immigrants. These agencies greatly influenced Israeli child welfare policy by establishing services around needs as they perceived them, leaving the governmental services to become residual, with widely different standards of public services for different population groups.[6]

The government expects that most innovation, demonstration, and research in the social services will be undertaken by voluntary agencies. Accordingly, governmental investment in research and demonstration has been minimal. Apart from a chronic lack of sufficient funds and staff for the basic education, housing, and welfare services, the low government priority assigned to research and demonstration is influenced by the British model, which looks to the private sector to pioneer and to demonstrate on a small, selective scale before risking large-scale governmental provision. Voluntary agencies are perceived as having the advantages of flexibility and freedom from bureaucratic rigidity in the employment of staff, in the procurement of supplies and equipment, and in operating programs. These advantages were recognized by the government when it created nonprofit corporations to manage some of its own institutional facilities, such as sheltered workshops for the retarded. Finally, the government can rely on the substantial research and demonstration capability of JDC-Malben.

The Statutory Framework

Israel — a unitary, multiparty, parliamentary democracy — has no formal constitution.[7] Instead, four basic laws have been passed estab-

6. Eliezer D. Jaffe, "Child Welfare in Israel: An Overview of Institutional Care, Foster Home Care and Adoption," and Hagith Shlonsky, *Welfare in Israel in a Comparative Perspective*, pp. 7–21.

7. Useful descriptions of the political system in Israel are: Eisenstadt, 285–367; Leonard J. Fein, *Politics in Israel*; Oscar Kraines, *Government and Politics in Israel*; David Lazar, "Israel's Political Structure and Social Issues"; Yael Yishai, "Interest Groups in Israel"; and Peter Y. Medding, *Mapai in Israel: Political Organization and Government in a New Society*.

lishing: (1) the Knesset, the single-chamber legislative body of 120 members elected every four years through a system of proportional representation; (2) the Cabinet, headed by a prime minister and collectively responsible to the Knesset; (3) the president, titular head of the state, elected by the Knesset for five years; (4) Israel's Lands. Because no party has ever received a majority of the votes, Israel has always been governed by coalitions, which until 1977 usually consisted of the Labor Party and a number of additional small parties. The major instruments of the state's authority are more than twenty cabinet ministries, which are headed by partners in the coalition. Among the most consistent of these partners has been the National Religious Party, which has long dominated the Ministry of Social Welfare, while Labor Party cabinet members have generally held the portfolios of Health, Labor, and Housing. Although power is concentrated in the central government, major policy decisions have usually been made in the parties' central committees and at the highest levels of the ministries that are controlled by the political party. The Knesset has a limited role as a source of new legislation because it tends to reflect previously determined agreements between top bureaucrats and party leadership.

The statutory basis for governmental services to the physically and mentally handicapped resides in relatively few laws with broadly stated provisions, supplemented by administrative regulations that are formulated by ministry officials and are subject to parliamentary review. Out of the more than 1,200 laws passed by the Knesset over a twenty-five-year period, six major laws, together with their amendments, have provided the legislative mandate for governmental responsibility for certain types of handicaps. These include: the Comprehensive Education Law of 1949; the Discharged Soldiers Pension and Rehabilitation Law of 1949 and 1974; the National Insurance Law of 1953 with major amendments in 1956, 1970, and 1973; the Social Welfare Law of 1958; the Supervision of Welfare Institutions Law of 1965; the Mental Retardation Law of 1969; and the General Disability Insurance Law of 1973.[8]

This small amount of legislation is typical of Israel and similar parliamentary systems. In the absence of a written constitution, the Knesset passes a few basic laws, usually initiated by the government ministries, which are amended over the years. As notable as the rela-

8. A comprehensive review of the statutory framework is Lotte Salzberger and Dan Schnitt, "Social Welfare Legislation in Israel."

tive sparsity of social welfare legislation is its unevenness; for example, an extensive and detailed network of statutory provisions deals with social security and labor, but housing and health are barely covered. The status of health legislation can be inferred from the fact that there is only one law, passed in 1955, pertaining to mental illness. The limited function of the Ministry of Health is explained by the dominant position of the Sick Fund of the General Federation of Labor, which provides basic health and medical services for 80 percent of the population.[9]

Vesting a high degree of discretion in the national and local officials responsible for implementing programs, social legislation in Israel contrasts sharply with the degree of specificity found in legislation in the United States. The advantages of Israeli practice, according to its supporters, are that it "allows the law to be relatively brief and the legislation is not obliged to deal with details. Flexibility is insured by the prerogative of the appropriate authority to modify the regulation within a short time, in accordance with actual needs."[10]

The civil servants who have this authority naturally prefer it because it gives them more discretion and bargaining power over the extent and definition of administrative authority. An extreme example is the program description of the Rehabilitation Section of the Department of Social Work in Jerusalem, which declares: "There is no legislation or administrative policy providing a basis for this program of rehabilitation services. The services are provided because of the need for them and because of the municipalities' ability to provide them."[11]

Although governmental service provision is usually believed to be more universalistic and voluntary agencies more particularistic, this is often more nominal than real. Virtually all legislation and the gov-

9. The Ministry of Health was established in 1948, not to replace the Sick Fund (Kupat Cholim), but to provide additional services and to assume a regulatory responsibility. The result is that, although Israel is a highly socialized country, it does not have a national health service. The Ministry of Health has far fewer resources than the Sick Fund, which receives over half of its funds from the government and represents the major membership strength of the General Federation of Labor. (Emmanuel Margolis, "Health Care in a Changing Society: The Health Services of Israel.")

10. Giora Lotan, *National Insurance in Israel*, p. 29.

11. S. Katz, K. Reagles, and G. Wright, eds., *Rehabilitation Services in Israel*, p. 15. It should be noted that the term *rehabilitation* as used by the Ministry of Social Welfare generally refers to the goal of placement in a sheltered workshop. A broader view of the voluntary sector in Jerusalem is Lotte Salzberger and Jona M. Rosenfeld, "The Anatomy of 267 Social Welfare Agencies in Jerusalem: Findings from a Census."

ernment programs based on it provide for specific population groups and specialized types of disabilities. Only in recent years has there been a tendency to refer to the "rehabilitation of the disabled," and to give less attention to the specific type of disability or its origin. In general, however, public policy relates services and benefits to the locus and the status of the disabled person at the time of injury. For example, services and benefits vary according to whether the disability occurred in the military or in the civilian population; at birth, at work, or at home; on a border, a hijacked airplane, or a soccer field; in an auto or on the street. Even the General Disability Insurance Law of 1973, which is regarded as comprehensive, applies only to eight types of disabilities; it is based on a percentage of functional disability and excludes persons covered by previous more selective legislation.

The statutory development of governmental programs on a categorical basis meant that certain handicapped groups, unless they were also financially needy, were not included for specialized services. This spurred a trend toward the development by voluntary agencies of separate programs and facilities for specific disability groups, such as victims of neuromuscular disorders, cancer patients, children with brain damage or with physical or other mental handicaps, school or work dropouts, and the chronically ill aged. Underlying this pattern are policy differences between officials in the Ministry of Social Welfare and leaders of voluntary agencies. The latter seek support for specialized facilities that serve only a single disability group, while the ministry, for reasons of fiscal efficiency, urges that such facilities as sheltered workshops, day care centers, vocational training programs, medical rehabilitation, social clubs, diagnostic and evaluation centers, and sports centers be available to a variety of handicapped groups.

Interorganizational Environment

While the scope of governmental programs is nominally comprehensive, there is little coherence and consistency in actual service provision and benefit systems. Twenty-two rehabilitation services are divided among eight ministerial domains, and there is no clear-cut pattern in the distribution of responsibility for the mentally and the physically handicapped among them. For example, four ministries are involved in various services for the mentally handicapped; only the Ministry of Social Welfare has a separate division for them and for the blind. The ministries differ among themselves in the extent to which authority is clearly divided between national and municipal administrations, as well as the extent to which services are decentralized.[12] The ministries also differ in fiscal policies. Their rates of reimbursement vary considerably; the Ministry of Education will pay 100 percent of the costs for certain types of institutional care for which the Ministry of Social Welfare will pay only 80 percent.

Access to, and utilization of, services are affected by the comparative organizational power and status of the ministries. Particularly important is the public image of the Ministry of Social Welfare, which has statutory obligation for the mentally retarded, the blind, and the deaf, as well as delinquent youth, the aged, and families and children in need. Because of the stigma attached to governmental charity and to the 180 local welfare bureaus, all the major disability groups have at one time or another tried to break out of its jurisdiction. Negative public attitudes toward the Ministry of Social Welfare have also been used to justify the development of parallel services by voluntary agencies on the grounds that it is easier for their clientele to utilize a nongovernmental service. The ministries differ considerably in the degree to which they are professionalized, bureaucratized, and politicized. Their meritocratic character, as well as their status and power, affects social policy and the allocation of funds. In this competition, the Ministry of Social Welfare has not fared well, and it ranks low, along with the Ministry of Health. It is perceived as a weak ministry in the intragovernmental competition for resources among the party-dominated ministries, largely because of its relegation for over twenty-five years to the National Religious Party, a small minority partner in the governing coalition.[13]

Direct responsibility for the provision of public assistance and the personal social services, in accordance with the Welfare Services Act of 1958, rests with the local authorities, whereas central government makes policy, proposes guidelines, supervises, and subsidizes an average of about 75 percent of the approved welfare expenditures. Local administration in a small, highly centralized state with a population of

12. Y. Freudenheim, *Government in Israel*, chapter 9. A critical analysis of public administration in Israel, together with an excellent bibliography, is Gerald E. Caidin, *Israel's Administrative Culture*. See also Shlonsky, pp. 22–49; Benjamin Akzin and Yehezkel Dror, *Israel: High Pressure Planning*; and Sharkansky, pp. 69–108.

13. In October 1977 the Ministry of Social Welfare, together with the National Insurance Institute and the Ministry of Labor, were merged by the Begin government into the Ministry of Labor and Social Affairs. Although the ministry was headed by a member of one of the new, small parties that emerged in the 1976 election, the control of the social welfare functions remained in the hands of the National Religious Party. The Israeli data was collected during 1972–1974, four years before the Ministry of Social Welfare was included in this merger.

about 3,000,000 and with a very weak local tradition is an anomaly, and there is enormous variation among the 180 welfare bureaus. In formal structure and official functions, the local welfare bureaus resemble their English counterparts, but only in the three large cities in Israel is there even a minimum number of professional staff. Most local authorities are fiscally weak and administratively incapable of fulfilling their obligations, and the welfare bureaus are often in the middle of three-way power struggles involving the Ministry of Social Welfare and the municipalities. The caseload of the local welfare offices consists of the most deprived and poorest clients and, outside of the three large cities, there are very few services for the handicapped.

The central government has, as we have noted, no authority to mandate services for the handicapped. Because there is no entitlement, an enormous amount of discretion is invested in the administration of welfare programs. The weak power of the central government, which has fiscal and administrative authority without direct program responsibility, results in inconsistent and inadequate services that are frequently unacceptable because of their stigma.[14] While some of the officials of the Ministry of Social Welfare would prefer to centralize the delivery of services to the handicapped because of the lack of local resources, such a policy change is not considered either politically or fiscally feasible.

Financial support for most health, education, and welfare services is a mixture of national and local governmental and nongovernmental funds. Most voluntary agencies receive government subsidies or are reimbursed for services to certain types of clientele. These arrangements are a type of deficit financing with little accountability. It is not unusual for voluntary agency programs to be funded by three or more ministries, four or five municipalities, and JDC-Malben, each with different criteria for support.

Voluntary agencies are generally perceived to be an economical substitute for governmental service provision. All but one of the voluntary agencies in the sample of fifteen received some funds from government, although this represented a smaller proportion of their

14. Doron and Kramer, pp. 146–48. A comprehensive study of local government in Israel is S. Weiss, "Local Government in Israel: A Study of Its Leadership." See also Fein, pp. 182–85; Ralph M. Kramer, *Community Development in Israel and the Netherlands*, pp. 37–44; and Fred Lazin, "Welfare Policy Formation in Israel: The Policy Role of the Local Agency." A different and more positive perspective on local government is offered by Daniel J. Elazar, "Local Government as an Integrating Factor in Israeli Society."

income than for agencies in the United States and the Netherlands. Because of the requirements of defense and immigrant absorption in a highly inflationary economy, there has been a long-standing moratorium on new governmental programs. This has enhanced the importance of voluntary agencies, which are most likely to improve or to start new programs.

Voluntary agencies in Israel can rely on the government to bail them out of serious financial crises. Typically, after initial financing by contributions in Israel or from abroad, it becomes increasingly difficult for a voluntary agency to maintain programs solely by contributions, and it then seeks funds from government. Because of the broad scope of governmental responsibility, practically any service can claim governmental support. One of the results of this policy — in the context of no long-term planning, rather low investment of government funds in research and development, and an absence of national structures for coordination — is that service trends tend to be shaped by the special interests of voluntary agencies, which "create facts" in the forms of programs for which they then request governmental support. In this way, voluntary agencies have a significant, if not a disproportionate, influence on the overall service pattern.

Most service programs for the physically handicapped, with the exception of victims of work accidents and war, originated in the voluntary sector, and they have continued with the aid of small amounts of government funds. Their existence, due in no small measure to the unacceptability and inadequacy of public programs, has also deterred government from developing better services, except for the expansion of its facilities for the mentally handicapped. In response to the consistent prodding of the association of parents of the mentally handicapped, more day care and sheltered workshops were established by the government, in addition to enlarging the capacity of some institutions. As a result, there are, in effect, two parallel networks of services to the mentally handicapped, with the nongovernmental one providing community-based services to different types of clientele, with higher standards.

In general, the service programs of the voluntary agencies are noninstitutional, highly specialized, and limited to particular groups of the handicapped. For example, there are no special governmental or voluntary programs for either the partially sighted or the hard-of-hearing. However, because the country is small, local branches of voluntary organizations have access to the resources of their national organizations and in some cases can offer services unavailable in the local welfare bureau.

Voluntarism and the Role of the State

Israel might appear to offer an inhospitable environment for voluntary agencies. It seems to lack many of the conditions regarded by social scientists as prerequisites for participation in voluntary associations, namely: (1) a tradition of limited central power; (2) the absence of a belief that the state will solve almost every problem; (3) the performance of social functions by numerous smaller units; (4) a middle class with sufficient discretionary time and income for voluntary activity.[15] In fact, Israel is highly centralized, politicized, and bureaucratized, a nation where society and polity overlap in a *parteienstaat*. There is no strong tradition of localism, and a belief prevails that the national government is responsible for taking care of virtually every problem. Its economy and defense require extremely high tax rates and full work schedules, so that very few persons have funds and leisure to support voluntary agencies. Paradoxically, not only are there large numbers of nongovernmental organizations in Israel, but their number has increased and new types of voluntary agencies have emerged.[16]

In Israel, however, forms of volunteerism differ in both motivation and expression. As an intrinsic part of the Zionist ideology of a pioneering, nation-building social movement, volunteerism in the Yishuv was oriented toward *collective* responsibility, in contrast to the *individualistic* person-to-person activities advocated today. The latter-

15. William A. Glaser and David L. Sills, eds., *The Government of Associations*, p. 3; and Gabriel A. Almond and Sidney Verba, *The Civic Culture: Political Attitudes and Democracy in Five Nations*, pp. 2–20, 29–35. For a historical view, see S. N. Eisenstadt, "The Social Conditions of the Development of Voluntary Associations—A Case Study of Israel."

16. An analysis of voluntary organizations in Israel depends on definitions and boundaries because there is considerable terminological confusion. In Israel, as in many European countries, the term *voluntary organization* implies a reliance on the unpaid efforts of members or other altruistic persons to perform socially desirable tasks, in contrast to the work of paid staff members. Accordingly, many persons in Israel will deny that there are any voluntary organizations in the health and welfare fields because most of the agencies employ professionals and pay their staff members or receive funds from the government. Others will contrast present-day voluntary agencies with those that existed in the prestate period, with the nostalgic implication that in those days there were voluntary organizations. There is also a tendency to restrict the term to the collective agricultural settlements (kibbutzim), or even to describe the Histadrut (the General Federation of Labor, Israel's "Second Government") as a voluntary organization. On the latter, see J. Joseph Loewenberg, "Histadrut: Myth and Reality," and Milton Derber, "Histadrut, an Industrial Democracy in Israel: An Interpretive Essay from an American Perspective."

day forms of volunteerism are much less egalitarian than their mutual aid form in the Yishuv because there is usually considerable social distance between the typical middle-class volunteer and the underprivileged recipient of services. Finally, there is an important religious differentiation between the two expressions of volunteerism: the contemporary form is, ironically, much closer to the individualism associated with Protestantism, whereas the earlier, prestate, ideological type is closer to the sense of obligation and commitment to equality found in the Jewish religion. There is little reliance in Labor Zionism or in Orthodox Judaism on autonomous individuals, freely choosing to volunteer and participate; rather, individual preferences are subordinate to one's religious obligation and social responsibility as a Jew.

In contrast to the Anglo-American tradition, in Israel no particular virtue is attached to voluntarism per se because it is not viewed as the preferred means of dealing with social problems. The role of government is not primarily one of encouraging or facilitating voluntary effort, nor is the existence of voluntary agencies or the nongovernmental sector justified, as it often is in the United States and England, on antimonopolistic grounds or because of the special values of choice and pluralism. There is no sense of an opposition between government and private or voluntary effort. The Lockean dichotomy of the individual versus the state is also absent, and there is no antistate philosophy that views with apprehension the expanding scope of the central government, as there is in the United States. Instead, state intervention is welcomed and the prevailing, somewhat paternalistic, expectation is that the government will take care of things, since the government is perceived as the central source of benefits to which everyone is entitled. Thus, a curious blend of paternalistic, individualistic, and collectivistic values reflects Israel's status in between the developed and the developing countries, having both socialistic and capitalistic tendencies, and historical affinities with both Western and Eastern Europe.

The outstanding feature of the Israeli power structure is the influence concentrated in a few, highly centralized bureaucratic and political institutions. Perhaps because present-day Israel is a very small state and a consciously created society, rather than one with a long history, the central government wields an authority that is possibly unparalleled in any other nontotalitarian state. No aspect of life is untouched by the state, acting either unilaterally or in partnership with other equally massive bureaucratic political institutions, such as the Histadrut and the Jewish Agency, which is responsible for the resettlement of immigrants. Owning more than 90 percent of the land and its resources, the state is the largest employer of labor, and, by means of subsidies and quasi-public partnerships, it is the dominant influence on the economic and social life of the country.

Given the primacy of the government, what is striking in Israel is the interpenetration among the three institutional sectors — governmental, public, and voluntary — and a blurring of divisions between their enterprises, resulting in a holism that contrasts sharply with the more dualistic system in the Netherlands. The public sector includes large, quasi-governmental organizations such as the Histadrut, a dozen or more political parties, women's auxiliaries that sponsor philanthropic services, and such organizations as Hadassah Medical Organization, Organization for Rehabilitation and Training (ORT), Women's International Zionist Organization (WIZO), and JDC-Malben, all of which obtain their funds from abroad. The voluntary sector includes the network of traditional religious organizations and charities, women's organizations, immigrant associations, various civic and service organizations, and voluntary social service agencies.[17] The three sectors can be arranged on a continuum based on the degree to which they utilize government funds and collaboration: the public organizations are involved in a co-mingling of government funds, whereas there is less government funding, participation, and joint planning in the voluntary social service agencies. All the sectors, however, sponsor services that could under other circumstances be provided directly by government.

The holistic character of the three sectors is manifested, for example, in the interchangeability of careers, allowing officials to move freely between government, the Histadrut, and the Jewish Agency. Funds from taxation and from philanthropic sources — both Israeli citizens and Jews abroad — are mingled to finance all health, education, and welfare services. In the social services, there is a widespread blurring of auspices, so that different organizations claim the same

17. Legally, there are three forms of nongovernmental organizations in Israel: (1) an Ottoman Society based on a Turkish law of 1909 that requires only a nonprofit purpose and that provides great autonomy for most voluntary organizations, including the political parties; (2) a charitable or religious trust, derived from a British law of 1924 that permits the use of quasi-governmental funds to accomplish public purposes without the need to conform to the usual bureaucratic restrictions; (3) a nonprofit, limited liability corporation based on a British law of 1929 and similar to its counterpart in the United States except that the Israel version has a much more restricted corporate structure. (Ralph M. Kramer, *The Voluntary Service Agency in Israel*, p. 5.)

service program as their own. The assumption underlying this holism is expressed by a government official who declared: "There is no real difference at all between governmental funds and those raised by our voluntary agencies here and abroad — they all come from the Jewish people." The attitude behind his statement grows out of the unique, 2,000-year-old history of the Jewish nation in exile and a tradition of financial support of institutions in the Holy Land by Jews in the Diaspora as a means of expressing their unity as a people. Thus, a combination of religious, ideological, and pragmatic elements sustains the holistic character of the relationships between the government and all other social institutions.[18]

The state of Israel, as well as the public sector and to a lesser extent the voluntary social service agencies, continues to depend for financing on external ties to Jewish communities abroad. Consequently, despite the socialist and highly centralized character of the society, there is a long-standing precedent of active support for nongovernmental initiative and relatively little concern with clarity of auspice and accountability.

Politics and the Civic Culture

Israeli political parties differ from those in the United States and England in the multiplicity and scope of their interests and resources. More comparable to their counterparts in the Netherlands, the political parties in Israel own and publish newspapers in several languages and operate economic enterprises such as banks, insurance companies, agricultural settlements, theaters, housing developments, health and welfare agencies, sports clubs, and community centers. As ideological social movements, they gain adherents by means of tangible services and facilities, with the result that members tend to support their parties as voters, clients, and fraternal brothers.

The power of the parties is particularly evident in the widespread use of political criteria in making all decisions on the allocation of resources, as well as in the more traditional area of patronage, which has been refined and routinized over a fifty-year period. Most positions in the government, the Histadrut, and the Jewish Agency are awarded to political parties on the basis of the percentage of votes obtained by them in the national elections. Based on a system of proportional representation, with the same lists presented throughout the

18. Different terminology to describe the holistic character of Israeli institutions is found in Caidin, pp. 20–34, and Akzin and Dror, pp. 1–38.

country, the local and national elections result in the selection of a party slate rather than individual candidates. The consequences are coalition governments and accountability to the central committee of the party, which originally selected the candidates, rather than to a geographically based constituency. The importance of local politics is also diminished because of the very small size of the country, the dominance of national issues and personalities, and the high degree of economic centralization. Nevertheless, even though local citizens have little direct voice in decisions affecting them, 80 percent of the citizenry votes in elections, which occur every four years and have a per capita campaign expenditure rate higher than that of any other nation in the world.[19]

Most citizen participation is structured within existing political parties and trade unions. Interests that cannot be represented within these established channels — and it is exceedingly difficult to organize a new political party — must resort to episodic protests, demonstrations, and other ad hoc strategies for influence. Ethnic interest and single-issue groups have not succeeded, and few voluntary civic associations function as advocates. Another characteristic of community decision making in Israel is that, whereas leadership is expected to provide an opportunity for membership to speak out, it may then act with little attention to minority opinion. Once a decision has been made — after opportunity has been given for the expression of different points of view — all members are expected to support it in a disciplined way.

Sanctioned by the dominant political and trade union decision-making systems, this type of participation varies from the idealized American notion of grass-roots or participatory democracy based upon shared, accountable leadership with widespread direct participation, along with the principles of majority rule and protection for the minority. Considerable difficulty has been encountered in Israel in trying to promote models of participation that vary from the prevailing political system and in dealing with the different cultural traditions of those who come from the patriarchal, traditional societies of the Middle East or the Soviet-type polities found in Rumania or Hungary.[20]

19. Fein, pp. 97–144, and Kraines, p. 62.
20. See also: Fein, pp. 182–85; Kraines, pp. 217–24; Alex Weingrod, *Israel: Group Relations in a New Society*, pp. 62–65; Moshe Lissak, *Social Mobility in Israel Society*, pp. 69–100; Curtis and Shertoff, pp. 281–362; and Judah Matras, *Social Change in Israel*.

Israel is a democracy, although it does not have a participant civic culture comparable to that in the United States or England. In this respect, it seems closer to the Netherlands. While the term *subject* is too strong and limiting to describe the Israeli civic culture, *participant* is also an exaggeration because of the relatively low degree of civic competence and opportunity. Most of the "participation space" in Israel, i.e., the small amount of discretionary time available for organizational work, is preempted by political and religious groups rather than by social service agencies.[21]

While the forms of volunteer participation encouraged by the voluntary agencies are similar to those in the United States, their public image is generally not a favorable one because of negative stereotypes associated with charity fund raising and women volunteers. In Israel, the role of a volunteer is not ordinarily a source of status or prestige, nor is it an aid to social mobility as it is in the United States.

For a variety of reasons, during the 1970s government and political leaders — including the prime minister and the heads of the Labor Party and the Histadrut — have called for more volunteerism to reduce the social gap between older settlers and newer immigrants and for greater use of the voluntary social framework to solve the pressing problems of poverty, disadvantaged youth, the integration of immigrants, literacy, delinquency, and the needy aged. Despite rhetoric and the establishment of a Volunteer Center in the Office of the Prime Minister in 1972, there does not seem to be much change in prevailing patterns. The social structure of Israeli life is not conducive to volunteerism because of inadequate socialization for citizenship roles and voluntary participation.[22] The dominant pattern of relationships in schools and youth movements, for example, is either European-authoritarian or benevolent-paternalistic, rather than democratic. The large part of the population that came from Moslem countries, for whom citizen participation is a foreign notion, still has a great respect for traditional authority. These factors may help explain the low "public-regardingness"[23] and the pervasive privatization of life noted by outside observers. Other constraints on volunteerism are, of

21. This aspect of the civic culture of Israel is discussed in Israel Ministry of Social Welfare, *Development and Participation: Operational Implications for Social Welfare.* See also Elihu Katz, "Culture and Communication in Israel: The Transformation of Tradition," and Kramer, *Community Development,* pp. 6–13, 114–16, 131–38.

22. Ben Lappin, "The Missing Volunteers in Israel's Struggle with Poverty."

23. James Q. Wilson and Edward C. Banfield, "Public Regardingness as a Value Premise in Voting Behavior."

course, the demands of daily living, the small amount of leisure time, the requirement of service in the military reserves (two months a year for most men), and the economic necessity for both husband and wife to work. The usual incentives for voluntary participation are also weak because most citizens believe that they are contributing adequately to the common welfare by paying extraordinarily high taxes and by performing military service.

Conclusions

Under the British Mandate a rich tradition of voluntarism existed within the organized Jewish community. Its infrastructure was transferred to the state of Israel, established in 1948. Confronted by the unprecedented, simultaneous demands of military defense, immigrant resettlement, and economic development, the state was content to leave the provision of many social services to voluntary organizations. Support for nongovernmental initiative was encouraged by the capacity of voluntary agencies to raise funds both in Israel and abroad for their specialized programs. Government programs for the physically and mentally handicapped are regarded as inadequate by the voluntary agencies, who have developed a complementary and often substitute network of services that acts as a deterrent to further governmental provision.

There is considerable interpenetration among the governmental, the public, and the voluntary sectors in Israel, with little concern with clarifying the auspices of a program or the division of service responsibility among different sponsors. The persistence of grave political and economic problems makes any serious change in governmental-voluntary relationships unlikely, except that national priorities may further enhance the value of voluntary agencies.

Table 1 summarizes three leading characteristics of sociopolitical contexts in the four countries.

TABLE 1.
Sociopolitical Contexts

	United States	England	The Netherlands	Israel
Governmental-Voluntary relationships	Mixed economy dominated by governmental financing with multiple service providers and diminishing organizational differences; voluntary agency functions as a vendor under contract.	Comprehensive statutory financing and direct provision through local Social Service Departments with some supplementation by voluntary agencies.	Voluntary agencies primary service providers with government subsidies.	Close partnership among all sectors. Voluntary agency supplements and often substitutes for government.
Civic culture	Extensive citizen participation, volunteerism, self-help and individualism; distrust of government.	Welfare state ideology, but with strong tradition of voluntarism; deferential toward government.	Religiopolitical stratification; corporatism prevails over voluntarism.	Collectivist, prestate tradition of voluntarism did not persist; little citizen participation outside political parties and unions.
Public policy environment	Federalism; decentralized three-level representative democracy with separation of powers; interest group pluralism; extensive output of laws and regulations.	Parliamentary democracy, dominated by central government bureaucracies, yet considerable local discretion.	Consociational democracy with policymaking vested in strong central government.	Unitary, multiparty state; highly centralized, politicized bureaucracies; weak Parliament and local government.

PART II

Internal Factors:
How Voluntary Agencies Are
Constituted and Maintained

Having noted the sociopolitical context in which voluntary agencies function in four countries, we now analyze the distinctive features of their organization. Relatively little research has been devoted to voluntary agencies, and chapter 5 begins with a brief assessment of the state of knowledge. Because of their reputed influence on organizational behavior, several dimensions of the structure, governance, and financing of voluntary agencies have been selected for analysis. Chapter 5 describes three salient features of the internal structure of voluntary agencies: size, formalization, and professionalization. In Chapter 6, governance and policymaking sytems are compared, including the size, composition, and role of the board of directors, and aspects of national-local relationships are examined. The fiscal resource systems of the voluntary agencies are then described. The subject of chapter 7 is contributed funds, and the use of government funds is discussed in chapter 8. Reliance on governmental funds is the most important trend since 1960, and I examine factors affecting the control and dependency of voluntary organizations and problems facing them when they become providers of public services. The effect of governmental funds on the roles of voluntary agencies and on their future is considered in Parts III and IV.

5.   Organizational Structure

Despite the prevalence and importance of voluntary organizations, there is no coherent theory to account for their development and change. There is not even a generally accepted classification of voluntary associations. As a substitute for the lack of theory, provocative metaphors have been employed, such as "loose coupling" and "organized anarchy." A garbage-pail model has even been elaborated, as well as the more conventional ones of system, organism, game, drama, and political economy.[1] As an organizational hybrid of a public-service bureaucracy and a voluntary association, the nongovernmental social service agency has been neglected by researchers. Most studies concentrate on other types of service-delivery structures, such as those listed below:

Primary groups (family and informal networks)
Mutual aid (self-help)
Alternative agencies
Formal voluntary associations (civic, professional, religious, ethnic)
Voluntary social service agencies
Quasi-nongovernmental organizations (QUANGOS)
Public bureaucracies

The paucity of data on voluntary agencies may also reflect difficulties in studying organizations whose record keeping is not extensive or systematic, and whose diversity does not lend itself easily to comparison.[2] Then, too, there may be ambivalence: voluntary agencies may be venerated because of their charitable work and may serve as quasi-sacred symbols, yet they may not be regarded as worthy of serious attention.

1. Some of the leading models and perspectives are summarized in J. Eugene Haas and Thomas E. Drabek, *Complex Organizations: A Sociological Perspective*, pp. 23–98.
2. The inadequate data base for the study of voluntary agencies in England is stressed by George J. Murray, "Voluntary Organizations in the Personal Social Service Field." The absence of adequate data for research purposes is a condition found in the Netherlands and Israel, where voluntary agencies have not previously been the object of the study. This is the first time they have been included in a research investigation of this type.

In recent years voluntary agencies have been included in a special class of human service organizations that, although differing in auspices (governmental or voluntary), functions, and client populations, share a set of common attributes and vulnerabilities. In contrast to other formal organizations, their "raw materials" are human beings, their goals are ambiguous and problematic, they rely on professionals and an indeterminate technology in which staff-client relations are the core, and they lack valid measures of effectiveness.[3]

When we seek the distinctive characteristics of voluntary social service agencies within this category of human service organizations, we find hortatory references to such qualities as uniqueness, flexibility, pioneering, and personal touch. Historically the following stereotypes have persisted for a century in both the United States and England:

Characteristics of Governmental Agency	Characteristics of Voluntary Agency
Rigid, slow to change	Flexible, adaptable
Only well-accepted services	Experimental and pioneering
Little citizen participation	Voluntary citizen participation
Mass, universal services	Individualized, personal, and selective services
Diffuse contacts	Intensive relationships
Remedial programs	Preventive services
Nonpartisan	Social change and reform
Nonsectarian	Religious and sectarian

A summary of the leading differences between governmental and voluntary agencies appears in Table 2.

Increasingly there is recognition that the polarities overlook significant differences within and a fading of distinctions between the two types of organizations, and that most governmental and voluntary agencies fall in between the extremes of commonly ascribed qualities. Furthermore, no attribute of organizational character is the exclusive property of either type of organization:

We need to break out of the categories of thought that make sharp distinctions between the private sector and the public bureaucracy, and that ascribe unambiguous virtues or vices to either. The reality of the contract

3. Yeheskel Hasenfeld and Richard A. English, eds., *Human Service Organizations*, pp. 8–22. See Richard Steiner, *Managing the Human Service Organization*, p. 30, for a detailed comparison of a human service organization with a business corporation, and Hal G. Rainey et al., "Comparing Public and Private Organizations."

TABLE 2.

Formal Differences between Governmental and Voluntary Agencies

	Governmental Agency	Voluntary Agency
Philosophy	Justice	Charity
Represents	Majority	Minority
Legal basis of service	Right	Gratuity
Source of funds	Taxes	Contributions, fees, payments, and grants
Determination of function	Prescribed by law	Selected by governing group
Source of policymaking authority	Legislative body	Charter and bylaws authorizing board of directors
Accountability	To the electorate via a legislative body	To constituency via board of directors
Scope	Comprehensive	Limited
Administrative structure	Large, bureaucratic	Small, bureaucratic
Administrative pattern of service	Uniform	Variable
Organization and program size	Large	Small

state is that there has been an extensive and probably irreversible inter-mingling of the public and private sectors, and a sharing of functions be-tween individuals who are public officials and those who are nominally private.[4]

In this study, I have tried to set aside conventional preconceptions and to demystify the voluntary agency by analyzing a comparable group of agencies in one field of service with some conceptual tools derived from organization theory. I begin with size, formalization, and professionalization. They are among the variables most fre-quently used to describe the internal structural characteristics of for-mal organizations. Also, in a large body of research they have been associated with innovation, change, and collaboration.[5] In these studies, however, auspice has not been considered an organizational variable except in some classifications, where it is related to the mode of financing. Although there are serious methodological deficiencies in much of the research on organizations, resulting in inconsistent and equivocal findings, existing research was nevertheless used as the source of a number of guiding hypotheses regarding the effects of bureaucratization and professionalization on voluntary agencies. For example, despite the fact that voluntary agencies are usually small, they are essentially bureaucratic in structure and presumably are subject to characteristic pressure toward ritualism, conformity, and insularity.[6]

Size

One feature of voluntary organizations is the tremendous difference in the scale of their operation. Variation in size, whether measured in terms of staff, clientele, or budget, makes it difficult to generalize about them as a class of organizations. Their diversity also constitutes a formidable obstacle to the development of typologies.[7] For example, it is possible to classify voluntary agencies according to the degree of

4. Bruce L. R. Smith, "Independence and the Contract State," p. 35. See also Eleanor Bril-liant, "Private or Public: A Model of Ambiguities," pp. 384–85.

5. Some of the major theories and supporting findings are conveniently summarized by Gerald Zaltman, Robert Duncan, and Jonny Holbek in *Innovations and Organizations*, pp. 34–86. See also Andre L. Delbecq and Jon L. Pierce, "Innovation in Professional Organizations."

6. Herman Stein, "Organization Theory — Implications for Administrative Research." See also Peter M. Blau, Wolfe V. Heydebrand, and Robert E. Stauffer, "The Structure of Small Bureaucracies."

7. One of the few typologies including both governmental and voluntary organizations and based on function, funds, personnel, and clientele is Raymond M. Weinstein and Jaroslov G. Moravec, "A Comparative Analysis of Health and Welfare Organizations."

TABLE 3.
Average Voluntary Agency Income, 1973–1974, in U.S. Dollars

	United States (N = 20)	England (N = 20)	The Netherlands (N = 20)	Israel (N = 15)
Mean	809,348	3,100,642	634,875	199,623
Median	305,120	1,224,693	178,621	90,830

TABLE 4.
Average Size of Voluntary Agency Staff, 1973–1974

	United States (N = 20)	England (N = 20)	The Netherlands (N = 20)	Israel (N = 15)
Mean	36	338	67	38
Median	22	40	24	10

consumer involvement (organizations of or for the handicapped); locus (national or local); size (income or staff); major source of funds (governmental or voluntary); function; structure; and technology. No single, overall classification proved useful in all countries, although the extent of client involvement, use of public funds, and size were illuminating in particular national contexts. In addition, the indicators of size that were used — income and the number of full-time equivalents of professional and administrative staff — were not always directly related to the scope, influence, and effectiveness of a voluntary agency.[8]

The average size of agency income and staff in the four countries is shown in Tables 3 and 4. In each case, much smaller medians reflect skewed distribution of income and staff between a few very large organizations and a more extensive number of smaller agencies. (See the appendix for details of the range in the size of agency income and staff.)

It is likely that there is as much variation among voluntary agencies on these measures as between them and governmental organizations. For example, how does one compare a voluntary agency that has two

8. There is no agreement in the research literature on appropriate and valid indicators of organizational size. See John R. Kimberly, "Organizational Size and the Structuralist Perspective: A Review, Critique, and Proposal," and James L. Price, *Handbook of Organizational Measurement*. The importance of large size and resources is stressed in Lawrence V. Mohr, "Determinants of Innovation in Organizations."

paid staff members with another organization that serves the same clientele but employs 80 persons and has an income 100 times as large? The small agency may have more in common with a mutual-aid association, while the larger one may be structurally and functionally closer to a government bureaucracy. Even the largest voluntary agencies, however, did not approach the local governmental social service departments in size, complexity, professionalization, and bureaucratization in England, the United States, and most parts of Israel. Size is probably the most consistent differential between governmental and voluntary social service agencies. This may explain the widespread belief that voluntary agencies have distinct advantages over governmental organizations in flexibility and capacity for adaptation, although these advantages are counterbalanced by greater fiscal uncertainty and limited service-delivery capability.

The small size of the staff may belie the scope and influence of the organization. For example, in five of the fifteen agencies studied in Israel, the executive was the only full-time paid staff member. (In the Netherlands there were two such agencies, and there was one each in England and the United States.) Two of the five Israeli agencies were ineffective in assisting the victims of auto accidents and tuberculosis. The other three, however, were successful in developing programs for school-age deaf children, the adult blind, and victims of work accidents. One agency had no executive other than its founder-president, who devoted several hours every day to the direction of the organization, and a part-time consultant. They served as advocates and managed to raise substantial funds to provide specialized equipment for schools, to sponsor teacher training, and to provide other direct services for deaf children and their families. Another agency resulted from the merger of two organizations, one *of* and the other *for* the blind. The executive, himself blind, was recognized as the spokesman for the blind in the country, and he exerted considerable influence on governmental legislation, regulations, and budgeting. He supervised a major network of sheltered workshops for the blind in Israel and oversaw twenty-three local programs of social and recreational activities for the blind.

One of the most effective voluntary organizations in Israel in fund raising and among the most active in volunteer utilization and program development — the Israel Cancer Association — had a professional staff of only three persons; they provided leadership for the organization's support of medical research, public education on cancer, and the sponsorship of sixty-five early-detection clinics. In England, the British Association for the Hard of Hearing had no paid staff; its rent was paid by a grant from the central government; and its national office was managed by the president with a budget equivalent to $28,000. Affiliated with it were 215 clubs with 8,000 members and four times as many active participants in their programs, which included advocacy, public education, and some social services.

Another effective agency with a small staff was the Cerebral Palsy Association of San Francisco, with only one and one-half full-time professionals but a budget of $214,000. It used most of its resources to induce other organizations to provide services for persons with cerebral palsy. The opposite approach was taken by an organization in Oakland concerned with cerebral palsy, which also had a small staff — two full-time and three part-time professionals, though it lacked an executive director for three years. In 1973 it used a modest budget of $105,000 for direct services to 184 individuals, including speech, occupational, and physical therapy; social, recreational, and educational activities; transportation, social work, and a vocational workshop in a campus setting. Finally, lack of correspondence between staff size and budget is illustrated in a San Francisco agency for the blind that had only six full-time professionals but had an operating budget of $1,200,000, in addition to a $3,500,000 endowment fund.

Thus size by itself does not tell the whole story. The type and number of functions and service programs sponsored by an agency are significant. Functions can be divided into direct services for the handicapped, which include residential care and community-based programs, and indirect functions, of which advocacy, support of medical research, and public education are the most common. Organizations that provide direct rather than indirect services have the largest staffs in all four countries, and those sponsoring various forms of residential care employ the largest number and most diverse types of employees. Whereas agencies raising large sums for research or sponsoring public education might not be expected to have sizable professional staffs, several of direct service agencies in the United States and England with large budgets also had small staffs; the San Francisco Lighthouse for the Blind and the National Society for Cancer Relief are examples. Two of the most complex organizations studied were the Royal National Institute for the Blind, with 1,500 paid staff members, and the Spastics Society in England, which employs almost 1,900 persons. A typical institution sponsored by the Spastics Society cared for 120 severely physically and mentally handicapped children, ages five to sixteen, and had 122 full-time and 25 part-time staff members with thirty-three job titles, among which were teacher, physiotherapist, occupational therapist, speech therapist, psychologist, nurse, psychiatrist, pediatrician, and social worker, in addition to house parent, matron, clerical staff, and domestic. The smaller size of staffs in the United States agencies, as well as in the other two countries, reflected differences in social policy. In the United States and Israel, most institutional care was under governmental auspices, and voluntary agencies usually sponsored small- or medium-size community-based programs for preschool children and adults, such as day care and sheltered workshops, which are not as labor intensive as institutions.

The history of voluntary agencies in England suggests that growth in size is not necessarily related to the age of the organization. Six of the English agencies were 75 to 150 years old, and all but one was in the lowest quadrant of income and staff size. Two of the agencies that had the largest staff, the largest facilities, and the highest income were established in the post-World War II period. The Spastics Society had the most remarkable growth of all. Starting with nothing but the initiative and determination of a group of parents, assisted by the imaginative skill of a public relations professional who promoted the spastics' cause by the first use of a football pool, this venture was so successful that in less than twenty years the Spastics Society accumulated the fourth highest assets (over £6,000,000) of any charity in Great Britain. It built more than one hundred specialized facilities, such as schools, day centers, residential homes, clinics, family-help units, hostels, holiday homes, work centers, industrial workshops, and hostels. In addition, it sponsored a £2,000,000 medical research program, teacher training, a Family Service and Assessment Center, and an extensive program of public information using the mass media. Almost 1,900 persons are employed in fifty-four programs that currently serve 3,600 persons. These achievements contrast sharply with the less spectacular development of cerebral palsy societies in the United States.[9]

Another example of exceptionally rapid growth is the Center for Independent Living in Berkeley, which, in a five-year period (1972–

9. The Spastics Society is discussed in Benedict Nightingale, *Charities*, pp. 316–19. The major sources of information on this and the other organizations cited are, unless otherwise indicated, derived from interviews and unpublished documents made available to the author by agency staff members.

1977), developed twenty-four programs serving over 2,000 disabled, blind, deaf, and elderly persons a month, with a budget of $1,000,000 and 110 staff members, of whom half are handicapped; by 1980, its budget exceeded $3,000,000. Evolving over a much longer period — it was started in 1952 by the present executive — the San Francisco Recreation Center for the Handicapped was supported by voluntary funds until 1964, when it began to secure government grants. It expanded rapidly to sponsor thirty-four programs serving 1,300 handicapped persons, with a paid staff of 80, 230 volunteers, and a 1976 budget of almost $1,000,000, of which five-sixths came from government sources. Its programs overshadowed those of the San Francisco City and County Recreation Department, which had only ten full-time staff members in its special division for handicapped persons, and, in a reversal of roles, seemed to supplement a voluntary agency.

Formalization

Voluntary agencies seem to retain their freewheeling, pioneering, and loose organization for only a short time during the early formative stages, while they struggle for identity and to establish their domain. Almost invariably, over time most of them grow and, like most organizations, become institutionalized — i.e., more bureaucratic and professional. Formalization, one dimension of bureaucratization, refers to the degree to which organizational work norms are made explicit, and in this study it was measured by the existence and use of written policies pertaining to staff (personnel practices, pay scales, and job classifications) and service delivery (eligibility and benefits).

In the four countries studied, organizations engaged in direct services to clients are more formalized — because of their larger staffs — than those that stress advocacy, public information, and support of research. Agencies in the United States and the Netherlands are, on the whole, more formalized than those in England; the Israeli agencies are the least formalized of all. In the United States, where formalization has progressed the furthest, it is not unusual for consumer-based, self-help, and alternative agencies to bureaucratize and professionalize within the space of a few years.

Because of the prevalence of a hierarchical pattern of authority, including a division of labor and policy rules, almost all of the agencies studied could be described as "mini-bureaucracies." This characterization may not apply to some of the smallest, most loosely structured organizations, which, because of their size and relative lack of hierarchy and professionalization, were unusually dependent on the quality of their leadership and were subject to idiosyncratic rather than to structural factors. The importance of personality variables rather than structural factors in such agencies may explain why, as James Q. Wilson has observed, "a non-pecuniary organization must tolerate a great deal of foolishness if it is to survive."[10] Charles Perrow may also have had such organizations in mind in his discussion of an insufficient level of bureaucratization as being at least as dysfunctional as the widely deplored excesses of "bureaupathology."[11] Voluntary organizations that grow beyond the first stage of charismatic or traditional leadership usually require more rational-bureaucratic or technical types of leadership as they become institutionalized.

One of the principal factors influencing the size of budgets, professional staff, and formalization is the character of the fiscal environment. In both the Netherlands and the United States, agencies have become dependent on highly centralized and bureaucratic funding sources in government, and, in the voluntary sector in the United States, on United Funds and federations. Relying on these fiscal sources for their existence, voluntary agencies in the United States and the Netherlands (much more so than those in England and in Israel), must take into account external demands for reporting, budgeting, management control, and other forms of public accountability. In the Netherlands, central government subsidies and, since 1970, social insurance payments have been the principal source of income for voluntary agencies. The necessity of complying with governmental requirements stimulated the formulation of job specifications, salary scales, and staffing and service norms. As a result, all twelve agencies providing services in the Netherlands have manuals for service policies and for personnel practices. In addition, government has deliberately used the subsidy policy to reduce the number of small agencies by requiring a minimum number of staff members in order for an agency to receive a subsidy. In some agencies, this policy has brought about an eightfold increase in staff over a ten-year period.

In the United States, eligiblity for government grants and service payments, as well as for membership in a United Fund, requires evidence of a minimum level of administrative, fiscal, and service capability. Consequently, all of the twenty U.S. agencies in the sample have service and personnel manuals, in contrast with England, where only eleven out of twenty agencies have statements of personnel practices

10. James Q. Wilson, "Innovation in Organization: Notes Toward a Theory," p. 210.
11. Charles Perrow, *Complex Organizations: A Critical Essay*, p. 6.

or use statutory pay scales as a salary guideline. Only one English agency reported the use of a service manual that specified eligibility criteria, and only three of the largest agencies had any regular procedures for staff evaluation.

In the United States, there is a trend toward the use of uniform financial reporting standards and, in some fields, standardized service statistics.[12] Widespread use of these measures of accountability by funding bodies is the source of a frequent complaint in the United States: excessive fiscal and service reporting requirements of the government and United Funds. In contrast, in England and Israel, where each agency raises its own funds and is not dependent on allocations from a single central source, there are few external pressures for these forms of bureaucratization. The regulations of the English charity commissioners are not very stringent, and most organizations have little difficulty complying.[13] The standards for the receipt of government funds by voluntary organizations are even less stringent in Israel, and only five agencies have formalized service and staffing policies.

In England, only two of the agencies have an information system or publish service statistics. This may be one reason why English agencies have rarely been the object of research. The lack of "businesslike management" in voluntary agencies has been discussed for many years in England, where the traditional charity image has persisted longer than in the United States. For example, in England it is not unusual for executive positions to be filled by retired army officers and former civil servants rather than by persons with social service experience. This contrasts with the requirement of the Department of Health and Social Security that the directors of the Social Service Departments in the local authorities be qualified social workers. There is also a high degree of staff discretion in most English voluntary agencies, although only two do not subject staff decisions to administrative review. The smallest organizations, as well as the largest, claim to exercise control over the authority to disburse funds by requiring the approval of someone on the next rung of the administrative ladder.

12. See American Institute of Certified Public Accountants, *Audits of Voluntary Health and Welfare Organizations;* National Health Council, *Standards of Accounting and Financial Reporting for Voluntary Health and Welfare Organizations;* and United Way of America, *UWASIS II: A Taxonomy of Social Goals and Human Service Programs.*

13. Goodman Committee, *Charity Law and Voluntary Organisations,* pp. 42–43, 89–90, 117–22; Nightingale, pp 277–82; and Wolfenden Committee, *The Future of Voluntary Organisations,* p. 161: "We do not believe that accountability is a real difficulty for the great majority of voluntary organizations."

Thus, to the factors conducive to formalization among voluntary agencies, such as professionalization and growth, we should add dependency on a centralized, bureaucratic funding source. Some consequences of formalization for the role performance of voluntary agencies will be discussed in chapters 9–12.

Professionalization

The task of comparing professionalization between, as well as within, the four countries was complicated by differences in the definition of the education and experience that qualify one as a professional. The ambiguity was increased by the variety of specialized medical and paramedical personnel involved in the assessment, care, treatment, and rehabilitation of the physically and mentally handicapped, virtually all of whom regard themselves as professionals, together with the members of the fund raising, public relations, and administrative staff of voluntary agencies. For example, of the more than 300 staff members of the National Society for Mentally Handicapped Children (NSMHC) in England, 40 to 50 percent are considered professional; another 20 percent, administrative; and the remaining 30 to 40 percent, clerical, maintenance, and domestic. Because of the absence of a more rigorous definition, I accepted each organization's own designation of "professional," which in most instances amounted to almost the entire staff, excepting clerical and custodial personnel but including all types of medical and nursing staff, social workers, counselors, teachers, therapists (occupational, physical, speech, etc.), recreational specialists — in short, all givers of service or care.

Although in all four countries the number of human service professionals of all types has increased as part of a societal trend, distribution and growth rates in the governmental and voluntary sectors are uneven, and within the latter, there are differences between the national and local levels. This is evident in social work, one of the key professions used to provide personal social services for the physically and mentally handicapped. Social workers in England are concentrated almost exclusively in the statutory agencies, which employ 85 to 90 percent of all qualified social workers, although only 40 percent of the social work staff in the local authorities is considered trained.[14] Furthermore, in the voluntary sector, almost all professional social workers are employed by such national organizations as the Invalid

14. Adrian Webb, Lesley Day, and Douglas Weller, *Voluntary Social Service Manpower Resources*, pp. 17–20.

Children's Aid Association, the Spastics Society, and the NSMHC, rather than by local affiliates, few of which sponsor professionally staffed programs or employ paid staff. This is due in part to the relatively small number of social workers in England and the recent development of professional education. A similar condition was found in Israel, where only five out of the fifteen agencies employ social workers and where professional education on the university level is a recent development. In Israel most university graduates in social work are employed in fields conferring higher status than does care of the physically and mentally handicapped.

English agencies have moved more slowly than those in the United States and the Netherlands from the patriarchal or matriarchal rule of their founders to a rational-bureaucratic structure. While the gap in staff qualifications and salaries between the English voluntary and statutory agencies has narrowed, a belief persists among leaders in both sectors that voluntary agency staffs are more idealistic and dedicated than their counterparts in the statutory agencies, although the two staffs often interact as professional peers.

The pattern in the Netherlands is the reverse of that in England: virtually all social workers and other professionals are employed by nongovernmental organizations responsible for the provision of health and social services. For example, in the field of care of the mentally handicapped, 180 social workers were employed in the voluntary sector and only 15 by government agencies. A further contrast is the high professional status accorded to socio-pedagogues who work with the mentally handicapped in the Netherlands. In other countries, this clientele has not been attractive to social workers and to other members of the helping professions. It is not clear how or why a different pattern emerged in the Netherlands, where most socio-pedagogues, in contrast to social workers in other fields, are men.

On the administrative level, Dutch professionals, supported by their peers in government, have tried to overcome the image of amateurism that the religious-charity origins of their organizations connote. They have succeeded to a considerable degree in attaining an image of managerial efficiency and professional-technical expertise. Apart from backgrounds in social work and socio-pedagogy, almost half of the Dutch executives have studied the social sciences, law, medicine, and business administration.

Despite belief by many social scientists and professionals in the incompatibility of bureaucracy and professionalism, very few such conflicts were reported in any of the countries. Indeed, in the Netherlands the power of the "techno-structure" (middle and upper echelon administrators, fund-raisers, public relations staff, social workers, and medical and other technical personnel) is very much in the ascendance and, as we shall see in the next chapter, is viewed by government officials and social scientists as seriously threatening the authority of the volunteer board of directors. This and evidence from other studies suggest that the assumption of a basic conflict between bureaucrats and professionals may be simplistic, and that there is a high degree of compatibility between them. Indeed, human service professionals seem to be effective in molding organizations to suit their interests.[15]

At the same time, there are two divergent professional ideologies, which can be described as technocratic and democratic. *Technocratic* refers to a belief that experts should have most of the power in policymaking and in the governance of an agency; this attitude is particularly evident in the Netherlands. From this perspective, the board member who is a citizen volunteer adds no particular value and makes no distinctive contribution to the process of policy formulation. A contrary view in the United States and England is based on democratic ideology and regards the relationship between professional and citizen volunteer as a democratic partnership in which each can bring something special to the policymaking process. This ideology also regards as a norm a professional obligation for educating citizen volunteers to enable them to develop their leadership abilities.[16] Although more often preached than practiced, the democratic ideology was more evident in responses of executive leadership in the United States and England than in the Netherlands and Israel. This reflects not only a difference in professional ideologies, but also a difference in civic cultures.

Variations in size, formalization, and professionalization are but three aspects of the structure of the voluntary agency. To complete the picture, we turn to the next level of the organizational hierarchy — the governance system.

15. Wolfe V. Heydebrand and James J. Noell, "Task Structure and Innovation in Professional Organizations"; Elizabeth Morrissey and David F. Gillespie, "Technology and the Conflict of Professionals in Bureaucratic Organizations"; and Richard Hall, "Professionalization and Bureaucratization."

16. Two representative examples of the belief that the ablest professionals attract and sustain the service of ablest lay leadership are: Brian O'Connell, *Effective Leadership in Voluntary Organizations: How to Make the Greatest Use of Citizen Service and Influence*, and Harleigh B. Trecker, *Citizen Boards at Work: New Challenges to Effective Action*.

6.   Governance Systems

Whereas organizational structure for service delivery expresses the bureaucratic character of a voluntary agency, its pattern of governance indicates its roots as a voluntary association. The distinctive, hybrid character of the voluntary agency brings together a group of citizen volunteers who serve as the governing body for a legally incorporated charitable organization and as employers of a staff who are responsible, in turn, for providing services to a selected clientele. Generally, the corporate board of directors has these responsibilities: policymaking, financing (securing funds and being accountable for expenditures), staffing (employing the executive and establishing personnel policies), interpretation (representing the agency in the community). Voluntary agencies in the four countries all included structures for legitimation in the form of a group of sponsors, patrons, notable citizens, or experts; for policy development, usually in an executive committee; for policy adoption, in the board of directors; and for implementation through an administrative hierarchy of paid staff and volunteers.

I considered five features of the board of directors: (1) size, (2) composition, (3) degree of activity (attendance, participation, and turnover), (4) policymaking patterns and internal democracy, with special reference to the distribution of power, and (5) national-local relationships.

Size and Composition of the Board of Directors

In the four countries, the number of members of a board of directors ranged from a minimum of 6 to 11 to a maximum of 25 to 120, as can be seen in Table 5. The average size of boards in the Netherlands was less than half that of their counterparts in the other countries.[1]

In none of the four countries was the size of the board of directors commensurate with the size of the budget or the target population.

1. In the Netherlands the term *volunteer* is not ordinarily used to refer to board members, who were traditionally known as "regents" and today as *bestuursleden*. The latter term approximates the English concept of "governor."

TABLE 5.
Range and Size of Agency Boards of Directors

	United States (N = 20)	England (N = 20)	The Netherlands (N = 20)	Israel (N = 15)
Range	11–64	10–120	6–25	8–71
Mean Size	24	23	11	23

More often, the reverse was found—the agencies with the largest budgets had the smallest boards of directors, clientele, and target populations. For example, in the United States two agencies with fifteen board members had budgets of $500,000 or more, while an agency with a board twice as large had a budget of less than $90,000. Furthermore, in the United States there was an inverse relationship between the size of the board and the use of public funds; the agencies that most relied on public funds had the smallest boards of directors.

In England, one of the three largest agencies, the Spastics Society, had only twelve members on its executive council, and thirteen persons, including seven top professional staff members, served as the policy-implementation body. Similarly, Cheshire Homes and the Shaftesbury Society, with their extensive network of institutions, had only eighteen persons on their boards of directors, whereas much smaller organizations with less than one-sixth of their income had thirty to forty persons.

In all four countries, business and professional men comprised from two-thirds to more than three-quarters of the board members. The community notables who provided legitimation for the agency were drawn from the Royal Family and nobility in England and from business and corporate leaders in the United States. Few politicians or elected officials served on the boards of directors; only one U.S. agency had such persons. In the Netherlands, seven organizations had public officials on their boards (no more than one or two), but the official was regarded as being like any other member. In Israel, two agencies had government representatives on their boards, but one of these agencies was in a state of receivership, and government was the primary referral source of clientele for the other. There was little support in any of the countries for the belief that when voluntary agencies receive a substantial amount of income from government, representatives of government should serve on the board, although this does occur in some local authorities in England.

TABLE 6.
Types of Voluntary Agencies in the United States

Degree of Consumer Involvement in Policymaking	Dependence on Government Funds	
	High	Low
High	Quasi-nongovernmental organization (QUANGO)	Alternative agency
Low	Private-public service provider (vendor)	Private service agency

SOURCE: "Future of the Voluntary Service Organization," by Ralph M. Kramer, *Social Work* 18, no. 6 (November 1973): 63. Copyright 1973, National Association of Social Workers, Inc. Reprinted with permission.

Women were least represented on boards in the Netherlands, where they comprised less than 20 percent of all board members, in contrast with about one-third in the United States, Israel, and England. The U.S. board members were, on the average, about ten years younger than their counterparts in the other countries, where the majority ranged in age from forty to sixty.

Another important characteristic of boards is the extent to which consumers are members. Indeed, the criterion of *cui bono* ("who benefits") is the basis of the well-known organizational typology of Blau and Scott.[2] Consumer involvement in policymaking and the degree of reliance on government funding were useful dimensions in classifying four types of voluntary organizations in the United States, as can be seen in Table 6.[3]

The degree of consumer involvement in governance systems varied considerably, both between and within the four countries. Clients or their family members were represented on the boards of seven of the fifteen voluntary agencies in Israel, but in the remaining eight agencies, there was little or no participation by consumers in policymaking bodies. Although handicapped persons or their family members were on the boards of all but four of the twenty U.S. agencies, they constituted only 14 percent of all board members in the sample, in contrast with England, where one-third of the total number of board members were consumers. Although mandated citizen participation is a well-

2. Peter M. Blau and W. Richard Scott, *Formal Organizations: A Comparative Approach*, pp. 42–58. The philanthropic organization is classified as a mixed type — part mutual-benefit and part service.

3. The organizational character and the futures of these four types of voluntary agencies are analyzed in Ralph M. Kramer, "Future of the Voluntary Service Organization."

established public policy in the United States, few voluntary agencies have any formal stipulation in their bylaws requiring the participation of consumers.

However, the presence of a high proportion of handicapped persons or their family members in policymaking roles does not mean that their views prevail, even when there is consensus among them. In the Spastics Society and the NSMHC, two of the largest agencies in England, consumer board members differed sharply on policy among themselves, often along generational lines, and disagreed with professional staff on such issues as the rights of the handicapped. In several episodes, a dissident faction seceded and formed its own group, challenging the right of the established organization to speak for it. This was the case of the Multiple Sclerosis Society in England and of the younger physically handicapped in Israel who rejected the efforts of the Israel Foundation for Handicapped Children (ILAN) to represent them and their interests. In the Netherlands, twenty-three national associations of the physically handicapped have resisted for years the government's efforts to organize them into a federation. In the United States there has been a slow growth, beginning in the mid-1970s, in the number of independent, self-help organizations controlled by the physically handicapped, which reject the tokenism of consumer participation in the established voluntary organizations.

Among the factors affecting the degree and nature of consumer participation is the type of handicap. The most successful forms of consumer participation were found among organizations of the blind and among parents of the mentally handicapped. Among the sensorially handicapped, the blind have been most assertive in pressing for greater participation. The Royal National Institute for the Blind, in response to the demands of an advocacy organization of the blind that had long been critical of the venerable Institute, increased the number of blind persons on its board of directors from 12 to 60 of a total 120 members. On the other hand, the specific nature of their handicap inhibited deaf persons in all countries from demanding more representation. They were shunned by the hard-of-hearing, who did not want to be associated with them, and their communication handicap made their organizations among the least effective in advocacy.[4]

Since the 1950s, in all four countries the parents of the mentally handicapped have founded consumer organizations with both service

4. The situation of the deaf in England is discussed in Benedict Nightingale, *Charities* pp. 213–17. See also Harry Best, *Deafness and the Deaf in the United States*, pp. 351–70.

and advocacy functions. They have succeeded in influencing public policy, in improving institutional care, and in promoting more community services. In the process, local associations have become professionalized — mainly in the United States, and to a lesser extent in England, where professionalization has occurred on national and regional levels, but rarely in the local community.[5] Some professionals and government officials are critical of parent associations because of the unrepresentative character of their leadership (middle- and upper-middle-class) and their primary interest in the kind of care needed by their own children. I shall note later the transformation of parent associations into large service bureaucracies as they become delegate agencies and vendors of services to government in the United States, England, and Israel, but not in the Netherlands.

Whereas the 1950s was a period of public awareness of the mentally handicapped, in the United States and, to a much lesser extent, in England the 1970s was a time when the physically handicapped received more attention and became the beneficiaries of significant legislation. Speedy, effective implementation of this legislation is one of the major objectives of a slowly growing number of self-help groups, such as the Center for Independent Living (CIL) in Berkeley. No organization comparable to it was found in any of the other countries, and only in the late 1970s did counterparts appear in the United States. The CIL operates an extensive array of service programs almost completely supported by governmental grants, employs only handicapped persons as staff members, and engages in vigorous advocacy.[6]

Board Member Activity

Despite the high rate (over 70 percent) of board member attendance reported in the four countries, the size of the boards and their schedule of infrequent meetings suggest that they are a policy-ratifying rather than a policy-formulating body. In England, where rates of attendance of 75 to 90 percent were reported, only seven out of the twenty boards met monthly; another four were convened bimonthly; and the remaining nine only three or four times a year.

5. On the evolution of organizations of parents and the conflicts between them and professional staff members, see Alfred H. Katz, *Parents of the Handicapped*. Another view is Robert M. Segal, *Mental Retardation and Social Action: A Study of the Associations for Retarded Children as a Force for Social Change*.

6. The Center for Independent Living is the subject of Hal R. Kreshbaum, Dominic S. Harveston, and Alfred H. Katz, "Independent Living for the Disabled."

Infrequent meetings might be explained by a paucity of policy issues other than routine organizational maintenance or fund acquisition. They may also result from a screening out by the executive of more controversial items through redefinition as technical or professional matters that do not appear on the agenda.[7] In contrast to the English boards, all but three of the U.S.-agency boards of directors met monthly, and their agendas indicated a more active board role in policy formulation than those of their English counterparts.

In all the countries there was an executive committee, even in the smaller boards, consisting of five to seven persons who made most of the policy decisions, which were then ratified by the board of directors. (This was less true in the Netherlands, where the small size of some of the boards did not require a subgroup for more frequent meetings.) Even the executive committees, presumably the most active decision-making units, met infrequently. Half of them convened once every month or two, whereas the remaining ten met only three to five times a year.

Only in the United States was there a concern with turnover among board members, and, although agencies varied, almost all the U.S. agencies reported annual rotation of about one-third of their board members. Half of the U.S. agencies reported terms of two to three years, with a maximum of six years, but one had no definite terms and another limited only the terms of nonphysicians on its board. The most extreme case of turnover was found in the CIL, which limited board member terms to one and one-half years and provided for an annual turnover of one-third. While bylaws might stipulate limits on terms, they were rarely enforced in the other countries, so that most members were continually reelected. This resulted in a turnover in England of about 10 percent, in contrast with the average of one-third in the United States. Among English agencies, four organizations had board members that served for seven to nine years; in seven agencies they were in office from ten to fifteen years; and two agencies reported board members' terms of fifteen to twenty-five years. The policy of reelecting the board members and of not replacing more than 10 percent each year probably explains why the recruitment of new members was not viewed as a serious problem by English executives.

In the Netherlands there had been a general diminution of board member activity and interest, particularly among the older, more traditional agencies. In addition to very little turnover in the agency

7. Ralph M. Kramer, "Ideology, Status and Power in the Board-Executive Relationship."

boards in the sample, three were reduced in size by 25 percent in the decade ending in 1975. Government officials stated that citizens refused to accept appointments to boards and that it became necessary to place ads in newspapers or to pay the president of an agency in order to ensure some measure of continuity and accountability. The Dutch government even considered paying board members a small stipend, apart from their expenses, to stimulate more active involvement.

Policymaking Patterns and Internal Democracy

The celebration of voluntary organizations as an important democratizing force has been challenged by those who note the prevalence of what has been termed "minority rule."[8] Functioning according to the "iron law of oligarchy," in which policymaking power is concentrated in a small number of self-perpetuating board members and an executive staff, the governance of voluntary organizations appears inconsistent with their espousal of democratic citizen participation. Some political sociologists have claimed, however, that internal democracy in voluntary organizations is less significant than their advocacy role in representing and advancing the special interests of diverse groups in society. Voluntary agencies, then, should be judged not by the norms of internal democracy, but by their contribution to pluralism in a society through advocacy and services for their clientele-constituency. Although this argument has considerable merit, the cost of a tendency to minority rule may outweigh or even cancel the contribution to pluralism. For example, lack of turnover within a leadership group can result in serious problems of succession, organizational unresponsiveness, an excessively narrow focus of interest, inflexibility, and resistance to change, thus vitiating the ostensible virtues of the voluntary agency.

My findings are in accord with the designation of voluntary agencies as "private governments,"[9] in which decision making is concentrated in relatively small, closed, self-perpetuating groups in the familiar pattern of minority rule found in other voluntary associations. Most boards were policy-ratifying bodies, with policy formulation emanating from the professional staff and the members of the executive committee. The dominant influence on decision making

8. David Sills, "Voluntary Associations: Sociological Aspects," pp. 368–69.

9. The term *private governments* is derived from Grant McConnell, *Private Power and American Democracy*, chapter 5. See also Constance Smith and Ann Freedman, *Voluntary Associations: Perspectives on the Literature*, pp. 33–76.

One-Man Domination   *Board Domination*

                          Strong professional   *Weak professional*
Executive or President   *leadership*   *leadership*

Concentrated   *Dispersed*
power   ◄─────────────────────────────────────►   *power*

Center for the Migdal Or NITZAN Cancer Association AKIM ILAN
   Blind   SHEMA   MICHA   Anti-TB League ANAT MATAV

Jewish Institute Disabled   Disabled
  for the Blind   Workers   Veterans
                  Association   Association

                                                       Association
                                                       of the
                                                       Deaf

Figure 1. Pattern of Distribution of Power in the Policymaking Body in
         Fifteen Israeli Voluntary Agencies

most often reported was one or more of three elements in the executive leadership system: (1) the executive or administrator (manager)
of the organization, (2) the president of the board of directors, and
(3) the executive committee, which was usually composed of five to
seven board members, including the officers and the administrators
who serve ex officio.

Because of the small number and size of organizations in Israel, it
was possible to make a systematic effort to study the distribution of
policymaking power. Four different patterns of power distribution in
the governance system were identified. They can be arranged on a
continuum; at one end power is concentrated in a single person —
either the executive or the president — and at the other end power
is dispersed, with different degrees of professional leadership. (See
Figure 1.) The voluntary agencies were almost equally distributed
between the patterns of monolithic and dispersed power, but the existence of the patterns did not seem to be associated with any particular
set of interests, issues, or values. For example, the type of power distribution did not appear to be related consistently to the degree of
active participation on the board or the rate of turnover.

Attempts to carry the analysis beyond this point were not productive because concentration of power in the executive leadership does not tell when and how it will be used — on behalf of what particular interests, values, and specific issues. It is difficult to avoid the pitfalls that have plagued studies of community decision making, which assume a stable, consistent, and fixed distribution of power that persists despite the issue and the particular situation.[10]

In both the United States and England, domination of decision making by the executive director was less prominent than was expected, particularly where a large number of high-status business or professional notables or parents were on the board. Under these conditions the executive director tended to take a back seat and to manifest a more reactive than active leadership style. As one U.S. agency executive declared: "My assistant and I try to be as nonvocal as possible at meetings. We really work for the volunteers (50 percent of the board are physicians) and only implement policy." A similar nonassertive style was found in four cases in England and the United States where the founder of the agency was still the executive, and in five of the fifteen agencies in Israel.

In the Netherlands, the ascendancy and increasing domination of professionals in policymaking and the resultant decrease in citizen participation in the management of voluntary agencies aroused more concern in governmental circles than in voluntary agencies themselves. An eminent Dutch sociologist who studied the conflicts between board and staff reported in the press from 1970 to 1975 ascribed this to such factors as the declining social status of the middle class (from which board members come), the lessening influence of established social institutions in Dutch society, the ambiguity of organizational goals, and lack of external controls by constituencies or by the government. He called for a new, broader governance structure in which there would be representatives of unions, politicians, and clients, as well as staff, on boards of directors to balance undemocratic domination by professionals, who could take over the entire apparatus.[11]

Paradoxically, professionals in the Netherlands have invoked the values and principles of participatory democracy to justify their claim

10. Some of the related methodological problems in the study of community decision making are considered in Thomas R. Dye, "Community Power Studies"; Terry Nichols Clark, *Community Power and Policy Outputs: A Review of Urban Research;* and Michael Aiken and Paul Mott, eds., *The Structure of Community Power.*
11. J. A. A. van Doorn, "De strijd om de macht in dienstverlenende organisaties."

for greater influence in the policymaking process, on the grounds that they are most affected by policy decisions and most competent to make them. At the same time, when there was a greater emphasis on managerial efficiency in the Dutch social services, there was increasing pressure by the government for decentralization and for democratization of the voluntary agencies. For example, all organizations in the Netherlands with more than one hundred staff members were required to have a council of staff members review nominations for the board of directors and to include some consumer representatives. In general, the relatively low level of internal democracy in the four countries did not prevent the effective functioning of a voluntary agency's service-delivery system. This was particularly evident in the Netherlands, where the professional and organizational ideologies of the nongovernmental sector, with their weak commitment to voluntary citizen participation, did not impair the continuing growth and the rising level of quality of services to the physically and mentally handicapped, a point that is overlooked by such critics as the authors of the *Knelpuntennota*.

Although a struggle for power between professionals and volunteers may be unavoidable, the situation was aggravated in the Netherlands. A plausible explanation is not difficult to find. The small size of the boards and their reputed loss of power to professionals reflected the reduced importance of the board in the fiscal resource system of Dutch agencies. Because the government, through subsidies and social insurance payments, had gradually assumed most of their financial responsibility, agencies were no longer as dependent on the status, prestige, and fund-raising abilities of their boards. The board of directors still performed a legitimating function as the nominal policymaking body, but it had little to do with financial support, since this was related to the agency's conformity to various government policies and regulations. Also, because salaries for professional staff were derived from government funds, the staff may have felt less accountable to and dependent upon the board members, although they were employed and could be dismissed by the board. Thus, a high degree of fiscal security may lead to diminished participation of board members in the governance structure of voluntary agencies.[12]

The growth in the power of the professionals and their influence on policy is also a consequence of increasing specialization and the tech-

12. A similar finding is reported in Greater New York Fund/United Way, *Impact of Government Funding on the Management of Voluntary Agencies*, pp. 21–22.

nical, complex, and bureaucratic character of an agency's services. The professionals' claim to expertise (based upon certification of technical competence required by government regulations for funding) encouraged them to assume a dominant role in policymaking. Furthermore, the tendency of professionals to convert such policy questions as the extension of services to the most handicapped into technical issues over which they can assert their authority was reinforced by the high degree of financial security most Dutch agencies enjoyed.

In both England and the United States, however, strong, countervailing fiscal and political factors militated against the erosion of the role of the volunteer board members and reinforced the need for active, prestigious boards of directors. Agencies in the United States and in England that received over half of their income from governmental bodies regarded board members as an important asset because of their influence in the highly politicized process of allocating public funds. In addition, the participant civic culture in the United States sanctions and encourages board member and consumer participation, which may account for more frequent meetings, a greater emphasis on turnover, and a more active role in deliberations. Because of different attitudes and policies in the United States regarding citizen participation, one might not expect the same outcome as in the Netherlands.

National-Local Relationships

In addition to the relationship between the executive leadership and the board of directors, there is another dimension of decision-making: the distribution of authority between national voluntary organizations and their local branches. The upward (decentralized) or downward (centralized) flow of authority is revealed in the degree of program autonomy of the branches and the percentage of funds they are expected to turn over to the national headquarters. Although most national organizations are formally structured as federations, the pattern of national-local relations varies.

In the United States, ten out of the twenty agencies in the sample were affiliated with a national organization. These included such highly centralized organizations as the American Cancer Society, which is structured on a hierarchical basis paralleling the structure of government, from the national policymaking body down to state divisions that authorize specific service programs sponsored by local units. The local chapters of the Multiple Sclerosis, Cerebral Palsy, and Heart and Lung associations are more loosely connected to their national organizations and have more freedom to select service programs, although they are required to allocate from 25 to 40 percent of their funds to support of the state and national research programs.

The allocation of funds between the national and local organizations is sometimes a contentious issue. Occasionally chapters disaffiliate, as did the Oakland Cerebral Palsy Society in 1969, preferring to use all of its funds for local services. Such other organizations as the Associations for the Mentally Handicapped or the Easter Seal Society have less obligation to a national organization. National advocacy and standard setting are supported through payment of dues rather than through an agreed-upon share of fund raising. In the Netherlands, only three of the eight national organizations included in the sample of twenty have branches. One of these is a pressure group with a membership of 30,000 that claims to speak for 400,000 invalids. The absence of affiliates in the Netherlands may stem from the lack of necessity for local fund raising as a result of the support of the national organizations by government subsidies. More prevalent than branches of national organizations is an extraordinarily complex pattern of 256 national federations ("roof" organizations), including many federations of federations, which reflect the social structure of *verzuiling* and the multiplicity of agencies under denominational auspices. Highly regarded by government officials because of its inclusiveness, the NOZ (the Dutch National Association for the Care of the Mentally Retarded) has since 1970 been the official, influential spokesman for a coalition of eight sets of interest groups concerned with the mentally handicapped:[13]

> Parents' associations
> Federations of social services
> Special school board members and teachers
> Sheltered workshops
> Residential institutions and psychiatric hospitals
> Hostels
> Day care centers
> Professionals and research scientists

A counterpart federation, the Netherlands Society for Rehabilitation (NVR), of almost 150 organizations is concerned with the physically

13. Jan B. Meiresonne, *Care for the Mentally Retarded in the Netherlands*, p. 41.

and sensorially handicapped, but it lacks the structure, resources, and power needed to function as more than a forum or clearinghouse. In practice, most of the national "umbrella" organizations have little authority over their constituent organizations, although they purport to speak on behalf of local agencies in consulting and negotiating with the ministries of central government.

All the Israeli organizations, with the notable exception of the Cancer Association, are completely decentralized, with autonomous branches.[14] Three organizations serving preschool deaf children use the same acronym (MICHA), but they have no affiliation with each other, although one described itself as a national organization. The agencies that have a more formalized national-local structure promote community service programs, but they often have difficulty in securing conformity to minimal standards of services or in getting the support of local chapters for decisions made by the national organization. In particular, local chapters have been reluctant to give up or transfer to government agencies such services as the provision of aids, appliances, and financial assistance to the physically handicapped.

Similar episodes were found in England, where devolution of authority is a basic principle in the polity and the society. Three types of national structures were found in England: highly centralized professional organizations, such as the Spastics Society; centrally coordinated networks of services coexisting as a federation of independent but affiliated organizations, such as the NSMHC, and confederations of independent organizations with national headquarters as a focal point.[15]

Almost all local organizations in England are referred to as affiliates and not as branches or chapters, which might imply some authorization from the top down. As affiliates, they are autonomous, with a weak link to a national policymaking body to which they may not even look for legitimation or information. In the federated structure of the English organizations, national and local are virtually two separate entities — similar to statutory and voluntary — that only occasionally

14. It is not clear why the Cancer Associations in the United States, Israel, and England are so much more centralized than other agencies that also support programs of medical research and provide some local social services, and whose boards of directors are also dominated by physicians. The remarkable similarity between the Israel Cancer Association and its U.S. counterparts may be due to their joint membership in the International Association of Cancer Societies and to the deliberate attempt of the Israeli executive to model his organization on the U.S. prototype following his study tour in the United States.

15. Judith Unell, *Voluntary Social Services: Financial Resources*, pp. 20–21.

intersect. Basic policy and program decisions are made centrally by the national organizations, but they differ in the extent to which they sponsor or even encourage local service programs. The most frequently reported function of the local affiliates is fund raising, but in contrast with the United States, where local branches forward 25 to 40 percent of their campaign income to their national associations, all but four affiliates in England kept all or most of the funds for themselves. The English affiliates, like those in the Netherlands and Israel, are closer geographically to their national organizations than are their counterparts in the United States. Consequently, it is unusual to find in England such a disparity in the degree of responsibility assumed by the local affiliates to their national organizations as exists in the United States.

The diversity in the degree of decentralization in England is considerable. The national staff of the Cheshire Homes — which has seventy-two residential centers under its auspices, each with its own management committee — consists of only five persons, in contrast with staffs of forty persons in the Shaftesbury Society and in the Royal National Institute for the Blind, both of which maintain closer supervision over their facilities. This disproportion may be due to the lack of financial responsibility by Cheshire Homes for any of the autonomous facilities using its name and to the fact that it is mainly a standard-setting body.

In England, two of the largest organizations, the Spastics Society and the NSMHC, maintain regional staffs to provide services to their local affiliates. Other national organizations have looser relationships with their affiliates. Interaction between the national organizations and their local affiliates in England is often depicted as a "love-hate relationship" because of continual tension and controversy regarding policy decisions made by the national organization. The attitude of one national organization towards its affiliates was expressed in the comment of its executive that "the less we tell our branches, the better." In another large English organization, the regional staff was occasionally used to "cool out" and bring into line local affiliates that disagreed with policy decisions at the national level or protested at their lack of involvement in the planning of facilities in their own communities. In another instance, national-local differences, reinforced by conflicts between professional staff members and volunteers, led to the formation of a new, nationwide professional organization providing a platform for executive staff members to promote policies that had been opposed by local societies. In England, the maintenance of the three levels of national, regional, and local organization, each independent of the other, often leads to considerable misunderstandings regarding mutual expectations, as well as to strong differences of opinion on policy matters. In part, this is because most of the national organizations in England were not created by concerted community efforts, but were organized from the top, and indigeneous community organizations later decided to affiliate with them.

Conclusions

Despite the diversity of voluntary agencies, a common pattern of increasing size and similar organizational careers marked by the growth of bureaucratization and professionalization can be discerned in all four countries. This development coincides with the growth of the welfare state, which expanded from the 1960s until the mid-1970s. Among the factors contributing to the growth of formalization and professionalization in voluntary organizations is progressive dependence on highly centralized and bureaucratized funding sources, a process that will be examined in more detail in the next two chapters.

The policymaking system of the voluntary agency — a blend of lay policy control and professional direction — exhibits the strengths and weaknesses of other citizen-sponsored organizations governed by democratic norms in a particular sociopolitical context. The power of the board of directors seems particularly sensitive to the impact of technocratic professionalism and public funding, which provides considerable fiscal security. By themselves, however, the factors affecting structure and governance are only part of the distinctive character of the voluntary agency. To fill in the rest, we next consider the fiscal resource system.

7. Fiscal Resource Systems

As Geoffrey Vickers has suggested, the source of resources determines the types of and standards for success and failure, the character of decision making, accountability, and the external relations of an organization. While voluntary agencies derive their income from many sources, only three principal, nongovernmental forms are considered in this chapter: endowments and bequests, sales, and contributions from independent and federated fund-raising campaigns. Government grants and payments for service, the fastest growing and most significant forms of voluntary agency financing, are the subject of the next chapter.

Uncertainty and Diversity

On a continuum of fiscal uncertainty, the voluntary, nonprofit organization stands midway between a government agency supported by taxes and a profit-making organization dependent on the relative unpredictability of the market. In contrast to other public-service organizations that operate on a budget rather than on the basis of performance or profitability, voluntary agencies have no legal mandate or claim on tax funds to assure them an annual renewal of financial support.[1] Ostensibly, there is an element of risk in relying on contributions, but the continued existence of most voluntary agencies shows that the risk is not as great as it may seem. Over a period of time, the processes of fiscal acquisition tend to become regularized and more or less predictable. The high birth rate[2] and low mortality rate among voluntary organizations indicate that most of them succeed in attracting enough support to maintain themselves on a minimum level.

1. Peter F. Drucker, "On Managing the Public Service Institution."
2. The recency of English voluntary organizations is illustrated by the finding that 25 percent were less than six or seven years old. (Wolfenden Committee, *The Future of Voluntary Organisations*, p. 184.) In the United States, it is estimated that 40,000 new organizations concerned with the environment have developed since 1970. (Commission on Private Philanthropy and Public Needs, *Giving in America: Toward A Stronger Voluntary Sector*, p. 47. Hereafter cited as Filer.)

The predictability of annual inputs of funds may contribute to the belief that voluntary agencies do not have to be efficient or effective to survive because fund raising has become institutionalized.[3] However, donor dependency remains an Achilles heel. Voluntary agencies must devote a greater proportion of their organizational resources to fund raising — or, as it is also called, "development" — than do governmental organizations. The fiscal environment of the voluntary sector contains many similar organizations, each representing a cause striving to capture public attention; hence, the unceasing search for appealing slogans and symbols and the widespread use of public relations and marketing techniques. Because of this, the charity market is probably one of the few remaining relatively free markets, where there are few external regulations or instances of interorganizational collusion. Although there may be service oligopolies, a spirit of competition and laissez-faire prevails.[4]

Income pluralism, the necessity to secure funds from a variety of sources such as fees, sale of products, grants from government and private foundations, endowments, special fund-raising events, and contributions, is generally regarded as highly advantageous because it prevents dependency on one type of income, which might fluctuate unpredictably or even disappear. Multiple sources not only minimize risks, they also represent a potential for developing constituencies to whom the agency's message may be communicated, reinforcing its identity and domain and generating sources of goodwill, support, and clientele.

With the exception of the Netherlands, the agencies in the countries studied expressed a strong preference for voluntary, rather than governmental, funding and for support from many sources. The U.S. agencies have the most varied, and the greatest number of income sources. One typical agency receives service payments and grants from ten different federal, state, and local government agencies; from the sale of products from its sheltered workshops, membership dues, and ten different types of fund-raising events; from fees, the United Way, individual and corporate contributions, rents, investments, and dividends. In the Netherlands, where the voluntary agencies usually obtain subsidies and payments from no more than two or three governmental bodies, agency executives believed that efficiency would be better served if they received funds from only one unit of government!

3. Peter Nokes, "Purpose and Efficiency in Humane Social Institutions."
4. On the charity market as an alternative to the political market for the provision of public goods, see David B. Johnson, "The Charity Market: Theory and Practice," pp. 81–101.

Bequests and Legacies

Because of their drive to achieve fiscal security, voluntary agencies in the United States, England, and Israel expressed a strong preference for one particular type of philanthropic contribution, namely, unrestricted bequests such as endowments and legacies. Apart from reducing an organization's dependence on the generosity of a great many contributors in a highly competitive market, bequests are attractive because of their low cost, since they do not require the mobilization of large numbers of volunteers. Usually the income from endowments is invested and the interest is not used for current operating expenses, but is held in reserve for capital expenditures, crises, or new programs.

In England, legacies and deeds of covenant and, in the United States, bequests and memorial gifts are the most prominent sources of income other than campaigns and payments for service. Eight of the twenty agencies in England derived from a third to three-quarters of their income from legacies and deeds of covenant. Deeds of covenant are the principal tax incentive for charitable contributions in England, although benefits accrue to the agency and not to the individual donor as in the United States. Charities are not liable to income tax, and they can obtain refunds if the tax has already been collected by the government for a gift made by means of a deed of covenant, in which an individual or a company designates an annual contribution for one or more charities for a period of up to seven years. The charity then receives the income tax on the contributed sum for seven years, enhancing the value of the gift by about 40 percent. Deeds of covenant provide a predictable source of income for seven years, even though their worth has depreciated substantially because of inflation.[5]

In the United States, only four of the twenty agencies received one-third to one-half of their income from bequests and memorial gifts, but in one agency this amounted to eight times the sum of other contributions from the public. In both the United States and England, this source of income is found mainly among the older, well-known, more traditional charitable organizations for the blind and the deaf and among the newer health agencies, for example, those concerned with cancer and heart disease in the United States and, in England, those dealing with rheumatism and arthritis. Health organizations are fortunate because there is a high degree of public acceptance of the

5. Deeds of covenant are discussed in Goodman Committee, *Charity Law and Voluntary Organisations*, pp. 51–52; and National Council of Social Service, *Fund-Raising by Charities*.

worthiness of their cause, in contrast to other types of voluntary agencies that have more abstract or controversial goals or exist to aid victims of a handicap that is not well known.

The value of large gifts from estates or from wealthy individuals can, however, be counterbalanced by restrictive uses imposed by the contributor, which may conflict with an agency's other priorities and interests. A gift is sometimes designated for the establishment of a particular facility to visibly demonstrate the donor's generosity, often by bearing his name. (This is sometimes known among fund raisers as "the edifice complex.") In Israel this practice has been criticized for indirectly contributing to the excessive use of institutions instead of alternative forms of community-based care.[6]

Fund-Raising Campaigns

The traditional image of a voluntary agency is that of a charity supported by contributions obtained from the public by volunteer solicitors. During the years following World War I, however, fund raising in the United States became a highly standardized, bureaucratized, and professionalized enterprise. Fund-raising campaign results fluctuated from year to year, but in the postwar years they showed a general upward trend. Voluntary agencies began to lose ground because of inflation and rising costs in the 1960s, when the proportion of income from contributions began to decline. In the United States, giving by individuals to all charities declined by 15 percent between 1960 and 1976, and since 1960 the income of the nonprofit sector as a percentage of the gross national product has grown only half as fast as the real national product. Similarly, in England contributions as a proportion of total agency income have been dropping by at least 1 percent a year since 1970.[7] The actual dollar amount of funds raised has grown enormously — in the United States they tripled between 1965 and 1977 — but inflation, particularly since the mid-1970s, has eroded most of the gains in a labor-intensive industry.

6. Eliezer D. Jaffe, "Substitutes for Family," pp. 129–44.

7. Judith Unell, *Voluntary Social Services: Financial Resources*, p. 11. In the United States, giving as a percentage of gross income has dropped 27 percent from 1960–1975, although at the same time all philanthropic giving has remained at a constant 2 percent of adjusted gross income for the total population since the 1930s. It should be noted that social welfare's share of all philanthropic giving is only about 10 percent, with religion accounting for almost half (46.5), health and education 14 percent each. As a result, contributions rarely exceed one-third the total income of voluntary agencies in the United States. (Filer, pp. 15 and 58, and F. Emerson Andrews, "Philanthropy in the United States: History and Structure," p. 94.)

In England, fourteen of the twenty agencies studied received less than 40 percent of their income from campaign contributions or other forms of internal fund raising, excluding legacies and deeds of covenant, during 1973–1974. Six of these agencies received less than 20 percent of their income from fund-raising campaigns, eight obtained 21 to 40 percent, and only three depended on campaign contributions for over two-thirds of their budgets. The fund-raising campaigns considered, included the ubiquitous Football Pool of the Spastics Society, which provides 42 percent of its income. Despite the fact that the legality of the football pool was challenged for many years, the Friends of the Spastics — a separate organization managed by professional promoters — was able to sell over 6,000,000 tickets weekly on a regular basis. The Football Pool competed successfully with commercial football pools because its prizes were bigger — less would have to be paid out in taxes because the Spastics Society was a charity. The pool organizers knew that eventually the tax authorities would catch up with them. When this occurred, they refused to pay and took the case on successive appeals to a higher court during 1968–1969. Although litigation involved substantial expenditures of funds, the society publicized its plight in being prosecuted by the government, and this enabled it to enlist further public support. Eventually, the Spastics' Football Pool lost its competitive edge because of the changing character of the gambling market, but many customers remain and the society is still able to raise over £2,000,000 annually in this way.

In the U.S. sample, nine out of the twenty agencies received less than 30 percent of their income from contributions, while eight received over half of their income from campaign contributions. The agencies in the United States and England that derive most of their income from campaigns tend to be newer, more individualistic, and smaller organizations, such as those concerned with cerebral palsy in the United States (but not in England) and the California League for the Handicapped. Also included in this group is the Lung Association, which derives most of its income from a mail solicitation, using its own computerized mailing list and requiring few volunteers.

In the Netherlands, only three of the twenty agencies received more than 80 percent of their income from contributions or dues. Two of these also obtained government funds indirectly. Eleven out of the twenty agencies received less than 6 percent of their income from campaigns, with nine reporting no contributions at all, making agencies in the Netherlands least dependent on this source of income.

TABLE 7.
Percentage of Voluntary Agency Income from Contributions,
1973–1974

	United States (N = 20)	England (N = 20)	The Netherlands (N = 20)	Israel (N = 15)
None	1	0	9	0
1–32	8	10	4	2
33–65	4	7	4	5
66–99	6	2	1	8
100	1	1	2	0
Mean	41	36	28	64

In Israel, a much higher proportion of income is derived from campaigns or, in the case of two agencies, from membership dues deducted from disability payments made by government to disabled war veterans and victims of work accidents. Although eight of the fifteen Israeli agencies received at least two-thirds of their budgets from campaigns, the amounts they raised were quite small: in 1973, when the Israeli lira was worth less than twenty-five cents, three agencies collected from 1,000,000 to 3,000,000 Israeli lirot; three others collected 500,000 to 1,000,000 lirot; and the rest collected less than 1,000,000 lirot. In contrast to Jewish giving in the United States, where approximately 15 percent of the contributors provide 85 percent of the funds, in Israel there are very few wealthy donors, resulting in a more equitable distribution in which 80 percent of the people contribute about 80 percent of the funds. What is unusual in Israeli fund raising is the existence of both a domestic and a foreign market: extensive campaigns, including those for capital purposes, are conducted annually among supporters in Jewish communities throughout the world. For example, two of the Israeli agencies serving the blind are completely supported by U.S. contributors and do not conduct any local campaign. The opposite case was found in England, where Cheshire Homes raises most of its funds in the United Kingdom, but also supports seventy-five homes in thirty-one countries. The percentage of voluntary agency income received from contributions in the four countries is shown in Table 7.

Apart from campaigns, income from the sale of products is the second most important source of support for three English agencies, providing almost one-third of their national budgets. Income is derived from the sale of greeting cards or from charity shops that sell used or special products, often made by disabled clientele. The most successful Christmas card campaign is conducted by the NSMHC, whose 40,000 volunteers in over 400 localities sell 22,000,000 cards, more than all other organizations combined. The campaign produces over £1,000,000 in gross sales, providing one-third of the total income that supports the national organization. Three agencies in the United States derived from 37 to 43 percent of their income from the sale of products made in sheltered workshops, and one of the sheltered workshops obtained 91 percent of its income from operations.

Federated Fund Raising

There is a long history of concern with the multiplicity of separate campaigns by voluntary agencies in the United States. The first attempts by business leaders to consolidate the annual, independent, competitive appeals of agencies occurred in the latter half of the nineteenth century, beginning in Cleveland and Denver. These efforts culminated in the Community Chest movement after World War I.[8] The concept of federated fund raising was broadened in the 1950s from a Community Chest to a United Fund, which included the American Red Cross and several national health agencies. Many health agencies do not permit their affiliates to participate in a local community United Fund — now called United Way — because they believe they can raise more money on their own, without risking loss of identity in a huge campaign involving more than one-hundred local agencies.[9] Other agencies do not participate because they cannot meet the minimum administrative and fiscal standards of a United Fund or because there may be a moratorium on the admission of new agencies.

The United Way seeks to reconcile the interests of donors, agencies, and consumers by imposing a greater measure of rationality and efficiency on fund raising. However, United Way organizations have

8. A classic study of federated fund-raising, which is described as "mass, operational, periodic and secular," is John R. Seeley et al., *Community Chest: A Case Study in Philanthropy.* United Funds are restricted to the United States and Canada, and it is not easy to explain why they have not caught on anywhere else in the world. Both countries have quite different characters, governments, and social problems, yet the fraction of income they devote to the United Funds is remarkably similar. For some speculation on this question see Thomas I. Ireland, "The Calculus of Philanthropy," pp. 77–78.

9. A more positive picture of the capabilities of United Way fund raising between 1964 and 1976 is Herbert S. Rabinowitz, Bruce R. Simmeth, and Jeannette R. Spero, "The Future of United Way." According to their analysis, which conflicts with most others, United Ways raised 7.6 percent more each year, while the annual increase in the Consumers' Price Index was only 4.9 percent (p. 278).

periodically been criticized.[10] They have been attacked because of their alleged control by business interests and their monopoly of payroll-deduction plans for employee giving. It is also claimed that United Way admission and allocation policies result in the maintenance of the status quo; safe, well-established organizations get most of the proceeds, while newer, smaller organizations serving minorities, women, consumers, and other more controversial groups are excluded.[11] Newer, activist groups have organized coalitions to oppose the United Way on both national and local levels and have pursued such strategies as lawsuits, boycotts, and the creation of competing federated campaigns. Considerable polarization has resulted in the U.S. voluntary sector on the merits of the United Way, as well as on the Filer Commission report.

Despite the active participation of corporate executives and trade union leaders, as well as the mobilization of millions of volunteers in 2,400 separate local campaigns, the United Way has not been able to keep up with the inroads of inflation, escalating costs, and pressures to admit new agencies. Consequently, while more funds have been raised each year, reaching $1,200,000,000 in 1978, the national average of the proportion of member-agency income derived from fund raising has dropped to about 20 percent.[12] This occurred during a period when more federal funds became available to voluntary agencies. By 1967, official United Way national policy had shifted from eschewing public funds to the active encouragement of a "partnership" with government. United Way allocations were used by voluntary agencies to meet the requirement of a local matching share, whereby certain federal grants were available on a three-to-one basis — i.e., for selected

10. See the critique in David Horton Smith, "The Philanthropy Business," and the rejoinders by John S. Glaser "Serving Community Needs," and Edmund M. Burke, "Defending the United Way." The traditional position of most national health agencies is presented in Richard Carter, *The Gentle Legions*, pp. 246–312.

11. The situation is not quite static because United Ways admitted over 1,000 new organizations throughout the United States during the period 1967–1975 and dropped 734; another 482 organizations were involved in mergers (Academy of Educational Development, *The Voluntary Sector in Brief*, p. 17). For an analysis of some of the factors responsible for the admission of these newer agencies, see Stanley Wenocur, "A Political View of the United Way."

12. Paul Akana, "The United Way System Needs No Defense." Reflecting the drop in the proportion of voluntary agency income derived from United Way, these allocations are redefined by the author as "essential, basic *start-up costs* and stable maintenance foundation on which the agencies build such other income as government contracts and fees for service" (italics mine). In the San Francisco Bay Area, United Way allocations averaged 32 percent of the budgeted income of the member agencies in 1973–1974, which was higher than the national average of 20 percent. By 1978, Bay Area United Way allocations had shrunk to an average of 10 percent of member-agency income, while governmental funds accounted for 40 percent.

programs one United Way or contributed dollar could bring three federal dollars. By this policy, the United Way accelerated and reinforced the use of government funds by voluntary agencies. Allocations to agencies obtaining such funds were, however, often reduced on the grounds that they had increased their income.

In our sample, the small share of United Way support is evident in that only ten of the twenty agencies were members of the Bay Area United Way in 1975. Of these, six received less than 12 percent of their income from this source, obtaining most of their funds from governmental purchase of service. Three agencies obtained 19 to 24 percent of their funds from the United Way, but only one received 46 percent.[13]

In none of the other countries was there any significant joint fund raising. In the Netherlands, the only combined campaign is the Princess Beatrix Fund, which was transformed from a polio campaign in the 1960s into a joint health agency appeal that provides support to agencies serving the physically handicapped, children, and persons with multiple sclerosis, muscular dystrophy, cerebral palsy, or polio. Despite some efforts by American-based agencies to encourage combined fund raising in Israel, the strongly independent agencies there have shown no interest.[14]

In England, fund raising has been transformed from the traditional, modest support of charities by a few wealthy donors to regularized mass appeals organized by professionals on the U.S. model, using media advertising and other marketing techniques. Over £100,000,000 is raised annually for all charities in England, and approximately one-third of all households contribute.[15] However, there has never been any support for federated fund raising in England. In fact, there is long-standing opposition to combined appeals. Several small-scale, episodic efforts in Liverpool and Manchester in the 1960s were not considered successful enough to be copied. Only a few consortia have been organized for charity stamps or Christmas cards, and the Common Good Fund, a pale imitation of the Community Chest, exists in

13. An extension of this practice of the use of contributed funds for matching purposes was found in one San Francisco agency that calculated the monetary value of the contributed services of its volunteers as worth $97,000 and used it as part of its matching funds for over $300,000 in federal grants. The Filer Commission has estimated the monetary value of volunteer work in the United States to be $26,000,000,000.

14. A. A. Kessler, "On the Study of the Financing of Jewish Community Activities."

15. Benedict Nightingale, *Charities*, p. 99. See also Wolfenden, p. 34, where it is estimated that the total income of all British charities in 1975 came to £1,500,000,000, and the income for social welfare purposes, to around £1,000,000,000, equal to about 3 percent of the total central and local governmental expenditure on social and environmental services.

only five small communities in all of the United Kingdom. There is no corporate interest, as in the United States, in joint fund raising; instead, there is a highly individualistic and competitive environment for voluntary agencies. Not only is there no combined campaigning by national organizations, there is usually little connection between their fund raising and that of their local affiliates. The branches of only four organizations turn over most of their funds to national headquarters, while the rest keep from 75 to 90 percent for their own purposes.

Beginning in the mid-1970s, there has been talk about a serious threat to the financial survival of many voluntary agencies, but the Wolfenden Report found "no evidence that the number of voluntary organizations in financial difficulty has risen dramatically." Another investigator reported that fifty-two out of sixty-four national agencies studied had actually doubled their income between 1970 and 1975.[16] The central government has provided no significant additional forms of aid to meet requests from some voluntary agencies to "inflation-proof" their budgets, although it did increase allocations to all types of national organizations from £19,000,000 to £35,000,000 between 1974 and 1976. This increase had no effect on the agencies in the sample because only six of the twenty reported receiving grants, and for four of them grants constituted less than 1 percent of total income.[17]

Few major changes are likely in the basic pattern of voluntary fund raising in England. Neither the Goodman Committee nor the Wolfenden Committee regarded joint fund raising, payroll deductions, or contribution deductibility as feasible or desirable. Instead, the Wolfenden Committee recommended modest increases in statutory funding to compensate for the decline in private giving and suggested that a small increase by local authorities to equal the level of grant aid by the more generous ones would be the best way to improve the position of voluntary organizations. The Goodman Committee placed more value on the security of income continuity through deeds of covenant and suggested reducing the covenanted period from seven to four years and simplifying the system. The members concluded that "[T]here is no evidence that the value of donations would increase if the covenant system was abandoned and there is a danger that the reverse would be the case."[18]

16. Unell, p. 12.
17. Unell also reports that the sixty-four agencies she studied were virtually untouched by governmental grant aid. She suggests that perhaps they do not seek grants or that different types of agencies receive them (pp. 8–9, 28).
18. Goodman, p. 53.

Fiscal Patterns

While the United States is alone in its commitment to consolidating or at least coordinating fund raising, its voluntary agencies share four characteristics with their counterparts in the other countries. First, the requirements of fund raising are so pervasive and recurrent that fund raising, rather than direct services, constitutes the primary function of volunteers.[19] It has been argued that the fiscal requirements of voluntary agencies preempt and divert resources of volunteers, leadership, and staff that might better be used for improved service to clientele or for innovative programs or leadership development. This view was found mainly in the Netherlands, where, according to one government official, it is "hopelessly old-fashioned to cover expenses by means of collections and contributions."[20] Several professionals in England suggested that the high quality of the social services in the Netherlands might be due to a smaller investment of resources in fund raising because most income is obtained from the government. It is doubtful, however, that most of the volunteers who participate in fund raising could or would be used for other purposes. In Israel the majority of the 30,000 to 40,000 volunteers who solicit door to door for a few hours each year are school children recruited through pressures exerted by teachers and adult leaders in the youth movements. The use of volunteers in capacities other than fund raising is, as we shall see in chapter 10, influenced more by factors in the agency structure and in the civic culture.

Few of the respondents claimed, as some U.S. partisans of voluntary fund raising do, that this type of participation has led to the development of a well-informed constituency for the agency. More attention is given in the United States to the nurturing of this positive side effect of involvement in fund raising.

The second fiscal pattern common to all the countries is that dependency on donors forces voluntary agencies to search for multiple income sources, which in turn leads to the institutionalization of fund raising and to possible deflection from goals.[21] The constant efforts necessary to maintain an agency easily take on a life of their own,

19. The English data is reported in Stephen Hatch, *Voluntary Work: A Report of a Survey.* See also Stephen Hatch and Ian Mocroft, "Voluntary Workers." For the U.S. data, see chapter 3, footnote 35.

20. A. Linde, "Services for the Mentally Handicapped in the Netherlands: A General Review," p. 68.

21. Norman Johnson, "The Finance of Voluntary Organizations for the Physically Disabled."

detracting from and competing with the service goals of the organization. Another consequence is that volunteers develop vested interests in particular programs and are often reluctant to change the programs or to transfer them to government, especially if they are tangible and appealing for fund-raising purposes. Affiliates of national organizations in both England and Israel resisted the policy of referring clients to government health services for aids, appliances, and other services. Several agencies in these countries, as well as in the United States, were described as "fund-raising instruments in search of a program" because they have an extraordinary capacity to continue to obtain substantial contributions, even though their clientele has drastically diminished.

Agencies concerned with fighting polio and tuberculosis were faced in the past with this situation, and most of them responded by a process of "goal succession," which meant taking on a new disease. This strategy was adopted by the Lung Association in the United States, formerly the TB Association, which branched out to include all types of respiratory diseases, allergies, and diseases caused by air pollution. It was also the path followed by the Chest, Heart, and Stroke organizations in England, which were formerly included in the TB Association founded in 1899. In Israel, the TB association continues despite a lower incidence of TB, but the original polio organization merged with a cerebral palsy parent group. The British Polio Foundation, in contrast to its U.S. counterpart, did not adopt a new set of goals, and it continues to exist in an attenuated form serving a dwindling number of older victims of the polio epidemics of the 1950s.

Other organizations have broadly stated goals that are unlikely to need to be changed because of a new discovery or improved method of treatment. For example, Action Research for Crippled Children emerged out of one of the early polio associations in England that was devoted solely to research. It took on the broadest of research missions when the polio vaccine was discovered — namely, to deal with all conditions affecting crippled children — a mission so open-ended that there is little likelihood it will ever have to change again. Many other agencies serving the physically and mentally handicapped have to face the natural aging of their clientele, as well as a lowered incidence of birth defects as a result of new medical technologies; hence, they, too, may have a declining number of possible future clients. However, since the gap between the number of persons afflicted with a particular handicap and those served is so vast, there is little danger that agencies serving the handicapped will not have clientele.[22] Organizations with a research mission have an even longer life expectancy.

A third characteristic, resulting from the competitive free enterprise system of fund raising in the four countries, is that the amount of money raised is not congruent with the incidence or seriousness of a particular handicap or the number of persons served. This point can be seen with particular clarity in England, where the income of the Spastics Society is seven and one-half times that of the Multiple Sclerosis Society, even though the total number of victims of each disease is about the same. The Muscular Dystrophy Group serves about half as many persons as suffer from cerebral palsy, but it raises less than half as much as the Multiple Sclerosis Society, or one-fifth as much as the Spastics Society. Least effective of all is the organization concerned with the victims of spina bifida, who increase by about 1,500 a year and may outnumber the spastics — it collects only one-fifth as much as the Muscular Dystrophy Group.[23] Similarly, in the United States the agency serving the smallest clientele — the blind — had the largest budget, twelve times that of the Multiple Sclerosis Society. Thus, popular perceptions and preferences, as well as fund-raising skills, are significant determinants of the amount of funds available to voluntary organizations.

Finally, the fourth characteristic is that the actual costs of fund raising remain controversial and indeterminate. Because of a lack of standardized accounting procedures and an agency's discretion in defining and assigning its expenditures, comparative judgments are almost impossible, except in extreme cases. It is known, for example, that direct mail and advertising are the most expensive forms of raising funds and that the use of volunteer solicitors is among the least. United Way organizations claim their administrative costs of 10 to 15 percent are among the lowest. Some U.S. national health agencies expend from 25 to 40 percent of their income for fund-raising, and their counterparts in England, from 11 to 18 percent.[24] In view of the close relation-

22. See Eda Topliss, *Provision for the Disabled*, on low "take-up." In the United States, less than half of the 7,000,000 children believed eligible for special education for the handicapped have been identified since the legislation was passed in 1975 ("A Bureaucratic Imperative," in *The Public Interest* 57 [Fall 1979]:115–17).

23. The lack of a positive relationship between the incidence of a disability and the fund-raising capacity of organizations concerned with it is discussed in Nightingale, 177–217.

24. Unell, pp. 17–18, estimated 14 percent for the administrative and fund-raising costs in her sample of sixty-four voluntary agencies. She also noted that expenditures of these agencies and the Local Authority Social Service Departments were in approximately the same proportion for administration and program, even though the statutory organizations' expenditures were ten times that of the voluntary agencies.

ship between the costs of administration, fund raising, and "public education," the percentage allocated to each is usually quite arbitrary. A study sponsored by the Filer Commission found that only 10 percent of a representative sample of New York State voluntary agencies reported fund-raising costs of more than 25 percent, but that 25 percent of the total representative sample made gross errors in reporting their fund-raising costs and percentages.[25]

Tax Incentives for Contributions

Like joint fund raising, a tax incentive for philanthropic giving by individuals is also peculiar to the United States. The tax policy of a nation has both direct and indirect influence on the fiscal resource system of voluntary agencies through its impact on the incentive to give, as well as on the amount of discretionary income available for possible contributions. The many indirect concessions and benefits available to voluntary agencies — such as tax exemptions on income, land, and property not used for commercial purposes and reduced postal rates — have been estimated as worth over £100,000,000 for all charitable organizations in England and $5,000,000,000 dollars in the United States.[26]

One powerful influence on contributions is a policy providing for some deductibility of contributions from a donor's income tax payments. The voluntary sector in the United States has long agreed that any change in the rate of deductibility of charitable contributions in computing the federal income tax has a significant effect on the level of giving. For example, between 1970 and 1978, changes in the law resulted in a decrease from 50 percent to 25 percent in taxpayers who itemize deductions, with an estimated loss of $1,500,000,000 in contributions.[27]

The subject of the charitable deduction in the United States is an extremely complex and controversial one. Arguments about it reflect opposing views on the roles of government and private philanthropy. Originally instituted in 1918, the charitable deduction was justified on the grounds that donated income did not enrich the giver and that an incentive was required to encourage private contributions for public

25. A. J. Grimes, "The Fund-Raising Percent as a Quantitative Standard for Regulation of Public Charities, with Particular Emphasis on Voluntary Health and Welfare Organizations." The study also found that the fund-raising cost percentages for national voluntary health agencies had no relationship to the total income raised by the organization or the relative rank among others in seriousness of the disease or disability for which they were appealing.

26. Goodman, p. 50, and Filer, p. 104.

27. Filer, p. 136.

purposes that the government would otherwise be required to support. The argument for its retention is based on a belief that the charitable deduction is efficient, since more money is contributed because of it than is lost to the Treasury. It has been estimated that, if the deduction was completely eliminated, contributions would drop by as much as 50 percent.[28] The inequity of existing deductions for contributions has been strongly criticized by the Donee group, consisting of social activists representing various minority, disadvantaged, and grass-roots interests that object to many of the recommendations of the Filer Commission. They have urged the use of tax credits so that benefits would be concentrated among low-income persons and thus would contribute to the democratization of philanthropy.[29] The future of the charitable deduction in the United States is uncertain, and it will undoubtedly continue to be attacked as an unjust tax loophole and to be defended as in the best interests of the public.

The lack of contribution deductibility in England may account in part for higher per capita giving in the United States, which, during 1971–1973, was fifteen times that in England. Although as a percentage of the total sums raised contributions have almost doubled, increasing from 6 to 10 percent during 1971–1973, in 1975 only about one-third of the 19,000,000 households in England contributed to charity, and the average donation amounted to only sixteen pence per week.[30]

In the United States, total contributions amount to less than 2 percent of the gross national product; in the United Kingdom, they amount to only .05 percent. In 1973, individuals in the United States gave nineteen times as much as corporations, while in the United Kingdom they gave only about four times as much as companies.[31] An English observer explained this by stating that "it is public policy to encourage

28. Filer, pp. 135–42. See also Martin S. Feldstein and Charles Clotfelder, "Tax Incentives and Charitable Contributions in the U.S.: A Microeconomic Analysis," and George F. Break, "Charitable Contributions under the Federal Income Tax: Alternative Policy Options."

29. The Donee Group Report and Recommendations, *Private Philanthropy: Vital and Innovative? or Passive and Irrelevant?*, pp. 26–32. The National Committee for Responsive Philanthropy is the successor organization to the original Donee Group.

30. There is a consistent decline in the proportion of private households reporting voluntary contributions in England between 1970 and 1975, with the result that the average weekly donation per household rose only by 26 percent during this five-year period, while disposable income rose by 112 percent. Similarly, the top twenty public companies increased their level of giving by 75 percent from 1969–1970 through 1974–1975, during which time their pretax profits increased by 136 percent. (P. Falush, "Trends in the Finance of British Charities.")

31. Wells Group of Fund-Raising Companies, *Wells Collection*, 1973 edition, pp. 7–8. See also Wolfenden, pp. 262–71.

charity in America; the attitude of the government here is that it is a useful supplement, little more."[32]

Similarly, in the Netherlands and Israel there are no tax advantages for contributors. In Israel tax write-offs are occasionally arranged on an ad hoc basis for large contributors through private negotiations with Treasury officials, but this is a special privilege rather than a matter of public policy. Instead of a positive direct tax policy to encourage voluntary contributions, tax policies in Israel have a deterrent effect on the capacity of citizens to contribute. This is also true in the Netherlands and England because of high individual income tax rates that reduce the amount of discretionary income available for contributions.[33] The higher tax rates in the Netherlands and England support a more extensive social service system under governmental auspices than is found in the United States; consequently, in these countries campaigns for voluntary agencies may appear superfluous. In the Netherlands, the small number of public campaigns, as well as their modest return, may result from widespread public knowledge of the system of subsidies, high tax rates, and comprehensive social insurance coverage. It is doubtful that the almost three thousand agencies receiving government subsidies in the Netherlands could or would be supported by the public if they were not subsidized by the government. At the same time, contributed funds are important because they are often the only source of support for new and experimental programs until these programs can qualify for subsidies.

Although contributions were the original source of voluntary agency income and are still the preferred mode of support, their importance has markedly declined. Contributions are necessary for an organization to be considered a voluntary agency in the countries studied, but contributions by themselves are rarely sufficient. We turn next to the use of government funds.

32. Nightingale, p. 99.

33. Arnold J. Heidenheimer, Hugh Heclo, and Carolyn Adams, *Comparative Public Policy: The Politics of Social Choice in Europe and America*, p. 228. No data regarding contributions comparable to those of the United States and England is available in the Netherlands or Israel.

8.   The Use of Governmental Funds

The conventional conception of voluntary agencies — free to choose their own clientele and mode of service, and financed mainly by philanthropic contributions — has been drastically altered since the 1960s as they have become more dependent on government funds. As nongovernmental providers of public services, voluntary agencies have become subject to the availability of tax funds and to governmental rules. This raises questions about their independence and accountability.

The growing reliance on governmental funding results from the convergence of: (1) the acute financial problems of voluntary agencies caused by a decline in real giving and increases in operating costs, both aggravated by an inflationary spiral; (2) the continuing expansion of governmental social service programs with more funds available for purchase of service from nongovernmental providers; (3) a lessened confidence, mainly in the United States, in governmental administration of social programs. Voluntary agencies are caught in a vicious circle in which declining income from contributions leads to increased dependency on government, which leads to the belief of donors that their support is no longer needed. This new cycle complements an older one in which a downturn in the economy generally increases the demand for voluntary agency services, while at the same time eroding their revenue base.[1]

Voluntary agencies in the four countries are used because government cannot meet its ever-growing responsibilities, as in England; because voluntary agencies are the providers of first choice, as in the Netherlands; or for more pragmatic reasons in the United States and Israel, where these agencies can provide an economical, flexible service with little red tape and can serve as a means of avoiding bureaucratic and policy constraints. Other advantages to government are the extension of services without a corresponding increase in staff and investment in facilities and the exporting of undesirable, impractical,

1. Dennis R. Young and Stephen J. Finch, *Foster Care and Nonprofit Agencies*, p. 17.

or low-priority tasks, particularly those involving highly specialized services to a very small clientele. For voluntary agencies, public funds not only compensate for the loss of contributed income, but also enable an agency to greatly enlarge the scope of its services.

Both sectors have something to gain as well as to lose in this exchange. We shall first review briefly the four national fiscal policies on the use of public funds by voluntary agencies and some of the consequences for their respective service patterns. This will provide the background for an analysis of three problems for voluntary agencies: vendorism, grantsmanship, and dependency. Because these trends have advanced most in the United States, the discussion will draw mainly on the experience of U.S. voluntary agencies. As a guide, Table 8 summarizes governmental-voluntary agency service patterns and fiscal policies in the four welfare states:

Four National Fiscal Policies and Their Consequences
The Netherlands

Although until 1976 no Parliament adopted legislation specifically authorizing the practice, subsidies to voluntary agencies serving the physically and the mentally handicapped have been included in the budget of the CRM since 1953, when they were introduced as an experiment. Because of their open-ended character, subsidies for all social services increased a thousandfold between 1952 and 1977, from Df. 1,400,000 to Df. 1,209,000,000, in addition to another Df. 500,000,000 from social insurance funds for the social services. (Of the total Df. 1,200,000,000, a little over one-third, or Df. 383,600,000, was for the handicapped.) The growth in subsidies was part of a general trend in the Netherlands from 1955 to 1971, when the ratio of government expenditures to GNP rose more sharply than in Great Britain or the United States: the proportion of tax revenue to GNP in Holland was twice that in the United Kingdom, six times that in the United States, and twice the average of six other European countries.[2]

As a result of this fiscal policy, almost all of the staff and program costs of voluntary agencies are paid by subsidies and social insurance payments. For example, of the twenty Dutch agencies, twelve received 75 percent of their total income from governmental sources, including six agencies supported by social insurance payments that amounted to 90 to 100 percent of their budget. Another four agencies

2. Arnold J. Heidenheimer, Hugh Heclo, and Carolyn Adams, *Comparative Public Policy: The Politics of Social Choice in Europe and America*, p. 228.

TABLE 8.

Governmental-Voluntary Service Patterns and Public Fiscal Policies

	Service Patterns	Fiscal Policy
United States	Mild preference for voluntary agency as an agent and sometimes as a partner, *complementing* a dominant, governmental system that uses a variety of service providers.	A decentralized, grants economy with over one-third of the governmentally financed personal social services provided by nonprofit organizations through purchase of service on a contractual or third-party payment basis.
England	Voluntary agency as a partner (junior or silent), *supplementing*, via gap-filling and substitution, for resource deficiencies in a system of primary statutory responsibility for direct administration of comprehensive, universal, personal social services.	Priority for statutory funding and provision. Very limited grant-aids for voluntary agency administration, with local authority payments for service mainly on a deficit-financing basis.
The Netherlands	Voluntary agencies are the primary service delivery system, based on the principle of *subsidiarity*, with government almost exclusively as financier, having only a residual role in service delivery.	Governmental subsidies for administration and social insurance payments provide at least 90 percent of the income of voluntary agencies.
Israel	High degree of interpenetration of institutional sectors, dominated by central government, with voluntary agencies as *complementary* but not necessarily as the preferred provider.	Limited governmental subsidies and deficit financing for a wide range of services.

SOURCE: Reprinted from "Public Fiscal Policy and Voluntary Agencies in Welfare States," by Ralph M. Kramer, *Social Service Review* 53, no. 1 (March 1979): 4, by permission of The University of Chicago Press. Copyright 1979 by The University of Chicago.

obtained 40 to 50 percent of their income from government. None of the nine agencies that received one-third or more of their income from social insurance obtained any income at all from contributions. (See Table 17 in the Appendix for additional details.)

Open-ended subsidies in the Netherlands have produced a tremendous expansion of most of the social services and a rising level of quality, at least as reflected in the increased number of professionals on agency staffs. The ability of subsidies to implement governmental priorities is illustrated in the doubling of the number of day care centers for the mentally handicapped and the tripling of the number of people served by them between 1969 and 1972.[3] Although subsidies might appear to be an uncertain source of income because they had no legislative sanction, they provided a stable and progressively larger proportion of agency income. One of the major deficiencies of subsidies is their reactive nature. They are more effective for the extension of current, conventional programs than for innovative services, which generally require three to five years of operation before they could be accepted for governmental support.

To the government, however, two other aspects of the subsidy policy were of greater concern: the decline of volunteer participation in the governance of the agencies as their dependency on subsidies increased and, perhaps more seriously, the runaway costs of expenditures for subsidies. One way of coping with the latter was to include coverage for some of the most expensive programs, such as day care centers for the mentally handicapped, in the scope of "extraordinary medical expenses" covered by social insurance. In addition, because of the growing number of small agencies eligible for subsidies since the mid-1960s, there have been mounting governmental pressures for mergers, "scale enlargement," and more efficient management of voluntary agencies. In an effort to bring together what the subsidy system had fragmented, a small beginning was made in 1976 to decentralize governmental decision making on subsidies for some social services and to create new structures for budgeting, planning, and coordination on the municipal level.

The subsidy system will probably not expand much further in the future if financing for additional social services can be obtained from the social insurance system. A new and more complex set of interorganizational relationships may then emerge, changing the distribution of power among the voluntary agencies and between them and local

3. Jan B. Meiresonne, *Care for the Mentally Retarded in the Netherlands*, p. 8.

and national government. This will have the effect of reducing some of the exceptional autonomy which the agencies have had.

England

In sharp contrast with the Netherlands, public fiscal policy in England has favored the utilization of the statutory system for both financing and service delivery. Since 1970, this policy has been implemented through the reorganized Social Service Departments in each local authority, which are responsible for an extensive array of personal social services. There is, however, official recognition that the demands for service have outstripped a statutory capacity reduced by the inroads of "stagflation." As a result, there is more emphasis on implementation of already promised benefits than on allocating funds to voluntary agencies for research and development or for the creation of new programs. Under these conditions, voluntary agencies continue to fill gaps, often substituting for government and compensating for the inevitable deficiencies of a system aspiring toward universalism.

Grant-aids for the administration of national voluntary agencies are provided by central government and, although these increased from £19,000,000 in 1974–1975 to £35,400,000 in 1976–1977, they have had a negligible impact on agencies serving the physically and mentally handicapped, which rarely receive or even seek such grants. A more realistic assessment of the role of central government in assisting voluntary agencies is evident in the rather modest increase in funds from the Department of Health and Social Security, which grew only from £1,800,000 to £2,800,000 and was divided among ninety-eight organizations during this two-year period. In addition, £4,600,000 was allocated by the Voluntary Service Unit in the Home Office, of which almost half went to the Women's Royal Voluntary Service.[4] For example, only one of the twenty agencies in the sample reported as much as nine percent of its income from central government, and these grants constituted less than 2 percent of the income of the other five agencies receiving such funds. A notable exception was the Spastics Society, which reported a tenfold increase in grants in the decade ending 1974–1975, when they went from £20,000 to £211,000.

Similarly, although grants made by the local authorities to nongovernmental organizations for all the personal social services in-

4. Unell, p. 9, and Wolfenden Committee, *The Future of Voluntary Organisations*, pp. 219–30.

creased from £2,500,000 in 1972–1973 to £7,900,000 in 1975–1976, these, too, have relatively little significance for most voluntary agencies. The grants consist of small sums, rarely exceeding several thousand pounds each. They are allocated to help relieve the deficits of more than one hundred organizations, and usually represent less than 1 percent of the total expenditures of a Social Service Department. Because statutory investment in the agencies is so small, there is little interest in any greater control over them or in integrating them into the statutory service system.

Of greater salience are local governmental payments for service, which rose throughout England and Wales from £45,000,000 to £61,500,000 in the year from 1974–1975 to 1975–1976. Twelve out of the twenty agencies studied received payments for service from local authorities; seven of the twelve relied on these fees for at least one-third of their income; and four obtained over 50 percent of their income from this source. Five agencies obtained from 25 to 50 percent and three, less than 25 percent of their income from these sources. (See Table 16 in the Appendix for additional details.)

These statistics should be viewed in the light of the claim by voluntary agencies that governmental payments usually cover only from two-thirds to three-quarters of real costs and that the difference between this and payments made by the local authority must be subsidized from other income. All but two agencies reported increases during the last ten years in all forms of income, mainly in fees for service from local authority. There is evidence that some voluntary agencies have substantially increased their charges to the local authority for the same level of service and that this may have more than compensated for the increase in consumer prices. For example, a survey conducted by the National Council of Social Service of sixty-four agencies providing personal social services found a 211 percent increase in income from residential care between 1970 and 1975![5]

Almost all the national agencies receiving payments from local authorities provide specialized forms of residential care to persons with particular handicaps. Local authorities usually buy such services from a voluntary agency because their own facilities are inadequate or because the voluntary agency can provide a service more cheaply. For these reasons, and because relatively few physically handicapped persons require residential care, voluntary rather than statutory in-

5. Unell, p. 9.

stitutions serve most of these persons. At the same time, there is often an exchange of funds and other resources in the local community between the Social Service Department and voluntary agencies, in which they tend to make up for each other's deficits.

Israel

As in England, practically any social service in Israel is eligible for some governmental support. Similarly, the reach of the welfare state exceeded its grasp, and voluntary agencies have filled in many gaps in governmental service programs. Within the social services, income maintenance for large families and the aged has had higher priority than services to the mentally and physically handicapped. The administration of the personal social services by 180 different local welfare offices, as well as the reimbursement formulas used by the national government, has further discouraged the development of new or improved services by the municipalities. Since the 1970s, due largely to persistent pressure from one voluntary agency, additional governmental funds have been allocated for the care of the mentally handicapped.

Although all but one of the fifteen voluntary agencies studied receive government funds, the amounts are relatively small. Only one agency obtains 80 percent of its income from governmental payments for service; another gets over half; and most of the rest receive less than 25 percent. (See Table 18 in the Appendix for details.)

As in the other countries, the policies of the different departments of central government that allocate funds to voluntary agencies are inconsistent. While the conditions under which funds are made available vary greatly, in Israel government funds are rarely used to raise standards among the voluntary agencies; instead, they are given to make up a deficit. Voluntary agencies are, however, expected to be the major source of innovation, and, consequently, there is a minimal governmental investment in research and development and in planning and coordination on both national and local levels.

The ability of voluntary agencies to "create facts" and then to request governmental support has given them a significant, if not a disproportionate, influence on overall service patterns. While it is not difficult for new agencies to emerge in Israel, once they can demonstrate a service, they can usually expect some governmental support or at least to be bailed out if they flounder. This practice is justified on the pragmatic grounds that auspices do not make much difference in Israel and that it is more important that a needed service be provided.

The United States

While governmental agencies are dominant in the United States, as in England, there is very little support in the United States for the British model of a single, comprehensive, "one-door," public social service center in every community. Instead, there is a strong tendency to separate financing from administration by purchasing services from both nonprofit and profit-making organizations. Over the five-year period from 1971 to 1976, the purchase of social services by government grew from 25 percent to approximately two-thirds of the total expenditures under Title XX of the 1974 Amendments to the Social Security Act. At the same time, public funds constituted a growing proportion of voluntary agency income, averaging about 40 percent.[6]

In the U.S. sample, seven out of the twenty agencies received over half of their income from payments for service and grants from governmental organizations. Five of the agencies had budgets of approximately $1,000,000, mainly from government funds for service payments. One agency received ten times as much from governmental fees for service as from all other funds contributed, and three other agencies quadrupled their income from governmental sources within a three-year period. (See Table 15 in the Appendix for additional details.)

The 1967 Amendments to the Social Security Act gave impetus to this trend by providing open-ended, matching grants that made possible the tripling of the value of contributed funds. This policy was in sharp contrast with the practice from 1930 to 1967, when public programs were implemented by government agencies, although there was always modest amount of use of voluntary agencies.

The rapid expansion of the social services since the 1960s, the loss of confidence in governmental capacity for implementation, and the preference for nongovernmental agencies has attracted new kinds of providers, particularly proprietary ones, so that the service system has become more complex. Such legislation as Title XX amending the Social Security Act in 1974 broadened the boundaries of eligibility and made it possible for government to purchase personal social ser-

6. Candace P. Mueller, "Purchase of Service Contracting from the Viewpoint of the Provider," p. 30. The voluntary agency's share of these purchase-of-service arrangements doubled to 40 percent within a five-year period from 1971 to 1976. There is great variation among states and between counties; in the San Francisco Bay Area, 40 percent of the voluntary agencies in 1979 received over half of their income from government funds. These patterns reflect a larger trend in which federal social service grants to the states tripled from 1963 to 1971 and then doubled once more between 1971 and 1972, reaching $1,700,000,000 (Alfred M. Skolnik and Sophie R. Dales, "Social Welfare Expenditures, 1950–75," p. 19).

TABLE 9.
Percentage of Voluntary Agency Income from Government Funds, 1973–1974

	United States (N = 20)	England (N = 20)	The Netherlands (N = 20)	Israel (N = 15)
None	5	8	2	1
Under 32	5	7	1	9
33–65	5	4	4	3
66–99	4	1	6	2
100	1	0	7	0
Mean	33	22	75	27

vices for a larger number of middle-class clients, who have traditionally been served by voluntary agencies. In addition to these service payments, a policy of "guided innovation," fueled by a grants economy, has been a source of government funds for agencies operating demonstration projects. These trends have led to governmental demands for greater efficiency, accountability, and service integration. They are reflected in the growing assumption of social planning responsibilities by local governments.[7]

To survive in the turbulent, competitive, and uncertain era of "private federalism," voluntary agencies in the United States have had to become more opportunistic, entrepreneurial, and political than their counterparts in the other countries. Operating in a context of policy direction and financial support by government, many voluntary agencies are experiencing an identity crisis and have expressed grave concern over their dependency and their future role, particularly in an era of cutbacks in public spending.

Table 9 summarizes the percentage of voluntary agency income from governmental sources in each country.

Three Issues in the Use of Government Funds by Voluntary Agencies
The increased reliance of voluntary agencies on public funds has generated a wide range of stresses on their fiscal resource systems. Three problems resulting from such stresses are most evident in the United States, although they are present in varying degree in the other countries: vendorism, grantsmanship, and dependency.

7. Richard S. Bolan, "Social Planning and Policy Development: Local Government."

Vendorism

As vendors, voluntary agencies sell social services to government for an agreed-upon price, usually on a unit-cost basis. Three fiscal dilemmas facing a voluntary agency stem from the gap between actual costs and the price paid by government for the provision of such services as day care, counseling, rehabilitation, and residential or home care. First, if the agency does not receive full reimbursement, then it must make up a deficit. Second, if it does charge the full cost, then the rate of reimbursement may be sufficient to attract competing profit-making organizations. Finally, unless there is some cost advantage, government may decide to operate the program itself.

If voluntary agencies are not reimbursed for their full costs — which is almost always the case in England as well as in the United States — they subsidize government and must seek additional funds to cover the deficit. Often it is not clear who is subsidizing whom because voluntary agencies invariably claim that government does not pay the full cost of care as they compute it.[8] In England, it is expected that, because voluntary agencies are charities, they will charge less than their actual cost and that they will make up the difference by seeking contributions from the public. In the 1960s, local authorities were urged by the central government to reimburse voluntary agencies up to 75 percent of their costs, but this was seldom done. One agency, Cheshire Homes, reported a deficit of £1,500,000, accumulated over a twenty-five-year period because local authorities insisted that, because they were a charity, they should absorb at least a third of the costs of maintaining residents. Similarly, several Social Service Departments observed that a number of voluntary agencies "acted like a charity" and did not even request specific rates for reimbursement. Instead, they approached the local authority informally with the modest request "pay us what you can." Other agencies expressed their belief in the priority of voluntarism, which they consider to be charity, by describing their function in terms that could be paraphrased as follows: "We make services available to the handicapped, but, unfortunately, they are very expensive and we cannot pay the whole cost. The SSD helps us because we happen to be out-of-pocket." Others,

8. A study of voluntary agency programs in New York City found an average differential of 16 percent between actual agency costs and government reimbursements, resulting in voluntary agencies "subsidizing" the governmentally funded child welfare programs with an additional $48,000,000 (Greater New York Fund, *Impact of Government Funding on the Management of Voluntary Agencies*, p. 10). See also Robert M. Rice, "Impact of Government Contracts on Voluntary Social Agencies," and William G. Hill, "Voluntary and Governmental Financial Transactions."

such as the Royal National Institute for the Blind, stated that they are committed to providing a service to the blind "as cheaply as possible" and viewed this as a favor or a discount offered to the government.

Some voluntary agencies, such as the Spastics Society, are more explicit about this policy than others and deliberately charge only from 60 to 80 percent of their costs in the belief that their independence would be endangered if they were reimbursed in full. In Israel, also, several agencies make a virtue out of necessity and give a concern for autonomy as their reason for not receiving full payment.

In England and the United States and, to a lesser extent, in Israel, determination of rates for reimbursement of costs on a per capita or unit basis is usually a matter of bargaining between buyer and seller. Through informal or formal consultation or, in the United States, through lobbying, voluntary agencies can influence the rate schedules. In England, each Social Service Department sets its own rates for payments to voluntary agencies, although there is some standardization in the Greater London area. In the Netherlands, voluntary agencies participate in rate setting through membership in the body that sets the rates for reimbursement under the social insurance system.

In the United States, maximum cost policies for reimbursement are sometimes established on a state or regional basis. These policies result in inequities when an agency cannot obtain needed services because allowable costs have been set at an unrealistically low level. The Golden Gate Regional Center in San Francisco, although incorporated as a nonprofit organization, receives all of its funds from the California State Department of Health, whose rigid spending limits on care for the mentally handicapped often make it practically impossible to provide required services. Many problems stemming from the differences between rates allowed by government and the actual costs of voluntary agency services are due to differences in accounting practices and to the administrative complexities of the eight possible payment mechanisms and eleven different variables that enter into rate determination.[9]

A second dilemma occurs if voluntary agencies charge rates that are closer to their actual costs because then competitive, proprietary, or

9. Norman V. Lourie, "Purchase of Service Contracting: Issues Confronting Governmental Sponsored Agencies," p. 22. The complexities of rate determination are also discussed in Gordon Manser, "Further Thoughts on Purchase of Service," and Ralph M. Kramer, "Voluntary Agencies and the Use of Public Funds: Some Policy Issues."

only nominally nonprofit organizations may be attracted to the market. This occurred in the United States and the Netherlands, where social insurance, third-party payments, and vouchers became available when the personal social services were defined as extensions of medical care. The Netherlands' system of third-party payments and social insurance has resulted in what many officials believe is an excess capacity in residential care. In the United States, where proprietary organizations were active mainly in residential care, the availability of government funds has encouraged their entry into the fields of day care, home medical care, vocational rehabilitation, and counseling.[10]

A third dilemma occurs when there is no cost advantage at all to the government in using a voluntary agency. Then, as in England, the local authority can decide to operate a program itself. In addition to pricing themselves out of the market, another threat facing voluntary agencies as vendors is that, as their services became larger in scale, standardized, routine, and organized on a bureaucratic basis, a public agency is more likely to want to take over and administer a program directly, particularly if there is no cost advantage in retaining the voluntary agency. In England, the volunteer meals-on-wheels programs were taken over by some local authorities when the programs became so extensive that they could no longer be run efficiently and reliably by volunteers.

The prospect of such takeovers is, however, not a real one in the Netherlands, where there is little sanction for direct governmental provision. Nor are takeovers likely to occur in Israel, where there are strong budgetary and political constraints on the expansion of any ministry's domain.[11]

Apart from the problems connected with rate determination, some other organizational costs of vendorism that were reported are: long delays in receiving funds from government, which often work to the disadvantage of small agencies that lack sufficient cash reserves to carry them until reimbursed and that are not usually in a position to borrow such funds; uncertainties regarding future funding, as well as the ever-present threat of loss of funding; the red tape involved in

10. A highly critical view of the role of profit-making organizations is Dan Rubenstein, R. E. Mundy, and Mary L. Rubinstein, "Proprietary Social Services." An opposing view is H. G. Whittington, "A Case for Private Funding in Mental Health." See also Donald Fisk, Herbert Kiesling, and Thomas Mullen, *Private Provision of Public Services: An Overview.*
11. Ralph M. Kramer, *The Voluntary Service Agency in Israel*, pp. 18–19.

complying with recording and reporting requirements; and the diminishing interest of board members and volunteers as government becomes more and more responsible for an agency's income.

Grantsmanship

Grants from governmental agencies or private foundations for specific programs are another source of income for voluntary agencies, in addition to payments for services they provide to designated individuals. Grantsmanship, the know-how required to obtain time-limited funds for a special purpose — research, demonstration, facility construction, or a service program for a particular clientele — has become a fiscal way of life for most public-service organizations in the United States. As a result, governmental and voluntary agencies are becoming more like each other because of their dependency on a grants economy with multiple funding sources in the "banker" state and federal government, as well as in private foundations.[12]

One of the major disadvantages of relying on grants, or "soft money," reported by U.S. agency executives is uncertainty. The vagaries of governmental funding, the frequent policy and regulation changes, legislative shifts, the threat of cutbacks, and the annual struggle over budgets all contribute to recurrent financial crises and a perennial state of insecurity in which program continuity is perpetually in doubt. This is particularly true when governmental spending is under attack and is being reduced. The precariousness of this way of life is evident in the experience of one U.S. agency, the Center for Independent Living, which depended almost entirely on $1,000,000 from eight government grants to support twenty-three different programs. In one fell stroke in 1978, one-fourth of its budget was eliminated within a month following the passage of Proposition 13 in California. At the same time, some voluntary agencies had their purchase of service contracts terminated, while many others were cut by 27 percent.

Another frequently voiced criticism is that the requirements for preparing proposals for funding and for complying with different and changing governmental procedures and regulations consume an ex-

12. Edward K. Hamilton, "On Non-Constitutional Management of a Constitutional Problem." Don K. Price has also observed that "governmental agencies now behave more like private institutions than they did before the Second World War, and private institutions are now more like governmental agencies in their subordination to public policy" ("Endless Frontier or Bureaucratic Morass?", p. 80).

cessive amount of staff time and that, by increasing the costs of organizational maintenance, they can deflect resources from the service
delivery mission of the agency. The hidden costs of grantsmanship
are thus similar to those of vendorism except that there may be an
even more disproportionate investment in administrative over program costs.

Finally, reliance on single, categorical, time-limited grants in the
United States is also believed to contribute to fragmentation and lack
of coordination in the social services. In the Netherlands, the great
expansion of publicly funded service programs and new agencies led
to the formation of a national commission, which has proposed a complete reorganization of the methods for allocating funds to the voluntary sector. In both of these countries, efforts have been made to
involve local government in social planning for the first time as a means
of promoting more service coordination.[13] There is little interest in
this type of social planning in England, where additional governmental
funding is being sought for local councils that would primarily be
concerned with strengthening the voluntary sector, rather than with
coordinating statutory and voluntary organizations. Similarly, in Israel
there is little governmental concern for local social planning, although
there have been several demonstration projects over the last decade.

Dependency

In the United States and, to a lesser extent, in England, the rapid
acceleration in public funding of voluntary agencies has stirred the
fear that their historical, indispensable independence may be lost. A
typical expression of this is the following:

> Volunteerism is in danger of obliteration . . . the services rendered by
> voluntary agencies are being displaced, changed, destroyed by the influx
> of government funds, which in turn demands accountability and adher-
> ence to regulations which are unreasonable and unmanageable . . . volun-
> tary agencies, by accepting government funds, participate in a process that
> will unavoidably lead them to disappear.[14]

The new alliance between voluntarism and vendorism in the United
States has raised with new sharpness the old question of What is vol-

13. See Robert Agranoff, "Services Integration," and Sheldon P. Gans and G. T. Horton,
Integration of Human Services: The State and Municipal Levels.
14. Greater New York Fund, p. 6. An eloquent and widely reprinted statement of this view
is Alan Pifer, "The Quasi-Non-Governmental Organization."

untary about an agency that receives most of its income from tax funds?[15] However, the findings of this study suggest that, posed in this way, the query is somewhat simplistic in its assumption that government funds inherently corrupt, co-opt, or constrain. An African proverb says that "if you have your hand in another man's pocket, you must move when he moves." Little evidence was found in any of the countries to support this belief. The executive leadership of the agencies reported few instances of unacceptable governmental requirements imposed on their service programs, governance, or administration. Nor did governmental funding seem to inhibit advocacy. This is not to say that there were no complaints about red tape or about the burdens of complying with an excessive number of regulations. These were, however, found almost exclusively in the United States, where there is a much greater emphasis on reporting and accountability, as well as more concern with the preservation of independence than in the other countries.

Paradoxically, ideological objections to "control by government" and preference for voluntary funding were expressed in England more often than in the United States. They were rarely expressed in Israel, where the Israel Cancer Association is the only agency that does not accept directly any government funds for its program on ideological grounds.[16] It was puzzling to find this belief about the corrupting influence of government funds in England, where voluntary agencies

15. Typical of many similar expressions of concern over the impact of governmental funds on voluntary agency independence are: Benjamin A. G. Jenvick, "The Voluntary Agency and the Purchase of Social Services," and Elizabeth Wickenden, "Purchase of Care and Services: Effect on Voluntary Agencies." One of the few dissents from the popular belief is found in a critique of the Filer Report by the Donee Group, which states: "[The commission's] fear of governmental interference is undocumented. It falsely pervades the recommendations and minimizes vouchers and matching grants." The authors also comment on the refusal of the report "to accept a larger role for government in the governance, access and accountability of voluntary agencies and foundations." The Donee report advocates a much larger share of direct service provision by government, which would then use its regulatory powers on behalf of certain disadvantaged groups, ("Private Philanthropy: Vital and Innovative? Or Passive and Irrelevant?", pp. 14–15).

16. In this respect the values and reference group of the Israel Cancer Association are closer to its U.S. counterparts than are those of any of the other agencies in Israel. The values and reference group are more influential in determining the association's fiscal policies than the political linkages of its executive and volunteer leadership to the highest levels of the Labour Party. Vehement ideological objections to the use of governmental subsidies for educational purposes are also found among some of the extreme Orthodox sects in Jerusalem, leading to bitter arguments and even violence between them and their opponents, who minimize the possibility of governmental control or cooptation. See *Jerusalem Post*, International Edition, November 4–10, 1979, p. 14.

receive relatively small amounts of statutory funds. In England, there were practically no complaints about governmental interference, partly because there are far fewer regulations than in the United States. For example, organizations that receive more than 50 percent of their income from central government must conform to governmental salary standards, may not locate their offices in central London, and must submit audited accounts and occasional reports. The perpetuation by voluntary agencies of the spectre of government encroachment by the use of an antibureaucratic, laissez-faire ideology and other "scare" tactics may be a political strategy to strengthen their claim on their respective domains and to win support from those opposed to governmental intervention.

That invoking the threat of governmental control over agency autonomy may be more ideological than real is also suggested by the continuing and unrestrained efforts of voluntary agencies in all four countries to secure more government funds. This was notable in England, where greater statutory funding for the voluntary sector was the principal recommendation of the Wolfenden Committee, which also reported that ". . . in general the amount of influence or control exercised by departments over voluntary organizations to which grants are made is remarkably small."[17]

Evidently, voluntary agencies in other countries have learned that they can have their cake and eat it, too. In the Netherlands, where there is the greatest dependency on governmental financing, voluntary agencies have even fewer constraints on their operations than do their counterparts in England and the United States. While it is not necessary to agree completely with Sidney Hook that "the increasing state control of the economy in democratic countries has not resulted in the progressive diminution of freedoms in political and cultural life,"[18] supporting evidence in the United States and Canada suggests

17. Wolfenden, p. 68. The absence of constraints is also mentioned by Eda Topliss, *Provision for the Disabled*: "There is no evidence that this dependence of voluntary bodies on the financial support of local authorities has seriously limited their activities" (p. 119). In commenting on a recent report showing that 40 percent of the income of voluntary agencies comes from government, endowments, interest, and rents, it was noted: "The usual warning was given that dependency on statutory funds could lead to loss of freedom, although no evidence before this has yet been produced since central-local government grants-in-aid first began." (Kathleen M. Slack, "Social Administration Digest: Voluntary Effort," p. 488).

18. "Socialism, Capitalism and Democracy: A Symposium," *Commentary* 65 (April 1978): 48.

that the impact of government funds in controlling voluntary social service organizations may be much less than is commonly believed.[19]

What might account for this finding in all four countries, which seems so contrary to the conventional wisdom that he who pays the piper calls the tune? Perhaps

> he who calls the tune [is] tone-deaf. That is, those who dispense funds may not have complete information, nor are they always rational and consistent. They may hold values that encourage them to react . . . in other than utilitarian terms. In addition and most important, funders are subject to the pressures of conflicting interests and reference groups.[20]

Among the external factors that appear to reduce the constraining effect of government funds on agency autonomy are the following: (1) the payment-for-service form of most transactions, (2) the diversity of income sources, (3) the countervailing power of a service monopoly and voluntary agency political influence, (4) low accountability due to the trade-offs in a mutual-dependency relationship.

The most frequent form of financial transaction between government and voluntary agencies is payment or reimbursement for a service provided by a voluntary agency to an individual for whom there is a public responsibility. Such arrangements generally involve fewer measures of control than grants or subsidies and are therefore less likely to weaken autonomy. In England and Israel, government payments are perceived by both parties to be a businesslike way of making up operating deficits. In England, the term *purchase of service* is rarely used. Instead, this type of income is usually recorded as "fees for service," making no distinction between payments from individuals and those from statutory bodies. In Israel, the president of an agency that received almost half of its funds from the government suggested the unimpaired freedom of his organization in its relation-

19. Representative examples are: Novia Carter, *Trends in Voluntary Support for Non-Governmental Social Service Agencies*, pp. 53–55; National Advisory Council on Voluntary Action to the Government of Canada, *People in Action*, pp. 20–21; Felice Perlmutter, "Public Funds and Private Agencies"; Young and Finch, pp. 232–38; William Burian, "Purchase of Service in Child Welfare: A Problem of Inter-Organizational Exchange"; Louis Levitt, "The Accountability Gap in Foster Care: Discontinuities in Accountability in the Purchase and Provision of Foster Care Services in New York City"; Maxine L. Harris, "Contracting with Private Agencies for the Delivery of Public Services: Policy Implications of an Emerging Trend"; and Trudy H. Bers, "Private Welfare Agencies and Their Role in Government-Sponsored Welfare Programs."

20. George Brager and Stephen Holloway, *Changing Human Service Organizations: Politics and Practice*, p. 43.

ship to government when he declared: "It's only the Golem [a nickname for the computer] that pays." Another agency executive stated: "Since the government doesn't pay the whole cost, they can't tell us what to do and besides they don't have the connections with the clientele that we have."

Although governmental payments for services provided by voluntary agencies contain the risks of vendorism cited earlier, the interorganizational relationship is generally perceived by both parties as essentially an exchange, a *quid pro quo* transaction rather than a threat to agency independence. When, as is most often the case in the United States, arrangements are formalized in a contract or written agreement — itself the product of a bargaining process — the rights and obligations of both parties are made explicit, including that of cancellation.

The agencies that depended on government for more than 40 percent of their income — from 20 to 25 percent of the sample in each country with the exception of the Netherlands — almost invariably received this income from a variety of public as well as voluntary sources. Although the proportion of an agency budget that can be obtained from any single source and not adversely affect the organization is a matter of dispute, there is considerable agreement on the importance of income diversity as a means of avoiding overdependency. This was not the case in the Netherlands, where all but eight of the agencies receiving government funds obtain them from only one government source; yet Dutch agencies have the greatest amount of freedom. In addition, the Dutch agencies receiving funds from several governmental agencies expressed their preference for obtaining them from only one!

There is, however, another side to diversity: while multiple funding sources may contribute to autonomy, some hidden administrative costs reported in the United States are the conflicting requirements of different regulations, standards of reporting and accounting, budget deadlines, standards of evaluation, and recording.

Also aiding independence is the distribution of power between governmental and voluntary organizations, including the strong resources for influence in the voluntary agencies' virtual monopoly of services required by government, as well as their ability to apply political pressure. In all four countries, the voluntary agency typically has a scarce, appropriate resource required by government for clients who have a right to the service. In economic terms, the supply of voluntary agency services and the demand of the governmental agency intersect at a price that is below the real cost for both parties. Government is often in the position of having authority and responsibility but lacking expertise, staff, facilities, and other necessary resources for service delivery. Having found a voluntary agency willing and able to provide the service, government officials are usually content to leave well enough alone because of their dependency on the agency.

The clearest example of a distribution of political power that favors the voluntary sector is in the Netherlands, where most of the agencies are connected with religious-political blocs. Because they have the support of the denominational political parties that are part of the coalition controlling the central government, voluntary agencies are well-protected against unacceptable bureaucratic demands.

Contrary to the belief that organizations might be afraid to bite the hand that feeds them, the most active advocates in the United States are among the agencies receiving the highest percentage of government funds, although the line between advocacy and self-interest in such instances is very thin. Reliance on tax funds in the United States requires continual monitoring of and involvement in the political process as part of the annual struggle for appropriations and the fight against cutbacks. Where voluntary agencies form an ad hoc coalition or are part of federations that negotiate with the government, as in the Netherlands and the United States, they are a formidable force with which government has to contend, often putting it on the defensive. This is particularly true of organizations serving the blind and the mentally handicapped.

Perhaps the most noteworthy condition mitigating any substantial challenge to the freedom of the voluntary agency is the low level of accountability demanded by government. This is epitomized in the candid statement of one government official who said: "If we knew more, we'd have to pay more."

Two principal forms of accountability are found mainly in the United States: fiscal and service reporting requirements and public policy restrictions on programs. Although extensive record keeping and burdensome reporting requirements were the most frequent complaints among voluntary agencies receiving public funds in the United States — in addition to the perennial objections to inadequate rates of reimbursement — they are not perceived as necessarily or even significantly impairing agencies' freedom. In several instances, United Way requirements in the United States were regarded as more unacceptable. Even in the United States, where there are governmental specifications regarding eligible clientele, staffing, and board representation for certain services,[21] these, too, were not generally viewed as a serious threat to independence, either because they were considered a legitimate and small price to pay for benefits, or because monitoring was insufficient to ensure compliance. Generally, agencies did what they always wanted to do, but for which they previously lacked the means. The use of public funds represented for virtually all of them an opportunity to be seized and enabled them to enlarge the scope of their services as much as tenfold.[22]

A question arises, however. Why was there such a low level of accountability and so little effort to control or regulate these vendors in the four countries? For example, governmental representatives were rarely found on the boards of directors except in Israel; when they were present in other countries, it was clear that they were serving in an unofficial capacity. Reporting requirements were ignored with impunity; one Dutch agency claimed that it had not submitted an annual financial statement for four years, yet its subsidy was continued.

Apparently the government bureaucrats in these countries lack the incentive and capacity for requiring stricter forms of accountability.[23] Although government officials complained about their lack of control over costs, the unevenness of voluntary agency services, and the difficulties of coordination, they are nevertheless dependent on what is in most cases a monopoly on service delivery. Also, governmental agencies lack sufficient personnel for close monitoring; in the Netherlands

21. Illustrations of sixteen types of federal and state regulations involved in purchase-of-service agreements are found in Ruth Werner, *Public Financing of Voluntary Agency Foster Care: 1975 Compared with 1957*, pp. 11–14, 17–19. Young and Finch, pp. 239–41, list thirty different requirements for voluntary agency reporting and notification required in New York City. See also Francine Rabinovitz, Jeffrey Pressman, and Martin Rein, "Guidelines: A Plethora of Forms, Authors, and Functions."

22. This was also one of the conclusions in Greater New York Fund, p. 8, and in Perlmutter, pp. 269–70. Some sense of the expansion of this mode of financing can be seen from the statistic that there was a 7,000 percent increase in the use of purchase of service by the voluntary agencies in San Diego County, California, from 1963 to 1978 (Martin C. Erwin and Jan K. Maiden, "Contracting for Human Services," p. 62).

23. The Greater New York Fund/United Way study found that program accountability was not as exacting as fiscal accountability, but that administrative costs had a higher priority than those for programs (p. 17). Other perspectives on these issues are: U.S. Department of Health, Education and Welfare, Social and Rehabilitation Service, *Purchase of Social Service: Study of the Experience of Three States in Purchase of Service Contracts under the Provisions of the 1967 Amendments to the Social Security Act*, and Bertram M. Beck, "Governmental Contracts with Non-Profit Social Welfare Corporations." p. 213–29.

this would be a staggering task because of the almost 3,000 agencies that would have to be inspected. The close links between agency sponsors and political parties also discourage a more assertive effort on the part of government supervisors.

In England, the Netherlands, and Israel, one by-product of mutual dependency is a network of informal, "cozy" relationships between the executive leadership of the voluntary agencies and government officials, among persons who share the same professional and administrative subcultures and who believe in live and let live. This condition has been described as "bureaucratic symbiosis" — i.e., a mutual co-optation in which both parties recognize their interdependency and are careful not to disturb it. From the standpoint of government, the use of voluntary agencies is a pragmatic policy and is rarely justified on ideological grounds. Most voluntary agency services in these countries are, in fact, less expensive than the same services provided by a governmental unit required to conform to civil service regulations. In Israel, it is easier for the Ministry of Social Welfare to obtain funds from the Treasury for service payments than to expand its own staff. Apart from economic advantages, there are organizational benefits to governmental agencies; they can obtain the loyalty of a constituency, extend their domain at a low cost, and, by showing that something is being done about a problem, sustain an impression of governmental responsibility and concern. For the voluntary agency, apart from helping to extend services, government funds constitute a means of access to government and an opportunity to influence public policy. However, once "addicted" to government funds, voluntary agencies are not likely to revert to soliciting contributions. Indeed, it seems reasonably clear that existing levels of services can no longer be sustained without tax funds.

Table 10 summarizes the principal advantages and disadvantages of the use of public funds by voluntary agencies.

I shall conclude with some generalizations on the effect of the intent of public funding and the type of service purchased on the possibility of governmental control of a voluntary agency, some implications of the trend toward bureaucratization and entrepreneurism, and the role of income diversity in mitigating dependency. (In chapter 14 I shall return to some of the issues surrounding the conflict between organizational autonomy and governmental accountability as they may affect the future of voluntary agencies in the welfare state.)

TABLE 10.

Principal Advantages and Disadvantages of the Use of Public Funds by Voluntary Agencies

Advantages to Voluntary Agencies	Advantages to Governmental Agencies	Disadvantages to Voluntary Agencies	Disadvantages to Governmental Agencies
Enlargement of scope of services; community utilization of specialized resources	More economical service	Inadequate rates of reimbursement	Lack of sufficient control over costs
Greater security of income	Extension of service without corresponding visibility or high fixed costs	Uncertainty of income; delays in cash flow	Unevenness of service delivery
Release of other funds for more particularistic purposes	Greater flexibility and responsiveness; easier to serve hard-to-reach groups; easier to initiate and to terminate funding	Red tape; excessive recording; reporting; and compliance with multiple, changing standards	Difficulties in maintaining standards and accountability

TABLE 10.

Principal Advantages and Disadvantages of the Use of Public Funds by Voluntary Agencies (continued)

Advantages to Voluntary Agencies	Advantages to Governmental Agencies	Disadvantages to Voluntary Agencies	Disadvantages to Governmental Agencies
Increased community status, prestige, and visibility	Bypass of bureaucratic and political constraints	Undesirable restrictions on service policies and on administration and governance	Fragmentation and less coherent social policy; weakened authority of government and chances of coordination
Access to governmental decision making	Transfer of unwanted tasks	Possible diminution in organizational autonomy, advocacy, and volunteer participation	Possible deterrent to assumption of governmental responsibility
	Gain of a supporting constituency or source of leverage to influence voluntary agency service standards	Becoming more bureaucratic and entrepreneurial; goal-deflection	
	Image of responsibility and cooperation		

Conclusions

The findings illustrate the principle that the degree of governmental constraint is a function of the method or form of financing.[24] It obviously makes a difference whether government funds are intended as a loan, a grant, a subsidy, or a payment, and whether they are for purposes of building construction, research, and demonstration, or reimbursement for services to persons who are entitled to them. Payments for service generally involve fewer measures of control and are less likely to threaten autonomy. Accordingly, there is a range of potential control by government, with grants at the top of the list, vouchers at the bottom, and service payments in the middle:

Categorical grants
Subsidies
Payments for service
Contracts for purchase of service
Third-party payments for service
Vouchers

While purchase of service requires a voluntary agency to channel its services into what the government defines as reimbursable, there is generally room for negotiation over respective interests. This is why contracts for purchase of service are increasingly regarded as one of the best means for balancing the value of a voluntary agency's independence and the government's need for accountability. Through a bargaining process, mutual expectations can be worked out, and each side has a better idea of what will be expected and required.[25] If a voluntary agency regards the conditions for government funds as unacceptable, it has the choice not to undertake the role of a vendor. As we have seen, the balance of power tends to favor the voluntary agency because of its usual service monopoly.

Another factor affecting the possibility of governmental control is the type of service to be purchased from a voluntary agency and the extent to which performance standards can be specified and monitored. While contracts that specify outcomes can be a major instrument of

24. Wickenden, "Purchase of Care and Services," p. 42. See also Edmond H. Weiss, "Grant Management: A Systems Approach."

25. Young and Finch, 238; Melvin Herman, "Purchase of Service Contracting: Promise or Threat to Social Services?" *Proceedings of the National Institute on Purchase of Service Contracting,* pp. 43–49. Pifer, p. 13, points out, however, that there is an inclination for contracting parties to compromise "so that the requirements of neither independence nor accountability are ever fully met."

accountability that can help government stay out of the internal operations of voluntary agencies and avoid infringing on the authority of
the management, these service outcomes are often very difficult to
define and to measure.[26] For example, it makes a difference whether
the service purchased involves meals, medical or nursing care, day
treatment, residential care, education or training, community organization, or counseling. These services vary greatly in the degree to
which performance criteria and outcomes can be specified. This is
why outputs — i.e., activities that easily lend themselves to quantifi-
cation, such as the number of interviews, meals served, and hospital
days — are usually substituted for outcomes. This practice contributes to charges of interference and overregulation stemming from excessive governmental reporting requirements.

Demands for information can be a particular problem for a small
voluntary agency because it lacks the administrative resources to comply without seriously cutting into its service capability. A New York
City study showed that small voluntary agencies spend proportionately more money to support their governmental programs than
do large and medium-size agencies.[27] The fact that purchase of service
arrangements may be more disadvantageous to a small agency is ironic
because small size, flexibility, and informality are supposed to be the
advantages of a voluntary organization when compared with a government bureaucracy. The virtues that make the voluntary agency a
valuable resource for government are at the same time the source of
conditions that militate against its complying with the demands of
accountability — to compete successfully and to comply with governmental regulations, the small agency must become more bureaucratic and must lose the very qualities that made it a desirable service
provider.

In addition to the dangers of bureaucratization, which are a particular concern of small agencies, there is a further fear that the voluntary
agency, as it becomes more preoccupied with efficiency and cost-
effectiveness, will inevitably become more like the profit-making
organizations with which it must compete. The growing entrepreneurism in the social services is regarded with concern by many government officials and social work professionals, who are inherently

26. Young and Finch, pp. 232–33. See also Lourie; Raymond M. Steinberg et al., "Area
Agencies on Aging: A Case Study of a Controversial Contract for Service"; and David Z. Robinson, "Government Contracting for Academic Research: Accountability in the American Experience," p. 110.

27. Greater New York Fund, pp. 15–16, 94–104.

suspicious of the profit motive and deplore its growing incursions into a field long dominated by charitable organizations.[28] However, there could be advantages in attracting profit-making organizations to the social services. These organizations would introduce choice into an area long characterized by scarcity and voluntary agency monopoly. Competition might even have the effect of raising standards or of strengthening the government's resolve to require compliance to higher standards. The latter, though, could lead to stronger regulatory mechanisms that, if effective, might reduce the independence of voluntary organizations and encourage adversarial relationships between government and social service providers similar to those found in other fields dependent on government funds.[29] Another possibility is that because of governmental deficiencies in monitoring the more subtle and indirect aspects of the social services, there will be a tendency to simplify and to reduce standards to quantifiable terms, and that voluntary agencies will be judged by profit-making criteria.

Finally, there is no agreement on the proportion of an agency's budget that can come from a single source without dominating the organization. Although some voluntary agency executives believe that an agency should not depend on any one source for more than 50 percent of its income, there is no evidence that this or any other percentage is an effective guideline for the acceptance of public funds or the preservation of autonomy.[30] There is, however, consensus on the

28. See footnote 10 and Alfred J. Kahn, "A Framework for Public-Voluntary Collaboration in the Social Services," and the rejoinders by Joseph M. Reid and Merle E. Springer. See also Kurt Reichert, "The Drift toward Enterpreneurialism in Health and Social Welfare: Implications for Social Work Education."

29. In addition to the long-standing opposition to government regulation by business and industry, increasingly adversarial relations have developed between universities and their federal funding sources in the United States. Paralleling the enormously expanded federal investment in university research and training programs have been widespread complaints of excessive regulation and interference with autonomy and academic freedom. See Price, pp. 75–92, and Derek C. Bok, "The Federal Government and the University." Influencing the degree of potential conflict between government and the providers of the personal social services is a high degree of dependency between the public funding agency and a small number of voluntary agencies, some of which practically have service monopolies. On the structural limits of governmental monitoring in this field, see Young and Finch, pp. 20–21, 89–93, and 232–34. The general inadequacies of governmental audits are outlined in General Accounting Office, *Grant Auditing: A Maze of Inconsistency, Gaps, and Duplication That Needs Overhauling.* See also Ira Sharkansky, *Wither the State? Politics and Public Enterprise in Three Countries,* pp. 130–44, on the problem of controlling "organizations on the margin of the State."

30. Kenneth R. Wedel, "Government Contracting for Purchase of Service," *Social Work* 21 (February 1976): 105; Filer, p. 17. On six other strategies for coping with dependency, see S. L. Elkin, "Comparative Urban Politics and Interorganizational Behavior." In addition to diversity, Pifer, pp. 12–13, posits a high degree of technical complexity, high prestige, size as important factors in minimizing dependency. Also see Burian, pp. 173–94.

importance of income diversity as a means of avoiding overdependency. To put it conversely, organizational autonomy is a function of multiple sources of financing; the lesser the dependency on any single source, whether voluntary or governmental, the greater the degree of freedom and choice and the possibility that an agency can determine its own destiny with an optimum degree of discretion. As the Filer Commission observed:

> Perhaps the most effective, and most possible, safeguard of autonomy is to have more than one purse to draw from. The presence of a firm core of private support, however small, in a private organization that gets major public funding can be of crucial importance in determining whether the managers of the organization regard themselves and behave as independent operators or as civil servants.[31]

Although income diversity may be good for a voluntary agency, it constitutes a formidable obstacle to efforts to coordinate agencies funded by a multiplicity of governmental agencies, foundations, and other private sources. Reliance by voluntary agencies on time-limited, categorical grants further aggravates the fragmentation, which continues to defy most governmentally sponsored efforts at service integration in the local community. Government grants might appear to be a way in which the voluntary sector could be influenced to develop a more integrated, comprehensive system to counteract the natural fragmentation that results from each agency going its own way. But this assumes a degree of intragovernmental collaboration and planning that does not often occur. Instead, there is an endemic lack of coordination among the federal agencies, which sponsor, among them, more than 400 separate categorical programs. Indeed, the lack of consistency and communication among governmental agencies and their conflicting policies and standards constitute one of the most serious administrative problems for voluntary agencies. Perhaps this is part of the price of pluralism and may necessitate lowered expectations about a more coherent service system.

31. Filer, p. 98.

PART III

Patterns of Organizational Behavior: How Voluntary Agencies Perform Their Roles

The internal structure of voluntary agencies, their governance, and their fiscal resource systems provide the basis for the performance of their organizational roles. Four functions have generally been expected of voluntary agencies: pioneering, the promotion of volunteerism, advocacy, and the provision of services. Each of the next four chapters is devoted to one of these roles, and similarities and differences in the ways in which they are performed in the four countries are described and explained. Among the internal organizational and external factors that account for the particular pattern in each country are professional ideologies, executive leadership, the public policy environment, and the civic culture. In each chapter theoretical and policy implications of the findings are also noted.

9. The Vanguard Role or Service Pioneer

The Pioneering Tradition

It has long been assumed that one of the primary functions of the voluntary agency is to pioneer in developing services and to pave the way for their adoption by governmental bodies. This trailblazing role was regarded by Lord Beveridge as responsible for "the perpetually moving frontier of voluntary action" and as the historical source of the welfare state, which has been described as "voluntary action crystallized and made universal."[1]

Strictly speaking, the term *pioneering* is most appropriate to describe voluntary agencies that served the physically and mentally handicapped during the nineteenth century. At that time, the prevailing social philosophies of Social Darwinism and individualism in both the United States and England assured voluntary organizations of a virtual monopoly on provision of the personal social services because of a lack of sanction for, and the incapability of government to undertake, such responsibilities. This was particularly evident in England, where, until the 1890s, local administration lacked even the authority to obtain the necessary resources for adequate sewerage, water supplies, and refuse collection. Not until 1893 was special education for blind and deaf children recognized as a governmental responsibility, many years after schools for such children had been established by voluntary organizations. In addition, voluntary agencies pioneered in the development of hospitals; health visiting; institutions for children, the aged, and the handicapped; labor exchanges; parks and open spaces; and most other social welfare functions subsequently assumed by the government. But by the time the essential foundation of the postwar welfare state was established in England and local authorities were given power for the first time to provide personal social services to the disabled, most of the pioneering programs of the voluntary agencies had already been transferred to or adopted by government.

1. Cited in David Owen, *English Philanthropy, 1660–1960*, pp. 534 and 575.

However, there was no single, consistent pattern in this field of service. The classic flow from private invention to public adoption is clearly revealed in the case of the mentally handicapped in England. Voluntary institutions and programs, originally developed in the latter half of the nineteenth century, exceeded their statutory counterparts in number and in rate of growth well into the 1920s. By 1938, however, most of them had been taken over by the local authorities.

This process continued well into the early 1950s, when parents of mentally handicapped children began to organize and later to establish a new network of community facilities for their children, while pressing government to expand and improve statutory services. Beginning in the late 1960s, a new cycle began when the National Society for Mentally Handicapped Children and the Spastics Society initiated efforts to transfer some of their institutions, schools, and day centers to local authorities, who had by then assumed responsibility for two-thirds of all the mentally handicapped receiving care. In a similar manner, institutions originally established by voluntary organizations, such as the Invalid Children's Aid Association for tubercular and crippled children, were taken over by statutory authorities, who also began to build their own institutions for care of the physically handicapped, a field that was dominated almost exclusively by voluntary organizations until World War II.

In sharp contrast to this pattern, however, the services pioneered in England by voluntary associations for the blind and the deaf produced very few adoptions by statutory bodies. Instead, the energies of the voluntary organizations were directed towards influencing public policy to obtain financial assistance for the blind and fees and grants for the voluntary organizations, which served as delegate agencies for the local authorities.[2]

Voluntary agency pioneering took a different form in the United States, where governmental responsibility came much later, reluctantly, and often in response to social action on the part of non-governmental organizations. Although many of the service modes adopted in public programs came from voluntary sources, typically the government assumed fiscal responsibility for service needs originally provided solely by voluntary organizations, and then relied on a combination of public and private agencies to deliver the service. There were significant regional variations in the United States. The

2. The development of the vanguard role in England is discussed in Ralph M. Kramer, "Voluntary Agencies in the Welfare State: An Analysis of the Vanguard Role."

British pattern of a voluntary organization preceding the development of governmental programs occurred less often in the West, where many nongovernmental organizations were founded after public responsibility was accepted. For example, all but four of the agencies in the San Francisco Bay Area were organized after World War II, in contrast to their English counterparts, one-third of which were established in the nineteenth century.

The dynamic of development in the U.S. public sector is thus more complex, and it is rarely the case that government is doing today what voluntary agencies did yesterday. Indeed, the idea of the voluntary agency as vanguard is regarded as an outdated myth by such policy analysts as Alvin Schorr, who stated:

> Most significant attempts at pioneering in the social services during the 1960s — innovative juvenile delinquency programs, community action, new services initiated under social security amendments, community care of the mentally ill, model cities — were largely inspired and set in motion by government. Thus the decade's major examples of pioneering have marginal connections with voluntary (or proprietary) social services or owe it nothing.[3]

In the Netherlands, a different process took place. The primary service delivery system of voluntary organizations under denominational auspices emerged only after World War II. Before that time, the personal social services were not a major concern of the confessional blocs, and very limited programs were sponsored by local governments or private organizations not affiliated with the religious denominations. In the postwar period, the nongovernmental organizational structure has become so institutionalized that there is little likelihood any of the operating programs will ever be taken over by government. Instead, pioneering takes the form of the diffusion of program ideas that may be adopted by other voluntary organizations. The major exception to this pattern is the sheltered workshops originally developed in the 1930s by a voluntary agency and adopted by most municipal governments. They are one of the few functions not sponsored by nongovernmental organizations in the Netherlands today.

In Israel, voluntary organizations pioneered in developing most social institutions in the prestate period under the British mandate from 1923 to 1948. The entire social, political, and economic infrastructure included a wide range of social services under voluntary auspices,

3. Alvin L. Schorr, "The Tasks for Volunteerism in the Next Decade," pp. 431–32.

which were rapidly transferred to governmental sponsorship after the declaration of statehood in 1948. However, because of the extraordinary demands on the state for defense and for absorption of almost a million immigrants, many programs — such as preschool education, day care, health services, and programs for the aged and the physically and mentally handicapped — were left in the hands of voluntary organizations. Despite the expanded scope of government, new voluntary agencies came into being in the 1950s, including all but two of the fifteen in the sample.

The Processes of Program Change
Extent of Innovation

The findings in all four countries suggest that, since World War II, much of what is termed "pioneering" or "innovation" in this field of service consists of the "discovery" of small groups of previously overlooked or underserved disabled persons. The arousal of public awareness usually comes from new, self-help associations of handicapped persons whose needs for care and treatment have been relatively neglected. In contrast, the older, more established agencies, such as most of those in the case studies, function as a vanguard only in a circumscribed way, rarely developing and transferring new methods or specific programs to statutory bodies, and tending rather to incorporate them into existing programs. Authentic social inventions, true innovations that are original or the first of their kind, are the exception. More common are "new programs" or changes that extend, expand, or improve an existing voluntary service.[4] Hence, *vanguard* may no longer be an appropriate term for describing such program changes, and the concept should be redefined to conform more closely to actual practice.

The agency executives in the study were asked to describe in detail the development of their most important new programs during the preceding ten to fifteen years. A program was accepted as "new" if it was perceived as such by the agency executive, even if it was not objectively new for the community or the field of service. It was believed that there would be a natural bias toward reporting in the most

4. The usage of the term *new program* in this study is similar to that described in Gerald Zaltman, Robert Duncan, and Jonny Holbek, *Innovations and Organizations*, pp. 7–14 — i.e., newness as subjectively perceived. See also Michael Aiken and Jerald Hage, "The Organic Organization and Innovation," p. 69. There are inherent methodological difficulties in studying innovation that, together with differences in understanding of the concept in the four countries, make quantitative comparisons rather crude, suitable only for cautious generalizations.

TABLE 11.
New Programs

	United States (N = 20)	England (N = 20)	The Netherlands (N = 20)	Israel (N = 15)
New Programs Reported	69	53	43	38
Agency Average	3.6	2.6	1.8	2.3

favorable way, and, therefore, that the findings, summarized in Table 11, could be interpreted on the assumption that the agencies were making the strongest possible case for themselves.

The small number of new programs for the entire sample is noteworthy. That this is not exceptional is suggested by a Canadian study of 208 agencies in twelve cities, which also found that executives reported an average of only 2.5 new programs between 1962 and 1972.[5] In addition, there were variations in each country — three or four agencies reported five or six new programs, whereas others had difficulty recalling more than one or two. In England, two voluntary agencies had to go back over twenty years to describe a significant program innovation. The U.S. agencies reported the largest number of new programs over the shortest period of time, and, in all four countries, the agencies that are the most active vanguards are also among the largest, most bureaucratic and most professional.

Types of New Programs

There were many more similarities than differences among the countries in the rate of development of new programs, as well as in some other attributes. Although the new programs were similar in function, scope, and content, they reflected the particular pattern of service distribution between governmental and voluntary agencies, the level of service development, and the fiscal resources available for different programs in each country.

Most new programs were rehabilitative or supportive rather than preventive. In the United States, the most frequently reported type of new program (one out of four) was vocational rehabilitation, followed by counseling or social work services and employment programs. The U.S. programs were much less building-centered than those in the

5. Novia Carter, *Trends in Voluntary Support for Non-Governmental Social Service Agencies*, pp. 61–63. Similar findings are reported in Jerald Hage and Michael Aiken, "Program Change and Organizational Properties: A Comparative Analysis."

other countries. In England, social work and counseling programs were most frequently mentioned, along with residential care, holiday homes, and professional-training programs. In the Netherlands, where professionalism in social work is more advanced than in England, such building-centered programs as schools, day care centers, sheltered housing, and recreation were reported most often. In Israel, vocational training, education, and recreational programs, as well as facility improvement, were the leading new programs.

Apart from these differences, the vanguard role in the four countries appeared to be quite similar: almost without exception, the service programs inaugurated are small-scale, noncontroversial, and incremental, if not marginal, extensions or improvements of conventional personal social services to a clientele previously underserved. Typical examples are toy libraries for mentally handicapped children, holiday homes for the disabled, respite programs and halfway houses, sports competition, infant stimulation programs, and activity centers.[6] Among the few truly innovative programs were those sponsored by three agencies in the United States that had no counterpart in any of the other countries and that in themselves exemplified an original social invention: the Golden Gate Regional Center, the Center for Independent Living, and the San Francisco Center for Recreation for the Handicapped.[7]

Program Origins

How do new programs get started? Who takes the initiative? At least two-thirds of the programs were initiated by professional staff members in the agency or in a governmental funding body. In the United States and England, the idea of inaugurating the remaining one-third of the new programs was ascribed to the community, the board members, or clientele.

6. A detailed list of the new programs of the Dutch agencies can be found in Gerrit J. Kronjee, *Particulier initiatief in de gehandicaptenzorg*, p. 36.

7. The Golden Gate Regional Center is one of twenty-three state-authorized and financed, nongovernmental organizations mandated to provide directly or through purchase all services needed by the developmentally disabled during their lifetimes. The Center for Independent Living in Berkeley is a consumer-operated agency, organized by disabled and blind persons, which provides over twenty-five different services in the East Bay area. It has served as the prototype for nineteen other Independent Living programs in California and seven others in the rest of the United States. See Hal R. Kreshbaum, Dominic S. Harveston, and Alfred H. Katz, "Independent Living for the Disabled," pp. 59–62. The San Francisco Center for Recreation for the Handicapped is one of the very few agencies in the United States with a full range of year-round indoor and outdoor social, recreational, and camping programs for severely mentally and physically handicapped children and adults, as well as emotionally disturbed children.

In at least 10 to 15 percent of the cases in the United States, representatives of governmental agencies approached voluntary agencies and suggested funding new programs. In the Netherlands, where few service programs are administered by government, officials in the CRM are also a source of innovation through planting ideas among nongovernmental organizations, as well as through launching such demonstration projects as day care for mentally handicapped in the early 1960s and volunteer centers in the 1970s. In Israel, the JDC-Malben professional staff provided the ideas and funds for at least one-third of the new programs launched by six of the fifteen Israeli voluntary agencies.

The more professionalized agencies in all countries tend to play a more active vanguard role. The new programs they initiate are essentially improvements and expansions of current services, rather than identification of an underserved population at risk. The latter function is more likely to be performed by voluntary associations composed of the handicapped themselves or of their families. The major exception to this pattern is the extension of services by some voluntary agencies for the blind and for victims of cerebral palsy to certain multiply handicapped groups, such as persons who are both blind and deaf or both mentally handicapped and cerebral palsied.

Despite their professional origins, few of the new programs were preceded by research or fact-finding. In England, less than one-quarter of the new programs reported any previous data collection to establish need and only about one-third were later evaluated. There was little demand to justify a decision on a more objective basis by reference to some previous assessment of needs as in the United States, where about one-third of the programs involved some sort of systematic fact-finding before they were launched. Generally, larger and more professionalized agencies are more research-oriented,[8] but the rational basis for the development of new programs is weak in all four countries. Most of the time, new services are offered in response to the multiple pressures of professional staff seeking to extend their

8. For example, the Invalid Children's Aid Association utilized empirical research data from one of their schools for handicapped children to justify the building of a new institution. A study of forty-nine children with severe speech and language disorders due to brain dysfunction who left the school between 1958 and 1965 showed that forty-eight of them were not able to cope with secondary education. On this basis, it was decided to establish a new school, one of three in the entire country to offer longer, more intensive, and more specialized educational and social experiences. The facility and the program are designed to permit experimentation with new methods to help the children to develop their powers of speech and the use of language.

technology, board members with personal interests in programs for their family members, and opportunities for support presented by funding bodies and individual donors.

In some situations the absence of prior study and analysis was explained by: (1) previously collected epidemiological data on the population at risk, (2) other information regarding the present scope of the agency's program and the nature of the target population, (3) a long-standing consensus on the desirability of certain forms of care, treatment, or rehabilitation, such as speech therapy or group counseling. Also, conventional programs may not require additional factual support because they are neither controversial nor risky. Only nine of the fifty-three new programs in England aroused any opposition, either within the agency or within the community. In the United States, less than a fifth of the programs involved some resistance, and this was usually caused by a dispute over organizational domain.[9]

The small scale and incremental character of most budgets, staffs, and clientele also contribute to the noncontroversial character of the new programs. One out of four of the new English programs required no additional funds, and less than half added more than ten new staff members. The average number of beneficiaries in the English programs was also correspondingly low, ranging from fifty to seventy-five. Over 50 percent of the programs had budgets of less than £20,000 in 1973–1974, and only one-third involved a larger sum. In the United States, the median budget of the new programs was $20,000; most of them served fewer than one hundred clients and employed fewer than ten staff members. (As we shall see, the small scale of these new programs may account for a lack of adoption by government, because they may not be suitable for larger populations.)

Despite their predominantly noncontroversial nature and small scale, the new programs take time to develop. About one-third of the programs in the United States and 40 percent of those in England took

9. More prevalent than opposition to those new program ideas was a lack of enthusiasm or readiness. Despite a board-staff consensus on the vast range of unmet needs, there may be a built-in conservative disposition in voluntary agencies that militates against any unfamiliar program idea constituting a substantial change. This resistance to change may be reinforced, paradoxically, by either the marginal or the consumer character of agency board members, the diversity of interests among professionals and volunteers, as well as among the various disciplines represented on the staff. See Kramer, "Ideology, Status and Power," pp. 108–14. The inhibiting effects of diversity and complexity on innovation are analyzed by James Q. Wilson, "Innovation in Organization: Notes Toward a Theory" pp. 195–218.

over two years to become established. In England, another third took
from two to five years to get started.

Financing New Programs

The role of the fiscal resource system is critical to the organization
of new programs because funds are rarely reallocated from existing
programs. Where do the new funds come from? In England, the
Netherlands, and Israel, contributed funds are the foremost source of
the initial financing of virtually all new programs, whereas in the
United States almost half of the new programs are started with government funds. In Israel, JDC-Malben is a major supplier of funds
for new programs, functioning much like a foundation or a U.S. governmental agency in providing seed money for demonstrations by voluntary agencies. Although government almost completely finances
the social services in the Netherlands, voluntary funds are necessary
for program initiation because the subsidy system can only support
well-established, ongoing programs. Ordinarily, only after three to
five years or more is a new service eligible for a subsidy. Therefore,
interim funds must be obtained from private foundations, from other
civic organizations, or through the few public campaigns in the
Netherlands. Such contributions are often difficult to obtain because
of widespread public knowledge of the system of governmental subsidies, which are assumed to meet all costs.

Fund-raising interests also affect the character of new programs because some donors are interested in such visible projects as buildings
and equipment. In one case, a public relations staff member per-
suaded an agency board to revive a listless campaign for funds by
launching the construction of continuing care units in hospitals as
memorials to athletes who had died from the disease.

Innovative Programs

The most vigorous performance of the vanguard role in producing
new programs or changes in programs is in the United States. In no
other country, of course, are newness and change as valued as in the
United States. Innovation is rarely questioned — the assumption is
that if a service or a product is new, it must be better. Accordingly, in
approaching public and private funding sources, voluntary agencies
customarily describe their programs as innovative; however, this is
more symbolic than real. In practice, new voluntary agency programs

are rarely demonstrations or pilot projects — less than half of the U.S. samples were even designated as such — but are instead a means for carrying out an agency's existing function. Because the static level of income from community campaigns requires a constant search for new funds, many voluntary agencies in the United States operate in an entrepreneurial and opportunistic manner.

The cult of innovation is coupled with a strong commitment to planned social intervention, reflected in the vast outpouring of legislation in the United States, where government is expected to respond to problem conditions with social programs or funds. No other country makes such an investment of government and philanthropic funds — embodied in a public policy of "guided innovation" and supported by a grants economy — for research and demonstration by voluntary organizations. In contrast, the other countries place a higher priority on the use of governmental funding for implementation of existing programs, and expect the voluntary sector to find its own resources for new projects. In England, the broad scope of the statutory personal social services means that new voluntary agency programs can be supported through fees for service or grant-aids only if they provide a resource needed by the local authority. The priority given to implementing existing programs explains in part the lack of statutory funds available to start new programs; in any case, the local authority would have prior claim on such funds. Voluntary agencies in England are also limited by a lack of professionalization on the local level and by the restriction of governmental grant-aids to national agencies for administrative purposes.

In the Netherlands, the fiscal system of subsidies and social insurance is oriented less toward innovation than toward extending current services to underserved groups. Substantial departures in the mode of intervention or the selection of a new clientele must first be demonstrated with nongovernmental funds. This is not as difficult as it appears because Dutch agencies are regarded by their professional peers as in the forefront of developing new ideas and of maintaining a high quality of service. Subsidies and social insurance, however, ultimately shape the character of new programs because programs must receive support from either or both of these sources if a service is to continue. As a result, there is an interaction between the relatively stable sources of funds — subsidies and insurance — and agency innovation, in which the governmental fiscal system has to be progressively enlarged in order to accommodate new needs and services. However, the reported

lack of use by voluntary agencies of the limited governmental funds
for research and development is surprising.

In Israel, the government has never made a strong policy commitment to research and demonstration in the field of services for the
physically and mentally handicapped or to promotion of new government programs in the personal social services. Government funds
have been more available for direct operation than for new programs,
so voluntary agencies rely on independent fund raising to support additional or improved services.

Adoptions and Transfers of New Programs

Once new programs are implemented, what happens to them? Are
they pioneered by voluntary agencies and then adopted by government? Despite the widespread belief that voluntary innovation paves
the way for eventual governmental operation, few of the programs
were adopted by government: in the United States, 5 percent; in England, 9 percent; in Israel, 3 percent; and in the Netherlands, none.
The rest were continued and institutionalized by the voluntary agencies that originally sponsored them. Half the programs that were continued in England received some form of statutory support in the form
of grant-aids or payments for service. That most of the projects were
not suitable for transfer or adoption is evident in the fact that only five
of the fifty-three were taken over by statutory bodies and that six
other program ideas were adopted by other voluntary agencies.

The facilities transferred from voluntary to statutory auspices include special schools, hospitals, short-stay homes, and other residential centers. One of the few that fit the ideal type is the Slough project
of the NSMHC. Six years of planning and discussion preceded the
establishment of this project in 1962, specifically for adoption by Buckinghamshire County Council. The purpose was to demonstrate that
mentally handicapped teenagers with IQs below 50 need not be hospi-
talized, but can live in a community hostel with house-parents rather
than uniformed staff and can be trained for full-time employment.
The idea for this project came from the research of Professor Jack
Tizzard of London University, who conducted a small residential-care
experiment in which mentally handicapped adolescents showed considerable progress in the new setting. The initiative for the NSMHC
project came from the director and some of the parent members of the
executive committee of the NSMHC, whose mentally handicapped
adolescents faced a dismal future in a subnormality hospital. In spite

of opposition from the residents of the community, the project began with funding from the society and, after seven years of what was considered to be successful operation by the NSMHC, the center was transferred to Buckinghamshire County Council. According to the agency, the center subsequently became a prototype for hostels and similar programs for the mentally handicapped operated by other voluntary and statutory organizations.

Other transfers of voluntary agency programs do not fit the ideal type. These include efforts by agencies operating residential institutions, day care centers, nurseries, hostels, and schools in England to rid themselves of the burdens of escalating costs by selling, transferring, or even giving the facilities to a local authority. Two of the largest British agencies have also tried to restrict new buildings or demonstration projects to those that can be transferred to a statutory body. In addition, four types of community program (home helps, meals-on-wheels, day centers, and holidays) were originally developed by voluntary agencies and were then progressively transferred to local authorities when they became too large for the original sponsor to manage or when they became too routine and standardized, and offered no cost advantage to the local authority. Because it is not always possible to determine whether a voluntary agency is being bailed out by a local authority, whether it is getting rid of an albatross around its neck, or whether the takeover results from mismanagement, adoption by a statutory agency may not be a reliable "vindicator" of the vanguard role.

The pilot study of eleven Social Service Departments in the Greater London area reported no voluntary agency pioneering during the past fifteen years that has resulted in statutory adoption of services. This response should be interpreted cautiously because it may reveal more about the perceptions and information of the directors of the social services than about the actual role of voluntary organizations in the community. Admittedly, the origins of new programs are often obscure, multiple, and difficult to recall, but it is significant that none of the twenty national agencies reported any service transfers in London, with the exception of the transfer of many of the NSMHC training centers to the educational authorities in 1971. Another possibility is that local innovative programs were started by indigenous, self-help associations rather than by the organizations in the sample.

In the United States, only four of the sixty-nine new programs were adopted by a governmental unit and three by other organizations, despite the fact that thirty out of the sixty-nine were described as pilot projects or demonstrations. In the United States and the Netherlands, the adoption of a program idea by other voluntary agencies is more typical than the transfer of a program to a governmental body.[10]

One of the best examples of an agency able to secure the adoption of its programs by government is JDC-Malben in Israel. The most extensive program transfer between 1971 and 1976 was a phased withdrawal from the JDC-Malben institutional and community service programs for the immigrant aged and disabled. These programs became part of a comprehensive community plan developed by new local and regional planning associations organized by JDC-Malben and funded by the national government. Earlier, JDC-Malben's pioneering assessment center for the mentally retarded, located in a general hospital, was adopted as a model by the Ministry of Social Welfare.[11]

There are two sets of reasons for the nonadoption of programs originally developed by voluntary agencies: (1) those related to national policy on the relationship between governmental and voluntary agencies, for example, the preference in England for statutory operation and in the United States for separation of financing and administrative responsibility; (2) interorganizational factors. Four interorganizational conditions can militate against the likelihood of governmental adoption of new voluntary programs. First, a demonstrated program may be inappropriate for governmental operation because of its *size*. Governmental provision to a small group may be difficult to justify, or a service modality may be effective for a small number of selected clients, but not if it must be available to all who might be eligible.

Second, apart from its scale, the *values* embodied in a demonstrated service may militate against adoption by government because they are sectarian, unpopular, controversial, or not yet considered legitimate

10. In a report on the United States prepared for an eight-country study of selected social services, it was observed that "in fact there are few illustrations in recent years of new service models being developed in the private sector and adopted subsequently by the public sector" (Sheila B. Kamerman and Alfred J. Kahn, *Social Services in the United States*, p. 449). Although organizations serving the mentally handicapped have been urged to transfer their service programs to government so that they can concentrate on advocacy, this seldom occurs. Virtually all of the "new" programs of the agencies in the San Francisco Bay Area were extensions and improvements made possible by government funds. Similar findings are reported in Greater New York Fund, *Impact of Government Funding on the Management of Voluntary Agencies*, p. 8.

11. The distinctive character of JDC-Malben is described in Ralph M. Kramer, *The Voluntary Service Agency in Israel*, pp. 46–47, 49–50. Also see Yechiel Eran, "A New Model of Voluntary Organization in Israel."

for the public domain. Services addressed to the sexual life of the handicapped might fall in this category.

Third, the absence of *congruent administrative boundaries* between national voluntary agencies and statutory organizations in England has made transfers difficult since the former operate on a regional basis, and there is no appropriate regional statutory authority to take over. The same difficulties are the source of one of the distinctive advantages of the voluntary agency, its "boundary-spanning" capabilities, which permit it to overcome some of the fragmentation of governmental jurisdictions and their geographic and functional "departmentalism."

Fourth, in addition to other fiscal, political, or administrative considerations, a particular clientele or service may have a *low priority* in governmental planning and budgeting.

Apart from limitations within government, there are also intrinsic resistances within voluntary agencies to the transfer of services. The fear that a service may be lower in quality when administered by government was found in England with reference to the blind, and in Israel in two of the largest agencies serving the mentally and physically handicapped. Similarly, service norms or a stigma attached to governmental operation may be unacceptable to the original sponsors. Other voluntary agency leaders stress the unique propensity of their organizations for pioneering and oppose the progressive enlargement of governmental responsibility for ideological reasons. Also, vested interests in programs persist for reasons of sentiment and of fund raising. Tangible service programs to the handicapped have always had great appeal for contributors; hence, voluntary agencies are reluctant to give them up.

Some of these attitudes were criticized by the executive of one of the largest voluntary agencies in England, who urged his colleagues "to withdraw from work that is duplicated by state services as and when the state can accept responsibility." But he added:

> Unfortunately [this] practice is contrary to the demand of human nature. Voluntary societies are apt to be terribly possessive about their work and most unwilling to concede that the march of progress has overtaken them. . . . There is, therefore, a contradiction between what we say and what we do. Far from being prepared to relinquish our work, we strive to show that the state cannot do without us, not because we are engaged in experimental pioneer work, that phase may be completed, but because we have a natural pride in the empire we have built and the money available

from public funds for the support of established work protects us from financial sanctions.[12]

Some voluntary agencies in England made a strong argument for retaining services they had pioneered because of their usefulness for research, training, and education. Other justifications included the provision of specialized services for very small groups for whom statutory programs would be uneconomical or not administratively feasible and offering opportunities for volunteer participation, choice, and functioning as a standard-setter. Because of changing attitudes toward government in the United States and the wide use of voluntary agencies as public-service providers, there the idea of transferring a program is given less serious consideration.[13]

The existence of parallel services under both governmental and voluntary auspices has often been labeled pejoratively as "duplication" and regarded as an obstacle to the efficient use of limited voluntary resources. There seems to be a double standard regarding the desirability of choice in a market economy and in the social services. It can be argued, however, that redundancy of services is not always a sign of waste and inefficiency, and that it is not necessarily dysfunctional. It can provide a safety factor and can permit more flexible responses and creative possibilities, in addition to promoting diversity and choice and increasing accessibility.[14]

Reevaluation of the Vanguard Role

The findings suggest a need for reconceptualizing the vanguard function. Despite a lack of supporting evidence, the mystique of the voluntary agency as a vanguard persists. Agencies in England continue to refer to themselves as "essentially a suicidal organization," as "practicing euthanasia," or, less dramatically, as "trying to put ourselves out of business" — although, like the state in Marxian theory, they fail to "wither away."

A less simplistic version of the vanguard role should provide for

12. Gordon Franklin, *Evangelical Charity in a Changing World,* p. 16.
13. In 1958, there was strong sentiment on the part of voluntary agency board members in the San Francisco Bay Area in favor of transferring many of their service programs to government (Ralph M. Kramer, "Governmental and Voluntary Agencies: A Study of Lay and Professional Attitudes.")
14. Martin Landau, "Redundancy, Rationality and the Problem of Duplication and Overlap." See also Harold L. Wilensky and Charles N. Lebeaux, *Industrial Society and Social Welfare,* pp. 255–57, for a critique of the concept of duplication and how its use obscures power struggles between groups with different values and interests.

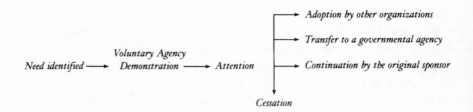

Figure 2. Possible Outcomes of Programs Initiated by Voluntary Agencies
(Reprinted courtesy of Cambridge University Press.)

several possible outcomes — intended or not — of voluntary agency
pioneering or program initiation. A program demonstration by a voluntary agency ideally draws attention to the program, which can then
be followed by one or more of the following: (1) adoption by *diffusion*
of the idea of the program to governmental or other voluntary agencies, (2) *transfer* to or takeover by a governmental body, (3) *continuation*
of the service by the voluntary agency as part of its ongoing program,
with or without governmental support, (4) *cessation* of the new program after the initial funding has expired because neither (2) nor (3)
has occurred.

These alternative outcomes are graphically portrayed in Figure 2.

It is widely believed that the propensity to innovate is found more
often among voluntary than among governmental agencies. An opposing view asserts that, while no organization has a monopoly on innovation, in the future it is more likely to occur within the governmental
sector.[15] Governmental organizations have a broader scope, greater
complexity, and more resources than voluntary agencies; in England,
they also have 90 percent of the professionally trained social workers.
All of these may be conducive to experimentation. There is considerable evidence of the ability of local authorities in England to initiate
new programs, particularly multiple-use facilities and services for the
multiply handicapped. However, one cannot ignore the persistent lack

15. Compare the conclusion of Barbara N. Rodgers, *Cross-National Studies of Social Service
Systems*, p. 47: "The British local authorities today do as much experimenting as do the voluntary
organisations."

of sufficient funds to carry out existing and mandatory, statutory responsibilities. Under these circumstances, a greater value may be attached to implementation than to newness per se.

In the United States, both governmental and voluntary organizations engage in research and demonstration projects, but governmental interests, priorities, and funds are unquestionably dominant in shaping the types of new programs developed by voluntary agencies.

If voluntary agencies are not pioneers in the sense that government adopts their new programs, then in what ways are they vanguards? One answer is that different types of innovation are produced at their inception and after they are more institutionalized. New, more indigenous, less bureaucratized and professionalized organizations are frequently regarded as demonstrating the cutting edge of voluntarism.[16] They usually identify previously neglected groups at the boundaries of government welfare programs, such as rape victims, battered wives, drug addicts, and sexual deviants. As one voluntary agency executive pithily put it, "It is the nonconformists who pioneer, the conformists who cooperate." Because voluntary agencies are more likely to be trail-blazers in their early stages, their high birth rate, more than their proverbial low mortality, helps ensure changes in the social services. Paradoxically, the oft-criticized "proliferation" of voluntary agencies expresses a resurgent vitality and constitutes one of the prerequisites for the performance of the vanguard function.

But the development of new programs is not restricted to less bureaucratized organizations at their inception when, literally, any program could be considered innovative because it did not previously exist, at least not under its new auspices. In the more institutionalized agencies, such as those in this study, forces inherent in the rationality of the bureaucratic structure, in the professional interests of the staff, and in organizational-maintenance needs are conducive to the development of new programs that extend and improve existing services.

This suggests that the idea of innovation is in need of conceptual clarification. Used indistinguishably with "experimentation," "demonstration," and "pioneering," "innovation" often becomes a ploy in the game of grantsmanship as agencies describe minor modifications and marginal extensions of conventional programs as original breakthroughs in order to compete for funding. Employed in this expedient

16. This principle can be inferred from the analysis of William R. Rosengren, "The Careers of Clients and Organizations." It is reaffirmed in Wolfenden Committee, *The Future of Voluntary Organisations*, pp. 46–48.

Modes of Intervention

Clientele	New	Current
New *(unserved)*	A "hot line" or respite care	Hostel for cerebral palsy
Current	Day centers for the handicapped	Additional social work staff

Figure 3. Two Types of New Programs
(Reprinted courtesy of Cambridge University Press.)

manner, the concept loses meaning and is trivialized. In addition, exaggerated emphasis on innovation by funding bodies in the United States may detract attention from other, more critical aspects of the social services system, such as access, choice, continuity, coherence, effectiveness, equity, and efficiency.

The meaning of *innovation* may be clarified if we distinguish between two kinds of new programs: programs pertaining to changes in a mode of intervention and those referring to services to a newly identified, previously unserved population at risk. This is conceptualized in Figure 3.

In the interests of a greater precision of language, the attribute *innovative* should be restricted to an original mode of intervention or service delivery system — i.e., one that is substantially different from previous efforts. In this sense, it can be used interchangeably with *pioneering*. Because of the social-utility character of the personal social services and the nature of the technology on which they draw, one would not expect to find many bold, innovative departures. Instead, program change or modification would tend to be the norm. It would refer to the extension, replication, or qualitative improvement of existing programs for either a new or a current clientele. The underlying principle is that, while all innovation implies change, not all change involves innovation.[17]

The preceding reevaluation of the vanguard role with its four possible outcomes and this redefinition of innovation both lead to the question of what organizational factors are associated with program change. Innumerable factors have been identified as positively correlated with organizational or program change. Among the most frequently cited are: large size, complexity, low formalization, decentralization, informal interpersonal relations, broad goals, absence of domination by a single professional ideology, executives' professional ideology, orientation toward change, and tolerance of ambiguity. Much research, however, has serious methodological flaws and has produced findings that are equivocal; for example, both large- and small-sized, centralized and decentralized, formal and less formalized organizations have been found to be associated with innovation.[18] The diversity and the idiosyncratic character of most voluntary agencies makes it unlikely that any one set of variables will be found to be conducive to the establishment of new programs. Indeed, it has even been proposed that "voluntary associations will display in exaggerated form the *contrary* tendencies that determine the innovative capacity of all organizations" (italics mine).[19]

The importance of personality variables, rather than structure, in voluntary organizations helps to explain the necessity of commitment and support by executive leadership as a prerequisite for program change.[20] Other facilitating factors are suggested by this study and by other organizational research. First is an organizational crisis affecting funds, management, clientele, and staff, or some other disruptive change in the external or internal environment. In accord with the proverb that "necessity is the mother of invention," a fiscal crisis may,

17. Zaltman, Duncan, and Holbek, p. 158. A similar distinction is made between innovation, development, and reform in social policy in Phoebe Hall et al., *Change, Choice and Conflict in Social Policy*, p. 19, where *development* refers to changes in the scale of an existing program, whereas reform is not a new or innovative departure, but rather a new way of doing something that the state is already doing.

18. Some of the inconsistencies in both concepts and methods in the study of innovation and organizational change are discussed in G. Downs and Lawrence Mohr, "Conceptual Issues in the Study of Innovation"; James Q. Wilson, *Political Organizations*, pp. 12–13; and Ronald G. Corwin, "Strategies for Organizational Innovation."

19. Wilson, "Innovation in Organization," pp. 209–10.

20. The critical role of the executive is the focus of Jerald Hage and R. DeWar, "Elite Values versus Organizational Structure in Predicting Innovation"; Howard B. Kaplan, "Implementation of Program Change in Community Agencies"; and Lawrence V. Mohr, "Determinants of Innovation in Organization," pp. 11–26.

for example, precipitate a creative response in the reorganization of a service delivery system. Second, new programs may be encouraged when a governmental agency is undeveloped and a voluntary agency is at an early stage of development. This condition prevailed until the end of the 1940s in both the United States and England, and in Israel until the 1960s. Third, a high level of professionalization may facilitate changes in the mode of intervention, and a low level contribute to the identification of new target populations. This suggests a differentiation of function between governmental and voluntary agencies whereby the discovery of persons who were previously underserved, as well as those requiring highly specialized care, occurs among small voluntary organizations in an early stage of development. Governmental and more established and professionalized voluntary organizations may then introduce new and different modes of intervention.

These hypotheses are derived from a study of only one field of voluntary service provision. They could be tested for relevance to other types of nongovernmental organizations in different fields of service.

Conclusions

The traditional concept of governmental adoption of voluntary agency pioneering no longer seems apt. There is little evidence that voluntary agencies are the chief sources of innovation for government. Among the possible intrinsic constraints on the transfer to or adoption by government of voluntary agency programs are inappropriate size, unacceptable values, low priority, and lack of administrative, fiscal, and political feasibility. More frequent than pioneering is the development of a small number of low-risk extensions or improvements of existing programs, which are then continued with government funds. Based on these findings and on a more critical view of the concept of innovation, the vanguard role can be reformulated to realistically reflect the multiple possibilities of program initiation.

10.   The Value Guardian Role and Volunteerism

The fact that voluntary service is
still given, and is apparently
still necessary, in an increasingly
egalitarian welfare society may seem
something of a paradox.

THE PRINCE OF WALES,
IN THE HOUSE OF LORDS,
25 JUNE 1975

Beginning with de Tocqueville, the literature on voluntarism is rich in testimonials to its unique and invaluable contributions to a democratic society. Cutting across the political spectrum in the English-speaking world is a virtual unanimity among heads of state, government bureaucrats, corporate, trade union, and military leaders, scholars, professionals, and others on the enriching and indispensable functions of volunteers.[1] An analysis of the reasons given to justify involvement of volunteers reveals a set of individual and social values that voluntary organizations are expected to "guard" — i.e., to protect and promote by offering opportunities for their active expression. These include: altruism, social integration, democratic collective action, self-help, pluralism, and the humanizing or personalizing of the provision of a social service. In addition, voluntary organizations are legitimated in democratic societies to preserve the particularistic interests and values

---

1. Representative of the literature on volunteerism are: Nathan Cohen, ed., *The Citizen Volunteer: His Responsibility, Role and Opportunity in Modern Society;* Eva Schindler-Rainman and Ronald Lippitt, *The Volunteer Community: Creative Uses of Human Resources;* John Cull and Richard Hardy, *Volunteerism: An Emerging Profession;* and Harriet H. Naylor, *Leadership for Volunteering.* Three U.S. journals are devoted exclusively to volunteerism: *Volunteer Administration, Voluntary Action Leadership,* and the *Journal of Voluntary Action Research.* For England, there are two notable books: Mary Morris, *Voluntary Work in the Welfare State,* and Geraldine M. Aves, *The Voluntary Worker in the Social Services.* There are few empirical studies of volunteers in the social services. Among the best are: David L. Sills, *The Volunteers: Means and Ends in a National Organization,* and Roger Hadley, Adrian Webb, and Christine Farrell, *Across the Generations: Old People and Young Volunteers.*

of religious, cultural, social, and other minority groups. Volunteer citizen participation serves separate functions for the individual and for society. The individual acquires organizational skills, political competence, personal satisfaction, integration into a larger milieu, and opportunities to learn norms, acquire information, and avoid loneliness. Voluntary associations mediate between groups of individuals and the larger society, integrating groups into that society and providing opportunities for value communication, development of community services, initiation of change, and the distribution of power.[2]

While few aspects of voluntary organizations are less disputed than the expectation that they nurture various forms of citizen participation, the distinction made in the Introduction between the organizational forms of *voluntarism* and *volunteerism* is important. Not all voluntary organizations involve volunteers in direct service giving, and not all volunteers are attached to voluntary organizations. Because the participation of volunteers in governance and fund raising has been described in chapters 6 and 7, this chapter is restricted to the direct service role of the volunteers — i.e., the person-to-person efforts of an unpaid volunteer in a local community to assist a handicapped person or his family. Often considered the highest form of volunteerism and altruism, this interpersonal help usually takes such forms as: visiting, transporting, shopping, tutoring, and other instances of individual care; offering advice, information, and emotional support; providing social and recreational experience; and advocacy. Sometimes service giving involves a dual function in which the volunteer helps to communicate the nature of the service and the agency to the client and, at the same time, interprets the interests and needs of the client to the agency and the community.

Found in both organizations of and for the handicapped, direct service volunteerism may be carried out by members on a mutual aid basis — for example, by parents of handicapped children — or through the recruitment of volunteers outside the organization. These types of voluntary service are often indistinguishable from help given within the family — which, incidentally, carries the bulk of the responsibility for caring for its handicapped members.[3] In this chapter, we are concerned only with the forms of volunteer service that are sponsored by

    2. David L. Sills, "Voluntary Associations: Sociological Aspects," pp. 372–76; Diana Leat, *Why Volunteers? Ten Points of View.*
    3. Robert Moroney, *The Family and the State: Considerations for Social Policy,* and Michael J. Bayley, *Mental Handicap and Community Care* and *Community-Oriented Systems of Care.* In the

organizations serving the physically and mentally handicapped. Naturally, this gives a very limited picture of the national patterns of voluntary service in England, the Netherlands, and the United States, where it is estimated that at least 15 to 25 percent of the adult population over sixteen years of age may be engaged in some form of voluntary work. Also, because this is a study of voluntary agencies and not volunteerism, such large organizations of volunteers as the American Red Cross and the Women's Royal Voluntary Service were not included.

Finally, there is another limitation, stemming from the composition of the sample and the lack of statistical data, on the extent to which comparative generalizations can be made about the use of service volunteers. All the twenty English voluntary agencies are national organizations, fourteen of which have local affiliates. This is also true of eight of the fifteen Israeli organizations and of eight of the twenty in the Netherlands. To the extent that service volunteers are used, they are found on the local, not the national, level. Unfortunately, few voluntary organizations outside of the United States keep records of their volunteers. This is due less to the small size of the usually overworked headquarters staff than to the high degree of autonomy of the local affiliates, which do not feel obligated to provide information on their activities to their national organizations. Hence, the picture must of necessity be incomplete.

Trends in Volunteer Services

Direct service volunteering can be viewed within the larger context of the great resurgence of volunteerism in the 1970s. A marked increase in the size, scope, and diversity of volunteer effort occurred in the United States and England and, to a lesser extent, in the Netherlands and Israel. In all these countries, there was greater public recognition of the value of volunteerism for society and of its contribution to pluralism, mutual aid, and individual well-being, as well as its usefulness as an organizational resource. Aided by an increase in leisure time, a rising standard of living in the advanced industrial democracies, and a wider diffusion of the norms of citizen participation and self-help, support for volunteer participation has broadened. This is manifested in the emergence of new forms of voluntary work, the changing composition of volunteers, the spread of mutual aid and al-

---

United States, studies show that two-thirds of the mentally handicapped are cared for at home (U.S. Department of Health, Education and Welfare, *Mental Retardation Sourcebook*, p. 24.)

ternative agencies, and an expansion of governmental responsibility for the promotion of volunteerism.

Chief among the new settings for volunteers in the United States and England are those in the public sector, such as courts, the correctional system, mental hospitals, and institutions and community facilities for the aged. In addition to college-educated, middle-class women, many of whom are entering the labor market in the United States, large numbers of students and young adults, as well as men and older retired persons, have entered the ranks of volunteers. In England, a national survey estimated that 16 percent of the population — 5,000,000 persons — work voluntarily for an organization each week. Almost half of the respondents were involved in fund raising, and 18 percent reported various forms of personal service: to the elderly (35 percent) and to the physically handicapped (21 percent), with virtually no mention of the mentally ill or the mentally handicapped.[4] In the United States, a widely publicized "guesstimate" is that one out of every four persons over the age of thirteen does some form of volunteer work weekly, of which at least 10 percent is in the field of social welfare. Studies by the U.S. Department of Labor show an estimated growth in the number of volunteers from 22,000,000 to 37,000,000 between 1965 and 1974, including 4,500,000 volunteers over the age of sixty-five, representing an almost fourfold increase in this category in a decade.[5] There are no comparable figures for Israel, but in the Netherlands, a government official estimated that there are 250,000 volunteers of all types, including 12,000 who work with the handicapped.[6]

New dimensions have been given to voluntary work in the United States by the provision of more tangible rewards, such as high school and university course credit for students and the use of volunteer experience to qualify for jobs or for admission to graduate schools. Also, there is more acceptance of modest payments or expense allowances for volunteers. Another trend is the increasing use of volunteer community service by courts in the United States and England as a form

4. Stephen Hatch, *Voluntary Work: A Report of a Survey,* pp. 1–6; and Wolfenden Committee, *The Future of Voluntary Organisations,* pp. 35–36. The survey of September 1976 consisted of a two-stage, stratified random sample of 2,114 persons sixteen years of age or more in Great Britain. Also notable were the statistically significant differences between social classes, in which the upper- and managerial-professional-class rate of volunteering was almost three times that of lower-skilled classes.

5. U.S. Department of Labor, Manpower Administration, *Americans Volunteer,* and Violet M. Sieder and Doris C. Kirshbaum, "Volunteers."

6. G. Hendriks, *New Trends in Social Welfare Policy in the Netherlands,* p. 82.

of restitution, substituting for punishment by imprisonment or fine. Surprisingly, few questions have been raised about the coercive character of this use of "volunteer" service, evidently on the assumption that it cannot help but be salutary and just.

In addition to new types of individual volunteers and modes of voluntary service, there is a proliferation of new voluntary organizations, particularly peer self-help groups and alternative agencies, in which the line between the helper and the helped, between board member, staff member, and client, is intentionally obscured. As we saw in chapters 1 to 4, during the 1950s, in the four countries studied and others in the Western world, there was a movement by parents and family members of persons suffering from mental handicaps, multiple sclerosis, polio, and cerebral palsy to found organizations to promote their mutual interests. In contrast to the traditional agencies for the blind and the deaf, organizations to benefit these more recently "discovered" handicaps are organizations *of* the handicapped and their guardians. This is less true of the new voluntary organizations launched to deal with such diseases as cancer, cardiac disorders, arthritis, and rheumatism, whose leadership tends to consist of physicians and other community notables. Concurrently, there has been an enormous growth in mutual aid and informal groups organized for purposes of self-fulfillment, advocacy, alternative patterns of living, or behavioral change.[7] All in all, the number of such organizations has grown rapidly, and several community studies in the United States and England show that 20 to 30 percent of the voluntary organizations in local communities were established in the last ten to fifteen years.[8]

At the same time that the number of volunteers and nongovernmental organizations increased, a spillover of this wave of volunteerism into the governmental sector resulted in a sharp rise in national responsibility for the promotion of volunteerism. In 1973, official bodies were established for the first time in the United States, England, and Israel to strengthen and extend volunteer service in both the governmental and the voluntary sectors.

7. Alfred H. Katz and Eugene I. Bender, eds., *The Strength in Us: Self-Help Groups in the Modern World*; Allan Gartner and Frank Reissman, *Self Help in the Human Services*; *Journal of Applied Behavioral Science*, Special issue on self-help groups; and *Social Policy*, Special self-help issue. Many of the self-help groups moved into being demonstration projects in the 1960s and from there to a greater concern with rights, becoming pressure groups demanding services in the 1970s.

8. Wolfenden, pp. 184–85; Commission on Private Philanthropy and Public Needs, *Giving in America: Toward a Stronger Voluntary Sector*, p. 47 (hereafter cited as Filer).

In the United States, in the early 1960s President John Kennedy gave a strong ideological impetus to enlarging the scope of volunteer effort with his famous injunction, "Ask not what your country can do for you, but ask instead what you can do for your country." During the 1960s, a host of new volunteer programs emerged under governmental auspices — for example, the Peace Corps, VISTA (Volunteers in Service to America), Foster Grandparents, RSVP (Retired Senior Volunteer Program), the Teacher Corps, and others concerned with fighting poverty, discrimination, pollution, etc. The newer programs built on the fifty-year experience of the Department of Agriculture with service volunteers and on the twenty-five years of experience of the Veterans' Administration with 110,000 volunteers who contribute 10,000,000 hours of service annually. In the United States, governmental involvement in volunteerism culminated in 1973 in the establishment by the White House of ACTION as a central coordinating body for more than forty volunteer programs under various governmental auspices, involving over 3,000,000 persons. Within the nongovernmental sector, national coordinating bodies were also established, so that by 1979 the Alliance for Volunteerism brought together twenty national organizations concerned with the promotion of volunteerism in more than 5,000 different communities.[9]

Two important books reflecting the enlarged scope of volunteerism appeared in England in 1969. Co-sponsored by two leading national organizations and written by an internationally known authority in the social services, Geraldine M. Aves, *The Voluntary Worker in the Social Services* summarizes the findings of a national study of over 800 direct service volunteers, including their recruitment, selection, preparation, functions, and relations with professional social workers.[10] The second volume, *Voluntary Work in the Welfare State*, by Mary Morris, is a wide-ranging, comprehensive review of various fields of service in which volunteers work — such as health and welfare, hospitals, service to children and youth, and prisons — and reveals the details of a burgeoning field of activity.[11]

As a follow-up to the recommendations of the Aves Report, the Volunteer Centre was established by central government in September 1973 to foster the development of new opportunities for volunteers. By

9. Harriet H. Naylor, *Volunteers, Resource for Human Services*, pp. 25–30; Susan R. Greene, "Network — Alliance — Style."

10. Footnote 1.

11. See footnote 1.

1976, it had taken over responsibility from the National Council of Social Service for all 140 Volunteer Bureaus in Great Britain and was moving into the development of support for "informal carers" — i.e., families, neighbors, and friends.[12]

The greatest growth in voluntary service in England occurred in the hospitals of the National Health Service, where the number of Volunteer Organizers employed increased from 68 to almost 300 between 1970 and 1975. By 1976, more than 700 additional persons were employed full-time — mainly in statutory agencies, but also in some voluntary agencies as organizers and coordinators of volunteer services. It is estimated that, by 1976, 15 to 20 percent of the volunteers in the personal social services were working for some statutory organization.[13]

A new and separate channel for recruitment has developed in England, through which many volunteers go directly to statutory agencies and not through a national voluntary organization. None of the ten London Social Service Departments surveyed relied on voluntary agencies for the physically and mentally handicapped to provide volunteers for their clientele. If the Social Service Departments use volunteers to any extent, they have someone on their own staff to supervise this work, or they utilize the Volunteer Bureau in the community. For example, Croydon is one of the local authorities that has made a substantial investment in mobilizing volunteers; in 1974 its staff of ten recruited and assigned 1,679 volunteers who served over 6,000 persons in the borough. The next most extensive volunteer program was in the borough of Camden, where each of the seven area offices had a volunteer organizer on the staff and, altogether, about 400 volunteers were assigned to work with persons served by the Social Service Department.[14]

12. *The Volunteer Centre: What It Stands For and What It Does* (Berkhamstead, England: The Volunteer Centre, 1974); Mike Thomas, "The Volunteer Centre"; Lee Brown, "Which Way Now for Volunteer Centre?"

13. Wolfenden, p. 35. The use of volunteers by Social Service Departments is analyzed in Giles Darvill, *Bargain or Barricade? The Role of the Social Services Department in Meeting Social Need through Involving the Community*. It is estimated that the total number of volunteers and staff in voluntary organizations in the personal social services exceeds that of the staff in social service departments. (Wolfenden, p. 36).

14. Annual reports for 1975 for the Camden and Croyden Social Service Departments. A representative national survey of 1,220 social workers employed in social service departments found that fewer than 60 percent were using the services of volunteers for one or two of their clients. A greater incidence of utilization of volunteers was found in the probation departments, where 70 percent of the staff members worked with volunteers and collaborated rather closely with them (Anthea Holme and Joan Maizels, *Social Workers and Volunteers*, p. 170).

One of the consequences of this trend in England is that volunteers who might have worked for a voluntary agency go instead to a statutory one. Some voluntary agencies regard this as competitive and are threatened by the statutory recruitment of volunteers, while others believe that different types of persons are recruited by the statutory agencies. There may now be two separate systems of volunteer activity in England, each stressing different functions and, through peer recruiting, attracting different types of persons. This pattern is reminiscent of the way in which statutory authorities took over other voluntary functions shortly after World War II. One thing is clear: voluntary agencies in England, as well as in the United States, no longer have a monopoly on the recruitment and utilization of volunteers.

In Israel, a Volunteer Center was established in the Office of the Prime Minister by Golda Meir in 1973, largely because of her interest and that of several other leading officials who sought to revive the volunteerism associated with the prestate period. Support for the establishment of the Volunteer Center was also stimulated by the 1972 report of the Prime Minister's Committee on Youth, which criticized the lack of service volunteers in contrast to the extensive use of volunteers in fund raising.[15]

Even though no new structure has been created within the governmental network in the Netherlands, interest in volunteerism in CRM is stronger than among many nongovernmental agencies and professional groups, with the possible exception of the National Council for Social Welfare. For example, the ministry took the initiative in sponsoring demonstration projects, completed in 1976, that involved volunteer bureaus in three cities. In the following year, it adopted a policy of supporting the establishment of Volunteer Centers throughout the country.[16] Except among a few government officials, the use of volunteers in the Netherlands is justified on pragmatic and cost-saving grounds rather than for the ideological reasons found in the United States and England.

Patterns in the Use of Volunteers

The most frequently reported use of volunteers in each of the four countries was not in direct service to a clientele, but in fund raising.

15. Prime Minister's Committee on Youth, "Report of the Sub-Committee on Voluntary Organizations," p. 10. See also Ben Lappin, "The Missing Volunteers in Israel's Struggle with Poverty," pp. 66–76.

16. Hendriks, p. 85.

This was as true of the local affiliates of national organizations as of other voluntary associations for the handicapped in the community. The fiscal resource system of the voluntary agency requires the recurrent mobilization of large numbers of volunteers for a succession of special money-raising events, projects, and an annual campaign. Although quantitatively impressive because of the large number of persons who participate, public solicitations have an inevitable mass, impersonal character and may not promote many of the values embodied in volunteerism. Unless special efforts are made, this form of participation may produce only a marginal identification with the agency and little satisfaction for the volunteer.[17] Rarely did an agency utilize the educational potential of fund-raising activities, perhaps because for many participation is less than voluntary. In Israel, for example, 30,000 school-age children were enlisted by teachers and other adults for a few hours once a year for a door-to-door campaign. In the United States, solicitors for three of the voluntary agencies were recruited by a random phone appeal by members of the fund-raising staff.

When the necessity of seeking public contributions declines, as it has in the Netherlands, and in the United States for agencies that receive most of their income from government funds, the number of volunteers drops because they are needed less. A few service volunteers are replaced by paid staff, who perform such typical volunteer tasks as transportation and tutoring. While there may be a reverse relationship between a high degree of fiscal security and volunteerism, agencies highly dependent on public funds, except in the Netherlands, still utilized direct service volunteers. As a prominent national agency executive in the United States declared: "Citizens can give just as much of themselves in an agency with heavy governmental funding as in an agency with little governmental funding."[18]

Not all voluntary agencies utilize direct service volunteers either from their own membership or from the outside. In England, eight

17. Research on why people volunteer and what keeps them going is a complex subject prone to all of the methodological hazards associated with self-reported motivation. In *The Volunteers*, Sills distinguishes between the satisfactions of those who are involved in direct service and those engaged in fund raising — i.e., the contrast between reaching goals using organizational skills, initiative, and imagination, as opposed to the personal satisfactions of helping and caring. Most studies of volunteer motivation report varying degrees of altruism, and self-interest, including recognition and sociability. One of the better studies using expectancy theory is Benjamin Gidron, "Volunteer Work and Its Rewards." See also Hazel Qureshi, Bleddyn Davies, and David Challis, "Motivation and Reward of Volunteers and Informal Care Givers."

18. Joseph L. Reid, "The Role of the Voluntary Sector," *Social Welfare Forum, 1976* (New York: Columbia University Press, 1976), p. 65.

out of the fourteen national agencies with local affiliates whose membership amounted to almost 100,000 did not use program volunteers at all. In the United States, the utilization of service volunteers was uneven: three of the twenty agencies had no program volunteers, and of the twelve organizations for the handicapped, only four made extensive use of service volunteers — e.g., involved more than 50 persons. There was no consistent relationship between the ratio of the number of service volunteers and the size of staff or the clientele. For example, of two U.S. agencies with similar programs for the mentally handicapped, one had 10 program volunteers and 13 professionals for 184 clients, while another had 75 program volunteers and 89 staff members to serve almost 800 clients. One agency that served 1,900 persons with cerebral palsy had 60 program volunteers, while another organization serving the same type of clientele had 25 volunteers for its 700 clients.[19]

In Israel, only five out of the fifteen agencies used service volunteers; in the Netherlands, twelve out of the twenty organizations had volunteer programs. One of the largest organizations in the Netherlands, serving 1,000 clients with a staff of 900 in a network of sixteen facilities, had only twelve weekly visitors in a children's institution of over 200, although arrangements were being made for another twenty volunteers to make weekly visits to hostels. Most of the volunteers in the Netherlands are obtained through the 113 branches of the National Union of Women Voluntary Workers. In contrast to the parent associations of the mentally handicapped in the other three countries, their counterparts in the Netherlands, originally organized by teachers and having a membership of over 50,000, are searching for a new set of functions because most of their service programs, including advocacy, have been taken over by other, more specialized nongovernmental organizations.

19. Most published statistics on volunteer activities should be used with great caution. For example, in all countries it was widely reported that the same people were volunteers in two and three different organizations, but it was not possible to verify this. Rarely is data about the duration, frequency, or intensity of volunteer service available to permit inferences about its impact on the volunteer or significance for the person receiving the service. One of the very few studies in this area is that of Hadley, Webb, and Farrow. Some studies suggest that there is at least three to four times as much volunteer activity undertaken informally as under the auspices of formal voluntary organizations. See James N. Morgan, Richard F. Dye, and Judith H. Hybels, "Results from Two National Surveys of Philanthropic Activity," pp. 167–73, and, on the great variation in the use of volunteers in different fields of service, United Way of America, "A Study of the Quantity of Volunteer Activity of United Way and Its Member Agencies," *Research Papers Sponsored by the Commission on Private Philanthropy and Public Needs*, vol. 2 (Washington, D.C.: Department of the Treasury, 1977) pp. 869–70.

In England, many of the associations of the parents of the mentally handicapped are suspicious or resentful of volunteers who do not have a handicapped child. Other strong, cohesive organizations of the handicapped also prefer using their own members to using outsiders, as a form of self-help. Organizations of the deaf in particular make limited use of outside volunteers, mainly because of the small number of persons who are willing to be trained in lipreading or sign language in order to communicate with the deaf. The blind, on the other hand, have traditionally been assisted by sighted volunteers. In these ways, the nature of a handicap influences the extent of volunteer activity.[20]

Self-Help Affiliates

One of the most distinctive features of the voluntary organizations of the physically and mentally handicapped is their capacity to provide a structure through which mutual aid can flourish. Many voluntary organizations in the local community grow out of self-help endeavors in which parents or other family members of a handicapped person come together with others who share a common concern. When it becomes evident that these informal methods are no longer adequate, the national voluntary organizations of the physically and mentally handicapped can offer resources whereby self-help can expand into a community service. The establishment of a formal voluntary organization as an affiliate or branch of a national organization is not only a way of obtaining resources that can provide support for existing informal networks, but it can also create new ones where none exist. By providing various forms of institutional care, day care, psychological support, information, and advice, voluntary organizations can relieve, replace, and reinforce existing informal networks and primary groups.[21] In organizations based on mutual aid principles, the lines between volunteer, member, and consumer overlap. The smaller the size of the affiliate or local organization, the more it will conform to the model of

20. The influence of the handicap itself, not only on volunteering, but also on other aspects of organizational behavior, has rarely been considered. Among the aspects of a disability that seem to have implications for both internal and external organizational behavior are: trends in incidence, epidemiological character, and the socioeconomic status of the handicapped; the diagnostic label and the extent to which the disability is defined as medical or social; public awareness and perception, as well as the stigma attached or the degree of social control required; economic consequences of impairment; the state of knowledge and technology; feasibility of assessment, training, education, rehabilitation, treatment, and prevention; and resources required. Stratification and labeling theories may illuminate some of these phenomena.

21. Wolfenden, p. 28. Voluntary self-help has been criticized when it serves as a substitute for what ought to be a right provided by government. See Bayley, *Community-Orientated Systems of Care*, pp. 39–40.

a peer self-help group in which emotional support and practical help will be the dominant activities.[22] As the chairman of a branch of the Multiple Sclerosis Society in London expressed it, "The branch offers a shoulder to cry on." A more service-oriented perspective is expressed in the statement of another chairman in London: "Where the borough (the Social Service Department) stops, the branch continues." The most elaborate panoply of services is in London, where up to ten different personal social services may be available among the affiliates of the NSMHC, depending on the initiative and resources of the local membership. These can include such services as: nurseries; classes; workshops; residential day care centers; respite facilities; home teaching; nursing and home help; occupational, physical, and speech therapy; and sitters. Two profiles of such affiliates follow.

The Westminster Society for Mentally Handicapped Children opened London's first five-day week nursery in 1963, and a second was opened in 1967. In 1966, the society began operating a special-care unit for children with multiple handicaps as an agent of the Westminster City Council. In 1971, it transferred this program to the Department of Education, although the society now runs the unit on behalf of the Inner London Education Authority. In 1970, the society opened its own residential home for twenty children between the ages of five and twelve. A welfare team visits parents in their homes, and meetings are arranged for parents as well as arrangements made for children to attend holiday events. A Gateway Club for mentally handicapped teenagers and young adults meets weekly, and twenty-seven persons participate in table tennis, dancing, painting, film shows, and bingo. Theater visits and outings also occur on a regular basis, along with the celebration of holidays and parties.

In Wandsworth, emphasis has been less on the establishment and operation of services or the purchase of facilities, and more on improving services for the mentally handicapped through making representations to the local council. The society has an active program of external relationships and participates in many community-wide or-

22. Jonathan Bradshaw, Caroline Glendinning, and Stephen Hatch, "Voluntary Organizations for Handicapped Children and Their Families: The Meaning of Membership." This survey of families caring for very severely disabled children at home revealed that about half belong to a voluntary organization, with membership varying according to disease, social class, income, family composition, and locality. The structure, function, processes, and phases of development of self-help groups as they become more formalized are summarized in Alfred H. Katz, "Self-Help Organizations and Volunteer Participation in Social Welfare." See also Donald Traunstein and Richard Steinman, "Voluntary Self-Help Organizations: An Exploratory Study."

ganizations. Committee members have been appointed governors for special schools in the borough, as well as to a college of further education. In addition to sponsoring four Gateway Clubs, a swimming club, and horseback riding, the society has been able to get the local authority's three youth centers to provide weekly programs for the mentally handicapped.

Volunteer activities in organizations of the handicapped contrast with others in being broader, more intensive, and more varied as they take on service functions in health care, recreation, education, and social work that are often assigned to professional paid staff. In Israel, because of the absence of social workers in many local communities, three organizations use volunteers extensively for interviewing clients, making plans and arranging referrals, and managing agency programs. They serve on thirty rehabilitation committees for the physically handicapped, eight counseling centers for parents of the mentally handicapped, and on all of the Cancer Association branch committees offering patient services. These volunteer-staffed service programs complement others that are likely to use no paid employees — for example, Reach to Recovery in Israel and the United States, through which women volunteers who have undergone mastectomies counsel others both before and after surgery.

The provision of services by affiliates is a matter of policy and not just dependent on the availability of resources. The Spastics Society, a much larger, more professionalized organization with three times the staff and income of the NSMHC, discourages individual welfare work by its affiliates. The NSMHC decided, however, that there is little likelihood in the future of adequate statutory funding of welfare services for the families of the mentally handicapped, and it has therefore taken the initiative in training its own volunteers to carry out these functions and, in this sense, to substitute for paid staff.

In their service programs, the NSMHC affiliates were quite similar to their U.S. counterparts. Insofar as comparisons can be made, proportionately more service volunteers are involved in the English agencies than in the U.S. ones, perhaps because the latter are able to obtain public funding for their paid staff.

In both Israel and the Netherlands, but to a lesser extent in the United States and England, volunteer involvement is an informal process. Only one of the Israeli executives had some professional training for and commitment to citizen participation, although three of the agencies sponsored some volunteer training programs.

The processes of recruitment, training, supervision, and evaluation in the United States are more formalized than in any of the other countries. Two-thirds (twelve) of the U.S. agencies have regular orientation programs for their volunteers, and half have in-service training programs, in contrast to England, where only five of the twenty agencies have some type of formal training program and none reported any procedures for the evaluation of volunteers. There is no consistent pattern in the reports on the experience of the agencies in recruiting volunteers. Almost equal numbers of informants said that recruiting new volunteers is more difficult, that it is easier, and that it is about the same; and there is no consistent pattern in the numbers recruited. Despite such social changes as the increased number of women in the labor force, none of the agencies in the United States reported any significant decrease in the use of women volunteers, although they may be used more for fund raising than for direct services. In England, thirteen agencies stated that there seemed to be an increased number of volunteers involved in fund raising, while only eight noted an increase in the number of volunteers in direct services.

Relationships between Professionals and Volunteers

It is widely believed that there is an inherent conflict between professionalism and volunteerism as, for example, that "all professionals are inherently anti-amateur." Less ominously, professionals have been described as the "full-time planners of other people's short-term bursts of energy and masochism."[23] In practice, however, the situation is more complex, and an appropriate functional separation between paid staff and volunteers is a controversial issue. The generally accepted view seems to be that if volunteers are used, they should extend or complement the work of paid staff, rather than substitute for it or threaten professionals' livelihood. This is illustrated in the definition of Mary Morris, who refers to voluntary work as consisting of the tasks that can't or won't be done by paid staff. She adds that volunteers should not be used just to save money.[24] Giles Darvill carries this one step further and finds that "the essence of the voluntary worker is that he performs an act of service which can only be adequately carried out if the service is seen to be unpaid."[25] This may be somewhat unrealistic and unduly restrictive if it confines voluntary work to situ-

23. Harold L. Wilensky and Charles N. Lebeaux, *Industrial Society and Social Welfare*, p. 304; and David Riesman, *Individualism Reconsidered*, p. 232.

24. Morris, p. xiii.

25. Darvill, p. 16.

ations in which friendship is essential and excludes such functions as education, recreation, and transportation.[26]

Opposition to volunteers' substituting for paid workers has come in the past not just from professionals, but also, in England, from trade unions. The Labour Party and its trade union members have a long history of rejecting philanthropic volunteering, particularly since it was identified with nineteenth-century concepts of self-help. This distrust is still found in Labour circles and among radicals who view volunteers and self-help as reactionary and diversionary from political and economic justice. In reviewing this background, Richard H. S. Crossman stated:

[In the 1930s] we all disliked the do-good volunteer and wanted to see him replaced by professionals and trained administrators in the socialist welfare state of which we all dreamed. Philanthropy to us was an odious expression of social oligarchy and churchy bourgeois attitudes . . . the only volunteers we approved of were volunteers for the struggle against the old oligarchy.[27]

In recent years, there have been jurisdictional disputes between low-paid staff and volunteers in the hospitals of the National Health Service, and in 1970 the Confederation of Health Service Employees passed a resolution condemning the use of volunteers in the National Health Service. Cutbacks in funds and shortages of personnel in the Social Service Departments stimulated the search for volunteers as a means of compensating for these deficits. In an effort to avoid future conflicts, a set of "Guidelines for Relationships between Volunteers and Paid Non-Professional Workers" was developed by a working party for the Volunteer Centre, headed by the General Secretary of the National and Local Governmental Officers' Association. It was published in 1975, and over 50,000 copies have been distributed.[28]

26. In England, a distinction between supplementary and complementary forms of volunteer service has been made. On the basis of a study of the use of volunteers in Social Service Departments and in probation departments, services are supplementary when volunteers are used mainly to carry out tasks that professionals feel ought to be done, but that they themselves cannot or should not do, and that without voluntary help would not be done. This was found to be the prevailing model in the Social Service Departments; it corresponds to the definition of Mary Morris. In the probation departments, a complementary model was found, in which volunteers are used in tasks that contribute to the achievement of casework objectives, and in which some form of close partnership is essential. (Holme and Maizels, pp. 172–76). See also Adrian Webb, Lesley Day, and Douglas Weller, *Voluntary Social Services Manpower Resources*, pp. 17–19.

27. Quoted in Bayley, *Community-Orientated Systems of Care*, p. 39.

28. Ian Bruce, "Volunteers and Labour Unions in Great Britain."

In the United States, the possible displacement of staff by volunteers is less of an issue, although when Proposition 13 passed in California in 1978 and public agency staffs were reduced, such services as libraries, recreation, and certain school programs were maintained on a limited basis by volunteers. (In chapter 14 I shall discuss the belief that, in the face of governmental budget cuts, volunteers can help maintain the social services.) In contrast to England, the AFL-CIO has officially endorsed volunteerism and the United Way and has encouraged union members to participate in various forms of community service. The reverse issue — i.e., the exploitation of volunteers — is a major concern among the feminist organizations in the United States, which have taken a strong stand against volunteer work by women. They have charged that most women volunteers in the social services function as substitutes for paid staff, and that this contributes to the low status of women in society and to the lack of adequate budgets for social agencies. Volunteers should concentrate on advocacy, they believe, and if a task is considered important, then someone should be paid to do it. This position is rejected by virtually all the other leading women's volunteer organizations on both ideological and practical grounds.[29]

An important element influencing the decision to employ volunteers is professional ideology, in particular the commitment of the executive to volunteerism. The value attached to technocratic management by professionals in the Netherlands was greater than their interest in the participation of volunteers as board members or in direct service. There was also relatively little executive commitment to direct service volunteers in the highly professionalized agencies in England and in the United States. Yet relatively little tension between staff and volunteers was reported in all four countries. This may be explained either by the relatively small number of professionals who actually have contact with volunteers, as in Israel or in England, or by the fact that the use of volunteers in certain agencies is not encouraged as a matter of policy, as in the Netherlands and the United States. When volunteers were utilized in professionally staffed agencies, though, few difficulties were reported.

29. National Organization for Women, *National Organization for Women — Why Not? Analysis and Answers.* An opposing view is found in Hilda Loeser, *Women, Work and Volunteering.* A different kind of controversy was stirred by Benjamin De Mott, who asserted that volunteerism is on the wane in the United States because of the women's movement, the growing political militancy of minorities, and a new enlightened selfishness and self-absorption ("The Day the Volunteers Didn't"). See the dissent by Kenn Allen and Arlene Schindler, "Is Volunteerism in Trouble?"

It is understandable that professional-volunteer relationships have been regarded as a problem area. Historically, social work emerged as a profession by displacing the volunteers who had founded an agency. Subsequently, as agencies became more bureaucratic and professionalized, volunteers came to be seen as inefficient, unreliable, unqualified to perform clinical tasks, and, at best, suited only for menial assignments.[30] Social work has been described as a "precarious profession," similar to nursing and teaching, because of its struggle to maintain exclusive control over its domain, and it has not yet succeeded in demonstrating the distinctive professional component in its practice. Volunteers can easily threaten this tenuous hold on professionalism, so they are traditionally looked down upon, or at least their contributions are not highly valued. Reflecting this attitude on the part of such professionals as social workers and teachers is the absence of any courses on work with volunteers in professional education for social work in the four countries.[31]

The lack of appreciation for volunteers is, however, more characteristic of a clinical or psychotherapeutic model of social work. There is a different perspective on volunteers in two other methods of social work, community organization and group work. Professionals in these fields do not perceive volunteers and professionals as locked in inevitable conflict, nor do they see the volunteer necessarily as a threat. Instead, there is an emphasis on process and on educational values in which the development and use of trained volunteers in a variety of supplementary tasks is regarded as an important professional responsibility.[32] This philosophy, however, is found only in a very small number of agencies in each country.

It is ironic that the further development of volunteerism is taking place through professionalization of the position of volunteer organizer in England or, as it is called in the United States, volunteer administrator or director of volunteers. This trend has not emerged at all in the Netherlands and in Israel, where the approach to volunteerism is more casual. The underlying assumption is that volunteer service is a valuable community resource for both governmental and

30. Roy Lubove, *The Professional Altruist: The Emergence of Social Work as a Career, 1880–1930*, pp. 51–119, 161–67, 170–71, and 218.
31. Adrienne A. Haeuser, "What the Graduate Social Work Curriculum Should Provide about Volunteerism for All Students."
32. See chapter 5, footnote 16, and Harriet H. Naylor, *Volunteers Today: Finding, Training and Working with Them.*

voluntary agencies and that it can be utilized most effectively under the direction of a professionally-trained staff person.

Conclusions

The future of organized volunteer services may depend not only on the existence of voluntary agencies, although they are the largest pro-moters and utilizers of such services, but also on such other factors as the type of sociopolitical context, public policy, professional ideology, and agency function. The value guardian role is facilitated by a civic culture whose norms and sanctions encourage various forms of citizen participation — hence, the more active performance of this function in the United States and England, compared with the Netherlands and Israel.

Public policy also has an impact on the different forms of volun-teerism. The increasing utilization of volunteers by governmental agencies can be supportive or complementary to the efforts of volun-tary agencies to recruit volunteers, but it can also become competitive, as it has to some extent in England and the United States. In the case of volunteer board members, the U.S. policy of mandated consumer participation in most federally sponsored programs has resulted in some broadening of representation in voluntary agency governance.

The extent to which the dominant professional ideology of the vol-untary agency staff values volunteer and consumer involvement is likewise influential. The more technocratic and precarious the profes-sionalism, the less likely will it be to encourage volunteerism. The more it aspires to a democratic partnership model, the greater the pos-sibility that volunteerism will be supported. These generalizations should be tempered somewhat because direct service or program vol-unteers can be nurtured both by an appropriate professional ideology and by the virtual absence of professionalism, in peer self-help organi-zations. This leads to the conclusion that the type of organization is important, as evidenced in the great variation in the use of volunteers in different fields of service, from leisure-time youth-serving agen-cies such as the Scouts — or in another category, the various Cross organizations — to family counseling agencies.

In this chapter we have been concerned with only one form of vol-unteerism, direct service giving, which, among agencies serving the physically and the mentally handicapped, was not found as frequently as volunteer involvement in fund raising, policymaking, and self-help. In this respect, it appears that such agencies are rather modest guardians of the values of volunteerism. Yet, nominally all voluntary agencies are basically voluntaristic because volunteers are a critical organizational resource necessary for legitimation, financial support, governance, advocacy, and occasionally direct service provision. The encouragement of the different forms of citizen participation, as well as the promotion of the values of diverse social, religious, ethnic, and cultural groups, constitutes an indispensable function of voluntary agencies in a democratic society.

Richard M. Titmuss and others have expressed great concern about the diminishing opportunities in the welfare state for altruistic behavior whereby one can "exercise a moral choice to give in non-monetary form to strangers."[33] Volunteerism is valued because "statutory functions alone can never hope to fulfill people's expectations for care, support and security in a modern society."[34]

While one can acknowledge the importance of sustaining altruism and citizen participation in a welfare state, there may be a tendency to exaggerate the virtues of both volunteerism and voluntary agencies. Volunteerism can be regarded inappropriately as a substitute for paid staff and can be expected to compensate for some of the fiscal and administrative deficiencies of government. Voluntary agencies' function as vendors of public services may also constrain the development of volunteerism. The inevitable bureaucratization, professionalization, and entrepreneurism that follow can easily diminish the role of volunteers. This may explain the fact that the growing edge of volunteerism is found less among the type of agencies in our study, and more among those stressing peer self-help and advocacy, and among certain volunteer programs sponsored by government.

In any event, although it may be more difficult to perform in the future, the value guardian role takes on greater significance in the welfare state. Another essential role of the nongovernmental sector is advocacy, and it is to this function that we now turn.

33. Richard M. Titmuss, *The Gift Relationship: From Human Blood to Social Policy*, p. 13.
34. Hadley, Webb, and Farrell, p. 4.

11. The Improver Role and Advocacy

Apart from their functions as pioneers and promoters of volunteerism, voluntary agencies are also supposed to serve as a progressive force for an enlightened and humane social policy. In pluralist democratic societies, where government is not expected to be its own critic or only source of change, there is both a moral and a legal sanction for voluntary agencies to mediate between the citizen and the state. Because innovation and volunteerism can also be promoted by government, the social change and advocacy functions of the improver role are often regarded as "the quintessential function of the voluntary sector."[1] A typical expression of this belief follows:

> Their (the voluntary agencies in general) role is not primarily to serve as an alternate to government, but, instead, to help keep government honest and responsible. The primary role of voluntary associations in American life is to continually shape and reshape the vision of a more just social order, to propose programs which might lead to the manifestation of that vision, to argue for them with other contenders in the public arena, and to press for adoption and implementation. For voluntary associations to do less than that is to abdicate their civic responsibility.[2]

The Filer Commission in the United States also noted the significance of this function:

> As government's role in many areas formerly dominated by nongovernmental groups grows ever larger, and the voluntary role grows correspondingly smaller, *the monitoring and influencing of government may be emerging as one of the single most important and effective functions of the private nonprofit sector.*[3] (Italics mine.)

1. Brian O'Connell, "The Contribution of Voluntary Agencies in Developing Social Policies," p. 1. (Note that in this chapter, the improver role and advocacy will be used interchangeably.)
2. Paul H. Sherry, "Getting It Together."
3. Commission on Private Philanthropy and Public Needs, *Giving in America: Toward a Stronger Voluntary Sector*, p. 45. (Hereafter cited as Filer.) See also Donald N. Michael, "Influencing Public Policy: The Changing Roles of Voluntary Associations."

Voluntary agencies have traditionally had the dual mission of providing social services and engaging in social action — of "case and
cause" — on behalf of their client constituencies. Throughout the
latter part of the nineteenth century, particularly in the United States
and England, private philanthropy supported and often initiated measures of social reform. In seeking to influence public policy and administration, charitable organizations drew on firsthand experience
with the problems of the handicapped, the poor, and other disadvantaged groups as they "witnessed" to the need for some form of government action.[4] With the expansion of public responsibility for both the
financing and administration of social services in new and complex
governmental bureaucracies, the improver role has become even more
important and specialized. In England it is believed that "voluntary
organizations are in a unique position to take action on issues which,
due to design, chance or history, do not fall clearly within the responsibility of any one governmental department."[5]

There is an acceptance of the improver role in the United States,
England, The Netherlands, and Israel, but fears regarding its future
have been expressed predominantly in the United States and England.
The possibility of losing their tax-exempt status as charitable organizations is said to deter some voluntary agencies from trying to influence legislation. The dangers of co-optation of voluntary agencies and
inhibition of their advocacy because of financial reliance on government is a recurrent theme in the United States and a rather prominent
one in England, but is not emphasized in Israel or, ironically, in the
Netherlands, where there is the greatest dependency on government
funds. Because of the necessity of extensive government support of
most voluntary agency programs for the handicapped, it has even
been proposed that the operation of direct service programs be abandoned because it generally preempts the advocacy function, which is
regarded as the most essential role. The strongest case for the substitution of "change agentry as the single perpetual focus" of voluntary
organizations serving the mentally handicapped has been made by
Wolf Wolfensberger. He has argued that long-term operation of services is "intrinsically maladaptive" for advocacy because it inevitably

4. Although George Bernard Shaw claimed that "charities are a bar to social progress," the
historical record of social reform in England and America shows an active role by private philanthropy. See James Leiby, *A History of Social Welfare and Social Work in the United States*, pp.
111–62, and David Owen, *English Philanthropy*, 1660–1960, pp. 211–442.

5. J. K. Owen, "Partnership with Government," p. 120. The "boundary-spanning" role of
voluntary agencies seems to be more significant for national agencies because the local organizations are more likely to have coterminous boundaries with local political jurisdictions.

TABLE 12.
Types of Advocacy

	United States (N = 48 episodes)	England (N = 45 episodes)	The Netherlands (N = 28 episodes)	Israel (N = 31 episodes)
Influencing legislation or regulations	21 (44%)	9 (21%)	4 (14%)	3 (10%)
Improving governmental service programs	8 (16%)	17 (40%)	3 (11%)	5 (16%)
Obtaining voluntary agency funding	12 (25%)	6 (14%)	12 (43%)	15 (48%)
Securing tax exemptions or benefits for clientele	7 (15%)	11 (25%)	9 (32%)	8 (26%)
	100%	100%	100%	100%

leads to conflict of interest, loss of autonomy, displacement of volunteers by professionals, the preemption of leadership, and increased bureaucratization.[6] We shall consider these and other internal and external constraints on advocacy after comparing the four national patterns of the improver role with respect to their objectives, political targets, strategies, and methods.

Four Objectives of Improver Activities

Table 12 summarizes the number of episodes reported by executives for the four types of objectives of their agencies' efforts to influence government.[7]

6. Wolf Wolfensberger, *The Third Stage in the Evolution of Voluntary Associations for the Mentally Retarded*, pp. 11–23. See also R. F. Dybwad, "The Voluntary Association on the International Scene."

7. Because all agencies were asked to describe in detail at least three of their major attempts to influence a governmental body during the last ten years, the total number of episodes reported is less significant than the distribution within each country among the four types of goals and the types of targets and methods.

Attempts to Influence Legislation or Regulations

There were twice as many legislative and policy-change episodes reported in the U.S. as there were in England; in the Netherlands and Israel, this type of improver activity was the least reported. This legislative activity, with a few notable exceptions, involved small-scale, relatively noncontroversial issues, and it usually represented differences in priorities between the specialized interests of the voluntary agency and the wider scope of governmental concerns. Typical examples are campaigns: to establish a national registry for the physically handicapped in the Ministry of Health (Israel); to adopt a city ordinance requiring wheelchair ramps at building entrances and at curbs (United States); to change a regulation that would have eliminated certain handicapped clients from social security benefits (United States); to prevent local governments from conducting a lottery (England);[8] to modify pension legislation for the dependents of handicapped persons (the Netherlands).

While there are isolated instances of involvement in broader social legislation in each country — the Chronic Sick and Disabled Persons Act of 1970 in England and the Mental Retardation Law of 1969 in Israel — voluntary agencies are consistently active on both the state and federal level only in the United States. Illustrations of this role include: the opposition of four of the U.S. agencies to a proposed merger of the State Department of Rehabilitation and the Department of Employment in California; lobbying for the Lanterman Mental Retardation Services Act of 1969, which created a statewide system of regional centers for developmental disabilities;[9] protests against U.S. Department of Health, Education and Welfare regulations concerning matching funds and Supplementary Security Income.

In contrast, none of the Israeli agencies presented testimony in the Knesset debates in 1974 on national disability and health insurance; only three of the fifteen agencies in Israel have ever been involved in legislative activities on the national level. In England, only four of the twenty agencies have been actively concerned with Parliamentary issues. Most of them have no stated policy on legislation, nor are any

8. In one of the few reported episodes of attempts to influence legislation in Parliament, the Spastics Society led a coalition to oppose the Government's Lottery Bill because it would have competed with the society's own lotteries in local communities. Ultimately, the Spastics Society and its allies were successful in imposing many restrictions on the use of lotteries by the local authorities.

9. See footnote 7, chapter 9, and Edgar W. Pye and Rhona S. Rudolph, "A California Regional Center Program."

board committees or staff assigned for such purposes, although their community-education activities may have had an indirect effect on public policy.

What may, however, appear as narrowness of vision or a lack of concern with public policy by some of the agencies is often a result of the different functions of national and local organizations. The national agencies in England and in Israel also operate service programs, in contrast to their counterparts in the Netherlands and the United States, which are almost exclusively concerned with national policies concerning income maintenance, housing, mobility, rehabilitation, and the rights of the handicapped. In England, there is an additional specialization among the national agencies whereby the Central Council for the Disabled is expected to press for housing, improved access, and mobility for the handicapped, while the Disablement Income Group and the Disability Alliance are active on income maintenance issues.[10] Because most of the changes in public policy affecting the handicapped in the Netherlands occur within the framework of the administrative regulations of central government and not through Parliamentary legislation, there the national organizations of the voluntary agencies are in close contact with the ministries.

Efforts to Improve Governmental Service Programs

The objective most frequently reported by the English agencies, comprising almost one-third of the improver episodes, consisted of efforts to prod the Department of Health and Social Security to allocate sufficient funds to the local authorities so that they could provide both mandated and optional services. The voluntary agencies usually sought priority for their particular clientele, as in the campaign to obtain special educational facilities for autistic children, or the attempts of the organizations for the sensorially handicapped to secure governmental provision of new or improved devices for the hard-of-hearing and the blind. Usually there were obstacles to the voluntary

10. The Disablement Income Group (DIG) was organized in 1966 because of the lack of pressure-group activity by the established voluntary organizations. It is a twofold organization: a pressure group and a registered charitable trust, both with identical aims — namely, to secure a national disability income and an allowance for the extra expenses of disablement. DIG is one of the few organizations to legally separate its lobbying from its status as a charitable organization. It offers no direct services. It has seventy local branches, but functions mainly through its London office. The Disability Alliance was organized in the mid-1970s by the sociologist Peter Townsend, a DIG patron, who brought together a coalition of about thirty groups representing the disabled themselves, unmarried mothers, the poor, and other minority organizations, despite the failure of previous attempts to organize a coalition of the poor and the handicapped.

agency's generating enough pressure to influence governmental policy if there was not already some predisposition to act. The appointment of a Minister for the Disabled in 1974 enlarged and strengthened advocacy within central government itself, and more than forty improvements in income, transportation, housing, employment, and the personal social services were claimed by the minister within a fifteen-month period.[11]

On the local level, where statutory responsibility for the social services is implemented, the ten London Social Service Department directors in the study reported a negligible amount of advocacy, criticism, monitoring, or prodding by the affiliates of the national agencies. Indeed, the directors expressed surprise that so little pressure was exerted by voluntary agencies in their communities in the face of sharp budgetary cuts in the personal social services during 1973–1975, as well as the acknowledged failure to implement the Chronic Sick and Disabled Persons Act of 1970.[12] More pressure was reported by the directors from their own staff than from the community at large. In general, the Social Service Departments make their decisions regarding priorities and levels of service with little interaction with any of the voluntary agencies. Evidently, few volunteers engaging in direct service use this experience as a basis for becoming advocates for the handicapped in the manner described by Mary Morris.[13]

11. Minister for the Disabled, "Checklist of New Help for the Disabled since March, 1974," pp. 1–6.

12. The failure of local citizen organizations to become pressure groups is not unusual; for example, only about 30 percent of the Social Service Department committees have representatives of voluntary organizations as members (The Volunteer Centre, *Encouraging the Community: Some Findings on the Social Service Department's Contributions*, p. 7). See also Terry Philpot, "Nurturing Pressure from Grass Roots." A different view is found in P. F. Cousins, "Voluntary Organizations and Local Government in Three South London Boroughs."

13. Mary Morris, *Voluntary Work in the Welfare State*, p. 210–12. The witness role for the volunteer is probably more normative than descriptive. Evidently the Seebohm Report also overestimated the amount of improver activity to be expected in the local community: "The local authority will need to tolerate and use the criticisms made by voluntary organizations and not expect the partnership to be without conflict. A certain level of mutual criticism between the local authority and voluntary organizations may be essential if the needs of the consumers are to be met more effectively and they are to be protected from the misuse of bureaucratic and professional power in either kind of organization" (Committee on Local Authority and Allied Personal Social Services, *A Report to Parliament*, p. 496). Similarly, Prime Minister Harold Wilson at the 1975 annual meeting of the National Council for Social Service spoke of "the distinct, indispensable and socially invaluable role that the voluntary organizations now play in tackling social problems and creating a better society. Nor is the role of voluntary organizations simply at the local level. There is also a central role in the formation of social policy at the national level" ("The Need for Voluntary Effort," *Social Service Quarterly* 49 [Winter 1975–1976]: 93).

An important exception to the relatively small amount of attention to governmental programs is the persistent and successful campaigns in all four countries to upgrade programs for the mentally handicapped. This may be due in part to the nature of mental handicaps, which require a wide range of services and facilities, from custodial to rehabilitative care, both institutional and community-based, extending over the lifetime of the retarded person. Some social provision must be made because a family is unable to provide the diverse forms of continuing care, treatment, and education required over the life span of a handicapped individual. Because the incidence of mental retardation is spread more or less evenly throughout the population, there is a cadre of middle-class persons who are directly affected as parents and have both the incentive and the necessary organizational skills to influence public policy.

Many parents' associations in these countries, notably the United States, have been transformed from a social movement of self-help groups into a more bureaucratic and professional community service provider, supported principally by public funds.[14] Over the years, there has been a shift in their organizational strategies from adversary to advocate, and from aggressive demands to cooperation and partnership. Many local authorities in England originally feared and resisted the parent groups, and often there was a standoff. One of the more controversial tactics of some local associations was to force the Social Service Department to pay for private care of the mentally handicapped, which would become uneconomical and would serve as an incentive for the local authority to set up its own group home. Institutions were sometimes pressured to release their patients prematurely in order to confront the local authority with the necessity of providing foster care in the community. As their children were increasingly provided for because of the growing availability of community services, parent groups became more understanding of the problems faced by overstrained local authorities. Although in all four countries many associations have modified their original adversarial stance to become partners with government, they have not ceased to be critics and prods for improved programs of institutional and community care. This was particularly true in Israel, where the Israel Association for the Rehabilitation of the Mentally Handicapped (AKIM) was second only to the Disabled Veterans Association as a gadfly to government.

14. See Alfred H. Katz, *Parents of the Handicapped*.

Governmental service programs for other types of handicapped persons receive relatively less attention in these countries partly because their clients are fewer in number and because many of the voluntary agencies are the principal service provider. In the Netherlands, for example, it is not clear who, apart from a few government officials, serves as the monitor, critic, or prod of the primary, nongovernmental service-delivery system.

Attempts to Secure Government Funds

A natural outcome of voluntary agencies' operation as a service provider for government is that they are led to seek grants, subsidies, fees, or payments for service. It may be questioned whether such actions, motivated primarily for financial benefit, should be considered a form of advocacy or change agentry; however, in seeking government funds, voluntary agencies interact with government officials and are involved in a political process. U.S. critics of the acceptance of public funds by voluntary agencies have warned that when a voluntary agency tries to influence appropriations from which it may benefit, this practice leads to conflict of interest and loss of credibility.[15] However, these charges rarely have been made by legislators or government officials, who seem less concerned with the issue of self-interest when nonprofit, charitable organizations seek funds from which their clientele may ultimately benefit.

Pursuit of government funds was the least frequently reported type of improver activity in England; only four out of the twenty agencies tried to obtain funds from the central government for their national headquarters. This did not mean, however, that the agencies failed to receive substantial proportions of their income from statutory sources; rather, most of their service programs were supported by payments from a number of local authorities.

In Israel, attempts to secure funds for the agency or its constituencies were the major form of interaction with the central government, and they were featured in twenty-three out of the thirty-one episodes reported. With two notable exceptions, the Israeli agencies did not try to prod government to extend, improve, or establish needed services. The fiscal career of most of the Israeli voluntary agencies began with a period of financing by contributions; when it became increasingly dif-

15. See footnote 15, chapter 8. In England, about half of the improver episodes were on behalf of a special constituency, and the other half were for broader groups, while in the United States about one-fourth of the episodes involved funds for the agency's own operations.

ficult for them to continue solely through independent fund raising, they sought and almost always received deficit financing from government. Thereafter, voluntary agency officials were involved in frequent and extended bargaining with government over rates and levels of support. These negotiations may have used up time that the leadership might have utilized for other agency purposes, such as advocacy.

In the Netherlands, subsidies and the regulations pertaining to them were the principal subject of discussion between the national federations and the government as part of the policy of corporate consultation. This phenomenon is not limited to the Netherlands; it is also found in the other countries.[16] The most politicized forms of this mode of improver activity are in the U.S., where eight out of the twenty voluntary agencies individually and in coalition were active in pressing legislative bodies at all three levels of government for increased or restored appropriations and for passage of legislation to benefit the physically and mentally handicapped. One-fourth of these episodes concerned social security benefits, local revenue sharing, and rate setting.

Special Benefits for Clientele

In this type of objective, the voluntary agency is an advocate striving for special concessions and tax exemptions for its clientele. Because of extraordinarily high tax rates and import duties, most Israeli agencies join other organized interest groups in requesting tax exemptions or reductions for the handicapped from the Treasury. Although the agencies cited these special benefits as a major accomplishment, the preoccupation with "hand-outs" was criticized by some of the blind as distracting from a more active legislative role and from attempts to raise the standards of governmental programs. In England, similar efforts, which constituted about one-fourth of the episodes, were also opposed by local affiliates and other consumer organizations on the grounds that seeking special privilege conflicts with the larger goal of normalization and integration of the handicapped into the mainstream of the community. Related to this controversy is the fact that some organizations for the handicapped conceive of themselves as a charity, which conflicts with growing emphasis on the rights of the handicapped.

In contrast to this pattern, only 15 percent of the episodes in the United States were attempts to obtain concessions for clientele. This

16. In the United States, it is estimated that there are over 1,200 advisory commissions on the federal level, of which over 400 are within the Department of Health, Education and Welfare.

may be due to the lack of discretionary authority in state and county governments to grant tax exemptions. In the Netherlands, the search by national agencies for special benefits for their constituencies was second only to contacts with central government on subsidy matters.

Targets of Advocacy

The targets of improver activities reflect the policymaking system in each country. Belief in the efficacy of law to bring about social change is reflected in the extraordinary volume and scope of legislation on all three levels of the federal system in the United States. As a result, voluntary agencies expend substantial effort in external relations in order to exert some control over the competitive and changing environment in their local communities and on the state and federal levels.

In contrast to the United States, the parliaments of the three other countries operate at a slower pace, producing a fraction of the legislation with less specificity and investing more power in the hands of central government bureaucrats. The U.S. agencies concentrate most of their action on legislative bodies — city councils, boards of supervisors, state legislatures, and Congress — while voluntary agencies in the other countries focus their attention on the bureaucracies of central government, with almost all advocacy occurring on the national level.

The United States tends to separate financing from administration. It makes greater use of voluntary agencies for purchase of service and, like England, makes extensive use of federal block grants to local government for financing social service functions. Given the character of the legislative system and public funding policy in the United States, where there is an annual political struggle to renew contracts and appropriations and to avoid cutbacks, voluntary agencies are continually drawn into the effort to influence the policy process as a means of assuring a major source of their income.

Strategies and Obstacles

Strategies for advocacy can be divided into two broad types: single agency and coalition. The most notable difference among the four countries is the greater use of ad hoc, interorganizational coalitions and citizen committees by voluntary agencies in the United States, as well as their greater participation in the political process. More than one-half (twenty-seven) of the forty-eight episodes reported in the United States — but less than one-third (fourteen) in England —

involved coalitions. Such alliances rarely occurred in the Netherlands and Israel. In the U.S., temporary coalitions of voluntary agencies were effective in defeating the promulgation of regulations that would have prevented the use of contributed funds to match federal allocations, in helping to persuade the legislature to override a governor's veto on the closing of state institutions, in obtaining a reduction of municipal bus fares for the handicapped, and in the adoption of federal regulations to implement the Rehabilitation Act of 1973 after three years of delay.

Coalitional strategies in the United States were also encouraged by legislative use of a functional definition of developmental disabilities. As part of a broadened government program, other handicaps requiring the same set of community services as mental retardation were brought into a single governmental budgeting and planning process, thus increasing the number of organizations with a common stake in the program.[17] Incentives for collaboration were also strengthened by such legislative changes as Title XX of the Amendments to the Social Security Act of 1974, which permits extensive purchase of social services by government. An expanded number of voluntary agency budgets are affected by these new laws and regulations, and this becomes the basis for ad hoc coalitions and coordinated strategies to influence public policy.

This pattern contrasts with England, where only an occasional attempt by Parliament to modify tax benefits is sufficiently threatening for temporary coalitions to be formed. In the field of services to the mentally handicapped there are five national organizations, each purporting to be a spokesman. Although this has produced some interorganizational conflict and public confusion, parallel and sometimes competing approaches have also had the unintended effect of bolstering one another's efforts. After the strident, adversarial stance of the Campaign for the Handicapped or the somewhat aggressive attitude of the Spastics Society, the assertiveness and reasonableness of the NSMHC is much appreciated by officials in the Department of Health and Social Security.

In all four countries, each handicapped group has negative stereotypes of others that prevent the formation of coalitions. The physically handicapped do not want to be associated with the mentally retarded,

---

17. The developmental disabilities include mental handicap, cerebral palsy, autism, epilepsy, and other handicapping neurological conditions.

and vice versa. In Jerusalem, when the Department of Education tried to combine mentally retarded children with those suffering from brain dysfunction, the parents of the latter, who had their own organization, went on strike and refused to send their children to school until the retarded children were removed.

Policy affecting one type of handicap is usually not of interest to those concerned with another. For example, the organizations for the physically — but not the mentally — handicapped in England took a major role in fighting for the Chronic Sick and Disabled Persons Act in 1970. Perhaps this was the foremost legislative victory of the voluntary agencies. In the struggle in California over the Lanterman-Petris-Short Act of 1969, concerning the mentally ill, the reverse was true: no organization for the physically or sensorially handicapped participated. The policy issues that lead to temporary coalitions are those pertaining to tax exemptions, architectural barriers to mobility, and, in the United States, contribution deductibility. The fear of being stigmatized or of losing a privileged status is reinforced by the intrinsic reluctance of organizations to cooperate unless they have to.[18] In the Netherlands, the fifteen national organizations for the blind and the deaf and the twenty-two separate national organizations for the physically handicapped have resisted for years government efforts to bring them into some kind of federation. In England, the Netherlands, and Israel, the lack of federated fund raising and structures for social planning or other occasions when common interests might draw agencies together also militates against collaboration in social action.

Except for the blind and the mentally handicapped, organizations *of* the handicapped are not more active in advocacy than organizations *for* the handicapped in any of the four countries. In England, the presence of handicapped persons in the leadership of six organizations did not make them more active advocates, nor did the absence of consumer representation on the Board of Directors of the Spastics Society keep it from being one of the leading and most successful pressure groups. Evidently, consumer participation is by itself an insufficient basis for expecting a high degree of advocacy because, for example, there may be substantial policy disagreements or factionalism among consumers. In England, the younger, more articulate spokesmen for

18. The experience with coalitions in England and the factionalism that resulted are described in Thomas Acton, "Charities and the Iron Law of Chaos." Some of the prerequisites for interorganizational collaboration are analyzed in Sol Levine and Paul E. White, "Exchange as a Conceptual Framework for the Study of Inter-Organizational Relationships."

the physically handicapped, especially among those who have not
been disabled from birth, strongly opposed efforts to improve institutional care and concentrated instead on improving community services. Older persons and others less able to function in the community
are much less articulate.

In England, there were also periodic consumer challenges to the
representativeness of the organizations for the blind and for victims of
multiple sclerosis. In the latter, a small group of young adults broke
with the national organization to establish their own action group in
1973, mainly because of the unwillingness of the national organization
to support the research of a particular scientist in whom they had great
confidence. Similarly, two large national organizations of the blind are
highly critical of the Royal National Institute for the Blind, which
they perceived to be paternalistic, outdated and unrepresentative of
the blind themselves. They claim that the RNIB has lost much of its
crusading political character, that it has not identified itself with the
struggle waged by organizations to improve income for disabled persons, and that it has resisted greater statutory control over welfare
services to the blind.

That there is no single set of homogeneous interests among persons
suffering from a particular handicap is also evident in the case of the
organizations for the mentally handicapped. When parents dominate
the agency board of directors, they are naturally concerned about the
fate of their children, and they evaluate organizational goals in terms
of their personal priorities. Positions taken on controversial issues concerning institutionalization, community care, or the improvement of
service programs usually reflect the age and special needs of the children of the dominant policymaking group of parents.

Methods and Processes

Voluntary agencies, like most other organizations, generally assume
that they will accomplish their advocacy goals best by cultivating informal, interpersonal relationships with government officials and legislators. Political connections are most evident in the United States,
where board members of ten out of the twenty agencies had contacts
directly or through intermediaries with elected officials in local, state,
and federal government. An outstanding example of this is the alliance that developed in the late 1960s between the associations for the
retarded and a leading Republican state legislator who originally opposed them. Because of his subsequent favorable experience as chair-

man of a legislative committee dealing with these groups, he became convinced of the merit of their proposals, eventually reversing his position to become their primary spokesman in the state legislature. His powerful political position enabled him to introduce and secure passage of a series of major laws improving community services for the retarded in California.

In the three other countries, there are long-standing, personal relationships among government officials and those representing the voluntary agencies. In England, the "old boy" network is epitomized by the statement of a leading voluntary agency executive that "my best friends are the civil servants I criticize." All of the organizations in England have direct personal contact with the Minister for the Disabled, and some are acquainted with the head of the Department of Health and Social Security. The English agencies were also effective in establishing two all-party Parliamentary groups for the physically and mentally disabled, with whom they meet on a regular basis.

The mutually dependent relationships between the voluntary agencies and the senior civil servants in central government rest on an unspoken agreement on the rules of the game and an exchange of needed resources. In Israel, the Ministry of Social Welfare successfully used voluntary agency pressure to persuade the Treasury to allocate funds for certain governmental programs when the Ministry itself was unable to do so. A possible exception to the pattern of trade-offs was the persistent and often strident campaign waged by AKIM on behalf of the mentally handicapped in Israel. The propriety of its lobbying and alarmist press releases was challenged by government officials who resented this type of citizen pressure. Numerous efforts were made by high-ranking officials to discredit AKIM's position on the grounds that the parents were a small, overly emotional minority, who lacked a professional point of view and who were motivated only by self-interest. Although AKIM's abrasive tactics may have engendered considerable ill will within the bureaucracy of the Ministry of Social Welfare, they resulted in rather substantial achievements, which were grudgingly acknowledged later by the same officials, who admitted that they could not have accomplished what they did without the voluntary agency.

In all four countries, ideas are "planted" among voluntary agencies by civil servants when they want to advance a particular program in order to be able to respond to citizen demand, without the risk of being charged with empire building. In this time-honored strategy, constituencies are cultivated and, occasionally, are co-opted by government. Despite official pronouncements to the contrary in England, central government officials do not value highly the improver role of the voluntary agency except when it supports their own positions. Like most civil servants, they believe that government is doing about the best that it can, and that pressure from voluntary agencies is unnecessary. There is no acceptance by government officials of the use of the media to generate pressure on government, of strident protest, or of the adversary strategies used by some consumer organizations. The bureaucrats naturally prefer informal, friendly relationships with the voluntary agencies and resent attempts to put pressure on them.

Among the techniques used in performing the improver role, there is more emphasis on formal communication with individuals by letter writing in the Netherlands and in England, while the U.S. agencies make more use of the mass media to organize campaigns and to influence public opinion, as well as presenting testimony at public hearings. In eighteen out of the forty-eight U.S. episodes, press releases were issued and there were appearances on tv and radio. Also confined to the United States and Israel are protest tactics, several of which were highly effective. For example, a three-week sit-in organized by the Center for Independent Living in the Regional Office of the Department of Health, Education and Welfare finally helped produce the long-delayed regulations implementing the 1973 Rehabilitation Act. In Israel, sit-in protests and demonstrations are widely used by many other groups, but such tactics were used by only two agencies and a parent organization in desperation after not receiving a reply to a request to government for over two years.

Another similarity in improver episodes is their duration. The average in all countries was between two and one-half and three years, although some processes were reported to have persisted for up to twelve years, and a campaign by English agencies serving the deaf lasted twenty years before it was able to persuade the government to take action against the deceptive practices of commercial hearing-aid companies.

Whether there is a preponderance of coalitions, as in the United States, or of more individualistic approaches to government, as in the other three countries, the resulting proportion of the attempts regarded as successful is quite similar: in the United States, thirty-five out of the forty-eight episodes; thirty-eight out of forty-five in England; about three-quarters of the ones in Israel; but less than half of those in the Netherlands.

TABLE 13.
Targets, Strategies, and Methods of Advocacy

	United States	England, The Netherlands, and Israel
Targets	Local, state, and national legislative bodies	Central governmental bureaucracies
Strategies	Coalitions of agencies	Single agency
Methods	Lobbying and use of the media	Informal and formal communications

Factors Affecting Advocacy

In the course of describing the processes of advocacy, we have noted how the particular targets, strategies, and methods of the voluntary agencies are influenced by their public policymaking systems.

The major differences are summarized in Table 13.

Among other factors, the differences in the patterns of the performance of the improver role also reflect civic culture. The interest-group pluralism in the United States helps account for the active efforts of the voluntary agencies to influence legislation and for their more extensive use of ad hoc coalitions, citizen's committees, lobbying, use of the media, and other more political means of pursuing goals. In contrast to the norms of citizen participation in the United States and England, the pattern of corporate consultation in the Netherlands and the absence of a tradition of social reform among the local Dutch social service agencies means that most of the responsibility for influencing policy is carried by the national "roof" organizations. In Israel, the civic culture associated with democratic centralism gives little encouragement or sanction to organizations outside the political party structure that try to affect legislation; the absence of such organizational structures may explain the widespread use of confrontation and other adversarial tactics. Much more prevalent is the practice of *protektzia*, which stresses interpersonal relationships between individuals, interest groups, and government.[19]

Another nominal restraint on such overt political activity as lobbying by voluntary agencies in both England and the United States is the fear of losing their tax-exempt status. In 1976, however, the Internal Revenue Service in the United States issued for the first time some clear guidelines permitting voluntary organizations to engage in a

19. An analysis of these modes of influence is Yael Yishai, "Interest Groups in Israel."

reasonable amount of legislative activity under the Tax Reform Act of 1976, whereby public charities may expend a certain percentage of their budgets on lobbying activities without fear of losing their tax-deductible status. If the total expenditure of an agency is under $500,000, it may expend 20 percent of the total for direct lobbying without being taxed. In addition, volunteers may still lobby freely for their organizations, and two of the most frequent forms of voluntary agency improver activity are not considered lobbying at all: making available the results of nonpartisan studies and research, and providing technical advice in response to a request by a governmental body.[20]

In England the picture is still ambiguous. It has been stated that, "in exchange for various benefits of the charity law, voluntary organizations are forced to be artificially cautious . . . it (the Charity Law) blackmails them into avoiding controversy and debate. It inhibits their natural development, distorts their character, imposes alien ways on them."[21] A contrary opinion is given in a series of case studies of changing social policy:

> The voluntary social services are good examples of pressure groups which maintain a low political profile; but their ability to apply pressure is real. In part their very existence can be a political pressure because they operate as an alternative to governmental provision, and as a source of comparison for the critics of government action or inaction. They may also step directly into the field of political action if they feel that a particular need is too large for them to cope with and that government should accept responsibility for it.[22]

The Goodman Committee concluded that the Charity Law did not present any serious obstacles to a typical voluntary agency in its efforts to influence public policy.[23] Yet there is a great gap between the few activist organizations and the rest that does not seem to be related to the fear of losing tax exemption. Of greater significance is the strength of the commitment of the executive leadership to advocacy

20. A description of this legislation is Eugene Goldman, "Conable Lobbying Bill Becomes Law." Although activist groups engage in litigation, monitoring, and lobbying in efforts to influence federal rules and regulations, there is little evidence that established voluntary organizations have taken advantage of the more liberal provisions of the Conable Bill of 1976 (Academy of Educational Development, *The Voluntary Sector in Brief*, p. 29). Also see R. L. Hubbard, *Lobbying by Public Charities*.

21. Benedict Nightingale, *Charities*, p. 52.

22. Phoebe Hall et al., *Change, Choice and Conflict in Social Policy*, p. 92.

23. Goodman Committee, *Charity Law and Voluntary Organisations*, pp. 41–47, 149–50.

and the related organizational self-image as a pressure group or as a charitable social agency.[24]

In investigating other factors limiting the performance of advocacy by voluntary agencies, it was found that, contrary to conventional wisdom, reliance on public funds is not constraining. As we have seen in chapter 8, four sets of factors mitigate dependency: the payment-for-service form of most fiscal transfers, the diversity of income sources, the countervailing power of the voluntary agency's service monopoly and political influence, and low accountability. The U.S. agencies that receive the largest amount in public funds are among the most active advocates. This includes four agencies serving the mentally handicapped that receive 80 percent of their income from public sources, as well as the Center for Independent Living, a consumer-managed agency whose income came almost entirely from governmental sources.

Advocacy in the United States is also facilitated by the multiplicity of governmental units on three levels of administration and policymaking. While the use of public funds produced relatively little loss of autonomy, conflict of interest, or co-optation, there was some impressionistic evidence, particularly in Israel, that a more active performance of the improver role could be inhibited by organizational-maintenance activities. A form of Gresham's Law may operate, in which fund raising and program management may drain off the time and energy of leadership that might be channeled into influencing social policy. It is for this reason that a prominent agency executive in the United States has recommended that a fixed percentage of organizational time be allocated to advocacy.[25]

24. Few of the voluntary organizations in England define themselves as part of a social movement, including those that are presumably representative of the handicapped themselves, such as members of the Disability Alliance. Only the Spastics Society and the NSMHC describe their advocacy function as at least on a par with service provision, and the NSMHC refers to efforts to prod government to assume its responsibility as the organization's basic purpose. In its 1970 annual report, the NSMHC approvingly quoted Harvey Cox: "The apathetic avoidance of politics is the way we, like Cain, club our brothers to death." The Central Council for the Disabled has urged English agencies serving the handicapped to become "streamlined professional organizations" instead of "amateur benevolent bodies" if they want to become effective. On the relationship between services and advocacy, see Arnold Gurin and Joan Ecklein, "Community Organization for What? Political Power or Service Delivery?"

25. O'Connell, p. 3. He adds, "The large provider of service which is substantially dependent on government funds tends to use up much of its social action time to deal with the legislative, appropriations, and administrative red tape which relate to the agency's own program." O'Connell does not recommend a specific amount of time, but suggests that somewhere between 25 and 50 percent might be justified.

Similar factors may explain the small amount of advocacy on the local level in England, where the leadership and members of the affiliates of the national agency do not give it high priority. Instead, they concentrate on fund raising and, in some cases, on service programs. They conceive of themselves as more a mutual aid association, particularly since so many of the members are handicapped themselves or have handicapped relatives. The demands of caretaking and other family roles leave very little discretionary time for organizational work. It is, therefore, composition, function, and organizational-maintenance requirements that probably limit the advocacy function in these affiliates, rather than the Charity Law or any dependence on the local authority.

Advocacy is also believed to be constrained by bureaucratization, professionalization, a federated structure, or service delivery. While this study was not a test of these hypotheses, in none of the four countries did the variables seem to function in this way.[26] For example, federated organizations were the major channels for advocacy in the Netherlands, where they had considerable influence on central government. In England, the national organizations were also federations, loosely connected with their affiliates but free to pursue their improver objectives as they chose to define them. In Israel, the most adversarial national organization, AKIM, was a federation of local chapters, but another organization (ILAN) with a similar structure was least active in this role. Federation per se did not seem to be a major determinant. The relatively more active improver roles of the U.S. agencies also had less to do with their organizational structure than with their environment, fiscal resource systems, and leadership.

Most of the active improver agencies in the United States, England, and, to a lesser extent, Israel were also among the biggest, most bureaucratized, and most professionalized service providers, as well as being receivers of large amounts of public funds. At the same time, some of the agencies that reported the fewest episodes of improver activities provided few direct services and emphasized research and public education. To put it conversely, neither the absence of service programs nor a low degree of bureaucratization and professionalization was conducive to advocacy. The ideological commitment of the

26. Martin Rein and Robert Morris, "Goals, Structures and Strategies for Community Change"; Wolfensberger, pp. 23–32; Richard Hall, "Professionalization and Bureaucratization," pp. 92–104; Mayer N. Zald, "Organizations as Polities: An Analysis of Community Organization Agencies."

executive leadership system to the performance of the improver role seemed to be more significant because the support, if not the initiative, of the executive or the volunteer officers of the board is necessary if influence is to be mobilized.[27]

Policy Implications

These findings have implications for the various roles of voluntary agencies. The mission of the voluntary agency to articulate the interests of neglected minority groups and populations at risk may take on greater significance as the social services in a welfare state become more universal in scope and benefit, overshadowing the service-provision functions of voluntary agencies. If neither the public nor the voluntary service system has a monopoly on service innovation or even on the use of volunteers, then the improver role, or what has been described as change agentry, comes close to being a unique organizational competence of the voluntary agency.

In considering how this role might best be defined, we can conceive of a flexible model whereby a voluntary agency's objectives could be guided by the level of development of universalism in governmental programs. If governmental responsibility has been assumed on a comprehensive basis for a particular population of concern to a voluntary agency, the voluntary agency could concentrate on the functions of external monitoring and safeguarding the quality of governmental services by means of independent advisory or watchdog committees.[28] The agency's new objectives could include a concern with more effective regulatory control, based on such principles as funding contingent upon externally evaluated performance, institutionalization of the ombudsman system, consumer participation in policymaking, and procedures for client feedback and grievance management. If, on the other hand, the universalism of the governmental program is more nominal than real or government is reluctant to assume operating responsibility, then the improver role of the voluntary agency would be to prod government to assure equitable coverage and legal entitlement

27. See Jerald Hage and R. DeWar; "Elite Values versus Organizational Structure in Predicting Innovation"; Howard B. Kaplan, "Implementation of Program Change in Community Agencies"; and Lawrence V. Mohr, "Determinants of Innovation in Organization."

28. These are some of the recommendations of Wolfensberger, pp. 25–32. The Donee critique of the Filer Commission also recommended that philanthropic funds be used primarily to support organizations monitoring or seeking change in government and other established institutions, or those aiding minorities to catch up, because these two functions are more important as government gets bigger and more remote.

so that adequate and appropriate services are available. Since all organizations require external sources of change, performance of the improver role by voluntary agencies can contribute to the more effective functioning of the entire social service system.

The argument for the primacy of change agentry rests on the belief that a strong and independent nongovernmental sector is needed to monitor and prod a sluggish bureaucratic system, as well as to serve as an advocate for clients. Because the organizational differences between governmental and voluntary sponsorship are lessening, the special value of the voluntary agency as a minority agency representing the interests of neglected groups may be considerably diminished, if not lost. In holistic, sociopolitical contexts such as Israel or the Netherlands, where there is usually a symbiotic relationship between agencies and government, the stimulating advantage of dialectic is lost. Greater differentiation might encourage each system to develop its distinctive competence.

Although in theory a strong case could be made for voluntary agencies' giving priority to social action, it is uncertain whether sufficient public support could be obtained for agencies that would be advocates exclusively. Most voluntary agencies have built their reputations on service programs, and it is on the basis of this appeal that funds are contributed by the public. It is doubtful that financial support and tax exemptions would still be forthcoming if service programs were substantially reduced in scope and social agencies became pressure groups like other types of voluntary associations, concerned only with the quality and quantity of governmental service. In addition, service delivery is the source of the legitimation and expertise underlying the credibility of the voluntary agency as an advocate. Hence, apart from the problems implied in expecting all service programs to be operated by government, it may be premature and unwise to call for such exclusive concentration on advocacy. We turn next to the service-provision function of the voluntary agency.

12. The Service Provider Role

Whereas pioneering is the most frequently mentioned value of voluntary agencies, their actual service role is less dramatic. In the past, voluntary organizations were the chief form of collective action for social service outside government. Public provision has, however, advanced so rapidly that the voluntary sector is usually viewed as a way of extending, improving, complementing, or substituting for government. Voluntary agencies are rarely the principal service providers, as they are in the Netherlands, except in certain fields, such as hospitals or leisure-time programs. More often a response to public policy and the level of development (qualitatively and quantitatively) of governmental provision, voluntary services can be assessed as one of the institutions of a pluralistic society, together with other nongovernmental service providers.

Many concepts and theories have been proposed to describe the actual and desired relationships between governmental and voluntary organizations in the provision of the social services. Typical of many concepts are the four functions ascribed to English voluntary agencies, which do work (1) that the welfare state will never do, (2) that the state might agree to do sometime, but does not at present; (3) that the state would probably be obliged to do if there were no voluntary agency, and (4) that is already being done, either well or inadequately, by the state itself.[1]

In the mid-1950s, in one of the few empirical studies of the subject, Samuel Mencher identified four major types of relationships in the British social services: (1) the voluntary agency administers the total service for the statutory agency; (2) the voluntary agency provides services for which the statutory agency has insufficient facilities; (3) the voluntary agency supplements a statutory agency where economy

1. Benedict Nightingale, *Charities*, p. 74. A parallel set of functions can be derived from the idea that voluntary agencies should do what government can't, should not, or won't do.

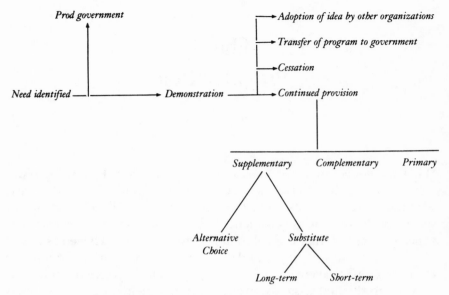

Figure 4. Typology of Service Provider Roles

or flexibility is desired; (4) the voluntary agency supplements a governmental agency with money or services for which there is no governmental provision.[2]

In analyzing the service provider role in the four countries, we shall use a slightly different threefold classification of relationships, in which: (1) the voluntary agency is virtually the only, or *primary*, provider because it has few if any governmental counterparts; (2) the voluntary agency *complements* governmental provision with services that are qualitatively different in kind; (3) the voluntary agency *supplements* or extends the governmental system with similar services, some of which may offer an alternative choice or serve as a substitute for a governmental service.[3]

2. Samuel Mencher, "The Relationship of Voluntary and Statutory Welfare Services in England," pp. 308–18.

3. Similar classifications have been used in England by the Personal Social Service Council and in the Wolfenden Report. The distinction between supplementary and complementary is also implicit in Burton Weisbrod's hypothesis that certain nongovernmental, public consumption goods are similar to and extend (supplement) governmental services, whereas their counterparts in the private market are qualitatively different in kind (complement) (*The Voluntary Non-Profit Sector: An Economic Analysis*, pp. 59–60).

Based on the reconceptualization of the multiple outcomes of the vanguard role in chapter 9, we can see in the schema below the subsequent, alternative forms of voluntary agency service vis-à-vis government, in which the voluntary agency may prod (improver), demonstrate (vanguard), or, by continuing to deliver the service, supplement, complement, or substitute for government, in addition to being a primary provider.

Primary Provider

While individual voluntary agencies may occasionally be the sole provider of a service in their localities, in few personal social services for the physically and mentally handicapped is a voluntary agency the sole sponsor using mainly nongovernmental funds. (The agencies in the Netherlands are, of course, an exception and they are not included in this analysis.) There are other exceptions. The only emergency ambulance service in Israel is operated by a voluntary agency that is supported solely by contributions from locally and abroad. In England, the manufacture and distribution of the many technical aids for the blind and the deaf are restricted largely to the Royal National Institutes for the Blind and the Deaf.[4] Outside the field of service to the handicapped, there is a virtual voluntary monopoly in England on animal welfare, sea rescue, and some forms of child protection. Social and recreational programs for the handicapped are found predominantly in the voluntary sector, but even in this traditional field there may be direct or indirect governmental support. This is also true for sheltered workshops, practically the only social service under municipal auspices in the Netherlands.

There is, of course, a limited period when voluntary agency services are the primary ones. This usually occurs in the early stages of organizational development, when voluntary agencies are the sole providers of services to controversial, stigmatized, or deviant groups, for whom government has not yet assumed responsibility. In England, this includes battered wives, victims of rape and other crimes, squatters, homeless persons, and homosexuals. In the long run there is, however, a tendency toward universalism in welfare states, and such groups tend eventually to be included in either governmental service

4. The Royal National Institute for the Blind, which describes itself as the largest voluntary agency for the blind in the world, reported over 30,000 orders for the 300 items listed in its catalog of aids.

programs or, more likely, through government financial support of voluntary efforts directed toward them.

The paucity of services for which the voluntary agency is the primary provider, with or without governmental support, in England, the United States, and Israel illustrates a fundamental feature of the welfare economy, in which most voluntary agency services either supplement or complement governmental programs. Although these two concepts are often used interchangeably, it is useful to distinguish them analytically. In addition to the distinction between services that are similar and those that are different in kind, supplementary and complementary services differ in symmetry and duration: *supplementary* refers to something added, often temporarily, to make up for a lack, where one element — the one being supplemented — is considered basic or most important. *Complementary* implies equivalence between the two elements, such as a circle divided into two sectors. Although governmental provision may be considered inadequate in both patterns, complementary services tend to continue for a long period because there is little likelihood of governmental provision, for example, preschool training for deaf children. In contrast, supplementary services are usually justified as only temporary because of a current lack of public resources or capability, for example, respite care or casework services for the parents of handicapped children.[5]

The three dimensions of the service relations between governmental and voluntary organizations are summarized in Table 14. They will be used first to analyze two types of service provision, later, to suggest ways of rethinking governmental-voluntary relationships.

Complementary Service Provision

At first glance, very few programs in England appear to fall into this category because of a long-standing commitment to universalism and statutory provision, which has progressed further than in the United States and Israel. As a result of the comprehensive scope of statutory responsibility, there are virtually no social services that a citizen could

5. This classification does not fit some of the more ambiguous patterns, whereby a service could reasonably be regarded as either a complement or a supplement. The distinction is not rigid, and it involves a value judgment. For example, if it is believed that the state should provide but it does not, voluntary provision is likely to be seen as a substitute rather than as a complement. This was the case in England and the United States when, until well into the twentieth century, the poor law filled the gap left by private charity and government was regarded as a substitute for philanthropy. Those who espouse empowerment theories regard voluntary organizations as primary and governmental services as supplementary or complementary.

TABLE 14.

Dimensions of Sectoral Relationships in Service Provision

	Supplementary Voluntary Services	Complementary Voluntary Services	Primary Voluntary Services
Basic character of voluntary service	Extension of similar governmental service	Qualitatively different from governmental service	No governmental counterpart of voluntary service provision
Power relationship	Asymmetrical: unequal power because one element (government) is basic or dominant	Symmetrical power relationships between voluntary and governmental organizations	Asymmetrical; voluntary agency is dominant
Duration of service	Ostensibly time-limited, until governmental provision	Long-term because governmental provision is unlikely	Uncertain; continues as long as there is no governmental provision

not claim. However, despite broad entitlement, there is a chronic unevenness and inconsistency in availability throughout the country.[6]

Examples of some complementary services offered by voluntary
agencies in England are: long-term counseling to families of handicapped children offered by the Invalid Childrens' Aid Association, as
well as their schools for asthmatic children and for those with speech
defects; the trusteeship program of the NSMHC; the Family Assessment Center of the Spastics Society; and the financial assistance given
to long-term cancer patients by the National Cancer Relief Society.
It is generally assumed in England that the long-term financial needs
of cancer patients will not and cannot be met by the local authority.
However, it is not clear what would happen if the agency did not
exist, because the staff of the Social Service Departments knows that
financial assistance from this voluntary agency is available and con-
tinuously refers cancer patients to it for needs that cannot be met by
the Supplementary Benefits Commission.

In addition to these instances of complementary services in England, one prominent set of services is not a gap-filling substitute for
governmental programs, but is substantially different in kind: namely,
the services offered through such indigenous, peer self-help programs
as the Center for Independent Living in the United States or the local
affiliates of the national organizations described in chapter 10 on the
value guardian role. In all four countries, these services and facilities
not only relieve and even replace the family, as do many governmental
programs, but at the same time, they can provide a unique reinforce-
ment of the family through parent-to-parent information exchange,
sharing, advice, and emotional support.[7] What is a clientele for a government agency is often, under voluntary auspices, a membership-
constituency for whom the voluntary agency operates as a service

6. Some sense of the scope of entitlement in England can be gained from the following list of
services which the 1970 Chronic Sick and Disabled Persons Act, Section 2, requires the Local
Authority Social Service Department to provide for disabled persons who need them: practical
assistance in the home; radio or tv, outings, and other recreational and educational facilities in
and outside the home; means of transportation to benefit from social activities; adaptations and
additional facilities for greater safety, comfort, and convenience in the home; holidays; meals;
phone; and necessary equipment.

7. Wolfenden Committee, *The Future of Voluntary Organizations*, p. 26. The report adds, "In
our view, the informal and statutory systems taken together constitute the principal means of
meeting social needs in our society." There is considerable evidence that most of the responsibility for the care and support of handicapped individuals rests on the family rather than on governmental or voluntary agencies. It might, therefore, be more accurate to describe the mutual aid
programs of voluntary agencies as complementary to both government and the family system.

provider, advocate, and bridge to government benefits. Although self-help service programs can also be considered a primary function of the voluntary sector, they are classified as complementary to emphasize both their difference in kind and the unlikelihood of governmental sponsorship.

Other examples of complementary services in England are the local associations for the deaf and for the blind, which the Social Service Departments have appointed as their delegate agencies. Apart from a lack of specialized personnel with the requisite skills to work with the sensorially handicapped, it is not economical for a single SSD to administer highly specialized residential or community-based services for very small population groups. Consequently, local authorities contract with the associations for the deaf and the blind in their communities to be the sole agents for these programs.[8]

In the United States, a wide range of voluntary agency services can be classified as complementary, not because they are different in kind from governmental programs, but because, although financed by tax funds, for reasons of public policy they are not likely to be provided directly by government. These include: sheltered workshops; day centers; social, educational, recreational, and camping activities; nutritional programs; employment training; job experience; and transportation.[9] In California, over fifty separate services are authorized for the developmentally disabled, few of which are provided directly by governmental agencies. Voluntary agencies also serve those who are ineligible for governmental programs, such as those regarded as insufficiently employable by the State Department of Rehabilitation. Therefore, some of these services are also substitutes, because if there were no qualified voluntary agencies government would have to provide the service or to assure that it would be offered by some other body, even if that meant creating a new organization. The latter

8. Up to 1948, virtually all services to the deaf in England were provided by over 200 local organizations, but by 1975 only about half of the local authorities still utilized voluntary agencies under religious auspices as their delegated agencies for serving the deaf. In contrast, almost three-fourths of the Social Service Departments used local associations for the blind and the physically handicapped until the 1970s.

9. Transportation services for the handicapped differ markedly in each of the countries. In the United States, transportation is considered a "case service," with matching federal grants available in a community for a very limited service. In England, however, it approximates a "social utility" and is provided to the extent possible by the Social Service Department's fleet of vehicles. In Israel, no transportation services are ordinarily available through governmental agencies, and this is also the case in the Netherlands. On the distinction between case services and social utilities, see Alfred J. Kahn, *Social Policy and Social Services*, pp. 76–78.

course was followed in the establishment of the Regional Centers for Developmental Disabilities in California as nonprofit corporations completely financed by government.[10]

To fulfill their service obligations, governmental agencies often have considerable choice. In California and in most other states, local government has four options in the provision of homemaker-chore services to the handicapped: (1) to employ its own staff, (2) to contract with a proprietary organization to deliver the service, (3) to purchase from or contract with a nonprofit organization such as a voluntary agency, (4) to give funds directly to the individual to buy his own services.[11] The greatest use of contracts is in the United States, together with a more extensive set of regulations concerning this practice. The "contract state" is seen vividly in California, where the Department of Rehabilitation contracts for all services for its clientele except counseling and case management. A similar policy is followed by the Crippled Childrens' Services of the California Department of Public Health.

In Israel, most voluntary agency services can also be classified as complementary, mainly because of the absence of governmental counterparts and the unlikely prospect of direct provision by government. This includes such programs as the preschool training of deaf children; the reach-to-recovery volunteer programs of the Cancer Association; sports centers; social and recreational programs for the deaf, blind, and disabled; homemaker services; and transportation. Among the factors that limit the direct involvement of the government in services for the mentally and physically handicapped in Israel are: the

10. Designed to establish a more comprehensive community service system for the mentally retarded that would offer alternatives to the state hospital, the Regional Center concept was first adopted by the California Legislature as a pilot project in 1964–1965, and was extended in 1969. It provided for state responsibility from the time of diagnosis of mental retardation, not upon admission to a state hospital. What was notable was the decision not to create another state agency, but instead to contract with a new voluntary organization in each region, which it was assumed would be better qualified to carry out the intent of the legislature to provide a lifetime resource for the individual and his family. This principle was challenged on constitutional grounds by the California State Employees Association, which held that the state must use its own qualified civil servants to expend state funds, but the Superior Court in Sacramento County ruled against it. The twenty-three Developmental Disabilities Regional Centers in California are nonprofit corporations that receive all of their funds from the State Department of Health. See footnotes 7, chapter 9, and 9, chapter 11.

11. It would be useful to compare these four modes of service delivery for different types of personal social services to identify their respective costs and benefits for the clientele and the organizations. For an example of some initial attempts at this type of research, see M. A. Garrick and W. L. Moore, "Uniform Assessments and Standards of Social and Health Care Services." Similar studies have been launched by the program on nonprofit organizations, Institution for Social and Policy Studies, Yale University.

priority given to defense of the state and the absorption of mass immigration in the early 1950s; the prior existence of voluntary agencies and the availability of philanthropic funds at home and abroad for their support; and, in contrast to the United States and England, a historical division of responsibility on the basis of age, with voluntary organizations expected to serve preschool children, while the government takes over most social services when children enter school. One consequence of the continued provision of services by voluntary agencies under these circumstances is that further governmental involvement in direct service provision has not been encouraged.

Many of these complementary programs are supported in Israel because their sponsors expect little or no change in the public policies that, in their view, make existing government programs inadequate or inappropriate. The lack of a strong commitment to prevention by the Ministry of Health, as well as by the Sick Fund of the General Federation of Labor, to which 80 percent of the population belongs, was given by the Israel Cancer Association as a major reason for the establishment of clinics for the early detection of breast cancer. The stigma attached to the municipal welfare offices, their lack of specialized, individualized services for the physically handicapped, and the absence of any specific ministerial responsibility for this clientele were cited by ILAN to justify its extensive network of seventeen programs for postpolio children and other young victims of neuromuscular disease. The momentum of ILAN's highly successful fund raising, which needed new and tangible services to enhance the annual appeal, also contributed to the maintenance of these separate programs. This was reinforced by the reluctance of volunteers to give up local programs to which they had become attached. As a result, 80 percent of ILAN's requests for service were from governmental agencies.

Another set of programs for the mentally handicapped in Israel was maintained by AKIM. These programs had significantly higher standards than their governmental counterparts, whose salaries, staff ratios, and services were regarded as unacceptable by AKIM board members. The voluntary agency also gave high priority to the development of hostels as opposed to closed institutions, and served persons who differed considerably in age and socioeconomic and ethnic status from those in government institutions and workshops.

The way in which a complementary service becomes self-perpetuating and ultimately deters governmental provision throughout the country is illustrated by the Homemaker Services Association (MATAV), started by a group of social workers in 1957 because neither the Ministry of Health nor the Sick Fund was willing to provide home care for their patients. This situation did not change for over twenty years, partly because MATAV offered a limited service in seven communities for a small number of persons for whom the partial cost of homemaker services was subsidized by government or the Sick Fund. In this way, the government and the Sick Fund had the best of both worlds; a modicum of service was provided to some of their clientele at less than cost, and they were in the virtuous position of supporting a charity.

Supplementary Service Provision

Supplementary services are of two types: those that are *alternatives*, offering a choice to the consumer, and those that are, in effect, *substitutions* for government provision. Because governmental agencies ordinarily cannot compensate for each other's deficiencies, supplementation is a special contribution of the voluntary agency that is influenced by public policy, the level of governmental provision, and, of course, the possession of appropriate resources. Substitutions can be classified into those that persist over a short period of time and are eventually adopted by a governmental body, and long-term situations in which the voluntary agency is a preferred provider or vendor, as in the United States, or a delegate agency for a statutory body, as in England.[12]

We can best examine the supplementary character of services provided by the voluntary agencies in England. Although there is comprehensive statutory responsibility for virtually all social services for the physically and mentally handicapped, the requisite funds, qualified staff, and facilities are often lacking or insufficient to carry out even mandatory duties, let alone discretionary functions. Accordingly, if an existing voluntary agency on either the national or the local level has the requisite resources, it is generally used to overcome the deficiencies and the constraints of the statutory system. In this way, English voluntary agencies extend the range of some rationed statutory services for constituencies that may have low visibility or low priority within the broad scope of the local authority, such as par-

12. The line between supplementary and complementary gets blurred at this point because the service provider role can also involve substitution — i.e., if the voluntary agency didn't do it, government would, but government prefers not to because using the voluntary agency is cheaper. At the same time, the service provider role complements government because of the assumption that voluntary auspices may make services qualitatively different — e.g., by improving access as a result of a more favorable perception of the service by the clientele or by providing a less bureaucratized, more individualized, and specialized service.

aplegics, deaf alcoholics, autistic children, or persons with multiple sclerosis, muscular dystrophy, or cerebral palsy.

Another type of supplementation is explained by the Invalid Childrens' Aid Association in describing their casework program: "This service is gap-filling insofar as the statutory social services are so overpressed and have a multiplicity of requirements as first call on their time that they cannot give such quality of service as ICAA workers who are without such commitments." As long as there is a gap between authorized services and available resources, there will be opportunities for voluntary agencies to help make good the promise of the welfare state by providing supplementary services.[13]

Some of the consequences of the service provider role are revealed in the experience of the Family Fund in England, a completely governmentally funded, nonprofit corporation set up in 1973 to meet the needs of all severely handicapped children, not just the victims of thalidomide.[14] Its original intent was to complement existing services, but very soon the Family Fund found itself supplementing such basic, statutory personal social services as laundry and transportation. In a short while, it became not only a substitute for many statutory services, but in some areas almost the primary provider, aiding far more persons and supplying more benefits than the local authority. Not until the third year of its existence in 1976 did the Family Fund change its policy and decide not to serve any longer as a substitute in the provision of aids, adaptations, and other benefits available through the Supplementary Benefits Commission.

A similar situation was faced by the Golden Gate Regional Center in the San Francisco Bay Area, which also had a broad mandate to serve all persons with a developmental disability. The Regional Center, which was perceived as a substitute rather than as a supplement to the existing service system, constantly struggled against the tendency of other agencies to "dump" their clientele onto it. The Regional Center sought to define its functions as advocacy and the stimulation

13. The special role of voluntary agencies in a period of declining support for governmental programs is discussed in greater detail in chapter 14. In a 1979 statement on behalf of Senate Bill 219 and House Resolution 1785 on charitable contributions, the Coalition of National Voluntary Organizations declared: "As government supported human services programs are reduced or eliminated under pressure for balanced budgets, Prop. 13-type cutbacks or the troubled economy in general, more and more of the gaps must be filled by charitable organizations." Some of the dangers of this position are discussed later in this chapter.

14. Lewis E. Waddilove, "The Family Fund," C. C. Hood and J. R. Bradshaw, "The Family Fund: Implications of an Unorthodox Agency."

of other agencies to serve persons with developmental disabilities as it tried with varying success to avoid becoming the primary service provider.

Sometimes a service may be initiated by a voluntary agency on the presupposition that it is a time-limited, supplementary one "until a statutory agency can take over." This aspiration, if taken seriously, assumes an ideal of the provision of universal services by government that is rarely attained. Implementation of policy is almost invariably blocked by resource deficits, administrative and professional inadequacies, or a highly politicized social service bureaucracy, such as one finds in Israel. In addition, new "needs" are always being discovered in a welfare state. Consequently, the time-limited, supplementary character of voluntary agency services may be a myth, because they almost always become institutionalized rather than remaining temporary.

While many voluntary agency services can be described as substitutes, the least frequent type of supplementary service is one which involves an alternative choice. Although the value of consumer choice is highly regarded in the economy, it has only recently been invoked in the social services, where there is typically a scarcity of resources and very little choice. A double standard is usually present, whereby consumer choice is regarded as desirable in competitive enterprise, but as "a proliferation of services, duplication and fragmentation in the social services."[15] Yet, in the provision of public goods, sometimes "the charity market" is preferred to the political market for economic or ideological reasons. Services provided by the voluntary sector may also be regarded as similar to the consumer services available through individual entrepreneurs, in contrast to the more standardized, impersonal services emanating from the public sector.[16] One of the few examples of this type of alternative service is the Assessment Center of the Spastics Society, which offers a choice to the families of handicapped children, since somewhat similar assessment services are available through the National Health Service in England. At the same time, the Spastics Society decided not to develop its own social work department as an alternative to those offered by most local authorities. It is not clear what criteria guided the society in offering its clients a choice for assessment, but not for social work services.

15. Some of the positive functions of duplication are discussed in Martin Landau, "Redundancy, Rationality, and the Problem of Duplication and Overlap."

16. On the charity market, see David B. Johnson, "The Charity Market: Theory and Practice," p. 100.

When a service is truly an alternative, both governmental and voluntary organizations offer similar services to the same clientele and may even compete with each other. This condition is found in some of the day care and social and recreational programs in England and the United States. Usually there is some special advantage to voluntary auspices, such as greater accessibility, less stigma, smaller scale, higher standards, or a more qualified, complete, or personalized service.

Some other complexities of the supplementary, gap-filling services are also more evident in England than in the other countries. We shall briefly note the supplementary character of residential care, the provision of holidays, and financial assistance by the English agencies.

Because the field of residential care for the physically handicapped in England has historically been dominated by voluntary agencies, there are few statutory counterparts of the institutions of the Shaftesbury Society, the Spastics Society, Cheshire Homes, and the Royal National Institutes for the Blind and the Deaf, which together provide for over half of all the physically handicapped requiring twenty-four-hour care. The prior existence of these facilities, as well as the recent entrance of government into this field (in the last thirty years), has made it uneconomical for local authorities to build institutions for small numbers of handicapped persons. They have instead utilized the existing national and regional institutions of the voluntary agencies on a payment-for-service basis, and the Social Service Departments have developed a very limited number of small residential units in the community. In residential care for the physically and sensorially handicapped in England, government supplements voluntary initiative, while the reverse is true in services for the mentally handicapped or in the provision of holiday homes, where the voluntary facilities are a specialized supplement to statutory provision.

So dominant is the voluntary agency in the field of residential care for the physically handicapped that several agencies have collected funds for the construction of such facilities as hostels, twenty-four-hour care institutions, training schools, and day care and then, after equipping and furnishing the facilities, have turned them over to the local authority. Typically, the local authority agrees to utilize a fixed number of places and, in a number of instances, to pay higher fees, sometimes up to eight times as much as the regular rate. In such cases, where the voluntary agency provides capital funds, both of the partners benefit. The voluntary agency has an attractive cause for fund raising and a place to invest its contributed funds. It secures a facility for the care of its constituency and the assurance of continued maintenance without having to worry about an annual deficit, and it usually obtains a voice in the management of the institution. On the other hand, the statutory agency is able to break through the government's freeze on new buildings and loans, and it acquires a capital investment free of charge. It can more easily include operating costs in its annual budget and can provide continuity and stability to the program. The voluntary agency service is also cheaper than if government provided the service directly. However, by substituting its capital funds for those of government, a voluntary agency may have been deflected from investing its resources in pioneering or experimental ventures.

In the provision of holidays (short-term vacations for the handicapped), a process of mutual-deficit financing is at work. In such arrangements, the local authorities pay the national voluntary agencies on a per capita basis for one- to two-week stays in voluntary homes for physically handicapped clientele for whom there is statutory responsibility. This is usually done because the voluntary vacation facilities are cheaper or because they offer a specialized form of care that is otherwise unobtainable in the countryside.

Voluntary agencies, on the other hand, subsidize the cost of holidays for other clientele for whom the local authority is unable or unwilling to pay, such as the spouses of handicapped persons. There is considerable variation in financing holidays because some Social Service Departments are prepared to pay the entire cost, while others authorize payment only if a voluntary agency is unable or unwilling to pay.[17] Governmental provision of holidays for the handicapped is far more advanced in England than in the other countries; only voluntary funds are available for this purpose in the United States and Israel.

In providing certain supplementary services, a voluntary agency is, as noted in Chapter 8, vulnerable as its costs approach those of direct governmental operation. Under these conditions, it is difficult to defend the use of a voluntary agency, particularly if the governmental agency is already offering a similar, if limited, service. Another problem arises when the scope of the voluntary program becomes increasingly standardized, routine, and bureaucratic, and its distinctive voluntary character is diminished. This occurred when many local

---

17. In a related, unpublished investigation by the Family Fund, the research staff found that almost half of the local authorities in the study relied on voluntary agencies and that without them, the provision of holidays for the handicapped would be "abysmally low."

authorities took over meals-on-wheels programs formerly under voluntary auspices. The experience in England suggests that unless there are compelling financial and administrative advantages to government to continue to pay for mainstream programs provided by voluntary agencies, their future is precarious.

A final example of supplementation is the provision of financial assistance on a case-by-case basis by many of the affiliates of the national agencies in England, as well as in Israel, for special needs that cannot adequately be provided by the local authority. Some handicapped persons are not sufficiently infirm to meet the eligibility requirements for a local authority facility, or they are above the level for supplementary benefits, or the monthly quota for certain kinds of aids has been exhausted.[18] Because the Social Service Departments never have enough funds and have other commitments and priorities, their social workers often seek additional financial assistance from voluntary organizations that have a specific interest in a particular type of handicapped person. Voluntary agencies are also used extensively as a way of circumventing onerous bureaucratic restrictions.

Universalism and Particularism

Underlying the distinctions between supplementary and complementary services are issues relating to universalism and particularism, as well as the desirability of achieving both mass coverage and individualization.[19] While, in general, voluntary agencies are centrifugal (separating out) and governmental organizations are centripetal (consolidating), there are important departures from these designations. Certain categories of the handicapped — such as the blind, the deaf, the mentally handicapped, and, most recently in the United States, the developmentally disabled — have historically been singled out for separate legislation or administrative treatments. The principles of universalism are further compromised by the great variation in the type and quality of public benefits in each country. Benefits are affected by the locus and circumstances under which a handicap originated — i.e., whether at birth, in an accident, at work, at home, on the street, on a sports field, or during a war.

Nevertheless, the tendency of government to be more universalistic and more generic in its approach provides much of the justification for

18. The vast range of financial need that could not be met by the local authority is evident in the existence of fifty-six categories of special need eligible for assistance from the Supplementary Benefits Commission.

19. Kahn, pp. 106–9, 155–57.

the specialized direct services and the educational and research programs of the voluntary agencies. The difference between contrasting governmental and voluntary perspectives was illustrated in 1975, when the Department of Health and Social Security in England requested the local authorities to report only the degree and not the type of disability of persons on the local authority register. Often its concern with the handicapped individual as a whole enables a voluntary agency to overcome the inherent fragmentation of departmentalized statutory services. As a prominent government official said: "Voluntary organizations at present are better able than government departments to respond to many-sided problems."[20]

There are, however, few exceptions to the single-handicap focus of most voluntary agencies. In England, the Invalid Childrens' Aid Association is the only agency that purports to serve any type of physically handicapped child. Its counterparts in the United States are such organizations as the Easter Seal Society, the California League for the Handicapped, and the Center for Independent Living, all of which offer their services to any handicapped person, regardless of his diagnostic label. These agencies contrast with the narrow focus of almost all the national agencies in England, the United States, and Israel, some of which have enlarged their scope by adding other systemically related handicaps, such as lung and heart. The prevalence of multi- rather than single-handicapped persons is the cause of criticism of voluntary agency overspecialization and selectivity, which has led to competition and jurisdictional disputes affecting the identification and affiliation of members. In each country, parents of a handicapped child can choose between four or five organizations, depending on which one conveys the least stigma to them. Curiously, there is a preference for forms of cerebral palsy or other neuromuscular conditions as a means of avoiding the stigma of mental handicap.[21]

20. Roy Jenkins, speech at the 1976 annual general meeting of the London Council of Social Services, partially reprinted in the *Lewisham Voluntary Action*, undated.

21. The socio-psychological factors relating to the differential perception of handicaps has been little explored. On the consequences of differences between organizational and individual definitions of a disability, see Mildred Blaxter, "'Disability' and Rehabilitation: Some Questions of Definition," and Robert A. Scott, "A Construction of Conceptions of Stigma by Professional Experts." The basic thesis of Scott's work, based mainly on his studies of the blind, is that the assumptions concerning the nature of a disability and stigmas on the part of various professionals constitute an ideology that shapes treatments and services. For example, he claims that the dominant professional ideology in the United States is essentially psychological; in England the emphasis is on "cheering up" the disabled; in Sweden the approach is much more technical. Permeating these cross-cultural comparisons is a relative emphasis on individual or collective responsibilities. Not only the professionals but also the laymen who control fund raising are

The experience in England with a more generic approach to the provision of the personal social services has not been very encouraging. The post-Seebohm goal of the Social Service Departments to become a one-stop, open-door provider of all the personal social services was, as we saw in chapter 2, beset by many organizational and financial obstacles. As part of a policy commitment to a generic approach, responsibility for the physically and mentally handicapped was dispersed throughout the entire case load in the decentralized area offices. To assist social workers in coping with their new kinds of clients, in-service training was provided, and some effort was made to use the specialized skills of the approximately one-third of the social workers who had been employed in mental health departments before 1971 by assigning them to emergency services or employing them as consultants to less-experienced staff. Nevertheless, there was an over-all impression that a leveling in the quality of service had occurred and that for some, such as the blind and the mentally handicapped, there was a setback. Whether this was temporary or not was unclear because two trends were at work. First, after the first three years many local authorities gradually abandoned the generic approach, and specialization by age, type of problem, or method slowly crept back in. Second, social workers were learning to deal more effectively with the specialized needs of the physically and mentally handicapped. This latter trend was vitiated by the rapid turnover of the front-line, least-experienced staff in the area offices, who had most contact with the handicapped, but who usually had insufficient time, ability, and inclination to work with them.[22]

Related to the identification of governmental organizations with universalism and a generic approach and of voluntary agencies with particularism and specialization is the conflict between the philosophy of normalization, or the integration of the handicapped into the main-stream of community life, and the maintenance of separate programs and facilities for each of the different handicapped groups. While governmental organizations are more active than voluntary agencies in promoting facilities for the multi-handicapped and in mixing various

influenced by values and assumptions concerning the nature of the disability. This includes attitudes toward the restorative and rehabilitative approaches, as opposed to the custodial approach, which has an easier time because of the community's need to stigmatize and isolate the handicapped person. Bureaucratic organizations, for example, require more legal and administrative definitions of disabilities so that there can be clear criteria in order to classify for eligibility. See also Chapter 10, footnote 20.

22. On the implementation of the Seebohm Report, see Eric Sainsbury, *The Personal Social Services*, pp. 77–78, 137–38; and Olive Stevenson, "Seebohm — Seven Years On."

groups of the physically and mentally handicapped, these efforts are constrained by a persistent set of negative stereotypes and by stigmas attached to various disabilities by the handicapped themselves. Many blind persons, most of whom were also aged, did not want to associate with other blind. The opposite attitudes were found in sheltered workshops and social clubs, where the physically handicapped and their families strongly prefer to exclude the mentally handicapped and vice versa.

The Dilemmas of Gap-Filling

Whether a voluntary agency service is a substitute, a supplement, or a complement may be of interest only to those who are specifically concerned with the survival of the nongovernmental sector or who have a research interest in the salience of auspices. Most persons probably regard governmental or voluntary sponsorship as less important than the way in which a service is provided. In this view, there is no need to tidy up the field with a formal delineation of responsibility; the particular auspice of a service provider is less significant than the quality, accessibility, cost, and accountability of the service. Others regard voluntary agencies as intrinsically preferable because of their presumed greater flexibility, capacity for innovation, and use of volunteers or, in some cases, because they serve as a brake on further expansion of the government bureaucracy. This position is opposed by still others who fear that one of the costs of voluntary agencies' functioning as partial subsidizers of the welfare state is that they may prevent government from implementing its mandate by masking the basic weaknesses in governmental provision. Under these circumstances, it is claimed, voluntary agencies risk perpetuating second-rate, substitute programs and thus in the long run depriving clientele of more effective services.

Despite the apparent hazards of substituting for government, few voluntary agencies in England were troubled by these possibilities, although most of them believed that "the voluntary agency should not be the local authority writ small." Obviously, it is not easy to identify the conditions under which voluntary agencies discourage statutory organizations from implementing their responsibilities or when the service would simply not be available without them. Furthermore, there may be a Fabian bias in the idea of a substitute service, whereby the governmental system is conceived to be the primary and ideal one, with the state meeting all areas of needs and the voluntary agency tolerated grudgingly until the state can take over. This belief is associated with the implicit assumption that the state ought to have a prior tax claim on discretionary income for public purposes.

While voluntary agencies may be gratified by the recognition by the statutory authorities in England that "we cannot do it all and we will increasingly have to call upon voluntary agencies in the future," the organizational costs of supplementation and particularly of substitution are not always fully appreciated. First of all, performance of the supplementer role can weaken the rationale for the voluntary agency, as well as its future, if the agency is shaped by the character of statutory policy and performance and uses little of its own potential discretion to choose more distinctive — i.e., complementary — areas of work. It is dismaying to learn that an opinion survey of national voluntary agencies in England in 1975 found that the most frequently cited justification for their programs was "the inability of the statutory services to reach all potential clients"; the least-mentioned reason was their "distinctive philosophy of approach."[23] Over a long period, supplementing or compensating for a lack of statutory resources is a weak rationale for a voluntary agency, which loses its distinctiveness by being just another nongovernmental public-service provider. Voluntary agencies will have to work hard to avoid being a tool of government, particularly when they work inside a framework determined by government and are dependent on it for funds.

Toward a Reformulation of Governmental-Voluntary Relationships

The foregoing analysis of the service provider role of the voluntary agency suggests the inadequacy of the traditional designations of "pioneering," "gap-filling," or the ambiguous "partnership." These terms not only mask actual power relationships, but they also obscure the existence of other service-providing systems in the family, in informal social networks, in the market, and in business, industry, and the trade unions.

Historically, two metaphors have been used in England to describe the preferred set of relationships between governmental and voluntary agencies. The earliest conception was the "parallel bars theory," in which the social services are bifurcated into a public and private sector operating quite independently, although the private agency is expected to have a favorable impact on government because of its stan-

23. Adrian Webb, Lesley Day, and Douglas Weller, *Voluntary Social Service Manpower Resources*, pp. 28–29. Also see Sainsbury, pp. 101–2.

dard setting, pioneering, and advocacy. An alternative conception was formulated by the Webbs in 1914, in which the public agency provides the basic minimum and the voluntary organization then supplements, enriches, and extends "the work of the public authorities to far finer shades of physical, moral, and spiritual perfection."[24]

Both of these notions have a quaint, old-fashioned character. As theories, they are anachronisms because of their underestimation of the growth of the public sector and its impact on the voluntary agency in a mixed social welfare economy, as well as their overestimation of voluntary advocacy, pioneering, and standard setting.

It may also no longer be appropriate to describe the relationship as a partnership, even if it is occasionally acknowledged that the voluntary agency is, at best, a junior partner if not a silent one. The U.S. literature on this subject is rich in metaphors that imply a coequal status in the partnership between government and voluntary organizations; for example, it has been called a marriage, branches of the same tree, two sectors of a circle, Siamese twins, a broad staircase with two railings, and two neighboring farms.[25] While the two sectors coexist, occasionally interacting and exchanging resources and often providing similar services to groups of vastly different sizes, their complex interrelationships cannot be captured in the simplistic notion of a partnership.[26] As early as 1963, Charles Schottland asserted that the concept of a partnership is obsolete because of great disparities in size, resources, scope, complexity, and accountability. Instead of attempting to forge a partnership, he suggested that new methods of interorganizational linkage be developed. These have proved to be elusive, and the myth of the partnership persists.[27]

A more valid model might be that of two coexisting organizational systems, occasionally cooperating and infrequently competing or in conflict, with four types of service relationships: primary, supplementary, complementary, and that of private, public-service provider or vendor — a new, hybrid role combining elements of the other three. The last service relationship is prevalent in the United States; in En-

24. Sidney and Beatrice Webb, *The Prevention of Destitution*, p. 252.

25. See, for example, Lester B. Granger, "The Changing Functions of Voluntary Agencies."

26. It is curious that concepts and theories that have been applied to other types of interorganizational relationships have so seldom been used where there are differences in auspice.

27. Charles Schottland, "Federal Planning for Health and Welfare." The vast differences in function, domain, interests, and resources between governmental and voluntary agencies are insufficiently appreciated in explanations for the lack of success of most intersectoral planning in England and the United States.

gland the voluntary agencies are supplementary to the statutory system; in the Netherlands they are the primary service providers; and they tend to be complementary in Israel.

In addition to its descriptive and ordering function, another value of this classification is that it suggests questions to be raised about the preferred or likely future pattern of interaction between government and voluntary organizations. Three different models of ideal relationship based on these principles have been proposed. In the first model, the state provides for most basic needs, and voluntary agencies are relatively minor supplementary specialists with a distinctive philosophy. In the second model, the state and voluntary organizations compete across the entire range of services, with voluntary organizations offering a choice of alternative philosophies of care. In the third model, the two are closely interrelated, but voluntary organizations extend the diversity and coverage of the hard-pressed governmental sector.[28]

In assessing the likelihood of each of these futures, we note that the first two seek to optimize choice on the basis of voluntary agency specialization or because of distinctive or alternative approaches to service. However, it is doubtful that society values choice in the social services. At best, ambivalence about its desirability is evident in the public concern with avoiding duplication and fragmentation. Reliance on a distinctive philosophical approach by voluntary agencies may also be unrealistic in view of the shared norms of the professionals who staff agencies in the two sectors. Even voluntary agencies under sectarian auspices have had increasing difficulty in identifying the religious component in their work as they have become more and more secularized. There may, however, be areas where nongovernmental auspices would be preferred, not so much because of a difference in philosophy or approach, but because they facilitate accessibility and more individualized, specialized care or because they are cheaper. Another advantage is the ability of some voluntary agencies to overcome the fragmentation of governmental departmentalization and to serve the whole person.

The first two models are based on a specific allocation of functions and clear statements on operating policy, both of which are unlikely to be forthcoming because of the long-standing lack of support for them in both sectors. Consequently, the present untidy state of the social services will probably continue, and the third scenario seems most

28. These three models are discussed in Webb, Day, and Weller, pp. 29–31.

probable. Essentially, though, it is an expedient, based on the assumption of continuing resource scarcity, and it emphasizes supplementary at the expense of complementary services. The British experience shows that long-term supplementation, by compensating for deficiencies in the statutory services, can displace such other voluntary agency roles as those of vanguard and advocate, and can deter or delay the implementation of governmental responsibility. Awareness of this possibility should stimulate the search by voluntary agencies for more distinctive or complementary service programs that cannot ordinarily be found under governmental auspices, as well as for means to improve and enrich, not just to extend, governmental services.

It becomes increasingly evident that the future of voluntary agencies in the welfare state will also depend on the priority that they place on their roles as vanguards, improvers, value guardians, and service providers. The implications of the reformulation of the service provision function for the distinctive competence and future of the voluntary agency and its relationship to the governmental sector will be considered in the next chapter.

PART IV

Conclusions

We have now concluded the comparative analysis of the internal structure, governance and fiscal resource systems, and performance of the roles of vanguard, improver, value guardian, and service provider of the voluntary agencies in four countries. What generalizations can we now draw about the distinctive organizational competence and vulnerability of the voluntary agency?

In Chapter 13, the findings are used to suggest a reformulation of the four traditional roles and to identify those functions that seem most appropriate for voluntary agencies. The analysis also discloses some of their characteristic vulnerabilities, and the chapter concludes with three recommendations to help organizations become more democratic, rational, and accountable.

Chapter 14 looks to the future by examining five possible roles for voluntary agencies in the welfare state in the 1980s. It concludes with a reevaluation of the central issue of voluntary autonomy and public accountability.

13. The Distinctive Competence and Vulnerability of the Voluntary Agency

In the preceding four chapters we have examined the performance of the four traditional roles ascribed to voluntary agencies. Despite different starting places, national settings, and public policies, there are more similarities than differences among the voluntary agencies serving the physically and mentally handicapped in the four countries. In all four countries, much of what has been regarded as innovative in recent years consists essentially of small-scale, low-risk, incremental improvements or extensions of conventional programs. Few agencies are distinguished by their pioneering qualities, nor are their services ordinarily available as alternatives to governmental provision. The small number of new programs started reflects the particular level of service developed in each country, professional and board member interests, and the availability of governmental funds for particular programs. Generally, the largest, most bureaucratic and professional agencies are the leading initiators of new programs, as well as being among the most active advocates and promoters of voluntarism.

With the exception of the Netherlands, a similar array of services is usually available under both auspices, except that the voluntary sector is subordinated to the dominant public system. Compared with their governmental counterparts, voluntary agencies are smaller in scope, less bureaucratic, and more specialized and individualized. In none of the countries did they have a monopoly on volunteerism; fund-raising events and public campaigns were the most frequent activities of the volunteers and not person-to-person service giving.

Active advocacy occurs mainly among the organizations for the blind and the mentally handicapped and a few other agencies in each country. Most of the issues with which the voluntary agencies are concerned tend to be narrow in scope and relatively noncontroversial, involving differences in priorities between government and themselves. Of critical importance in influencing the extent of advocacy, as well as direct service volunteerism, was the extent of the commitment of the executive leadership of the agency. Other differences in the patterns of organizational behavior were due mainly to the external influence of the civic culture and public policy.

If we can generalize from these findings and apply them to other types of voluntary agencies, similar in structure and function but serving different kinds of clientele, some of the conventional conceptions of voluntary agency function will need to be reformulated.

Basic Characteristics

Before undertaking the task of generalization and reformulation, three prominent features of the organization of voluntary agencies should be noted because of their influence on its distinctive competence and vulnerability.

First, voluntary agencies are interest groups in both a literal and a political sense: they manifest a special concern for a particular group of persons or a specific problem, which is expressed in a commitment both to specialized services for their client-constituency and to acting as an advocate for them. In this latter capacity, voluntary agencies share some properties with other interest groups: they try to influence public policy; they are themselves sources of power; they have administrative functions; they are narrow in focus; and they are usually deficient in internal democracy. They combine the character of a voluntary association–interest group and a social service bureaucracy and contribute to pluralism in the society and polity.[1]

Second, voluntary agencies have a considerable degree of discretion in the allocation of their resources, more than they often use or believe they can use. While it must be chartered by government, a voluntary agency is not mandated to serve a particular population in a particular way; its clients do not have a legal claim or right to a service. The agency can choose to deliver a service that will be paid for by government, or it can decide to seek funds elsewhere or to invest its efforts in functions other than service provision — e.g., advocacy, research, or

---

1. On voluntary organizations as interest groups, see J. Rowland Pennock and John W. Chapman, eds., *Voluntary Associations, Nomos*, pp. 147–232; Constance Smith and Ann Freedman, *Voluntary Associations: Perspectives on the Literature*, pp. 38–85; and William D. Amis and Samuel E. Stern, "A Critical Examination of the Theory and Functions of Voluntary Associations." For a different view of interest-group pluralism, see T. H. Lowi, *The End of Liberalism: Ideology, Policy and the Crisis of Public Authority*, pp. 238–73.

public education. Thus, it has the freedom to choose what groups it will serve, when, and in what ways; although when such choices are made, the voluntary agency tends to become institutionalized and, like other formal organizations, to seek stability and to avoid uncertainty. Over a period of time, it develops traditions and acquires obligations that limit its freedom of action.

Third, voluntary agencies are heavily dependent on the quality of their executive leadership, more so than on other structural features, because of their considerable discretionary power, relatively small size, and reliance on intangible incentives for participation and support.[2] The commitment and capability of the executive leadership is a necessary if not a sufficient requisite for the performance of any voluntary agency role. This factor helps account for the great variability among voluntary organizations; their idiosyncratic behavior is both an essential weakness and a strength.

Four Unique Functions

These three characteristics underlie the following reformulation of the roles of vanguard, improver, value guardian, and service provider. The roles are presented in the form of four functions that are more likely to be found in voluntary than in governmental or profit-making organizations and that represent what might ideally be expected from a voluntary organization.

The first salient attribute of a voluntary agency is not pioneering or experimentation, for reasons shortly to be described, but rather *specialization* in a problem, a group of people, or a method of intervention. Like all interest groups, voluntary agencies are minority agencies. As nongovernmental, nonprofit organizations, they are intrinsically particularistic, in contrast with the more universal and comprehensive scope of a governmental agency. The voluntary agency can be a specialist because government is responsible for the basic services. This does not mean that government cannot supply specialized services to selected categories of persons; rather, a voluntary agency can legitimately and more easily be selective and exclusive. As Lord Beveridge

2. On the decisive role of executive leadership systems in voluntary organizations, see Jerald Hage and R. DeWar, "Elite Values versus Organizational Structure," pp. 279–90. Wolf Wolfensberger, *The Third Stage in the Evolution of Voluntary Associations for the Mentally Retarded*, p. 11, states that "quality depends much more on the ideologies of key leaders in the locality and within the service system, than upon the nature of the auspices." On the relationship between incentives and participation in voluntary organizations, see Peter B. Clark and James Q. Wilson, "Incentive Systems: A Theory of Organization."

put it, "The philanthropic motive is in practice a specialist motive; it drives men to combat a particular evil, to meet a particular need that arouses their interests."[3] The other side of specialization is a fragmentation caused by the natural proliferation of voluntary agencies in pluralist societies. Paradoxically, because they can often more readily serve the whole person voluntary agencies are also able to put together what governmental agencies fragmentize through departmentalization.

The specialized aspects of the voluntary agency also make it possible for consumers and other constituencies to identify with the organization. The particular problem area selected by the agency serves as a basis for service delivery and support by individualizing groups that may be overlooked or may have a low priority in government or the market. Like a brand name, specialization contributes to the preservation of organizational identity and enables a voluntary agency to assert jurisdiction over a domain. While the voluntary agency has no necessary monopoly, its specialized knowledge and experience are a major source of legitimacy and credibility, which are expressed in a structured way in both service provision and advocacy.[4]

In the search for what is distinctive about the voluntary agency, emphasis on specialization rather than pioneering, experimentation, or innovation does not necessarily mean the dethronement of the vanguard role. Rather, as shown in chapter 9, innovation may be more appropriately conceived as one of several possible outcomes of program change and not as a basic purpose of the voluntary agency. Some dysfunctional aspects of the exaggerated stress on innovation are the trivialization of the concept and the deflection of the organization from other service goals, such as improved access, effectiveness, efficiency, and equity.[5] Conceivably, of course, a voluntary agency could specialize in the development of innovative programs, but this seldom occurs. While the belief persists, there is little evidence that the volun-

3. Lord William Beveridge, *Voluntary Action: A Report on Methods of Social Advance*, p. 26.

4. Alfred J. Kahn and Sheila B. Kamerman, *Social Services in International Pespective: The Emergence of the Sixth System*, and the Wolfenden Report both refer to the importance of specialization and expertise as justification for the voluntary agency, but the former regards the voluntary agency as an obstacle to the development of a comprehensive system of personal social services, a point that will be discussed in chapter 14. The Wolfenden Report, while acknowledging specialization, tends to subordinate it to pioneering, even though it acknowledges that there is relatively little pioneering within the voluntary sector. The Commission on Private Philanthropy and Public Needs, *Giving in America: Toward a Stronger Voluntary Sector*, pp. 42–46 (hereafter cited as Filer), identifies eight functions for the voluntary agency, most of which are contained within our definition of the four roles.

5. See footnotes, 2, 3, 10, and 16 in chapter 9.

tary agency is the primary source of innovation for government.⁶ Instead, the development of new programs and methods by voluntary agencies is highly dependent on outside financing by government and, to a lesser degree, philanthropic foundations. The priorities and interests of these funding sources naturally have a major influence in shaping the character of the new programs and methods that are developed by voluntary agencies. Because of this dependence, voluntary agencies may have more freedom in choosing their area of specialization than in the type of "innovation" they undertake. Consequently, because change and experimentation can be promoted and supported under government auspices, a stronger case can be made for specialization than for innovation as a unique function of the voluntary agency.

A second function characteristic of voluntary agencies is *advocacy*, which stems from their organizational status as specialized interest groups. There is little disagreement in a democratic society on the necessity for a strong and independent voluntary sector to monitor and pressure government in order to safeguard and to raise the quality of public services. The mission of defending and articulating the interests of underserved populations at risk takes on more importance as the social services in a welfare state become universal. This does not imply the absence of advocacy or support for these groups within government or among professional associations; rather, it affirms that advocacy is a more consistent and legitimate expectation of voluntary agencies.

As noted in chapter 11, advocacy can be constrained by the demands of organizational maintenance, by cooptation engendered by excessive closeness to government, by the absence of a suitable civic culture, by lack of appropriate resources, and by insufficient commitment by the executive leadership of the voluntary agency. Advocacy is also more likely to be found among newer, less institutionalized organizations that have considerable consumer involvement. In the field of service to the handicapped, advocacy has been proposed as the primary function of voluntary agencies in welfare states that have extensive programs of social service. For ideological and practical reasons, this is not feasible, since most of the public support for voluntary agen-

6. That the absence of innovation or even of sufficient funds is not the major obstacle to the improvement of the social services is persuasively argued by Paul Berman, "Buying Social Reform with Federal Dollars." Berman identifies lack of organizational or administrative capacity to implement programs as the crucial factor.

cies and most of their influence are derived from their legitimacy, credibility, and expertise as service providers. While it may be unwise to call for exclusive concentration on advocacy, there is justification for a greater stress on this function.

Because various types of volunteerism can also be promoted by government, the third special contribution of a voluntary agency is, strictly speaking, *consumerism*, which is expressed in peer self-help and in associations organized by the clientele themselves. In the four countries, the most distinctive voluntary agency activity that is not a substitute for or a duplication of government is the mutual aid and advocacy sponsored by peer self-help groups, either by the local affiliates of national organizations or by indigenous organizations of the handicapped themselves. This type of consumerism will probably increase because of diffusion of the emphasis on citizen participation, the rights of disadvantaged populations, and the continual discovery of new needs and underserved groups.

Many, if not most, voluntary agencies do not give high priority to consumer involvement. Nonprofit organizations are the principal users of the time of unpaid volunteers, whose extensive participation in fund raising, service giving, and policymaking distinguishes voluntary from profit-making and governmental organizations. But if we seek an activity that is more exclusive, one that will not be nurtured in the same way if at all under other auspices, then the value guardian role, if it is to be truly distinctive, should be reformulated more narrowly to emphasize the participation of persons affected by a problem. From this perspective, an organization is voluntaristic to the extent that it significantly involves the intended beneficiaries in decision making concerning program policy, a practice other service providers do not ordinarily engage in. If a voluntary agency does not go beyond the use of volunteers for its own support or actively seek consumer participation, then the value guardian role is more a maintenance than a task function, and is not on the same level as advocacy or service provision.[7] If the fulfillment of this special potential is considered too stringent and unrealistic, an alternative formulation is to combine the third function into volunteerism-consumerism.

7. This approach to the use of volunteers as part of the maintenance system of a voluntary agency is derived from the systems model described by Amitai Etzioni, "Two Approaches to Organizational Analysis: A Critique and a Suggestion." For research purposes, voluntary agencies could be classified by the types and extent of volunteer resources on which they rely. Charles Perrow, *Organizational Analysis: A Sociological View*, pp. 93–116, has already pointed toward this.

The emphasis on consumerism does not limit or exhaust the potential for citizen participation in the value guardian role. Voluntary agencies also protect and promote other social, religious, cultural, and ethnic values through their service programs and their advocacy. The uniqueness of this function is underscored because it operates in an area that is proscribed for state agencies in pluralist democracies.

The last and most pervasive role is that of a *service provider*. An expanded version of this customary and least distinctive function is necessary to reflect the changed character of the social service economy, which has become more complex, competitive, and entrepreneurial, particularly in the United States, and in which government funds provide a principal source of income for voluntary agencies. Historically, voluntary organizations were the main source of social services, but public provision has expanded so rapidly that there are relatively few services now in which voluntary agencies are the primary providers, relying on contributed funds. Because governmental agencies are ordinarily not able to make up for the deficiencies of other governmental departments, supplementation, or the extension of similar services, is almost by definition a distinguishing attribute of voluntary agencies. Voluntary services can be an alternative, but usually they are a supplementary substitute for government. The role of substitute may deflect the voluntary agency from performing its other functions and also may deter the governmental agency from fulfilling its responsibilities. More desirable for both sectors are complementary services — i.e., those that are qualitatively different and that enrich rather than just extend government programs. Consequently, as we saw in chapter 12, there are not one but four different modes of service provision: primary, supplementary, complementary, and a new hybrid, that of vendor, each with its respective costs and benefits. The particular mode of voluntary service provision is largely dependent on public policy and the level of public provision.

While some minimize the importance of auspice for service provision, there are special advantages in the use of voluntary organizations because of their small size and scope, their capacity for more individualized (i.e., less standardized) services, and, at the same time, a more holistic approach. They seem particularly suitable for services to clientele who have highly specialized needs or who are ineligible or not likely to use governmental services. At the same time, because of the diversity and idiosyncrasy of voluntary organizations, public policies relying on them will be uneven in their impact.

We can now sum up this reformulation of the roles of the voluntary agency. As a social service provider, the voluntary agency functions as an indispensable part of a three-sector social service economy along with government and, in a growing number of instances, profit-making organizations. It may substitute for, influence, extend, and improve the public sector; replace, reinforce, and relieve the primary social systems; and compete with profit-making organizations in some fields. As an organization, the voluntary agency has four distinctive competencies: specialization, advocacy, consumerism and other forms of volunteerism, and the provision of services, which can be primary, supplementary, complementary, or those of a public agent or vendor.

These concepts can provide a vocabulary for further research on the organizational behavior of voluntary agencies. They offer conceptual categories that can be used in posing questions, and, as a classification, they constitute the first step in theory building. For example, the four competencies suggest four ideal types of priorities. While some voluntary agencies stress advocacy, others emphasize service supplementation, self-help, or specialized expertise. Most voluntary agencies try to pursue these goals at the same time, although different parts of an organization may concentrate on one or the other.

Similarly, these concepts can be used to describe the phases of an organizational career. Historically, many voluntary organizations have shifted from being a cause to being a function, and from being a voluntary association to being a social agency. In this process they often start with some form of consumerism or mutual aid and advocacy and then proceed to develop specialization and, later, governmental service supplementation. In a proposed future third stage in the evolution of voluntary associations, advocacy has been prescribed as the foremost role, to prevail over service delivery.

Another set of stages of organizational development is based on four types of agencies differentiated by the extent of their reliance on government funds and by consumer involvement; thus, many voluntary agencies have progressed from being an alternative agency to being a private service agency, to being a vendor, to being a QUANGO.[8] To the extent that these and other models of the life cycle of different voluntary organizations lend themselves to research, we can add to

8. These four types of voluntary agencies and their organizational careers are described in Ralph M. Kramer, "The Future of the Voluntary Service Organization," pp. 63–67. For a somewhat different perspective on these types of organizations, see Bertram M. Beck, "The Voluntary Social Welfare Agency," pp. 147–54.

our fragmentary knowledge of how organizations are created, develop, and change, and of why some succeed better than others.

Vulnerabilities

Like all organizations, voluntary agencies not only have special capacities, they also have a particular set of weaknesses. Four characteristic vulnerabilities of voluntary agencies have been identified: (1) institutionalization, (2) goal deflection, (3) minority rule, (4) ineffectuality.[9]

(1) Institutionalization refers to a process of "creeping formalization," a sequential development leading to greater bureaucratization in an organization. According to organization theory, formalization as an aspect of bureaucratization can produce greater efficiency, reliability, and accountability, but an organization's need for control often results in rigidity, inertia, and resistance to change, as well as in ritualism and insularity. Formalization usually accompanies an increase in the size and resources of a voluntary agency and it can lead to a diminution of the special attributes for which the agency is valued: flexibility, responsiveness, and risk taking.[10]

In the United States many alternative agencies evolved from consumer domination of board and staff to increased status differentiation between them, as the agencies became more specialized. In this way, the agencies became almost indistinguishable from the older, well-established, more conventional social service agencies. Similarly, for many of the Dutch agencies and the associations for the mentally handicapped in the other countries, institutionalization was one of the consequences of a reduction in fiscal uncertainty as organizations gradually took on the character of the highly centralized and bureaucratic funding sources on which they became progressively dependent.

At the same time, bureaucratization and professionalization did not hamper the development of new programs, advocacy, or the promotion of volunteerism in the four countries. Undoubtedly, the development of new programs was related to the ability of the organizations, particularly the larger ones, to acquire resources and to secure more control over their environment. This does not mean that there is a necessary connection between institutionalization and effectiveness;

9. The source of many of these ideas is David L. Sills, "Voluntary Associations: Sociological Aspects," pp. 367–72.

10. James G. March and Herbert A. Simon, *Organizations*, pp. 36–47; Perrow, pp. 50–91; and Herman Stein, "Organization Theory — Implications for Administrative Research," pp. 80–90.

rather, that bureaucratization and professionalization do not preclude it. Yet, as we shall see, because of insufficient formalization, voluntary agencies are unusually prone to ineffectiveness. The truth is that the appropriate balance between formalization and effectiveness or other desirable attributes is elusive. Institutionalization is a two-edged sword; it enables and disables for precisely the same reasons.

(2) Goal deflection, the displacement of ends by means, is another vulnerability of voluntary agencies. In formal organizations, purposes can be subverted by many factors, including informal structures that develop, overly strict application of rules, and the self-serving activities of leadership. Although these are also present in voluntary agencies, more typical is the displacement of service goals by maintenance needs, as illustrated in the preemption of volunteers and staff time and energy by fund raising in the United States, England, and Israel, but not in the Netherlands. Agency leadership can also be deflected from advocacy by the demands of fiscal acquisition and system maintenance. Other examples of goal displacement found in voluntary agencies pertain to "donor dependency," where the emphasis is on tangible and visible projects undertaken to please potential contributors. It is often argued that goal displacement also occurs when voluntary agencies, to secure governmental funds, design programs whose purposes are at variance with their stated goals, policies, and priorities. This is, however, the exception rather than the rule.

(3) Another characteristic deficiency of voluntary organizations is their rule by a self-selected and self-perpetuating minority. As private governments drawing their board members from a narrow social stratum, most voluntary agencies are more representative of their philanthropic origin than of their clientele. Although some progress in greater consumer involvement has occurred in the United States and the Netherlands, efforts to broaden the base of agency policymaking have yet to deal effectively with the inherent problems of the lack of representativeness and accountability of these new board members. Thus, the voluntaristic character of an organization can still be called into question by the consistently oligarchical character of its governance system, which challenges the celebration of voluntary agencies as an important democratizing force in society. On the other hand, as noted in chapter 6, some social scientists have argued that internal democracy in voluntary associations is less significant than their role in representing and advancing the special interests of diverse groups in the community. From this perspective, a voluntary organization

should be judged, not by the norms of internal democracy, but by its contribution to pluralism in society. But some of the observed costs of the tendency to minority rule may easily outweigh the contribution to pluralism, for example, a lack of turnover within the leadership group often results in serious problems of succession, organizational unresponsiveness, a narrow focus of interest, inflexibility, and resistance to change, thus vitiating most of the ostensible virtues of the voluntary agency.

(4) A final vulnerability of voluntary agencies is the conglomerate term *ineffectuality*, which includes inefficiency, insularity, low accountability, a casual, muddling, and bumbling style of operation, and other administrative deficiencies. The managerial inefficiency of voluntary agencies is rooted in the context of a charity market, dominated by a spirit of independence and laissez-faire, which strongly resists any pressures for mergers or any changes that might reduce freedom. Many of these frequently cited faults can be traced to small, often marginal size and resources that keep an organization in an ineffectual or early stage of development. Some voluntary agencies never develop beyond this initial, fumbling stage, while others that do remain on a plateau and fail to achieve more organizational capability. This is not to say that all organizations must inevitably grow, but there may be a requisite level of size, degree of bureaucratization, and professionalization for providing a minimum level of service and for retaining voluntary leadership, clientele, and public support.

Three Recommendations

What, then, can voluntary agencies do to optimize their special capabilities and to cope more effectively with some of their inherent disabilities? Most of the recommendations that have been addressed to voluntary agencies over the years, urging them to put their house in order, are contained in the injunction that they must become more democratic, accountable, and rational.[11]

Voluntary agencies have been advised to become more *democratic* by seeking broader and more diverse constituencies and by providing for

11. There is an enduring quality to these recommendations because most of the subsequent prescriptions for voluntary agencies differ little from those prepared in the early 1940s, as in Selskar M. Gunn and Philip S. Platt, *Voluntary Health Agencies, An Interpretative Study*, pp. 296–306. It is important to distinguish between recommendations directed to enabling individual voluntary agencies to fulfill their organizational potential and those addressed to the voluntary sector as a whole, which tend to be primarily concerned with the effects of tax policy and governmental influence on the autonomy of voluntary organizations.

their active participation in policymaking. Wider representation would help ensure that different priorities and issues might be considered, particularly if there is greater involvement of consumers in program decisions. The time when a voluntary agency could function without some consistent and structured provision for consumer input seems to be at an end, and there will be mounting pressure on voluntary agencies to demonstrate that they are operating less in the interest of staff and board and more on behalf of their intended beneficiaries. A more representative board of directors, acting more openly and in a democratic way, can help contribute to the legitimacy and community support required by voluntary agencies.

In addition to a greater measure of internal democracy in their governance systems, voluntary agencies can also make a greater contribution to the pluralist character of a society by investing more of their resources in the roles of monitor, prod, and critic to improve the quality of service in the public sector.

Accountability ought to be stressed by voluntary agencies at least as much as, if not more than, autonomy. To be more accountable implies conceiving of the agency as the property of the community, rather than of the board and staff, and would at least be reflected in more frequent and more extensive public disclosure of information regarding income sources and services. For virtually all voluntary agencies, implementation of this recommendation would require the development of more reliable information systems than they now have, better-functioning boards of directors, and a more substantial investment in program evaluation.

Greater administrative *rationality*, in the sense of more congruence between organizational ends and means, is the third essential requirement for voluntary agencies. It can begin with a review by each agency of its mission, priorities, and organizational capacities in the light of future trends in the social services. Such basic questions as the following can be the basis for the redesign of agency structure and function to be more appropriate for the organizational character and environment: What kind of an organization do we want to be? To what extent do we — can we — demonstrate, supplement, or substitute for governmental services or function as an advocate? How can we best use our resources to deal with the aspects of the problem or condition we have selected for our work? One of the most effective means of facilitating organizational revitalization is to provide for periodic, systematic reviews of goals, functions, policies, and programs.

This can take the form of agency self-studies every three to five years, with an independent outside evaluation every seven to ten years.

In a broader context, a reformulation of the strengths and weaknesses of the voluntary agency will also be useful in future public policy decisions regarding the choice of the most appropriate sector — governmental, profit-making, or voluntary — for the delivery of social services.[12] The extent to which voluntary agencies will be able to perform their special roles will depend on the nature of their political and economic environment, on the choices they make in reevaluating their mission, and on their capacity for organizational self-renewal. It is these alternative futures that we consider next in the final chapter.

12. Apart from ideological factors, decisions regarding the appropriate sector for the delivery of a particular service are difficult to make on a rational basis because of a lack of information regarding the intrinsic capacity of the different types of organizations to achieve such service system goals as continuity, efficiency, equity, effectiveness, coherence, and accountability. Only a beginning has been made in studying some of these relationships in the health field with reference to the differences among similar services under different auspices. There are, however, considerable data comparing the costs of profit-making and governmental organizations in carrying out various municipal functions; the former seem to be more economical. See, for example, E. S. Savas, "Municipal Monopolies versus Competition in Delivering Urban Services," and Lyle C. Fitch, "Increasing the Role of the Private Sector in Providing Public Services."

14. Alternative Futures
for Voluntary Organizations
in the Welfare State

The Crisis of the Welfare State

The future of the voluntary agency is indissolubly tied to the future of the welfare state, and both are increasingly perceived to be in crisis. Such spokesmen for the voluntary sector as John Gardner and Alan Pifer warn of its "steady deterioration in the U.S. due to government encroachment and discriminatory tax policies" in their call for a new movement to defend and revitalize a beleaguered voluntarism.[1] Other observers conclude that the democratic welfare state, which sanctions and supports voluntary agencies and whose policies define the boundaries of voluntary opportunities and constraints, is in trouble at the end of thirty years of unprecedented expansion.

Despite its extensive benefits, the welfare state has become the "source of both conservative fears and liberal disillusionment."[2] Once seen as an important mechanism for alleviating poverty and distress, the welfare state has come under increasing fire from critics on both the left and the right. It has been attacked by the radical left for its failure to redistribute wealth, status, and power or to change class relations. Instead of eliminating poverty, radicals argue, most of the benefits of the welfare state have gone to the middle class and organized labor, who have been coopted to keep the capitalist state from achieving social justice and equality. Democratic socialists agree with

1. "A Group to Save 'Non-Profit' Sector," *San Francisco Chronicle*, November 30, 1978, p. 9. Called the Independent Sector, a new coalition "to preserve and enhance our national tradition of giving, volunteering, and not-for-profit initiative" was established in March 1980 through the joint efforts of the National Council on Philanthropy and the Coalition of National Voluntary Organizations. See also Alan Pifer, "The Jeopardy of Private Institutions"; Waldemar A. Nielsen, *The Endangered Sector;* and Jonathan Kandell, "Private Charity Going Out of Style in West Europe's Welfare States."

2. Peter L. Berger and Richard John Neuhaus, *To Empower People: The Role of Mediating Structures in Public Policy*, p. 5.

this indictment, but have more faith in politics and social planning to bring about a more equitable distribution of wealth through more democratic, mixed modes of ownership and the control of resources.[3] The classic conservative objections to the welfare state are in terms of morality and efficiency — i.e., it weakens the work ethic and individual initiative by rewarding improvidence and encouraging dependency. The welfare state is wasteful and inefficient in its expenditures, bureaucratic administration, excessive taxation, and governmental regulation, which undermine economic and political liberty.[4]

A group of neo-conservatives asserts, both on ideological and on empirical grounds, that government has undertaken responsibilities far beyond its function and capacity, resulting in a disproportionate growth in the public sector and a swollen bureaucracy that overregulates the economy and the society. Because the obstacles and limits to administration have been underestimated, there have been unintended and unanticipated negative consequences that require still further corrective action. Legislative efforts to achieve ill-conceived and unwarranted goals of equality and redistribution have generated a revolution of rising entitlements and endless expectations exceeding what can possibly be provided. The parallel growth in centralized, professionalized, service bureaucracies with wide powers over the lives of citizens has also contributed to alienation and to a diminution of social control. Altogether, widespread dissatisfaction with the costs and results of governmental programs has led to a backlash in some European countries and in the United States in the form of national public resistance to increased taxes and governmental spending, coupled with a strong antibureaucratic sentiment.[5]

3. The case for conservative democratic socialism is eloquently stated in Peter Clecak, *Crooked Paths: Reflections on Socialism, Conservatism and the Welfare State*. See also Lewis Coser and Irving Howe, eds., *The New Conservatism: A Critique from the Left*.

4. The conservative argument is stated succinctly and rebutted in Harold L. Wilensky, *The Welfare State and Equality*, pp. 107–19. More complete accounts of the conservative position are: Milton Friedman, "The Role of Government in a Free Society"; Robert A. Schoenberger, ed., *The American Right Wing: Readings in Political Behavior*, pp. 280–98; Richard Cornuelle, *Reclaiming the American Dream;* and Roger A. Freeman, *The Growth of American Government: A Morphology of the Welfare State*.

5. A definitive analysis is Peter Steinfels, *The Neo-Conservatives: The Men Who Are Changing America's Politics*. Typical examples of this point of view are: Nathan Glazer, "The Limits of Social Policy"; Daniel Bell, "The Revolution of Rising Entitlements"; Irving Kristol, "Taxes, Poverty and Equality"; Daniel P. Moynihan, "The American Experiment." A useful critique is Amitai Etzioni, "Societal Overload: Sources, Components, and Corrections." On the welfare backlash, see Harold L. Wilensky, *The "New Corporatism," Centralization and the Welfare State*, pp. 14–18, 23–30.

However, another, more positive perspective sees the welfare state as "a victim of its success, not of its failures. It has succeeded in banishing the specter of material deprivation through illness, loss of employment, disability, and old age that has haunted past generations. But the abolition of the threat has also abolished the fear it engendered. The collective memory of the population is short; political allegiance is often based on past wrongs, rarely on past achievements."[6] From this point of view, the welfare state is not in crisis, but is experiencing an inevitable contraction, a natural tapering off with a slower rate of growth, having peaked in the early 1970s, followed by a downturn in a spending cycle that was the culmination of a set of conditions not likely to recur. The rapid establishment, particularly in the United States, of long-delayed welfare-state programs within the space of a few decades in which nondefense spending as a proportion of GNP almost doubled is over. Once the welfare state is established, a plateau is reached. Future changes will be incremental, paralleling population growth and other demographic changes and influenced by alternating periods of liberalism and conservatism. The shift by the welfare state and its social programs into low gear is thus largely a result of its past successes in providing so many benefits and services to so many groups that there are now fewer remaining groups to be included. Consequently, while public spending may rise in constant as well as in current dollar values and even as a share of GNP, the overall rate of increase in the 1980s will be much lower.[7]

Is the welfare state intended to bring about adequacy, equity, or equality? Should it be expected to compensate for past injustices and misfortunes or to invest in the future? Is it supposed to supplement or to replace income? To what extent should it allocate cash, in-kind benefits, social services, and power? The manner in which we answer

6. John Logue, "The Welfare State: Victim of Its Success," p. 85. Logue explains that "the welfare state does not attempt to re-distribute income among classes as much as even out income throughout life. . . . The welfare state has abolished want, not class differences in consumption" (p. 72).

7. James N. Tattersall, "The Crisis of the Public Economy," pp. 1–8. See also Richard E. Wagner and Warren E. Weber, "Wagner's Law, Fiscal Institution, and the Growth of Government." The authors cite evidence that tends to disprove "Wagner's Law," formulated toward the end of the nineteenth century, which forecasts an indefinite expansion of government as income rises. The reduced growth of governmental expenditures is related to predictions of very modest growth in the economy and a growing acceptance of limits to material resources. See Mayer N. Zald, "Demographics, Politics, and the Future of the Welfare State," p. 120; Freeman, pp. 185–90; and Clecak, pp. 8–11.

	Reprivatization	Empowerment	Pragmatic Partnership	Governmental Operation	Nationalization
Role of voluntary agency as:	Alternative	Substitute	Supplement Complement	Obstacle	Marginal

P = Profit-making organizations
G = Governmental organizations
V = Voluntary organizations

Figure 5. Alternative Sectoral Relationships in the Delivery of the Personal Social Services

these questions determines the way we assess criticisms of the welfare state.[8]

With these divergent views as background, we shall examine five alternative futures of the welfare state in terms of possible types of sectoral relations among providers of the personal social services. They run the ideological gamut from right to left, as seen in the continuum in Figure 5, in which the voluntary agency is regarded as a bulwark against, an alternative to, a substitute for, or a complement or supplement to, government, or as an obstacle to a more universal and comprehensive system of personal social services.

While the continuum is based on increasing governmental operating responsibility, with considerable overlap between each type, we shall consider the five policies in ascending order of their likelihood in the United States — i.e., nationalization, governmental operation, reprivatization, empowerment, and pragmatic partnership. In evaluating

8. Adam Graycar, "Backlash, Overload and the Welfare State." See also Mark F. Plattner, "The Welfare State vs. the Redistributive State"; Martin Rein, "Economy and Social Policy"; William A. Robson, *Welfare State and Welfare Society: Illusion and Reality*, pp. 11–32; Richard M. Titmuss, "Welfare State and Welfare Society."

these alternative futures, I shall make some broad generalizations from this limited study of organizations for the physically and mentally handicapped in four countries. I shall be particularly concerned with their implications for a more rational and equitable delivery system for the personal social services and with their impact on voluntarism and pluralism.

All of these future sectoral relationships are based, of course, on the assumption that governmental financing of the social services will continue, and that the welfare state will not be dismantled. Although dismantlement is theoretically possible, it is not seriously advocated, although it is often implied by the rhetoric of conservatives. There have been proposals to eliminate this or that program, or even such essentials as the social security tax,[9] but the number of beneficiaries of the welfare state is now so great that it would be politically unthinkable to advocate scrapping it. Despite the bitterness of initial and persistent conservative opposition, the welfare state has proven to be compatible with governments of both the center and right in the United States and Europe, which have not tampered with basic programs.

Nationalization

Another rather unlikely prospect is nationalization of the voluntary sector.[10] One of the few instances of nationalization occurred as part of a reorganization of the health and social services in Quebec in 1973. Following the incorporation of all hospitals into one governmental network, fourteen Regional Social Service Centers were established throughout the province to consolidate into one governmental system all existing social work services in schools, hospitals, and courts, as well as those of forty-two voluntary agencies. Although voluntary or-

9. David H. Fisher, *Growing Old in America*, p. 204, proposes the substitution of a grant of capital at birth for each individual instead of the payment of social security taxes. Typical of those critics who advocate major changes in funding while keeping the basic principles is Nathan Keyfetz, "Why Social Security Is in Trouble." Other attacks on the social security system have come from more conservative forces that have urged a return to the principles of individual thrift.

10. There is evidently a place for voluntary organizations, or at least a desire for them, even in totalitarian countries. Joseph L. Reid reports that the Child Welfare League of America was approached in the mid-1970s by representatives of two Iron Curtain countries, who asked how to establish voluntary agencies in their countries in order to provide for more diversity ("The Role of the Voluntary Sector," *Social Welfare Forum, 1976* [New York: Columbia University Press, 1976] p. 69). According to Alfred J. Kahn and Sheila B. Kamerman, *Social Services in International Perspective: The Emergence of the Sixth System*, p. 392, Poland makes extensive use of volunteers, particularly in providing certain services to the aged.

ganizations could elect to remain outside the new regional structures, they would not be eligible for governmental funding. In Montreal, eight Catholic agencies, six Protestant agencies, and one Jewish agency were incorporated into three new Social Service Centers for their respective constituencies. Other changes that occurred included a tremendous expansion of the administrative staff — threefold in the case of one Social Service Center — with no significant increase of clientele, and a reduction in the number of active board members from seventy-five to thirteen.

It is risky to generalize from this limited experience, particularly because of the presence of a unique combination of religious and political-separatist influences on the social services in Quebec. Many of the important features of the plan were not implemented due to underfinancing and administrative difficulties, nor has the changeover been evaluated. Nevertheless, there is considerable impressionistic evidence that the new, "para-public" Social Service Centers have fallen far short of their objectives of providing a wide range of integrated and accessible health and social services, together with extensive citizen participation.[11]

The Quebec experience suggests one of the prerequisites for a takeover of voluntary organizations by government: namely, that voluntary agencies, which receive most of their income from government, be used almost exclusively to carry out a public function because there are few, if any, governmental agencies able to do so. Although these conditions exist in the Netherlands, as well as in the field of children's foster care in New York City, the countervailing political power of sectarian interest groups in both cases is sufficiently strong to render such a possibility unlikely. In the absence of appropriate political con-

11. There are no adequate accounts in English of the radical changes in the social service system in Quebec as a result of Bill 65, Chapter 48, of 1971. Most of the information cited is derived from my interviews with government officials and social service executives and staff members in Montreal during November 1978. Representative publications are: J. L. Torczyner, "Centralization and Participation in Conflict: Social and Health Services in Montreal"; Patrick Deehy and Claire Fainer, "The New Social Service System in Quebec: Organizational Myths and Professional Responses"; Fred R. MacKinnon, "Changing Patterns in Public-Voluntary Relationships in Canada"; Solomon M. Brownstein, " 'La Reforme' in Quebec Health and Social Services: Impact on Jewish Case Work Services"; and Sidney S. Lee, *Quebec's Health System: A Decade of Change, 1967–77.* An opposing view of these changes is Frédérick Lesemann, "The Local Community Service Centres and the Democratization of Health." On the political background of these social policies, see Leon Dion, *Quebec: The Unfinished Revolution,* and Douglas M. Fullerton, *The Dangerous Delusion: Quebec's Independence Obsession.*

ditions, then, nationalization of voluntary agencies is not a realistic option. There is little support in the United States for governmental monopolies in the social services; the trend is, as we shall see, in the opposite direction.

Governmental Operation

This model, with intellectual roots in the Seebohm Committee Report and in the writings of Richard M. Titmuss, assumes that only the state can administer a system of comprehensive personal social services that will be universal, equitable, accountable, and available as a right. As many services as possible are provided directly by local government social service departments; although a voluntary agency may be called upon to fill gaps or to supplement with some specialized, sectarian, or unconventional service, it has a subordinate if not a marginal role, as in England. In transferring this model to the United States, it has been suggested that some voluntary organizations could stress advocacy or rely on contributions for their service programs, but those that receive most of their income from tax funds would be regarded as quasi-nongovernmental organizations, subject to the same rules and regulations as a governmental agency, including the presence of governmental representatives on the board of directors. In this view, the values of a rational service-delivery system prevail over those of pluralism, voluntarism, or political ideology.

Some empirical support for this model is based on the Kahn and Kamerman study of eight countries, where it was observed that "equality, coverage and accountability are increasingly expected in the personal social services . . . as [countries] assume financial obligations and recognize service rights, [they] must modify the voluntary sector, take it over as a quasi-governmental operation and/or separate some of it out so as to enhance certain functions essential to the overall services concept."[12] Because voluntary agencies are by nature particularistic, singling out certain categories of persons for special treatment from the mass of public welfare clients, they are regarded by Kahn as an obstacle to the achievement of a more coherent and equitable system of personal social services. Therefore, the basic issue in the United States is "whether the bulk of the base-line and specialized service will

12. Kahn and Kamerman, p. 383. This is prefaced by an earlier statement that "there may continue to exist a related and voluntary personal social services section devoted to innovation, specialization, and advocacy with the latter development affected by the general nature of the polity" (p. 382).

be established in public social service agencies or assigned to the voluntary sector through public funding."[13]

In considering this alternative, we note that it involves a further extension of the welfare state — the institutionalization of a fifth social service system in addition to education, income maintenance, health, and housing. Because it would probably require additional funds and enlarged governmental responsibilities, it is more in tune with the ever-expanding frontier of the welfare state during the 1950s and 1960s than with the backlash temper that followed; consequently, its political feasibility in the United States is dubious.

While in theory the public sector may best be able to achieve the goals of a comprehensive, universal, and accountable system of personal social services, actual experience with the one-stop, generic, social service center in England reveals a great performance gap between formal responsibilities and implementation. Objectives have been insufficiently realized because of policy ambiguities, lack of funds, excessive bureaucratization, and other administrative and professional staff deficiencies, as well as political factors. In England, as in the United States, despite the right to services, there is enormous variability among the Social Service Departments, so that the service one gets depends upon where one lives, a long-standing condition known as "territorial injustice." The ostensible universal coverage under the system is also contradicted by the low "take-up," and service integration is belied by the lack of coordination between the statutory programs in health, social services, housing, education, and employment, a condition that is not notably different from that in the United States. However, the fact that the same deficiencies in coordination, coherence, and efficiency are also found in the Netherlands, where voluntary agencies predominate, suggests that we may be dealing less with the attributes of a particular auspice than with the essential nature of a social service system, regardless of whether the major providers are governmental or voluntary.

Two other factors make this alternative less appropriate for the United States. First, public policy in the United States has encouraged a more pluralistic economy in the social services than that of England, with extensive governmental purchase of service from vol-

13. Kahn and Kamerman, p. 384. At the same time, the authors are cognizant of the obstacles to the development of a more coherent system inherent in the structure of government, with its multiple layers of administration and tendencies toward fragmentation through the proliferation of new categorical grant programs and agencies.

untary and profit-making organizations. This trend has become more pronounced with the lessening of public confidence in government bureaucracies as instruments for service delivery. The second factor is the persistently unfavorable public image of welfare departments in the United States (as in Israel). They have been identified with the poor, with scandals, and with fraud, which would seriously detract from their becoming a central, one-stop social service center.

While these factors may constitute obstacles to the implementation of a preeminently public model of the personal social services in the United States, the recommendation of the Filer Commission should be kept in mind:

> The [voluntary] sector should not compete with government so much as complement, help humanize it, however. Nor because of institutional inertia or self-protectiveness should it or parts of it stand in the way of proper extension of government into areas where, because of the demands of scale or equity, the private sector simply cannot fill a collective want.[14]

Reprivatization

The traditional conservative and the neo-conservative views of the welfare state urge two contrasting policy alternatives: reprivatization and empowerment. Reprivatization, or entrepreneurism, requires the use of the profit-making sector whenever possible and relies on competition in the market to deliver the best-quality service at the most reasonable price. Empowerment places its faith in the nonprofit sector and encourages greater utilization of voluntary associations, religious institutions, neighborhoods, and the primary social systems. Both aim at reducing the overload on government, lessening its power, and each seeks to provide decentralized, high-quality services at reduced costs. In both strategies, government sets standards, finances, and oversees lightly, but does not offer the service directly. Profit-making organizations are the favored providers of reprivatization, whereas advocates of empowerment believe, as did Titmuss, that altruism is superior to the market in the production and distribution of social services. Not surprisingly, the United States is the home of both theories, and only empowerment has much support in England. (It will be recognized as another version of the concept of subsidiarity that underlies the social services in the Netherlands.)

14. Commission on Private Philanthropy and Public Needs, *Giving in America: Toward a Stronger Voluntary Sector*, p. 48. (Hereafter cited as Filer.)

Strictly speaking, the term *reprivatization* is a misnomer in referring to the social services because they have rarely been provided by commercial organizations. Only in recent years, with the advent of purchase-of-service contracts and third-party payments, have business corporations and proprietary organizations found it as profitable to supply various health, welfare, and educational services as they have other public services. Their entry into the social services, although still quite limited, has made this field more competitive, narrowing the gap between profit-making and traditional voluntary agencies because both are subject to the same policies and regulations. The future of profit-making organizations seems assured in the United States by the refusal to exclude such contractors from eligibility for purchase of service under Title XX of the Social Security Act.[15] There is also more interest in the Netherlands in the use of the market as a means of reducing social service expenditures.

The growing entrepreneurism in the social services is distrusted within the voluntary sector because of the assumption of an irreconcilable conflict between social service provision and the profit motive. Typical is the belief that "proprietary social services [are] deficient, discriminatory and dehumanizing. Social welfare service for profit is neither humane nor social, even its service is misdirected."[16] While there are few empirical studies, there is much anecdotal data to suggest the truth of some charges. Evidence is usually cited of scandals and inefficiency in the Job Corps, nursing homes, Medicare, children's institutions, day care, home health, dialysis centers, and others. Critics of the profit motive claim that it fails to result in more efficient service, and government officials complain about the subversion of regulations and standards by proprietary providers, making them difficult to monitor and to hold accountable.

One of the consequences of a greater use of profit-making organizations is stratification among clientele because proprietary agencies are usually least willing to serve the most troublesome and handicapped persons. Because of the reluctance of nongovernmental organizations to serve them, the most difficult and hopeless cases are the victims of a

15. *Federal Register*, June 27, 1975, p. 27354.
16. Dan Rubenstein, R. E. Mundy, and Mary L. Rubenstein, "Proprietary Social Services," p. 140. A brief and typical statement of the case for reprivatization is E. S. Savas, "Doing More with Less: Getting Public Services into Private Hands." See also the debate "Can the Businessman Meet Our Social Need?" between Peter F. Drucker and Edward K. Hamilton.

"creaming" process and usually end up in public institutions and programs. Accordingly, Amitai Etzioni has questioned whether "human services [can] really generate a legitimate profit without skimping on quality or quantity, without weeding out the really ill and giving unnecessary services to the relatively healthy."[17]

Entrepreneurism in the social services has been significantly advanced by the use of both cash and service strategies. Among the advantages of cash and voucher policies is the possibility of greater consumer choice. Supporters of entrepreneurism assume that competition among providers will bring about the best quality of service because informed users will seek out the better services and the second-best will not survive.

Unfortunately, these conditions are rarely found: the self-regulatory market, the purifying process of competition among an adequate number of qualified providers, and meaningful opportunities for consumer choice occur infrequently in the social services, even if they are occasionally found in the economy. At the very least, the alleged merits of reprivatization are "not proven," and considerable skepticism is warranted concerning the ability of the market to bring about equity or coverage.

The extensive use of profit-making organizations also presents an additional set of obstacles to coordination and efforts to bring a greater measure of rationality into the social service system. Despite these misgivings, the use of profit-making organizations, together with vouchers, performance contracting, and purchase of service as means of de-bureaucratizing and decentralizing the social services will probably increase in the United States. This will mean that profit-making organizations will continue to challenge, threaten, and compete with voluntary nonprofit organizations.

Empowerment of Voluntary Organizations

Amidst signs of the contraction of the welfare state, the special advantages of nongovernmental organizations are being rediscovered, particularly in the United States and England. This is a new development because during the debate on the welfare state in the 1960s, there was

17. Amitai Etzioni, "What To Do About the Nursing Homes," p. 26. See also the criticism of profit-making organizations in the social services by Kurt Reichert, "The Drift Toward Entrepreneurialism in Health and Social Welfare: Implications for Social Work Education." The experience with the use of profit-making corporations in performing other public functions is analyzed in Herbert Kiesling and Donald Fisk, *Local Governmental Privatization/Competition Innovations*.

virtually no mention of voluntarism.[18] There is powerful ideological support for the strengthening of voluntarism, both as a means of recovering the lost sense of community, and as a bulwark against further state intervention in the affairs of citizens. Hoping to regenerate social institutions on the local level, Morris Janowitz argues that greater volunteer participation can humanize the welfare state, revive a sense of community, and transform the welfare state into a welfare society:

> Citizen participation in the management of social welfare institutions is an integral aspect of the . . . management of stagflation. . . . The frontier in citizen participation rests on the specific purpose local voluntary association and on the direct involvement of local citizens in directing and administering particular social welfare agencies.[19]

To reduce the distance between institutions and citizens, Janowitz recommends the regrouping of agencies on a geographic basis, the integration of health, welfare, and educational services, and the greater use of self-help and paraprofessionals.

Similarly, in a manifesto pitting liberty and voluntarism against the bureaucracies of the overregulated society, Peter L. Berger and Richard J. Neuhaus offer a solution to the dilemma that people want more governmental services and, at the same time, less government. Rejecting any attempt to dismantle the welfare state, they assert that "the welfare state is here to stay, indeed that it ought to expand the benefits it provides — but that *alternative mechanisms are possible to provide welfare state services.*"[20]

Rooted in the venerable sociological tradition of Durkheim, Toennies, and Simmel, Berger and Neuhaus make an eloquent case for the greater use of the mediating structures of neighborhood, family, church, and voluntary association, which are essential for a vital democratic society and which stand between the individual and his

18. A representative selection of the views during the 1960s showing the range of ideological positions but with no mention of volunteerism is Charles I. Schottland, ed., *The Welfare State: Thirty Selected Essays.*

19. Morris Janowitz, *Social Control of the Welfare State*, p. 126; see also pp. 132–33. The experience of neighborhood groups providing various types of law enforcement services is the subject of the entire issue of *The Journal of Voluntary Action Research* 7 (Winter-Spring, January-April 1978): 4–108. The roots of the faith in neighborhood groups as deliverers of social services go back to the 1920s. See, e.g., John Dewey, *The Public and Its Problems;* Mary P. Follett, *The New State.*

20. Berger and Neuhaus, p. 1. See also Theodore Levitt, *The Third Sector: New Tactics for a Responsive Society,* and Brian O'Connell, "From Service to Advocacy to Empowerment." The use of nongovernmental organizations for the provision of public services has also been advocated by Gunnar Myrdal, *Beyond the Welfare State,* p. 70.

private life and the megastructures of public life. Two broad policy recommendations are made to ensure pluralism. Public policy should protect and foster the mediating structures: first, minimally, they should not be damaged by government; second, maximally, wherever possible, government should empower them with the resources for the realization of public purposes.[21]

Coincidentally, the same set of values and guiding principles is found in the Wolfenden Report in England. The Wolfenden Committee declared that the rate of statutory growth cannot continue, nor should it because it is too costly, too big, monopolistic, inflexible, and resistive to innovation, as well as making it difficult for citizens to be involved both in policymaking and in the delivery of the social services. Although the statutory should remain dominant, it is possible to halt the increasing scale of government by changing the direction of provision by making greater use of voluntary organizations as alternative public-service providers, particularly where the community and the clientele can be involved directly in the provision of services.[22] The voluntary agency is presented as a way of obtaining more choice and specialization, as well as an antidote to bureaucratization, professionalism, and paternalism in the governmental sector.[23]

A more detailed explication of the philosophy behind the Wolfenden Report is offered by one of its members, Roger Hadley, who also believes that "we have come to the end of the era of the expansion of the statutory services."[24] He observes that the voluntary sector, which includes both formal organizations and the informal network of social relationships, is already the major provider of services for such groups as the infirm, the elderly, the chronically sick and disabled, the mentally ill and handicapped, preschool children, and youth. The com-

21. The utilization of voluntary, nonprofit organizations as an alternative to the political market (government) for the provision or "co-production" of public services is of special interest to public choice economists, who have pointed out the vast underestimation of the economic value of the voluntary sector. See: Gary S. Becker, *The Economic Approach to Human Behavior;* T. F. Stinson and J. M. Stam, "Toward an Economic Model of Volunteerism: The Case of Participation in Local Government," *Journal of Voluntary Action Research* 5 (1976): 52–60; Burton A. Weisbrod, *The Voluntary Non-profit Sector: An Economic Analysis.*

22. Wolfenden Committee, *The Future of Voluntary Organisations*, pp. 187–88. The report adds that voluntary agencies should be of, for, and by the people.

23. The authors of the Wolfenden Report do not go as far as E. F. Schumacher *(Small Is Beautiful)*, who, at the annual meeting in 1976 of the National Council of Social Service in London declared: "One of society's foremost tasks is to devise a system by which government collects the necessary funds for non-governmental voluntary organizations to spend it."

24. Roger Hadley, "Beyond the Limits of the Welfare State: Social Policy and Community Resources."

munity, through its voluntary organizations and networks, is also a supplementary resource for the services for which government is the main provider. With more positive public policies, the voluntary sector has the potential to make a greater contribution and, at the same time, to lead to a strengthening of the statutory sector and citizen participation.[25]

Historically, we seem to have veered 180 degrees from the time in the 1930s and 1940s when government took over unemployment relief in the United States because voluntary organizations were no longer able to meet the demands; now we call for a greater use of the voluntary sector because government seems to have reached the limits of its capacity and legitimacy. However, in this attempt to reverse the process of *gemeinschaft* to *gesellschaft*, it may be unwise to assume too soon that "we have reached the limits of state welfare." A facile acceptance of the end of the welfare state can become a premature, self-fulfilling prophecy, too easily tolerating governmental failure to implement existing commitments to continue providing benefits that only the state can ensure. Voluntarism is no substitute for services that can best be delivered by government, particularly if coverage, equity, and entitlements are valued.[26] True, a few neo-conservatives believe that the United States and England still have a long way to go to provide the universal minimum that is regarded as essential; nor do they all believe that United States taxes have reached the limit. Nevertheless, there is a danger that those who have jumped on the bandwagon of the era of limits, signaling the end of the welfare state by advocating more volunteerism, are being coopted by others who have less concern with social justice than with tax reduction. There is no evidence to suggest that the extension of social services would be more acceptable to taxpayers if provided by nongovernmental organizations. The spread of public support for limiting taxation and government spending seems to preclude this.

25. There seems to be more interest in England than in the United States in the development of closer links between statutory organizations and the family and informal networks in the provision of community care. See, for example, Michael F. Bayley, *Community-Oriented Systems of Care*, pp. 42–43; and Gerald Caplan, *Support Systems and Community Mental Health*. On some of the limitations of the family and the prerequisites for it to carry out some of these support and care functions, see Steven P. Segal, "Community Care and Deinstitutionalization: A Review," and Abraham Monk, "Family Supports in Old Age."

26. Alfred J. Kahn, *Social Policy and Social Services*, pp. 52–56. For an unusual case study of some of the problems — and advantages — of using a nongovernmental organization to carry out governmental functions, see C. C. Hood and J. R. Bradshaw, "The Family Fund: Implications of an Unorthodox Agency," and J. R. Bradshaw, *The Family Fund: An Initiative in Social Policy*.

Enthusiastic supporters of empowerment tend to lump together indiscriminately all forms of volunteerism and mediating structures and to regard them as equally desirable and effective in combating excessive governmental size. There are, however, considerable differences between the use of volunteers as unpaid staff and peer self-help, between mutual aid, neighborhood, and community-based service organizations, and between the forms of citizen participation, as well as in the institutional structures of family and religion. It is quite understandable in a shrinking economy that, for example, there would be a revival of interest in the use of volunteers as a substitute for paid staff. In California, supporters of reduced taxation fantasized about a wave of good-neighborliness that would sweep the state in a collective volunteer effort to restore services lost as a result of budget cuts. But experience has shown that, as a cheap form of labor, volunteers can exacerbate tensions among staff and between nongovernmental organizations and trade unions. They are no substitute for necessary services best delivered by professionals and other types of paid staff.

Sufficient attention has not been given to the great diversity in the effectiveness of voluntary organizations as service providers and in nurturing citizen participation. Proponents of the voluntary sector often fail to appreciate that its strengths are at the same time the source of its limitations. Whether based on locality, ethnicity, religion, or another sectarian interest, voluntary organizations as service providers are inherently narrow and exclusionary in their interests. Because the individual is dependent for social services on the initiative, resources, and capabilities of a particular group with which he is administratively identified, the substitution of voluntary for governmental agencies can result in uneven, inconsistent, and inequitable services. Although evidence of their service delivery capability is rather sparse, experience with various forms of neighborhood organization suggest that they can become just as institutionalized, rigid, inaccessible, unresponsive, and undemocratic as professionalized bureaucracies.[27]

27. On some of the limitations of decentralized neighborhood groups in the social services, see Neil Gilbert and Harry Specht, *The Dimensions of Social Welfare Policy*, pp. 174–77; David J. O'Brien, *Neighborhood Organization and Interest-Group Processes*; Grant McConnell, *Private Power and American Democracy*, p. 107; Norman Furniss, "The Practical Significance of Decentralization"; Harold Weissman, *Community Councils and Community Control*; and Ralph M. Kramer, *Participation of the Poor: Comparative Community Case Studies in the War on Poverty*. A strong counterargument is made by Milton Kotler, *Neighborhood Government: The Local Foundation of Political Life*, and Richard C. Rich, "The Roles of Neighborhood Organizations in Urban Service Delivery."

The use of small voluntary organizations (particularly alternative and more loosely-organized ones in which advocacy, flexibility, responsiveness, and citizen involvement are sought) is often seriously compromised by the administrative demands of service delivery. For example, while contracts may be a highly desirable way of utilizing the resources of more established voluntary agencies to ensure accountability, formalization can vitiate the very qualities sought in alternative agencies or self-help groups, in which responsibilities are more diffuse. Often there is a choice between the haphazard performance and uncertain quality of a small-scale, voluntaristic, community-based program and larger organizations that may be able to provide better services but are more bureaucratic and professional. This is part of an inherent conflict between pluralism-voluntarism and the desire for comprehensive, cost-effective, and integrated services. Still another consideration in the use of small, neighborhood-based, informal, consumer-oriented voluntary organizations is the possibility of their cooptation and subsequent decline as advocates because of the greater demands of service delivery. While there will probably be increased pressures for greater utilization and support of the nongovernmental sector, the extent to which voluntary organizations and the citizen participation they promote can humanize or "save" the welfare state is an open question.

Pragmatic Partnership

The last and most likely of the five types of relationship between the governmental and voluntary sectors is a projection of the pattern that prevailed during the 1970s in the United States. The characteristic features of this social service system, which relies on governmental funding and provider pluralism and faces the dilemmas of vendorism and grantsmanship, have been described in chapters 3 and 8.

In this model, there is a policy of increasingly comprehensive services as a right, as in the alternative of governmental operation, but, in contrast to a free-standing, comprehensive public social service center, there is a strong pragmatic preference for contracting with nongovernmental organizations. This is part of a highly dispersed, uneven "nonsystem," which has defied periodic efforts to impose more efficiency, accountability, and rationality, but which is conducive to pluralism and voluntarism. Although it falls far short of the ideal of a universal, accountable, and equitable system of personal social services, the channeling of tax funds to voluntary organizations typifies the traditional incremental approach to social change in the United

States, as well as the historical ambivalence toward government. Despite the perennial calls for service integration, there are few incentives for more planning or a more formal division of responsibility between the sectors. Because of the multiplicity of funding and provider interests served by this pragmatic partnership[28] and the absence of sufficient forces to alter the equilibrium between the sectors in either direction, this policy is likely to continue.

It is possible to project a few "surprise-free" changes that might occur in the personal social services system in the United States in the context of anticipated economic, political, and demographic trends during the 1980s. There will probably be increased competition between health, welfare, and educational programs for funding, both among nongovernmental providers and between them and governmental agencies. Demographic trends will make social services for the aged one of the strongest claimants for governmental support, with the interests of older persons competing sharply with those of children and youth. This will be particularly true in the field of the handicapped, where the incidence of disability is expected to decrease and a larger number of the handicapped persons will be older because of a decline in the birth rate and improved life-saving medical technology.[29] In a no- or slow-growth economy, governmental spending for normal population groups will vie more keenly with services for the handicapped, and among the latter there will be competition between different disability groups, each with a right to education, independent living, care, and treatment, as well as a struggle between the support of mainstream and specialized services.

In the battle over priorities, it is likely that the larger, more bureaucratic and professional voluntary agencies with the greatest visibility and popularity will increase their advantage over smaller organizations because of their superior ability to respond to increased demands for fiscal and program accountability. Only as the less formalized volun-

28. More apt, though perhaps clumsier, would be a designation of this model that refers to the transactional or exchange character of the relationship between a buyer and a seller, or the special features of a social service economy with multiple providers and govenmental financing. Although, as suggested in chapter 12, the concept of partnership may imply a spurious equality and obscure vast differences in power, it may be warranted in this case because it is the customary term used in the United States and England. Also, its normative connotations are pertinent if it conveys the ideal of an interdependent relationship in which there is respect both for the autonomy of the voluntary agency and for public accountability.

29. Duncan Guthrie, "The Future Role of the Local Voluntary Organisations for the Disabled"; John Gliedman and William Roth, *The Unexpected Minority: Handicapped Children in America.*

tary agencies become more bureaucratic will they be able to improve the efficiency of their programs and to comply with other requirements for receiving government funds. At the same time, voluntary agencies will be competing with large, profit-making organizations, which may be in a better position to guarantee quality control for certain services. As they compete for contracts with other nongovernmental agencies and profit-making organizations, voluntary agencies will have to define and demonstrate their competence and accountability more persuasively. When they become public service providers, they will have to strive for greater efficiency and equity in service delivery, will have to improve managerial capability, and will have to learn to accept more paperwork and some program restrictions.

These trends may hasten the development of additional ad hoc coalitions and more permanent confederations within the voluntary sector to enable it to deal with government on a more equal basis. Within a more turbulent, competitive, and increasingly complex interorganizational environment, a continued blurring of organizational character can be expected as both the governmental and voluntary sectors become more entrepreneurial. Within the United States, one can anticipate further pressures for de-bureaucratization, decentralization, and deprofessionalization, as well as the expanded use of contracting for the provision of governmental service programs. While this may strengthen pluralism and voluntarism, it will do so at the expense of a progressive loss of coherence and diminished possibilities for a more integrated system.

Because they are less costly and ideologically more acceptable, some voluntary agencies may benefit from the backlash against public bureaucracies. More likely, however, in an era of cutbacks in governmental spending is a decline in governmental support for the type of social services provided by voluntary agencies. This occurred in California, where, in the wake of Proposition 13, voluntary agencies under contract with local governments were hard hit when funds for their programs were eliminated. At the same time, there were additional pressures on voluntary agencies for even more services following reductions in governmental programs.[30]

This presents voluntary agencies with a dilemma: if they do not offer services that supplement or substitute for government, they will be ineligible for public funding and will have great difficulty in sup-

30. Paul Terrell, *California Human Services Two Years after Proposition 13: An Analysis of Budget, Personnel, Organizational and Client Impacts in 13 Counties*, pp. 38–44.

porting their programs through contributions. If they do offer mainstream programs, they can lose a substantial portion of their income when government funds are cut.

While it is not possible to identify the choices that individual voluntary agencies will make under these circumstances, we can, on the basis of our analysis of the four countries, project the likelihood of certain future patterns: in the United States, more extensive reprivatization and greater utilization of voluntary organizations; in England, a modest increase in the use of voluntary organizations and empowerment of the family and informal networks; in the Netherlands, a stronger role for government in the regulation, planning, and coordination of social services, but not in service delivery; in Israel, expanded use of voluntary organizations, less for ideological reasons than because of the inability of government to provide services.

If, as seems reasonable to assume, there will be greater interdependence between government and voluntary organizations, then issues pertaining to the relationships between the two sectors become more important. Most of the problematic aspects revolve around the conflict between voluntary agency autonomy and the accountability required by government. It is with the clarification of these two concepts that we shall conclude.

Autonomy and Accountability: A Reevaluation

The existence of different interests and values underlies much of the confusion surrounding the respective virtues and vices of voluntary agency autonomy and public accountability. For example, the much-vaunted independence of a voluntary agency may be viewed by outsiders as arbitrary, idiosyncratic, or self-serving behavior, just as pluralism is frequently regarded as duplication, fragmentation, or even "organizational anarchy."[31] Autonomy is naturally prized by the supporters of a voluntary agency, but others may be more concerned with the consequences of governmental domination by private interests or other dysfunctional aspects of bureaucratic symbiosis. Government or an underserved population at risk will not consider a reduction in the autonomy of a voluntary agency a calamity if it means that the agency functions with a broader or different conception of the public

31. "Yesterday's pluralism has become today's disorganization." The same principle is involved in the belief that the solutions to problems become problems themselves over a period of time (Paul Starr, "Medicine and the Waning of Professional Sovereignty," p. 181).

interest, or if it operates more according to the wishes of certain groups of clientele and less according to those of the staff and board.

Conversely, governmental demands for service and for fiscal accountability may be perceived by voluntary agencies as excessive or as unnecessary intrusions, resulting in administrative busywork and giving an illusion of "businesslike" efficiency. Voluntary agencies usually interpret governmental concern with procedures and forms as counterproductive controls, deflecting resources from the goal of service provision. They also challenge the belief that there is more accountability in the public services on the grounds that governmental agencies are usually reluctant to disclose information concerning their operations and often fail to respect a client's entitlement to service and redress of grievance.

On the other hand, the conventional dualism between autonomy and accountability may be more artificial than real. They may be less opposed than many people believe.[32] For example, a strong, independent agency can be more accountable because government can pinpoint responsibility. Furthermore, accountability requirements may be beneficial to a voluntary agency as it seeks to improve the efficiency and effectiveness of its performance. In any case, it is evident that both terms are ambiguous and value-laden and require analysis. For example, how autonomous should, or can, a voluntary organization be, and with respect to what aspects of its functioning? To whom should a voluntary agency be accountable, for what, when, and how? How much accountability should government require and in what forms?

To begin with autonomy, it is obvious that no organization can be completely independent, because all of its policy decisions are subject to many external and internal constraints. Autonomy is obviously a matter of degree — i.e., it is relative and conditional. Autonomy is also not an end in itself, but a necessary means for the accomplishment of an organization's task and maintenance goals, justified pragmatically by its contribution to more effective performance. The distinctive nature of organizations is that, like persons, they are not self-sufficient or wholly self-determining, but instead are inescapably dependent on their environment and operating systems for essential resources. The

32. That the relationship between independence and accountability may be more complex than a zero-sum game is persuasively argued by Harvey C. Mansfield, "Independence and Accountability for Federal Contractors and Grantees."

prevailing natural state of organizational life is one of interdependency, in which organizations "use" each other — i.e., there are trade-offs in which resources are exchanged for a measure of control.[33] Furthermore, voluntary agencies are not wholly private, freewheeling enterprises; they are, in many ways, public agencies because they require sanction from the state in the form of a charter or legal recognition of their nonprofit, charitable, tax-exempt, corporate status, and they must often be licensed. The community in which they function is the source of their legitimation, service mandate and domain, good will, and more tangible resources such as funds, clientele, staff, and information.

What, then, is autonomy? The term seems to refer to the freedom of an organization to make decisions with an optimal degree of discretion, or, to put it conversely, with relative freedom from the imposition of unwanted restrictions on service-delivery policy and practices (who may be served, by whom, and under what conditions), on governance (composition of the board or advisory committee), and on administrative requirements pertaining to staffing, service standards, costs, reporting, and so on. Autonomy is diminished to the extent that an organization accepts a reduction in its discretionary power and, in so doing, acknowledges the superior power of another group over its area of jurisdiction.

There is, however, nothing unique in voluntary agencies' concern with autonomy. All types of organizations face challenges to their freedom to decide their own fate. Wealthy donors, third-party payments, United Way allocations, and community and professional groups can also constrain an agency's independence.

It is even harder to grapple with the concept of accountability. Its popularity in the human services is exceeded only by the lack of agreement about its meaning. It has been viewed as both an end and a means; it has been defined in terms of procedures, results, disclosure of information, recourse, and compliance with regulations; and it is often indistinguishable from such concepts as evaluation, efficiency, effectiveness, control, and responsibility. At a minimum, accountability means having to answer to those who control a necessary,

33. This view of organizational behavior is articulated in: David Jacobs, "Dependency and Vulnerability: An Exchange Approach to the Control of Organizations"; Sergio E. Mindlin and Howard Aldrich, "Interorganizational Dependence: A Review of the Concept and a Reexamination of the Findings of the Ashton Group"; J. Kenneth Benson, "The Interorganizational Network as a Political Economy"; Michael Aiken and Jerald Hage, "Organizational Interdependence and Intra-Organizational Structure."

scarce resource. Therefore it involves an obligation to report how the organization is discharging its service and fiscal responsibilities in appropriate detail so that decisions can be made. This type of reporting or "public accounting," which is so essential to accountability, should, however, be distinguished from restrictions on agency functioning that might limit its autonomy. Although reporting requirements and red tape may be costly nuisances and may even deflect agency resources, they do not necessarily impair an agency's freedom.[34]

Voluntary agencies, like other organizations, have multiple accountability: to their boards of directors, to by-laws, to stated goals and policies, and to various constituencies, including clientele, contributors, and other funding sources.[35] Accountability for what? The simple answer — that they are accountable for doing what they are supposed to do — immediately raises another question: According to whom? Not only do various interest groups in agencies and the community have different expectations of organizational purpose and performance, but the desired results of the work of voluntary agencies are notoriously difficult to demonstrate. This inherent weakness in the social services is masked by the overriding importance attached to independence and innovation among voluntary agencies. The characteristic diffuse goals and technology of social agencies, as well as their inability to produce evidence of effectiveness, help to explain the substitution of outputs (processes and activities) for substantive outcomes and also contribute to the frequent extremes of over- or underregulation by governmental agencies.[36]

This study found that voluntary-agency autonomy is seldom compromised by the accountability requirements of governmental funding sources. More often, there is a low level of regulation and a closeness

34. A useful overview of the different meanings of accountability is Amitai Etzioni, "Alternative Conceptions of Accountability: The Example of Health Administration." Typical approaches in the social services are: George Hoshino, "Social Services and the Problem of Accountability"; Edward Newman and Jerry Turem, "The Crisis of Accountability"; Emmanuel Tropp, "Expectation, Performance and Accountability"; J. J. Stretch, "Increasing Accountability for Human Service Administration"; and Theodore R. Marmor and James Morone, "Representing Consumer Interests: Imbalanced Markets, Health Planning, and the HSAs," pp. 132–33.

35. Because accountability is generally viewed as an external demand or the sole concern of government, there is insufficient recognition of the internal organizational supports for quality control, such as formal review procedures, and the informal controls of the professionalism of the staff and membership in standard-setting national organizations. Some of the special problems of service provider accountability are cogently analyzed in Bruce L. Gates, *Social Program Administration: The Implementation of Social Policy*, pp. 83–95.

36. Dennis R. Young and Stephen J. Finch, *Foster Care and Nonprofit Agencies*, pp. 233–34.

based on mutual dependency. Because pluralism requires a clear separation between public and private, greater distance and differentiation between the two sectors would enable each to optimize its special competence. Perhaps the issue can be rephrased, not as the preservation of voluntary agency freedom, but rather as how to make public-service providers more accountable without restricting the very qualities of flexibility and individualization that make voluntary agencies desirable. At the same time, to prevent the regulated from regulating the regulators, we need to discover an appropriate social distance between governmental and voluntary agencies — a midpoint that is not so close as to produce excessive restrictions, overenforcement of rules, or co-optation, or so distant that it is not possible to protect the public's interests and to assure compliance with stated objectives.

The quest for principles to bring about a better balance between voluntary agency autonomy and accountability will be elusive and demanding, but the search is essential if pluralism and voluntarism are to be preserved in the welfare state.

Appendix:
Voluntary Agencies
Included in the Sample

Because this was an exploratory study of voluntary agencies in four countries, the sample was purposive (not statistically representative), with the selection based primarily on geographic scope, size, and function.

The initial aim was to select twenty agencies in each country that, in the opinion of local experts, included representative small, medium, and large organizations providing direct services to handicapped clientele, with some distribution between organizations of and for the handicapped. Thus, organizations concerned primarily with fund raising, advocacy, research, public education, information, coordination, or standard setting were eliminated from consideration, although some of these indirect functions were performed by many agencies selected for study.

To facilitate data collection, the agencies chosen were concentrated in selected metropolitan areas of the four countries: Greater London; Amsterdam, The Hague, Rotterdam, and Utrecht; Tel Aviv and Jerusalem; and, in the United States, the San Francisco Bay Area in California. Comparability of direct service functions in the four countries was obtained by selecting national agencies in England and Israel; regional and national agencies in the Netherlands; and local and regional agencies in the San Francisco Bay Area.

In the Netherlands, I relied on the information and recommendations of executive staff members from the Netherlands Society for Rehabilitation, the Dutch National Association for the Care of the Mentally Retarded, and the Netherlands Institute for Social Work Research. In England, staff members of the National Institute of Social Work, the National Council of Social Service, and the Wolfenden Committee served as consultants in the selection of the sample. Officials of the Jewish Agency, JDC-Malben, and the Ministry of Social

Welfare in Israel gave advice on selecting agencies. For the United States, I relied on information in the files of the Bay Area United Way, supplemented by my own knowledge of these agencies.

In Israel there were an insufficient number of agencies offering direct services to the handicapped, so the sample included four agencies with similar functions for victims of road accidents, victims of work injuries, and those disabled in the defense of their country, as well as an agency serving the chronically ill at home. The Dutch organizations fell into two classes, whose differences in corporate form and degree of service provision corresponded to the distinction between organizations of and for the handicapped. Eight organizations were associations of the handicapped themselves or of family members; they received little governmental support and provided few services. The remaining twelve organizations provided services for various types of physically handicapping conditions, for the mentally handicapped, and for the blind and the deaf. They were heavily concentrated among agencies with facilities for rehabilitation, education, day care, treatment, and sheltered workshops. In England, six of the agencies, like those in the Netherlands, operated extensive residential-care institutions throughout the country, and almost all the other national agencies administered a small number of holiday homes for their constituents. None of the U.S. voluntary agencies operated twenty-four-hour residential facilities, as did their Dutch and English counterparts, although they did sponsor day care, treatment centers, and sheltered workshops.

The study was conducted in Israel during 1972–1973; in the Netherlands and the United States during 1974–1975, and in England during 1975. In addition to the fiscal and other data obtained during 1972–1975, more recent relevant information was utilized when available.

Tables 15–18, which follow, list the agencies included in the sample in each country, the percentage of income they received from government in 1973–1974, and the total number of their staff.

In addition to the interview and documentary data obtained from the 75 voluntary agencies included in the sample, between 1972 and 1976 I conducted over 300 interviews with 251 respondents representing 111 organizations, including 23 in the sample, in the United States, England, the Netherlands, and Israel. These interviews were a major source of data on the sociopolitical context and the public policy and interorganizational environment of the voluntary agencies in the four countries.

TABLE 15.

Voluntary Agencies in the United States Included in the Sample

	1973 Income (in $)	Percentage of Income from Government Funds	Number of Staff
Alameda County Association for the Mentally Retarded, Oakland	946,000	63	115
Aid Retarded Children, San Francisco	280,000	44	37
American Cancer Society, San Francisco Chapter	922,000	0	19
Bay Area Hearing Society, San Francisco	142,000	0	10
Contra Costa County Association for the Mentally Retarded, Walnut Creek	416,000	68	38
California League for the Handicapped, San Francisco	126,000	28	9
Center for Independent Living, Berkeley	330,000	75	99
Cerebral Palsy Center for the Bay Area, Oakland	105,000	20	11
Easter Seal Society for Crippled Children and Adults of Alameda County	558,000	17	23
Easter Seal Society for Crippled Children and Adults of San Francisco County	260,000	5	13
Golden Gate Regional Center, San Francisco	4,500,000	100	91
Lung Association of Alameda County, Oakland	214,000	0	5
National Multiple Sclerosis Society, Northern California Chapter, San Francisco	96,000	0	4
Recreation Center for the Handicapped, San Francisco	607,000	90	97
San Francisco Community Rehabilitation Workshop	565,000	44	26
San Francisco Hearing and Speech Center	307,000	22	29
San Francisco Heart Association	772,000	35	19
San Francisco Lighthouse for the Blind	1,160,000	0	21
United Cerebral Palsy Association of San Francisco	214,000	44	3
Westcom Industries (Mt. Diablo Rehabilitation Center), Pleasant Hill	941,000	70	55

NOTE: All of the agencies are located in the San Francisco Bay Area.

TABLE 16.
Voluntary Agencies in England Included in the Sample

	1973 Income (in $)	Percentage of Income from Government Funds	Number of Staff
Association for Spina Bifida and Hydrocephalus	234,436	9	27
British Association of the Hard of Hearing	28,875	0	1
British Polio Fellowship	324,365	27	21
British Rheumatism and Arthritis Association	746,926	0	80
Cheshire Homes	9,038,873	60	2,017
Chest and Heart Association	234,436	1	25
Invalid Children's Aid Association	918,427	57	245
Jewish Blind Society	1,609,549	22	65
Multiple Sclerosis Society of Great Britain	2,333,917	0	19
National Deaf Children's Society	172,843	0	6
Muscular Dystrophy Group of Great Britain	1,520,960	0	20
National Society for Autistic Children	545,171	64	7
National Society for Cancer Relief	3,537,573	0	40
National Society for Mentally Handicapped Children	2,504,179	31	343
Royal Association in Aid of the Deaf and Dumb	499,928	0	58
Royal National Institute for the Blind	15,079,341	27	1,525
Royal National Institute for the Deaf	2,061,511	40	40
Shaftesbury Society	1,597,929	74	340
Spastics Society	17,632,000	29	1,874
Spinal Injuries Association	38,657	0	2

NOTES: Based on £ = $2.895.
All of the agencies are located in Greater London.

TABLE 17.
Voluntary Agencies in the Netherlands Included in the Sample

	1973 Income (in $)	Percentage of Income from Government Funds	Number of Staff
Algemene Nederlandse Invaliden Bond (ANIB), Haarlem (Association of Disabled Persons)	107,135	20	17
Ammanstichting, Rotterdam (Rehabilitation and Training for the Deaf)	2,453,571	90	170
Amstelrade, Amstelveen (Residential Care for the Severely Physically Handicapped)	897,857	99	124
AVO, Nederlandse Vereniging Sociale Zorg voor Mindervaliden, The Hague (Sheltered Workshops for the Handicapped)	535,714	73	42
AVO-Dagverblijf, Rotterdam (Day Care Center for the Physically Handicapped)	111,327	100	14
Bond van Nederlandse Militaire Oorlogslachtoffers (BNMO), The Hague (Disabled Veterans Association)	36,347	0	18
BOSK, Bond van Motorisch Gehandicapten, The Hague (Parents of Brain Damaged Children)	45,714	40	3
Effatha, Christelijk Instituut voor Dove Kinderen, Voorberg (Deaf Children)	2,143,781	94	147

TABLE 17.

Voluntary Agencies in the Netherlands Included in the Sample (continued)

	1973 Income (in $)	Percentage of Income from Government Funds	Number of Staff
Gehandicapten Organisatie Nederland, Doorn (Organization of the Handicapped)	25,411	71	4
Haags Mytyl Vormingscentrum, The Hague (Day Care Center and School for the Mentally Handicapped)	928,571	100	17
Instituut de 'Hartekamp', Haarlem (Day Care and Foster Homes for the Mentally Handicapped)	4,643,000	100	346
Katholiek Instituut voor Maatschappelijke Dienstverlening aan Geestelijk Gehandicapten, Uitgeest (Catholic Social Services for the Mentally Handicapped)	142,857	93	26
Kinderdagverblijk Ellemare, Rotterdam (Day Care Center for the Mentally Handicapped)	214,285	100	22
Nederlandse Multiple Sclerose Stichting, The Hague (Netherlands Multiple Sclerosis Association)	21,429	0	0
Nederlandse Vereniging voor Slechthorenden, Zutphen (Netherlands Association for the Deaf)	33,122	40	3
Stichting St. Christofoor, Utrecht (Social and Community Services for the Mentally Handicapped)	357,143	100	47

TABLE 17.

Voluntary Agencies in the Netherlands Included in the Sample (continued)

	1973 Income (in $)	Percentage of Income from Government Funds	Number of Staff
Stichting voor Geestelijke Volksgezondheid in Zuid-Holland, Zoetermeer (Social Services for Mental Health)	2,029,142	100	138
Van der Woudenstichting, Delft (Foster and Day Care for the Physically and Mentally Handicapped)	1,321,429	100	108
Vereniging het Nederlandse Blindenwezen, Amsterdam (Netherlands Association for the Blind)	109,231	50	12
Vereniging Spierdystrofie Nederland, Amersfort (Muscular Dystrophy Association)	30,186	37	2

NOTE: 2.781 Df. (guilder) = $1.

TABLE 18.
Voluntary Agencies in Israel Included in the Sample

	1972–1973 Income (in $)	Percentage of Income from Government Funds	Number of Staff
AKIM (Israel Association for the Rehabilitation of the Mentally Handicapped)	309,524	46	110
ANAT (Israel Association for Rehabilitation of Traffic Accident Victims)	28,571	11	2
Association of the Deaf	88,810	61	35
Anti-Tuberculosis League	63,631	10	2
Center for the Blind	45,238	20	3
Disabled Workers Association	71,429	15	1
ILAN (Israel Foundation for Handicapped Children)	714,286	10	113
Israel Cancer Association	642,857	0	6

TABLE 18.
Voluntary Agencies in Israel Included in the Sample (continued)

	1972–1973 Income (in $)	Percentage of Income from Government Funds	Number of Staff
Jewish Institute for the Blind	309,529	25	31
MATAV (Homemaker Services Association)	218,095	80	217
MICHA (Association for the Rehabilitation of Deaf Children)	80,952	21	10
Migdal Or (American-Israel Lighthouse for the Blind)	92,857	34	10
Nechei Zahal (Disabled Veterans Association)	547,619	25	34
NITZAN (Organization for Children with Developmental and Learning Difficulties)	19,048	20	4
SHEMA (Organization of Parents of Deaf and Hard-of-Hearing Children)	71,428	15	1

NOTES: Based on IL4.20 = $1.00.
     All the agencies are located in Tel Aviv or Jerusalem.

In each country the executives of the voluntary agencies in the sample were interviewed by experienced professionals, whom I trained and supervised. The same interview schedule was used in each country and required four to five hours for completion, usually in two sessions. In Israel and the Netherlands the interviews were conducted in Hebrew and Dutch, respectively.

Table 19 shows the distribution of respondents by country and type of organization.

TABLE 19.
Respondents By Organization and Country

	United States		England		The Netherlands		Israel	
	Number of Organizations	Number of Respondents	Number of Organizations	Number of Respondents	Number of Organizations	Number of Respondents	Number of Organizations	Number of Respondents
Voluntary agencies in the sample	20	22	20	25	20	23	15	24
Other local and national voluntary social service agencies (executives, professional staff, and presidents)	3	4	12	18	6	7	3	7
National associations of voluntary agencies	3	5	8	16	7	15	7	9
Governmental ministries (senior officials in departments of health, welfare, education, or labor)	4	8	3	11	5	10	5	18

TABLE 19.
Respondents By Organization and Country (continued)

	United States		England		The Netherlands		Israel	
	Number of Organizations	Number of Respondents	Number of Organizations	Number of Respondents	Number of Organizations	Number of Respondents	Number of Organizations	Number of Respondents
Local governmental social service departments (directors and department heads)	3	7	12	26	3	5	5	7
Professionals, experts and researchers		5		11		6		12
Legislators and elected officials		4		3		2		3
Miscellaneous foundations, fundraising bodies, and journalists		5		6		5		6
TOTALS	33	60	55	116	41	73	35	86

BIBLIOGRAPHY

Abrams, Burton A., and Schitz, Mark D. "The 'crowding-out' effect of governmental transfers on private charitable contributions." *Public Choice* 33 (1978):29–39.

Academy of Educational Development. *The Voluntary Sector in Brief.* New York: Academy of Educational Development, 1979.

Acton, Thomas. "Charities and the iron law of chaos." *New Society* 30 (1974):477–80.

Addams, Jane. *Twenty Years at Hull House.* New York: New American Library, 1961.

Agranoff, Robert. "Services integration." In *Managing Human Services*, edited by Wayne F. Anderson, Bernard J. Frieden, and Michael J. Murphy. Washington, D.C.: International City Management Association, 1977. Pp. 527–64.

Aiken, Michael, and Hage, Jerald. "Organizational interdependence and intra-organizational structure." *Administrative Science Quarterly* 33 (1968): 912–30.

———. "The organic organization and innovation." *Sociology* 5 (1971):63–82.

Aiken, Michael, and Mott, Paul, editors. *The Structure of Community Power.* New York: Random House, 1970.

Akana, Paul. "The United Way system needs no defense." *Community Focus* 2 (1978):17–18.

Akzin, Benjamin, and Dror, Yehezkel. *Israel: High Pressure Planning.* Syracuse, N.Y.: Syracuse University Press, 1966.

Allen, Kenn, and Schindler, Arlene. "Is volunteerism in trouble?" *Voluntary Action Leadership* (Summer 1978):35–36.

Almond, Gabriel A., and Verba, Sidney. *The Civic Culture: Political Attitudes and Democracy in Five Nations.* Boston: Little, Brown & Co., 1965.

American Institute of Certified Public Accountants. *Audits of Voluntary Health and Welfare Organizations.* New York: 1974.

Amis, William D., and Stern, Samuel E. "A critical examination of the theory and functions of voluntary associations." *Journal of Voluntary Action Research* 3 (1974):91–99.

Amos, F. J. "An opportunity missed." *Social Service Quarterly* 51 (1978):129–30.

Andrews, F. Emerson. "Philanthropy in the United States: history and structure." In *Philanthropy in the 70s: An Anglo-American Discussion*, edited by John J. Corson and Harry V. Hodson. New York: Council on Foundations, 1973. Pp. 89–114.

Aves, Geraldine M. *The Voluntary Worker in the Social Services*. London: George Allen & Unwin, 1970.

Bagley, Christopher. *The Dutch Plural Society: A Comparative Study in Race Relations*. London: Oxford University Press, 1973.

Bakal, Carl. *Charity U.S.A.: An Investigation into the Hidden World of the Multi-Billion Dollar Charity Industry*. New York: Times Books, 1979.

Bayley, Michael J. *Mental Handicap and Community Care*. London: Routledge & Kegan Paul, 1973.

——— . *Community-Orientated Systems of Care*. Berkhamstead, England: The Volunteer Centre, 1978.

Beck, Bertram M. "The voluntary social welfare agency: a reassessment." *Social Service Review* 44 (1970):147–54.

——— . "Governmental contracts with non-profit social welfare corporations." In *The Dilemma of Accountability in Modern Government*, edited by Bruce L. R. Smith and D. C. Hague. New York: St. Martin's Press, 1971. Pp. 213–29.

Becker, Gary S. *The Economic Approach to Human Behavior*. Chicago: University of Chicago Press, 1976.

Bell, Daniel. "The revolution of rising entitlements." *Fortune* 71 (April 1975):98–103, 182, 185.

Benson, J. Kenneth. "The interorganizational network as a political economy." *Administrative Science Quarterly* 20 (1975):229–49.

Benton, Bill, et al. *Social Service Federal Legislation versus State Implementation*. Washington, D.C.: The Urban Institute, 1978.

Berger, Peter L., and Neuhaus, Richard John. *To Empower People: The Role of Mediating Structures in Public Policy*. Washington, D.C.: American Enterprise Institute for Public Policy Research, 1977.

Berman, Paul. "Buying social reform with federal dollars." *Taxing and Spending* 2 (1979):22–25.

Bers, Trudy H. "Private Welfare Agencies and Their Role in Government-Sponsored Welfare Programs." Ph.D. dissertation, University of Illinois, 1973.

Best, Harry. *Deafness and the Deaf in the United States*. New York: Macmillan, 1943.

Beveridge, Lord William. *Voluntary Action: A Report on Methods of Social Advance*. London: George Allen & Unwin, 1948.

Beveridge, Lord William, and Wells, A. F., editors. *The Evidence for Voluntary Action*. London: George Allen & Unwin, 1949.

Bevier, Michael. *Politics Backstage: Inside the California Legislature*. Philadelphia: Temple University Press, 1979.

Blau, Peter M., and Scott, W. Richard. *Formal Organizations: A Comparative Approach.* San Francisco: Chandler Publishing Co., 1962.

Blau, Peter M.; Heydebrand, Wolfe V.; and Stauffer, Robert E. "The structure of small bureaucracies." *American Sociological Review* 31 (1966):171–91.

Blaxter, Mildred. " 'Disability' and rehabilitation: some questions of definition." In *A Sociology of Medical Practice*, edited by Caroline Cox and Adrianne Mead. London: Collier-Macmillan, 1975. Pp. 207–23.

——— . *The Meaning of Disability: A Sociological Study of Impairment.* London: Heinemann Educational Books, 1976.

Blommestijn, Pieter J. "Implementation and administration of legislation concerning the handicapped: The Netherlands Contribution to the Second International Conference on Legislation Concerning the Disabled, 16–20 January 1978, Manila, Philippines." The Hague: Ministry of Culture, Recreation and Social Welfare, 1978 (mimeographed).

Bok, Derek C. "The federal government and the university." *The Public Interest* 58 (1980):80–101.

Bolan, Richard S. "Social planning and policy development: local government." In *Managing Human Services*, edited by Wayne F. Anderson, Bernard J. Frieden, and Michael J. Murphy. Washington, D.C.: International City Management Association, 1977. Pp. 85–127.

Boorstin, Daniel J. *The Americans: The National Experience.* New York: Vintage Books, 1965.

Boswell, David M., and Wingrove, Janet M., editors. *The Handicapped Person in the Community.* London: Tavistock Publications, 1974.

Braam, G. P. A. "Social work as a means to social change." *Sociologia Neerlandica* 6 (1970):155–67.

Bradshaw, J. R. "The origins of the Family Fund." *Journal of Voluntary Action Research* 8 (1979):17–24.

——— . *The Family Fund: An Initiative in Social Policy.* London: Routledge & Kegan Paul, 1980.

Bradshaw, Jonathan; Glendinning, Caroline; and Hatch, Stephen. "Voluntary organizations for handicapped children and their families: the meaning of membership." *Child: Care, Health, and Development* 3 (1977):247–60.

Brager, George, and Holloway, Stephen. *Changing Human Service Organizations: Politics and Practice.* New York: Free Press, 1978.

Break, George F. "Charitable contributions under federal income tax: alternative policy options." In *Research Papers Sponsored by the Commission on Private Philanthropy and Public Needs*, II. Washington, D.C.: Department of the Treasury, 1977. Pp. 1521–42.

Bremner, Robert. "Scientific philanthropy, 1873–93." *Social Service Review* 30 (1956):168–73.

Brilliant, Eleanor L. "Private or public: a model of ambiguities." *Social Service Review* 47 (1973):384–96.

Brown, Josephine C. *Public Relief, 1929–39.* New York: Holt, 1940.

Brown, Lee. "Which way now for Volunteer Centre?" *Community Care*, March 17, 1976, pp. 11–13.

Brown, R. G. S. *The Management of Welfare: A Study of British Social Service Administration*. London: Fontana/Collins, 1975.

Brownstein, Solomon M. " 'La Reforme' in Quebec health and social services: impact on Jewish case work services." *Journal of Jewish Communal Service* 51 (1974):162–70.

Bruce, Ian. "Volunteers and labour unions in Great Britain." *Volunteer Administration* 11 (1978):2–9.

Bruce, Maurice. *The Coming of the Welfare State*. London: B. T. Batsford, 1961.

Bruno, Frank J. *Trends in Social Work*. New York: Columbia University Press, 1948.

"A bureaucratic imperative." Current Reading in *The Public Interest* 57 (1979):115–17.

Burian, William. "Purchase of Service in Child Welfare: A Problem of Inter-Organizational Exchange." Ph.D. dissertation, University of Chicago, 1970.

Burke, Edmund M. "Defending the United Way." *Society* 15 (1978): 18–21.

Burns, Eveline M. *Social Security and Public Policy*. New York: McGraw-Hill, 1956.

———. "Letter to the editor." *Social Service Review* 36 (1962):234–35.

Cahn, Frances, and Bary, Valeska. *Welfare Activities of Federal, State and Local Governments in California, 1850–1934*. Berkeley: University of California Press, 1936.

Caidin, Gerald E. *Israel's Administrative Culture*. Berkeley: University of California, Institute of Governmental Studies, 1970.

Camden, London Borough of. *Annual Report of the Social Service Department, 1975*. Pp. 8–10.

Caplan, Gerald. *Support Systems and Community Mental Health*. New York: Behavioral Publications, 1974.

Carrier, John, and Kendall, Ian. "The development of welfare states: the production of plausible accounts." *Journal of Social Policy* 6 (1977):271–90.

Carter, Novia. *Trends in Voluntary Support for Non-Governmental Social Service Agencies*. Ottawa, Ontario: Canadian Council on Social Development, 1974.

Carter, Richard. *The Gentle Legions*. Garden City, N.Y.: Doubleday & Co., 1961.

Clark, Peter B., and Wilson, James Q. "Incentive systems: a theory of organization." *Administrative Science Quarterly* 6 (1961):129–66.

Clark, Terry Nichols. *Community Power and Policy Outputs: A Review of Urban Research*. Beverly Hills: Sage Publications, 1973.

Clecak, Peter. *Crooked Paths: Reflections on Socialism, Conservatism and the Welfare State*. New York: Harper & Row, 1977.

Cloward, Richard A., and Epstein, Irwin. "Private social welfare's disengagement from the poor: the case of family adjustment agencies." In *Social Welfare Institutions*, edited by Mayer N. Zald. New York: John Wiley & Sons, 1965. Pp. 623–43.

Cohen, Nathan E. *Social Work in the American Tradition*. New York: The Dryden Press, 1958.

Cohen, Nathan E., editor. *The Citizen Volunteer: His Responsibility, Role and Opportunity in Modern Society*. New York: Harper & Row, 1962.

Commission on Private Philanthropy and Public Needs. *Giving in America: Toward a Stronger Voluntary Sector*. Washington, D.C.: 1975.

Committee on Local Authority and Allied Personal Social Services. *A Report to Parliament*. London: HMSO Cmnd. 3703, July 1968.

Cornuelle, Richard. *Reclaiming the American Dream*. New York: Random House, 1965.

Corwin, Ronald G. "Strategies for organizational innovation." *American Sociological Review* 37 (1972):441–54.

Coser, Lewis, and Howe, Irving, editors. *The New Conservatism: A Critique from the Left*. New York: Quadrangle Books, 1974.

Coughlin, Bernard J. *Church and State in Social Welfare*. New York: Columbia University Press, 1965.

Cousins, P. F. "Voluntary organizations and local government in three South London boroughs." *Public Administration* 54 (1976):63–82.

Croydon, London Borough of. "Summary of Statistics." *Croydon Voluntary Services of the Social Service Department*. London: 1975. Pp. 1–9.

Cull, John, and Hardy, Richard. *Volunteerism: An Emerging Profession*. Springfield, Ill.: Charles C. Thomas, 1974.

Daalder, Hans. "The Netherlands: opposition in a segmented society." In *Political Opposition in Western Democracies*, edited by Robert Dahl. New Haven: Yale University Press, 1966. Pp. 188–236.

——— . "On building consociational nations: the cases of the Netherlands and Switzerland." In *Consociational Democracy: Political Accommodation in Segmented Societies*, edited by Kenneth McRae. Toronto, Ontario: McClelland & Stewart, 1966. Pp. 102–24.

Darlove, Jay. *The Politics of Policy in Local Government*. Cambridge: Cambridge University Press, 1973.

Darvill, Giles. *Bargain or Barricade? The Role of the Social Services Department in Meeting Social Need through Involving the Community*. Berkhamstead, England: The Volunteer Centre, 1975.

Deehy, Patrick, and Fainer, Claire. "The new social service system in Quebec: organizational myths and professional responses." *Intervention* 42 (1975):3–15.

Delbecq, Andre L., and Pierce, Jon L. "Innovation in professional organizations." *Administration in Social Work* 2 (1978):411–24.

De Mott, Benjamin. "The day the volunteers didn't." *Psychology Today* 11 (1978):23–24, 131–32.

Derber, Milton. "Histadrut: an industrial democracy in Israel, an interpretive essay from an American perspective." In *Israel: Social Structure and Change*, edited by Michael Curtis and Mordecai Shertoff. New Brunswick, N.J.: Transaction Books, 1973. Pp. 257–80.

Derthick, Martha. *Uncontrollable Spending for Social Service Grants*. Washington, D.C.: Brookings Institute, 1975.

de Tocqueville, Alexis. *Democracy in America*. Edited by J. P. Mayer. Garden City, N.Y.: Doubleday & Co., 1969.

Dewey, John. *The Public and Its Problems*. New York: Henry Holt & Co., 1927.

Dion, Leon. *Quebec: The Unfinished Revolution*. Montreal: McGill-Queens University Press, 1976.

The Donee Group Report and Recommendations. "Private philanthropy: vital and innovative? or passive and irrelevant?" In *Research Papers Sponsored by the Commission on Private Philanthropy and Public Needs*, vol. 1. Washington, D.C.: Department of the Treasury, 1977. Pp. 49–88.

Doron, Abraham, and Kramer, Ralph M. "Ideology, programme and organizational factors in public assistance: the case of Israel." *Journal of Social Policy* 5 (1976):131–49.

Downs, G., and Mohr, Lawrence. "Conceptual issues in the study of innovation." *Administrative Science Quarterly* 21 (1976):700–714.

Drucker, Peter F. *The Age of Discontinuity: Guidelines to Our Changing Society*. New York: Harper & Row, 1969.

———. "On managing the public service institution." *The Public Interest* 33 (1973):43–60.

Drucker, Peter F., and Hamilton, Edward K. "Can the businessman meet our social need?" *Saturday Review of the Society*, April 1973. Pp. 41–53.

Dybwad, R. F. "The voluntary association on the international scene." In *Mental Retardation and Developmental Disabilities: An Annual Review*, edited by J. Wortis. New York: Brunner/Mazel, 1974. Pp. 273–87.

Dye, Thomas R. "Community power studies." In *Political Science Annual, II*, edited by James A. Robinson. Indianapolis: Bobbs-Merrill Co., 1969. Pp. 35–70.

Ebenstein, William et al. *American Democracy in World Perspective*. 4th ed. New York: Harper & Row, 1976.

Educational Care of the Handicapped Child. The Hague, The Netherlands: Ministry of Education and Science, 1970.

Eisenstadt, S. N. *Israeli Society*. New York: Basic Books, 1967.

———. The social conditions of the development of voluntary associations — a case study of Israel." *Journal of Voluntary Action Research* 1 (1972):2–13.

Elazar, Daniel J. *Israel: From Ideological to Territorial Democracy*. New York: General Learning Press, 1971.

————— . "Local government as an integrating factor in Israeli society." In *Israel: Social Structure and Change*, edited by Michael Curtis and Mordecai Shertoff. New Brunswick, N.J.: Transaction Books, 1973. Pp. 15–26.

Elkin, S. L. "Comparative urban politics and interorganizational behavior." *Comparative Urban Research II* 5 (1974):5–22.

Elon, Amos. *The Israelis: Founders and Sons*. New York: Holt, Rinehart & Winston, 1971.

Eran, Yechiel. "A new model of voluntary organization in Israel." *Journal of Jewish Communal Service* 54 (1978):262–65.

Erwin, Martin C., and Maiden, Jan K. "Contracting for Human Services." Master's thesis, School of Social Work, San Diego State University, 1978.

Etzioni, Amitai. "Two approaches to organizational analysis: a critique and a suggestion." *Administrative Science Quarterly* 5 (1960):257–78.

————— . "The decline of neo-feudalism: the case of Israel." In *Papers in Comparative Public Administration*, edited by Ferel Heady and Sybill Stokes. Ann Arbor: University of Michigan Press, 1962. Pp. 229–43.

————— . "Alternative conceptions of accountability: the example of health administration." *Public Administration Review* 35 (May–June 1975):279–86.

————— . "What to do about the nursing homes." *Juris Doctor* 6 (1976):26–31.

————— . "Societal overload: sources, components, and corrections." *Political Science Quarterly* 92 (1977–1978):607–31.

Falush, Peter. "Trends in the finance of British charities." *National Westminister Bank Quarterly Review*, May 1977. P. 33.

Family Fund Research Project. *The Prevalence of Children with Very Severe Disabilities in the United Kingdom*. York: University of York, Department of Social Administration and Social Work, 1976 (mimeographed).

————— . *Variations in Provision by Local Authority Social Service Departments for Families with Handicapped Children*. York: University of York, Department of Social Administration and Social Work, 1976 (mimeographed).

Farrell, Gabriel. *The Story of Blindness*. Cambridge: Harvard University Press, 1956.

Federal Register. June 27, 1975, p. 27354.

Fein, Leonard J. *Politics in Israel*. Boston: Little, Brown & Co., 1967.

Feldstein, Martin S., and Clotfelder, Charles. "Tax incentives and charitable contributions in the U.S.: a microeconomic analysis." In *Research Papers Sponsored by the Commission on Private Philanthropy and Public Needs*, vol. 2. Washington, D.C.: Department of the Treasury, 1977. Pp. 1393–418.

Fine, Sidney. *Laissez-faire and the General Welfare State*. Ann Arbor: University of Michigan Press, 1956.

Finer, S. E. *Comparative Government*. London: Allan Lane, 1970.

Fiorina, Morris P. "The decline of collective responsibility in American politics." *Daedalus* 109 (1980):25–46.

Fisher, David H. *Growing Old in America*. New York: Oxford University Press, 1977.

Fisk, Donald; Kiesling, Herbert; and Mullen, Thomas. *Private Provision of Public Services: An Overview*. Washington, D.C.: The Urban Institute, 1978.

Fitch, Lyle C. "Increasing the role of the private sector in providing public services." In *Improving the Quality of Urban Management*, edited by W. D. Hawley and D. Rogers. Beverly Hills, Calif.: Sage Publications, 1974. Pp. 501–59.

"Five years of enabling legislation: the 1970 act and its consequences." *Contact*, no. 10 (1975):3–9.

Fogarty, Michael P. *Christian Democracy in Western Europe, 1820–1953*. London: Routledge & Kegan Paul, 1957.

Follett, Mary P. *The New State*. New York: Longmans, Green, 1918.

Franklin, Gordon. *Evangelical Charity in a Changing World*. London: Shaftesbury Society, 1967.

Fraser, Derek. *The Evolution of the British Welfare State: A History of Social Policy since the Industrial Revolution*. London: Macmillan, 1973.

Freeman, Roger A. *The Growth of American Government: A Morphology of the Welfare State*. Stanford, Calif.: Hoover Institution Press, 1975.

Freudenheim, Y. *Government in Israel*. Dobbs Ferry, N.Y.: Oceana Publications, 1967.

Friedman, Milton. "The role of government in a free society." In *Private Wants and Public Needs*, edited by Edmund Phelps. New York: W. W. Norton, 1962. Pp. 104–17.

"Friendly satellites." Editorial. *New Society* 42 (1977):11.

Fullerton, Douglas M. *The Dangerous Delusion: Quebec's Independence Obsession*. Toronto: McClelland & Stewart, 1978.

Furniss, Norman. "The practical significance of decentralization." *Journal of Politics* 36 (1974):958–82.

Gans, Sheldon P., and Horton, G. T. *Integration of Human Services: The State and Municipal Levels*. New York: Praeger, 1975.

Garrick, M. A., and Moore, W. L. "Uniform assessments and standards of social and health care services." *Social Service Review* 53 (1979):343–57.

Gartner, Allan, and Reissman, Frank. *Self-Help in the Human Services*. San Francisco: Jossey-Bass, 1977.

Gates, Bruce L. *Social Program Administration: The Implementation of Social Policy*. Englewood Cliffs, N.J.: Prentice-Hall, 1980.

General Accounting Office. *Grant Auditing: A Maze of Inconsistency, Gaps, and Duplication That Needs Overhauling*. Report to the Congress by the Comptroller General of the U.S. (June 15, 1979). Washington, D.C.: General Accounting Office, 1979.

Gidron, Benjamin. "Volunteer work and its rewards." *Volunteer Administration* 11 (1978):18–25.

Gilbert, Charles, "Welfare policy." In *Policies and Policy Making: Handbook of*

Political Science, 6, edited by Fred Greenstein and Nelson Polsby. Reading, Mass.: Addison-Wesley Publishing Co., 1975. Pp. 111–240.

Gilbert, Neil. "The transformation of the social services." *Social Service Review* 51 (1977):624–41.

Gilbert, Neil, and Specht, Harry. *The Dimensions of Social Welfare Policy*. Englewood Cliffs, N.J.: Prentice-Hall, 1974.

Glaser, John S. "Serving community needs." *Society* 15 (1978):16–17.

Glaser, William A., and Sills, David L., editors. *The Government of Associations*. Totowa, N.J.: Bedminster Press, 1966.

Glazer, Nathan. "The limits of social policy." *Commentary* 52 (1971):51–58.

Gliedman, John, and Roth, William. *The Unexpected Minority: Handicapped Children in America*. New York: Harcourt, Brace and Jovanovich, 1980.

Goldman, Eugene. "Conable lobbying bill becomes law." *Voluntary Action Leadership* (Winter 1977):7–8.

Goodman Committee. *Charity Law and Voluntary Organisations*. London: Bedford Square Press of the National Council of Social Service, 1976.

Goudsblom, Johan. *Dutch Society*. New York: Random House, 1967.

Granger, Lester B. "The changing functions of voluntary agencies." In *New Directions in Social Work*, edited by Cora Kasius. New York: Harper & Brothers, 1954. Pp. 68–86.

Graycar, Adam. "Backlash, overload and the welfare state." *Australian Quarterly* 51 (1979):16–28.

Great Britain, Minister for the Disabled. *Checklist of New Help for the Disabled since March, 1974*. London: Minister for the Disabled 1974 (mimeographed).

Greater New York Fund/United Way. *Impact of Government Funding on the Management of Voluntary Agencies*. New York: Greater New York Fund/United Way, 1978.

Greene, Susan R. "Network — alliance-style." *Voluntary Action Leadership* (Winter 1979):17.

Grimes, A. J. "The fund-raising percent as a quantitative standard for regulation of public charities, with particular emphasis on voluntary health and welfare organizations." In *Research Papers Sponsored by the Commission on Private Philanthropy and Public Needs*, vol. 5. Washington, D.C.: Department of the Treasury, 1977. Pp. 2899–914.

"A group to save 'non-profit' sector." San Francisco *Chronicle*. November 30, 1978.

Grushka, Th., editor. *Health Services in Israel*. Jerusalem: Ministry of Health, 1968.

Gunn, Selskar M., and Platt, Philip S. *Voluntary Health Agencies, an Interpretive Study*. New York: Ronald Press, 1945.

Gurin, Arnold, and Ecklein, Joan. "Community organization for what? Political power or service delivery?" *Social Work Practice, 1968*. New York: Columbia University Press, 1968. Pp. 1–15.

Guthrie, Duncan. "The future role of the local voluntary organisations for the disabled." Address at the 1976 Harding Award of the Central Council for the Disabled. Guildhall, London.

Haas, J. Eugene, and Drabek, Thomas E. *Complex Organizations: A Sociological Perspective.* New York: Macmillan, 1973.

Hadley, Roger, 1978. "Beyond the limits of the welfare state: social policy and community resources." Ninth World Congress of Sociology, Uppsala, Sweden, August 1978.

Hadley, Roger; Webb, Adrian; and Farrell, Christine. *Across the Generations: Old People and Young Volunteers.* London: George Allen & Unwin, 1975.

Haeuser, Adrienne A. "What the graduate social work curriculum should provide about volunteerism for all students." *Voluntary Action Leadership* (Summer 1978):1–6.

Hage, Jerald, and Aiken, Michael. "Program change and organizational properties: a comparative analysis." *American Journal of Sociology* 72 (1967):503–19.

Hage, Jerald, and DeWar, R. "Elite values versus organizational structure in predicting innovation." *Administrative Science Quarterly* 5 (1973):279–90.

Hall, M. Penelope. *The Social Services of Modern England.* New York: Humanities Press, 1960.

Hall, Phoebe. *Reforming the Welfare: The Politics of Change in the Personal Social Services.* London: Heinemann Educational Books, 1976.

Hall, Phoebe, et al. *Change, Choice and Conflict in Social Policy.* London: Heinemann Educational Books, 1975.

Hall, Richard. "Professionalization and bureaucratization." *American Sociological Review* 33 (1968):92–104.

Hamilton, Edward K. "On non-constitutional management of a constitutional problem." *Daedalus* 107 (1978):111–28.

Hamlin, Robert. *Voluntary Health and Welfare Agencies in the U.S.: An Exploratory Study by an Ad Hoc Committee.* New York: Schoolmaster's Press, 1961.

Harris, A. I. *Handicapped and Impaired in Great Britain*, Part I. H.M.S.O.: Office of Population Censuses and Surveys, 1971.

Harris, Maxine L. "Contracting with Private Agencies for the Delivery of Public Services: Policy Implications of an Emerging Trend." Ph.D. dissertation, University of Southern California, 1975.

Hartz, Louis. *The Founding of New Societies.* New York: Harcourt, Brace & World, 1964.

Hasenfeld, Yeheskel, and English, Richard A., editors. *Human Service Organizations.* Ann Arbor: University of Michigan Press, 1974.

Hatch, Stephen. *Voluntary Work: A Report of a Survey.* Berkhamstead, England: The Volunteer Centre, 1978.

Hatch, Stephen, and Mocroft, Ian. "Factors affecting the location of voluntary organization branches." *Policy and Politics* 6 (1977):163–72.

————. "Voluntary workers." *New Society* 42 (1977):24.

Haveman, Robert H. *A Benefit-Cost and Policy Analysis of the Netherlands Social Employment Program.* Madison: University of Wisconsin, Institute for Research on Poverty, 1977.

————. *Public Employment of Less Productive Workers — Lessons for the U.S. from the Dutch Experience.* Madison: University of Wisconsin, Institute for Research on Poverty, 1977.

Heidenheimer, Arnold J.; Heclo, Hugh; and Adams, Carolyn. *Comparative Public Policy: The Politics of Social Choice in Europe and America.* London: Macmillan, 1976.

Hendriks, G. "Scale enlargement and democratization." In *Community Development and Democratization.* Rijswijk, The Netherlands: Ministry of Culture, Recreation, and Social Welfare, 1974. Pp. 31–43.

————. *New Trends in Social Welfare Policy in the Netherlands.* Rijswijk, The Netherlands: Ministry of Culture, Recreation, and Social Welfare, 1978.

Heydebrand, Wolfe V., and Noell, James J. "Task structure and innovation in professional organizations." In *Comparative Organizations*, edited by Wolfe V. Heydebrand. Englewood Cliffs, N.J.: Prentice-Hall, 1973. Pp. 294–322.

Hill, Christopher P. "The English system of charity." In *Philanthropy in the 70s: An Anglo-American Discussion*, edited by John J. Corson and Harry V. Hodson. New York: Council on Foundations, 1973. Pp. 61–88.

Hill, William G. "Voluntary and governmental financial transactions." *Social Casework* 52 (1971):356–61.

Hinton, Nicholas. "Building for the future." *Social Service Quarterly* 51 (1978):125–29.

Holme, Anthea, and Maizels, Joan. *Social Workers and Volunteers.* London: George Allen & Unwin, 1978.

Hood, C. C., and Bradshaw, J. R. "The Family Fund: implications of an unorthodox agency." *Public Administration* 56 (1978):447–64.

Hook, Sidney. "Capitalism, socialism and democracy: a symposium." *Commentary* 65 (1978):48–50.

Hoshino, George. "Social services and the problem of accountability." *Social Service Review* 47 (1973):373–83.

House of Commons Debates, Hansard, 1975. Vol. 895, no. 154, cols. 345–405.

House of Lords Debates, Hansard, 1975. Vol. 361, no. 110, cols. 1389 and 1397.

Hubbard, R. L. *Lobbying by Public Charities.* Washington, D.C.: National Center for Voluntary Action, 1977.

Ireland, Thomas I. "The calculus of philanthropy." In *The Economics of Charity.* London: The Institute of Economic Affairs, 1973. Pp. 63–78.

Israel Ministry of Social Welfare. *Development and Participation: Operational Implications for Social Welfare.* Report submitted to the Seventeenth International Conference on Social Welfare, Nairobi, Kenya. Jerusalem: Israeli National Committee for Social Service, 1974.

Jacobs, David. "Dependency and vulnerability: an exchange approach to the control of organizations." *Administrative Science Quarterly* 19 (1974):45–59.

Jaehnig, Walter. "Seeking out the disabled." In *Yearbook of Social Policy in Britain, 1972*, edited by Kathleen Jones. London: Routledge & Kegan Paul, 1972. Pp. 168–84.

Jaffe, Eliezer D. "Substitutes for family: on the development of institutional care for dependent children in Israel." *Journal of Jewish Communal Service* 42 (1967):129–44.

————. "Child welfare in Israel: an overview of institutional care, foster home care and adoption." *Journal of Jewish Communal Service* 55 (1978):170–82.

Janowitz, Morris. *Social Control of the Welfare State*. New York: Elsevier Scientific Publishing Co., 1976.

Jefferys, Margot. *An Anatomy of Social Welfare Services*. London: Michael Joseph, 1965.

Jenvick, Benjamin A. G. "The voluntary agency and the purchase of social services." In *Social Work Practice, 1971*. New York: Columbia University Press, 1971. Pp. 152–59.

Johnson, Arlien. *Public Policy and Public Charities*. Chicago: University of Chicago Press, 1930.

Johnson, David B. "The charity market: theory and practice." In *The Economics of Charity*. London: The Institute of Economic Affairs, 1973. Pp. 79–106.

Johnson, Norman. "The finance of voluntary organizations for the physically disabled." *Social and Economic Administration* 12 (1978):169–81.

Jones, Kathleen. *A History of the Mental Health Services*. London: Routledge & Kegan Paul, 1972.

Journal of Applied Behavioral Science. Special issue on self-help groups. Vol. 12, 1976.

Journal of Voluntary Action Research. Special issue: "Citizen participation in law enforcement." Vol. 7, 1978.

Judge, Ken. *Rationing Social Services: A Study of the Allocation of the Personal Social Services*. London: Heinemann Educational Books, 1978.

Kahn, Alfred J. *Social Policy and Social Services*. New York: Random House, 1973.

————. "A framework for public-voluntary collaboration in the social services." In *Social Welfare Forum, 1976*. New York: Columbia University Press, 1976. Pp. 47–62.

Kahn, Alfred J., and Kamerman, Sheila B. *Social Services in International Perspective: The Emergence of the Sixth System*. Washington, D.C.: Government Printing Office, 1976.

Kaim-Caudle, P. R. *Comparative Social Policy and Social Security: A Ten-Country Study*. London: Martin Robertson, 1973.

Kamerman, Sheila B., and Kahn, Alfred J. *Social Services in the U.S.* Philadelphia: Temple University Press, 1976.

Kandell, Jonathan. "Private charity going out of style in West Europe's welfare states." *New York Times*, July 2, 1978.

Kaplan, Howard B. "Implementation of program change in community agencies." *Milbank Memorial Fund Quarterly* 45 (1967):321–32.

Katz, Alfred H. *Parents of the Handicapped.* Springfield, Ill.: Charles C. Thomas, 1960.

————. "Self-help organizations and volunteer participation in social welfare." *Social Work* 15 (1970):51–60.

Katz, Alfred H., and Bender, Eugene I., editors. *The Strength in Us: Self-Help Groups in the Modern World.* New York: New Viewpoints, Franklin Watts, 1976.

Katz, Elihu. "Culture and communication in Israel: the transformation of tradition." *Jewish Journal of Sociology* 15 (1973):5–21.

Katz, S., Reagles, K., and Wright, G., editors. *Rehabilitation Services in Israel.* Madison: University of Wisconsin, Department of Behavioral Disabilities, Rehabilitation Research Institute, 1972.

Keeton, G. W. *Government in Action in the United Kingdom.* London: Ernest Benn, 1970.

Kessler, A. A. "On the study of the financing of Jewish community activities." *Jewish Journal of Sociology* 12 (1970):89–100.

Keyfetz, Nathan. "Why Social Security is in trouble." *The Public Interest* 58 (1980):102–19.

Kiesling, Herbert, and Fisk, Donald. *Local Governmental Privatization/Competition Innovations.* Washington, D.C.: The Urban Institute, 1973.

Kimberly, John R. "Organizational size and the structuralist perspective: a review, critique, and proposal." *Administrative Science Quarterly* 21 (1976): 571–97.

————. "Hospital adoption of innovation: the role of integration into external informational environments." *Journal of Health and Social Behavior* 19 (1978):361–73.

Kleinberger, Aharon K. *Society, Schools and Progress in Israel.* New York: Pergamon Press, 1969.

Kotler, Milton. *Neighborhood Government: The Local Foundation of Political Life.* Indianapolis: Bobbs-Merrill, 1969.

Kraines, Oscar. *Government and Politics in Israel.* Boston: Houghton Mifflin Co., 1961.

Kramer, Ralph M. "Governmental and voluntary agencies: a study of lay and professional attitudes." In *Community Organization, 1961.* New York: Columbia University Press, 1961. Pp. 160–74.

————. "Ideology, status and power in the board-executive relationship." *Social Work* 10 (1965):108–14.

————— . "Voluntary agencies and the use of public funds: some policy issues." *Social Service Review* 40 (1966):15–26.

————— . *Participation of the Poor: Comparative Community Case Studies in the War on Poverty*. Englewood Cliffs, N.J.: Prentice-Hall, 1969.

————— . *Community Development in Israel and the Netherlands*. Berkeley: University of California, Institute of International Studies, 1970.

————— . "Future of the voluntary service organization." *Social Work* 18 (1973):59–69.

————— . *The Voluntary Service Agency in Israel*. Berkeley: University of California, Institute of International Studies, 1976.

————— . "Governmental-voluntary relationships in the Netherlands." *Netherlands Journal of Sociology* 16 (1979):155–73.

————— . "Voluntary agencies in the welfare state: an analysis of the vanguard role." *Journal of Social Policy* 8 (1979):473–88.

Kreshbaum, Hal R.; Harveston, Dominic S.; and Katz, Alfred H. "Independent living for the disabled." *Social Policy* 7 (1976):59–62.

Kristol, Irving. "Taxes, poverty and equality." *The Public Interest* 37 (1974): 3–28.

Kronjee, Gerrit J. *Particulier initiatief in de gehandicaptenzorg*. The Hague: Netherlands Institute of Social Work Research, 1976.

Kruijt, J. P. "The Netherlands: the influence of denominationalism on social life and organizational patterns." In *Consociational Democracy: Political Accommodation in Segmented Societies*, edited by Kenneth D. McRae. Toronto: McClelland & Stewart, 1974. Pp. 128–36.

Lally, Dorothy, *National Social Service Systems: A Comparative Study and Analysis of Selected Countries*. Washington, D.C.: U.S. Department of Health, Education and Welfare, Social and Rehabilitation Service, 1970.

Landau, Martin. "Redundancy, rationality and the problem of duplication and overlap." *Public Administration Review* 29 (1969):346–58.

Lappin, Ben. "The missing volunteers in Israel's struggle with poverty." *Journal of Jewish Communal Service* 49 (1972):66–76.

Lazar, David. "Israel's political structure and social issues." *Journal of Jewish Sociology* 15 (1973):23–43.

Lazin, Fred. "Welfare policy formation in Israel: the policy role of the local agency." *Policy Sciences* 12 (1980):193–214.

Leaper, R. E. B. "Subsidiarity and the welfare state." *Social and Economic Administration* 9 (1975):82–97.

Leat, Diana. *Why Volunteers? Ten Points of View*. Berkhamstead, England: The Volunteer Centre, 1978.

Lee, Sidney S. *Quebec's Health System: A Decade of Change, 1967–1977*. Monographs on Canadian Public Administration, No. 4. Toronto: Institute of Public Administration of Canada, 1979.

Leiby, James. *A History of Social Welfare and Social Work in the United States.* New York: Columbia University Press, 1978.

Lesemann, Frédérick. "The local community service centres and the democratization of health." *Canada's Mental Health* 26 (1978):14–17.

Levine, Sol, and White, Paul E. "Exchange as a conceptual framework for the study of inter-organizational relationships." *Administrative Science Quarterly* 5 (1961):583–601.

Levitt, Louis. "The Accountability Gap in Foster Care: Discontinuities in Accountability in the Purchase and Provision of Foster Care Service in New York City." Ph.D. dissertation, New York University, 1972.

Levitt, Theodore. *The Third Sector: New Tactics for a Responsive Society.* New York: Macon Press, 1973.

Lijphart, Arend. "Comparative politics and the comparative method." *American Political Science Review* 65 (1971):682–93.

——— . *The Politics of Accommodation: Pluralism and Accommodation in the Netherlands.* 2nd ed. Berkeley and Los Angeles: University of California Press, 1975.

Linde, A. "Services for the mentally handicapped in the Netherlands: a general review." In *Talking about Integration.* Rijswijk, The Netherlands: Ministry of Culture, Recreation, and Social Welfare, 1973. Pp. 50–56, 81.

Lissak, Moshe, *Social Mobility in Israel Society.* Jerusalem: Israel Universities Press, 1969.

Loeser, Hilda. *Women, Work and Volunteering.* Boston: Beacon Press, 1974.

Loewenburg, J. Joseph. "Histadrut: myth and reality." In *Israel: Social Structure and Change,* edited by Michael Curtis and Mordecai Shertoff. New Brunswick, N.J.: Transaction Books, 1973. Pp. 249–56.

Logue, John. "The welfare state: victim of its success." *Daedalus* 108 (1979): 69–88.

Lotan, Giora. *National Insurance in Israel.* Jerusalem: National Insurance Institute, 1969.

Lourie, Norman V. "Purchase of service contracting: issues confronting the governmental sponsored agency." In *Proceedings of the National Institute on Purchase of Service Contracting: Child and Family Services,* edited by Kenneth Wedel et al. Lawrence, Kansas: University of Kansas, School of Social Welfare, 1978. Pp. 17–28.

Lowi, Theodore J. *The End of Liberalism: Ideology, Policy and the Crisis of Public Authority.* New York: W. W. Norton & Co., 1969.

Lubove, Roy. *The Professional Altruist: The Emergence of Social Work as a Career, 1880–1930.* Cambridge: Harvard University Press, 1965.

——— . "The welfare industry: social work and the life of the poor." *The Nation* 202 (May 23, 1966):609–11.

McConnell, Grant. *Private Power and American Democracy.* New York: Alfred A. Knopf & Co., 1966.

MacKinnon, Fred R. "Changing patterns in public-voluntary relationships in Canada." *Child Welfare* 50 (1973):633–42.

McRae, Kenneth D., editor. *Consociational Democracy: Political Accommodation in Segmented Societies*. Toronto: McClelland & Stewart, 1974.

Manser, Gordon. "Further thoughts on purchase of service." *Social Casework* 55 (1974):421–34.

Manser, Gordon, and Cass, Rosemary. *Voluntarism at the Crossroads*. New York: Family Service Association of America, 1975.

Mansfield, Harvey C. "Independence and accountability for federal contractors and grantees." In *The Dilemma of Accountability in Modern Government*, edited by Bruce L. R. Smith and D. C. Hague. New York: St. Martin's Press, 1971. Pp. 319–35.

March, James G., and Simon, Herbert A. *Organizations*. New York: John Wiley & Sons, 1958.

Marcus, J., and Russell, A. "The vulnerable and the handicapped." In *Children and Families in Israel: Some Mental Health Perspectives*, edited by A. Jarus et al. New York: Gordon & Breach, 1970. Pp. 385–426.

Margolis, Emmanuel. "Health care in a changing society: the health services of Israel." *Medical Care* 13 (1975):943–55.

Marmor, Theodore R., and Morone, James A. "Representing Consumer Interests: Imbalanced Markets, Health Planning, and the HSAs." *Milbank Memorial Fund Quarterly* 58 (1980):125–65.

Marshall, T. H. *Social Policy in the Twentieth Century*. London: Hutchinson & Co., 1970.

Matras, Judah. *Social Change in Israel*. Chicago: Aldine Publishing Co., 1965.

Medding, Peter Y. *Mapai in Israel: Political Organization and Government in a New Society*. Cambridge: Cambridge University Press, 1972.

Meiresonne, Jan B. *Care for the Mentally Retarded in the Netherlands*. Utrecht: Dutch National Association for the Care of the Mentally Retarded, 1975.

Mencher, Samuel. "The Relationship of Voluntary and Statutory Welfare Services in England." D.S.W. dissertation, New York School of Social Work, Columbia University, 1957.

——— . "Factors affecting the relationship of the voluntary and statutory child care services in England." *Social Service Review* 32 (1958):24–32.

——— . "Financial relationships between voluntary and statutory bodies in the British social services." *Social Service Review* 32 (1958):138–51.

——— . *Poor Law to Poverty Program*. Pittsburgh: University of Pittsburgh Press, 1967.

Michael, Donald N. "Influencing public policy: the changing roles of voluntary associations." In *Readings in Community Organization Practice*, 2nd ed., edited by Ralph M. Kramer and Harry Specht. Englewood Cliffs, N.J.: Prentice-Hall, 1975. Pp. 81–86.

Mindlin, Sergio E., and Aldrich, Howard. "Interorganizational dependence: a review of the concept and a reexamination of the findings of the Ashton Group." *Administrative Science Quarterly* 20 (1975):382–92.

Mishra, Ramesh. "Welfare and industrial man: a study of welfare in Western industrial societies in relation to a hypothesis of convergence." *Sociological Review* 25 (1973):535–60.

Moberg, David O. "Religion and society in the Netherlands and in America." *American Quarterly* 13 (1961):172–78.

————. "Social Differentiation in the Netherlands." *Social Forces* 29 (1961): 333–37.

Mohr, Lawrence V. "Determinants of innovation in organizations." *American Political Science Review* 53 (1969):11–26.

Monk, Abraham. "Family supports in old age." *Social Work* 24 (1979):533–39.

Morgan, James N.; Dye, Richard F.; and Hybels, Judith H. "Results from two national surveys of philanthropic activity." In *Research Papers Sponsored by the Commission on Private Philanthropy and Public Needs*, vol. 1. Washington, D.C.: Department of the Treasury, 1977. Pp. 157–324.

Moroney, Robert. *The Family and the State: Considerations for Social Policy.* London: Longmans, 1976.

Morris, Alfred, and Butler, Arthur. *No Feet to Drag: Report on the Disabled.* London: Sidgwich & Jackson, 1972.

Morris, Mary. *Voluntary Work in the Welfare State.* London: Routledge & Kegan Paul, 1969.

Morris, Robert. *Toward a Caring Society.* New York: Columbia University, School of Social Work, 1974.

Morrissey, Elizabeth, and Gillespie, David F. "Technology and the conflict of professionals in bureaucratic organizations." *Sociological Quarterly* 16 (1975):319–32.

Moynihan, Daniel P. "The American experiment." *Public Interest* 41 (1975):4–8.

Mueller, Candace P. "Purchase of service contracting from the viewpoint of the provider." In *Proceedings of the National Institute on Purchase of Service Contracting: Child and Family Services*, edited by Kenneth R. Wedel, Arthur J. Katz, and Ann Weick. Lawrence, Kansas: University of Kansas, School of Social Welfare, 1978. Pp. 29–36.

Murray, George J. *Voluntary Organizations and Social Welfare.* Edinburgh: Oliver & Boyd, 1969.

Murray, George J. "Voluntary organizations in the personal social service field." In *Reviews of United Kingdom's Statistical Sources*, vol. 1, edited by W. F. Maunder. London: Heinemann Educational Books, 1974. Pp. 1–54.

Myrdal, Gunnar. *Beyond the Welfare State.* New Haven, Conn.: Yale University Press, 1960.

National Council of Social Service. *Fund-Raising by Charities*. London: National Council of Social Service, 1973.

National Advisory Council on Voluntary Action to the Government of Canada. *People in Action*. Ottawa, Ontario: National Advisory Council on Voluntary Action to the Government of Canada, 1977.

National Health Council. *Standards of Accounting and Financial Reporting for Voluntary Health and Welfare Organizations*. 2nd ed. New York: National Health Council, National Assembly of Voluntary Health and Social Welfare Organizations, and United Way of America, 1974.

National Organization for Women. *National Organization for Women — Why Not? Analysis and Answers*. Chicago: Task Force on Women Volunteerism, 1973.

Naylor, Harriet H. *Volunteers Today — Finding, Training, and Working with Them*. Dryden, N.Y.: Dryden Associates, 1973.

————. *Leadership for Volunteering*. Dryden, N.Y.: Dryden Associates, 1976.

————. *Volunteers, Resource for Human Services*. Occasional Paper Series, Project SHARE. Washington, D.C.: Department of Health, Education and Welfare, Office of the Assistant Secretary for Planning and Evaluation, 1979.

"The need for voluntary effort." *Social Service Quarterly* 49 (1976):93.

Neipris, Joseph. "Social Services in Israel." *Journal of Jewish Communal Service* 47 (1971):289–315.

The Netherlands Ministry of Culture, Recreation and Social Welfare. *Netherlands Reply to the Questionnaire of the Council of Europe on "Social Welfare Planning and Organization."* Rijswijk, The Netherlands: 1972 (mimeographed).

————. *Rapport van de beraadsgroep knelpunten, harmonisatie welzijnsbeleid en welzijnswetgeving*. Rijswijk, The Netherlands: 1974.

————. *The Public Assistance Act in the Netherlands*. Rijswijk, The Netherlands: 1977.

————. *Social Policy on the Handicapped in the Netherlands*. Rijswijk, The Netherlands: 1977.

Newman, Edward, and Turem, Jerry. "The crisis of accountability." *Social Work* 19 (1974):5–17.

Nicholson, J. H. *Help for the Handicapped: An Inquiry into the Opportunities of the Voluntary Services*. London: National Council of Social Service, 1958.

Nielsen, Waldemar A. *The Endangered Sector*. New York: Columbia University Press, 1979.

Nightingale, Benedict. *Charities*. London: Allan Lane, 1973.

Nisbet, Robert A. *The Quest for Community: A Study in the Ethics of Order and Freedom*. New York: Oxford University Press, 1953.

————. *The Sociological Tradition*. New York: Basic Books, 1966.

Nokes, Peter. "Purpose and efficiency in humane social institutions." *Human Relations* 13 (1960):141–56.

O'Brien, David J. *Neighborhood Organization and Interest-Group Processes.* Princeton, N.J.: Princeton University Press, 1975.

O'Connell, Brian. "The contribution of voluntary agencies in developing social policies." Sidney Hollander Colloquium, Council of Jewish Federations and Welfare Funds, April 24, 1976 (mimeographed).

——— . *Effective Leadership in Voluntary Organizations: How to Make the Greatest Use of Citizen Service and Influence.* New York: Association Press, 1978.

——— . "From service to advocacy to empowerment." *Social Casework* 59 (1978):195–202.

Owen, David. *English Philanthropy, 1660–1960.* Cambridge: Harvard University Press, 1964.

Owen, J. K. "Partnership with government." *Social Service Quarterly* 49 (1976):120.

Palumbo, Dennis J. "Comparative analysis: quasimethodology or new science?" *Comparative Urban Research* 4 (1973–1974):37–53.

Pennock, J. Rowland, and Chapman, John W., editors. *Voluntary Associations, Nomos,* XI. Yearbook of the American Society for Political and Legal Philosophy. New York: Atherton Press, 1969.

Perlmutter, Felice. "Public funds and private agencies." *Child Welfare* 50 (1971):264–70.

Perrow, Charles. *Organizational Analysis: A Sociological View.* Belmont, Calif.: Brooks/Cole Publishing Co., 1970.

——— . *Complex Organizations: A Critical Essay.* Glenview, Ill.: Scott, Foresman & Co., 1972.

Philpot, Terry. "Nurturing pressure from grass roots." *Community Care,* April 7, 1976. P. 18.

Pifer, Alan. "The quasi-non-governmental organization." *1967 Annual Report of the Carnegie Corporation of New York.* New York: Carnegie Corporation, 1967.

——— ."The Jeopardy of Private Institutions." In *The New Political Economy: The Public Use of the Private Sector,* edited by Bruce L. R. Smith. New York: John Wiley & Sons, 1975. Pp. 68–82.

Pinker, Robert. *Research Priorities in the Personal Social Services: a Report to the Research Initiatives Board.* London: Social Science Research Council, 1977 (mimeographed).

Plattner, Mark F. "The welfare state vs. the redistributive state." *Public Interest* 55 (1979):28–48.

Price, Don K. "Endless frontier or bureaucratic morass?" *Daedalus* 107 (1978): 75–92.

Price, James L. *Handbook of Organizational Measurement.* Lexington, Mass.: D. C. Heath & Co., 1972.

Prime Minister's Committee on Youth. *Report of the sub-committee on voluntary organizations.* Jerusalem: 1972 (mimeographed).

Public Health in the Netherlands. The Hague, The Netherlands: Ministry of Public Health and Environmental Hygiene, 1972.

Pumphrey, Ralph E., and Pumphrey, Muriel W. *The Heritage of American Social Work.* New York: Columbia University Press, 1961.

Pye, Edgar W., and Rudolph, Rhona S. "A California Regional Center Program." Annual Meeting, American Association of Mental Deficiency, Toronto, 1974.

Querido, A. *The Development of Socio-Medical Care in the Netherlands.* London: Routledge & Kegan Paul, 1968.

Qureshi, Hazel; Davies, Bleddyn; and Challis, David. "Motivation and reward of volunteers and informal care givers." *Journal of Voluntary Action Research* 8 (1979):47–55.

Rabinovitz, Francine; Pressman, Jeffrey; and Rein, Martin. "Guidelines: a plethora of forms, authors, and functions." *Policy Sciences* 7 (1976):399–416.

Rabinowitz, Herbert S.; Simmeth, Bruce R.; and Spero, Jeannette R. "The future of United Way." *Social Service Review* 53 (1979):275–84.

Rainey, Hal G., et al. "Comparing public and private organizations." *Public Administration Review* 36 (1976):233–44.

Redman, Eric. *The Dance of Legislation.* New York: Simon & Shuster, 1973.

Reichert, Kurt. "The drift toward entrepreneurialism in health and social welfare: implications for social work education." *Administration in Social Work* 1 (1977):123–34.

Reid, Joseph L. "The role of the voluntary sector." In *Social Welfare Forum, 1976.* New York: Columbia University Press, 1976. Pp. 63–69.

Rein, Martin. "Economy and social policy." *Social Service Review* 51 (1977):565–87.

Rein, Martin, and Morris, Robert. "Goals, structures and strategies for community change." In *Social Work Practice, 1962.* New York: Columbia University Press, 1962. Pp. 127–45.

Rice, Robert M. "Impact of government contracts on voluntary social agencies." *Social Casework* 56 (1975):387–95.

Rich, Richard C. "The roles of neighborhood organizations in urban service delivery." *Urban Affairs Papers* 1 (1979):81–93.

Richardson, Eliot L. *Responsibility and Responsiveness, II.* Washington, D.C.: Department of Health, Education and Welfare, 1973.

Riesman, David, *Individualism Reconsidered.* New York: Free Press, 1954.

Rimlinger, Gaston V. *Welfare Policy and Industrialization in Europe, America and Russia.* New York: John Wiley, 1971.

Robinson, David Z. "Government contracting for academic research: accountability in the American experience." In *The Dilemma of Accountability in Modern Government,* edited by Bruce L. R. Smith and D. C. Hague. New York: St. Martin's Press, 1971. Pp. 103–17.

Robson, William A. *Welfare State and Welfare Society: Illusion and Reality.* London: George Allen & Unwin, 1976.

Rodgers, Barbara N. *Cross-National Studies of Social Service Systems.* United Kingdom Reports, vol. 1. New York: Columbia University, School of Social Work, 1976.

Rodgers, Barbara N., and Dixon, Julia. *A Portrait of Social Work: A Study of Social Services in a Northern Town.* London: Oxford University Press, 1960.

Rodgers, Barbara N.; Greve, John; and Morgan, John S. *Comparative Social Administration.* London: George Allen & Unwin, 1971.

Rodgers, Barbara N., and Stevenson, June. *A New Portrait of Social Work: A Study of the Social Services in a Northern Town from Younghusband to Seebohm.* London: Heinemann Educational Books, 1973.

Rooff, Madeline. *Voluntary Societies and Social Policy.* London: Routledge & Kegan Paul, 1957.

Rose, June. *Changing Focus: The Development of Blind Welfare in Britain.* London: Hutchinson & Co., 1970.

Rosen, M., et al. *The History of Mental Retardation: Collected Papers.* 2 vols. Baltimore: University Park Press, 1976.

Rosengren, William R. "The careers of clients and organizations." In *Organizations and Clients: Essays in the Sociology of Service,* edited by William R. Rosengren and Mark Lefton. Columbus, Ohio: Charles E. Merrill, 1972. Pp. 117–36.

Rowe, Andrew. "The voluntary service unit." In *Yearbook of Social Policy in Britain, 1974,* edited by Kathleen Jones. London: Routledge & Kegan Paul, 1974. Pp. 179–95.

Rubenstein, Dan; Mundy, R. E.; and Rubenstein, Mary L. "Proprietary social services." In *Social Welfare Forum, 1978.* New York: Columbia University Press, 1979. Pp. 120–40.

Sainsbury, Eric. *The Personal Social Services.* London: Pitman Publishing, 1977.

Salzberger, Lotte, and Schnitt, Dan. "Social welfare legislation in Israel." *Israel Law Review* 8 (1973):550–79.

Salzberger, Lotte, and Rosenfeld, Jona M. "The anatomy of 267 social welfare agencies in Jerusalem: findings from a census." *Social Service Review* 48 (1974):255–67.

Savas, E. S. "Municipal monopolies versus competition in delivering urban services." In *Improving the Quality of Urban Management,* edited by W. D. Hawley and D. Rogers. Beverly Hills, Calif.: Sage Publications, 1974. Pp. 473–500.

———. "Doing more with less: getting public services into private hands." *Taxing and Spending* 2 (1979):10–11.

Schindler, Reuben. "The pioneering ideology and the roots of social welfare in the pre-state period of Israel." *Journal of Jewish Communal Service* 52 (1976):384–92.

Schindler-Rainman, Eva, and Lippitt, Ronald. *The Volunteer Community: Creative Uses of Human Resources.* Washington, D.C.: The Center for a Voluntary Society, 1975.

Schoenberger, Robert A., editor. *The American Right Wing: Readings in Political Behavior.* New York: Holt, Rinehart, & Winston, 1969.

Schorr, Alvin L. "The tasks for volunteerism in the next decade." *Child Welfare* 49 (1970):425–34.

Schottland, Charles I. "Federal planning for health and welfare." In *Social Welfare Forum, 1963.* New York: Columbia University Press, 1963. Pp. 97–120.

Schottland, Charles I., editor. *The Welfare State: Thirty Selected Essays.* New York: Harper & Row, 1967.

Scott, Robert A. "A construction of conceptions of stigma by professional experts." In *The Handicapped Person in the Community*, edited by David M. Boswell and Janet Wingrove. London: Tavistock Publications, 1974. Pp. 108–21.

Seeley, John R., et al. *Community Chest: A Case Study in Philanthropy.* Toronto: University of Toronto Press, 1957.

Segal, Robert M. *Mental Retardation and Social Action: A Study of the Associations for Retarded Children as a Force for Social Change.* Springfield, Ill.: Charles C. Thomas, 1970.

Segal, Steven P. "Community care and deinstitutionalization: a review." *Social Work* 24 (1979):521–27.

Sharkansky, Ira. *Wither the State? Politics and Public Enterprise in Three Countries.* Chatham, N.J.: Chatham House, 1979.

Sherrill, Robert, et al. *Governing America.* New York: Harcourt, Brace & Jovanovich, 1971.

Sherry, Paul H. "Getting it together." *Journal of Current Social Issues* 9 (1971):2.

Shlonsky, Hagith. *Welfare in Israel in a Comparative Perspective.* Chicago: University of Chicago, School of Social Service Administration, Center for the Study of Welfare Policy, 1971.

Sieder, Violet M., and Kirshbaum, Doris C. "Volunteers." In *Encyclopedia of Social Work*, 17th issue, vol. 2. Washington, D.C.: National Association of Social Workers, 1977. Pp. 1582–90.

Sills, David L. *The Volunteers: Means and Ends in a National Organization.* Glencoe, Ill.: The Free Press, 1957.

———. "Voluntary associations: sociological aspects." In *International Encyclopedia of the Social Sciences*, 16, edited by David L. Sills, New York: Macmillan, 1968. Pp. 362–79.

Skolnick, Alfred M., and Dales, Sophie R. "Social welfare expenditures, 1950–1975." *Social Security Bulletin* 39 (1976):3–20.

Slack, Kathleen M. "Social administration digest: voluntary effort." *Journal of Social Policy* 7 (1978):488.

Smith, Bruce L. R. "Independence and the contract state." In *The Dilemma of Accountability in Modern Government: Independence vs. Control*, edited by Bruce L. R. Smith and D. C. Hague. New York: St. Martin's Press, 1971. Pp. 3–69.

Smith, Constance, and Freedman, Ann. *Voluntary Associations: Perspectives on the Literature.* Cambridge: Harvard University Press, 1972.

Smith, David Horton. "The philanthropy business." *Society* 15 (1978):8–15.

Social and Cultural Planning Office. *Social and Cultural Report.* Rijswijk, The Netherlands, Social and Cultural Planning Office, 1974.

Social Policy. Special self-help issue. Vol. 7, September–October 1976.

Stanton, Esther. *Clients Come Last: Volunteers and Welfare Organizations.* Beverly Hills, Calif.: Sage Publications, 1970.

Starr, Paul. "Medicine and the waning of professional sovereignty." *Daedalus* 107 (1978):175–94.

Stein, Herman. "Organization theory — implications for administrative research." In *Social Science Theory and Social Work Research,* edited by Leonard S. Kogan. New York: National Association of Social Workers, 1960. Pp. 80–90.

Steinberg, Raymond M., et al. *Area agencies on aging: a case study of a controversial contract for service.* Los Angeles: University of Southern California, Andrus Gerontology Center, 1976 (mimeographed).

Steiner, Richard. *Managing the Human Service Organization.* Beverly Hills, Calif.: Sage Publications, 1977.

Steinfels, Peter. *The Neo-Conservatives: The Men Who Are Changing America's Politics.* New York: Simon & Schuster, 1979.

Stevenson, Olive. "Seebohm — Seven Years On." *New Society* 43 (1978):249–51.

Strange, John J. "Citizen participation in community action and model city programs." *Public Administration Review* 32 (1972):655–69.

Stretch, J. J. "Increasing accountability for human service administration." *Social Casework* 59 (1971):267–77.

Swift, Linton B. *New Alignments between Public and Private Agencies in a Community Family Welfare and Relief Program.* New York: Family Service Association of America, 1934.

Tattersall, James N. "The crisis of the public economy." *Public Affairs Report.* Berkeley: University of California, Institute of Governmental Studies, 1979.

Terrell, Paul. "Private alternatives to public human services administration." *Social Service Review* 53 (1979):56–74.

——— . *California Human Services Two Years after Proposition 13: An Analysis of Budget, Personnel, Organizational and Client Impacts in 13 Counties.* Millbrae, Calif.: National Association of Social Workers, California Chapter, 1980.

Thomas, Mike. "The Volunteer Centre." In *Yearbook of Social Policy in Britain, 1973,* edited by Kathleen Jones. London: Routledge & Kegan Paul, 1974. Pp. 234–43.

Titmuss, Richard M. *The Gift Relationship: From Human Blood to Social Policy.* New York: Vintage Books, 1971.

——— . "Welfare state and welfare society." In *Commitment to Welfare.* London: George Allen & Unwin, 1973. Pp. 124–37.

Topliss, Eda. *Provision for the Disabled*. London: Martin Robertson, 1975.

Torczyner, J. L. "Centralization and participation in conflict: social and health services in Montreal." *The Social Worker (Le Travailleur)* 44 (1976): 54–61.

Traunstein, Donald, and Steinman, Richard. "Voluntary self-help organizations: an exploratory study." *Journal of Voluntary Action Research* 2 (1974): 230–39.

Trecker, Harleigh B. *Citizen Boards at Work: New Challenges to Effective Action*. New York: Association Press, 1970.

Tropp, Emmanuel. "Expectation, performance and accountability." *Social Work* 19 (1974):139–48.

Trustees of Dartmouth College vs. *Woodward* 17 U.S. 518, 647 (1819).

Unell, Judith. *Voluntary Social Services: Financial Resources*. London: Bedford Square Press of the National Council of Social Service, 1979.

U.S. Census Bureau. *Americans Volunteer, 1974*. Study for ACTION. Washington, D.C.: Government Printing Office, 1975.

U.S. Department of Health, Education and Welfare. *Mental Retardation Sourcebook*. Washington, D.C.: Government Printing Office, 1972.

U.S. Department of Health, Education and Welfare, Social and Rehabilitation Service. *Purchase of Social Service: Study of the Experience of Three States in Purchase of Service Contracts under the Provisions of the 1967 Amendments to the Social Security Act*. Washington, D.C.: Department of Health, Education and Welfare, 1971.

U.S. Department of Labor, Manpower Administration. *Americans Volunteer*. Manpower-Automation Research Monograph No. 10. Washington, D.C.: Government Printing Office, 1969.

United Way of America. *UWASIS II: A Taxonomy of Social Goals and Human Service Programs*, 2nd ed. Alexandria, Va.: United Way of America, 1976.

van Doorn, J. A. A. "De strijd om de macht in dienstverlenende organisaties." *Beleid & Maatschappij* 2 (1975):111–17.

The Volunteer Centre. *Encouraging the Community: Some Findings on the Social Service Department's Contributions*. Berkhamstead, England: The Volunteer Centre, 1976.

Vorwaller, Daryl. "The voluntary agency as a vendor of social services." *Child Welfare* 51 (1972):436–42.

Waddilove, Lewis E. "The family fund." *In The Yearbook of Social Policy in Britain, 1973*, edited by Kathleen Jones. London: Routledge & Kegan Paul, 1974. Pp. 203–20.

Wagner, Richard E., and Weber, Warren E. "Wagner's law, fiscal institutions, and the growth of government." *National Tax Journal* 30 (1977): 59–68.

Warham, Joyce. *Social Policy in Context*. London: B. T. Batsford, 1970.

Warner, Amos G. *American Charities: A Study in Philanthropy and Economics.* New York: Thomas Y. Crowell, 1894.

Warwick, Donald T., and Osherson, Samuel, editors. *Comparative Research Methods.* Englewood Cliffs, N.J.: Prentice-Hall, 1973.

Watson, Frank. *The Charity Organization Movement in the U.S.: A Study in American Philanthropy.* New York: Macmillan, 1922.

Webb, Adrian. "Voluntary action: in search of a policy?" *Journal of Voluntary Action Research* 8 (1979):8–16.

Webb, Adrian; Day, Lesley; and Weller, Douglas. *Voluntary Social Service Manpower Resources.* London: Personal Social Services Council, 1976.

Webb, Sidney, and Webb, Beatrice. *The Prevention of Destitution.* London: Longmans, Green, 1916.

Weingrod, Alex. *Israel: Group Relations in a New Society.* London: Pall Mall Press, 1965.

Weinstein, Raymond M., and Moravec, Jaroslav G. "A comparative analysis of health and welfare organizations." *Pacific Sociological Review* 20 (1977): 79–104.

Weisbrod, Burton A. *The Voluntary Non-Profit Sector: An Economic Analysis.* Lexington, Mass.: D. C. Heath & Co., 1977.

Weiss, Edmond H. "Grant management: a systems approach." *Socio-Economic Planning Sciences* 7 (1973):457–70.

Weiss, S. "Local Government in Israel: A Study of Its Leadership." Ph.D. dissertation, Hebrew University of Jerusalem, 1968.

Weissman, Harold. *Community Councils and Community Control.* Pittsburgh: University of Pittsburgh Press, 1970.

Wells Group of Fund-Raising Companies. *Wells Collection.* London: Wells Group of Fund-Raising Companies, 1975.

Wenocur, Stanley. "A political view of the United Way." *Social Work* 20 (1975):223–29.

Werner, Ruth. *Public Financing of Voluntary Agency Foster Care: 1975 Compared with 1957.* New York: Child Welfare League of America, 1976.

Whittington, H. G. "A case for private funding in mental health." *Administration in Mental Health* 2 (1975):23–28.

"Why our social service volunteers need backing." *London Times,* November 23, 1977.

Wickenden, Elizabeth. "Purchase of care and services: effect on voluntary agencies." In *Proceedings of the First Milwaukee Institute on a Social Welfare Issue of the Day: Purchase of Care and Services in the Health and Welfare Fields,* edited by Iris Winogrond. Milwaukee: University of Wisconsin, 1970. Pp. 40–58.

————. "A perspective on social services: an essay review." *Social Service Review* 50 (1976):586–600.

Wilensky, Harold L. *The Welfare State and Equality: Structural and Ideological Roots of Public Expenditures.* Berkeley and Los Angeles: University of California Press, 1975.

——— . *The "New Corporatism," Centralization and the Welfare State.* Sage Professional Papers in Contemporary Political Sociology. Beverly Hills, Calif.: Sage Publications, 1976.

Wilensky, Harold L., and Lebeaux, Charles N. *Industrial Society and Social Welfare.* New York: The Free Press, 1965.

Wilson, James Q. "Innovation in organization: notes toward a theory." In *Approaches to Organization Design,* edited by James D. Thompson. Pittsburgh: University of Pittsburgh Press, 1966. Pp. 193–218.

——— . *Political Organizations.* New York: Free Press, 1973.

Wilson, James Q., and Banfield, Edward C. "Public regardingness as a value premise in voting behavior." *American Political Science Review* 58 (1964): 876–87.

Witmer, Helen. *Social Work: An Analysis of a Social Institution.* New York: Farrar & Rinehart, 1942.

Wolfenden Committee. *The Future of Voluntary Organisations.* London: Croom Helm, 1978.

Wolfensberger, Wolf. *The Third Stage in the Evolution of Voluntary Associations for the Mentally Retarded.* Toronto: National Institute on Mental Retardation, 1973.

Woodroofe, Kathleen. *From Charity to Social Work in England and the United States.* London: Routledge & Kegan Paul, 1962.

Yin, Robert K., et al. *Citizen Organizations: Increasing Client Control over Services.* Prepared for the Department of Health, Education and Welfare. Santa Monica, Calif.: Rand Corporation, 1973.

——— . *Citizen Participation.* Washington, D.C.: Community Services Administration, 1978.

Yishai, Yael. "Interest groups in Israel." *Jerusalem Quarterly* 11 (1979):128–44.

Young, Dennis R., and Finch, Stephen J. *Foster Care and Nonprofit Agencies.* Lexington, Mass.: D. C. Heath & Co., 1977.

Zald, Mayer N. "Organizations as polities: an analysis of community organization agencies." In *Readings in Community Organization Practice,* 2nd ed., edited by Ralph M. Kramer and Harry Specht. Englewood Cliffs, N.J.: Prentice-Hall, 1975. Pp. 87–96.

——— . "Demographics, politics and the future of the welfare state." *Social Service Review* 51 (1977):110–24.

Zaltman, Gerald; Duncan, Robert; and Holbek, Jonny. *Innovations and Organizations.* New York: John Wiley & Sons, 1973.

INDEX

The following abbreviations are used to identify organizations, legislation, and documents that pertain to the four countries in the study: United States (US); Israel (IS); England (E); the Netherlands (N).

Accountability: and autonomy, 289–292; and formalization, 109; for governmental funds, 163–169; requirements, 260. *See also* Governmental funds; Autonomy
ACTION (US), 198
Action Research for Crippled Children (E), 139
Advocacy: for client benefits, 220–221; constraints on, 227–231; models, 231–232; sanction for, 212–213; and service delivery, 232; styles, 222; as unique function, 261–262; use of media in, 226
AKIM (IS): as advocate, 218, 225; federated structure of, 230; programs maintained by, 241
Alliance for Voluntarism (US), 198
Almshouse (US), 59, 61, 63
Altruism, 193, 211
American Cancer Society, 66, 123–124
American Heart Association, 66
American Red Cross, 134, 195
American Society for the Hard of Hearing, 66
Auspices: as organizational variable, 102; significance of, 12–13, 250
Autonomy: and accountability, 288–292; and discretion, 258–259; influence of governmental funds on, 158–160
Aves, Geraldine, 198

Backlash, 277, 287
Ben-Gurion, David, 79
Berger, Peter L., 281
Beveridge, Lord William, 6, 260
Beveridge Report (E), 39
Boards of Directors: consumers on, 115–117; functions of, 113; participation of, 117–123
Boorstin, Daniel J., 58

British Association for the Hard of Hearing, 105
British Polio Foundation, 139
Bureaucratization. *See* Formalization
Burns, Eveline M., 15, 72–73

California League for the Handicapped, 298
Campaign for the Handicapped (E), 222
Canada, 4, 5, 11
Categorical programs (US), 67, 157
Center for Independent Living (US): and advocacy, 226; effect of Proposition 13 on, 156; as self-help program, 117–118, 178, 196–197, 248
Central Council for the Disabled (E), 47, 52, 216
Cerebral Palsy Association (US): national organization of, 67, 124; of Oakland, 105; of San Francisco, 105
Charitable deductions. *See* Tax exemptions
Charity Law (E), 228
Charity Organization Society (US), 62–65
Cheshire Homes (E), 114, 126, 133, 153, 245
Chest, Heart and Stroke Association (E), 139
Choice in the social services, 244, 253
Chronic Sick and Disabled Persons Act of 1970 (E): benefits of, 288n; implementation of, 47, 215, 217, 223; significance of, 46–47
Church-state separation: in the Netherlands, 20–21; in the U.S., 59, 72
Civic culture, influence of: on advocacy, 227; on board member participation, 123; on volunteerism, 210
Coalitions, 221–222
Commission on Private Philanthropy and Public Needs. *See* Filer Commission
Common Good Fund (E), 136–137
Community Chest, 134. *See also* United Way
Consumer participation: and advocacy, 223–224; on boards of directors, 115–117; unique function of, 262–263. *See also* Self-help organizations; Volunteerism
Contracting. *See* Purchase of service
Crossman, R.H.S., 207

Compositor: Viking Typographics
Printer: Vail-Ballou Press
Binder: Vail-Ballou Press
Text: 11/13 Janson
Display: Janson